MW00325615

CREATIVE
SYNERGY:

CREATIVE SYNERGY:

Using Art, Science, and Philosophy to Self-Actualize Your Life

Bunny Paine-Clemes, PhD

Joy to you on your creative path!

Bunny Paine-Clemes

4th Dimension Press ■ Virginia Beach ■ Virginia

Print made by William Blake 1757-1827
Repository title: *Europe. A Prophecy, Plate 1, Frontispiece*
1794
Color-printed relief etching in dark brown with pen and black ink, oil and watercolor
Sheet: 14 3/4 x 10 1/2 inches (37.5 x 26.7 cm)
Plate: 9 1/8 x 6 5/8 inches (23.2 x 16.8 cm)
Spine: 15 3/8 inches (39.1 cm)
Yale Center for British Art, Paul Mellon Collection
3878 - B1992.8.4(1)

Contents

Acknowledgments

Like any other creator, I couldn't have completed this project without help. My first thanks go to my husband and creative partner, Dr. Jack Clemes, who endured months of solitary days while I was secluded in my study and immersed in this project. Without his help I couldn't have completed this book in any sort of timely fashion. He did the household chores, built a special bookshelf for my materials, and supplied crucial creative backup with fresh ideas and perspectives on the book as a whole.

My next thanks go to my two main creative boosters, the pair who have cheered me on and believed in me for over sixty years: my parents, Harry and Gloria Paine. I especially thank my father, who made many suggestions that enriched the content appreciably. Next, I'd like to thank Dr. Steve Pronchick, an engineering professor at the Cal State Maritime Academy, who agreed to peruse three chapters of my original draft. Because Steve is a fine writer with impeccable scientific and engineering credentials, as well as a cultivated reader with broad tastes and acute intelligence, I knew I could trust him to provide a vital additional perspective. It is Steve who suggested that I consult the work of Roger Penrose, who proved a vital source.

Next, I would like to thank the library staff at Cal State Maritime Academy, especially Fran Fraser, Mark Stackpole, and Jean Walker, who went out of their way to find obscure journal articles through interlibrary loan. In addition, I'd like to thank science professors Jim Wheeler and Lloyd Kitazono for their remarks on symmetry and Professors Tuuli Messer-Bookman, Peter Hayes, and Jim Buckley for their discussion of teamwork in Marine Transportation. Finally, I would like to thank Cal State Maritime itself for approving a sabbatical so that I could work on this book and the wonderful folks at A.R.E. Press, especially copy editor Stephanie Pope and Director Cassie McQuagge.

Preface

The Mystery of Creativity

This book explores the mystery of creativity: the why, the what, and the how. We will trace some of its manifestations in the fields of science, spirituality, literature, the arts, engineering, psychology, business, sports, and philosophy—as well as traditions both Eastern and Western.

What makes this book different is its focus on *synergy*—the interactive synthesis of many parts and wholes. Ken Wilber (after Arthur Koestler's nomenclature) calls such units *holons*: they can be whole in and of themselves but are also parts of larger wholes. So math and literature are both whole fields, but they are usually parts of a college education. Your background is a whole, but it is also only a part of you, and in itself it is composed of many parts, such as your reading, your experiences, and your synthesized ideas about life.

Organization of the Book

The first three chapters establish a theoretical framework.

Chapter 1 and 2, while dissecting the paradoxes involved in the study of creativity, indicate how some thinkers have viewed it from ancient times to the present. Particularly germane is the notion of the universe as a great thought, a web of interrelated ideas and possibilities, available to those who know how to access it. This concept may seem controversial but is by no means new—sources ancient and modern, Eastern and Western will be cited to document it.

Chapter 3 outlines the ten–step process that you can use to activate *Creative Synergy*. You immerse yourself in the formulas of your craft, then activate the flow state, center your awareness, relate to the center of what is trying to happen through you, and let the inspiration flow. You also allow for incubation, synchronicity, and feedback to support the process. For this method I am deeply indebted to Swami Kriyananda (a.k.a. Donald Walters).

Chapter 4 summarizes the Integral Operating System of Ken Wilber. If you find the ideas a bit dense and the descriptions a bit confusing, feel free to skip this chapter. Wilber's system is complex, developed over the course of many books and articles as well as many years of deep thought and prolific writing. The ideas in this chapter will be explained in greater depth later since his system will provide the structure that organizes Chapters 5–13.

Chapters 5–13 provide the practical application of *Creative Synergy* to the individual, the work, the artistic community, and the domain. The organizational framework is Ken Wilber's Integral Operating System: "5 elements" that provide a "comprehensive map of human potentials."[1] For *the first aspect*, Wilber divides a square into four equal quadrants: the *I* or sense of individual self (subjective singular), the *we* or sense of community (subjective plural), the *it* or artifact (objective singular), and the *its* or organizing system (objective plural). (See Figure 2, Chapter 4.) These four universal categories, derived from the pronoun systems of "all major languages," classify a culture's **art, morals,** and **science,** "the Beautiful, the Good, and the True."[2] The *next two aspects*, *lines* and *levels*, are components of developmental stage theory. Human beings mature through various *lines* of development, some of the most famous of which are psychosexual (Freud), psychosocial (Erikson), cognitive (Piaget), and moral (Kohlberg and Gilligan). While progressing through

---

1 Ken Wilber, "The Integral Operating System: An Integral or Comprehensive Map," (February 19, 2012), retrieved from http://integrallife.com/integral-post/integral-operating-system, 1.
2 Ken Wilber, "The Integral Operating System: How It All Fits Together: The Four Quadrants," (February 19, 2012), retrieved from http://integrallife.com/integral-post/integral-operating-system, 6.

these lines, people advance to various *levels* or *stages*. Because each *line* develops separately, maturation is uneven: someone with a highly developed intellect may have immature social skills. *Two other aspects are states and types.* All human beings fluctuate among various states of consciousness, the most familiar of which are waking, dreaming, and deep sleep. Also recognized have been differences between masculine and feminine viewpoints.[3]

Using this system, Chapters 5–13 *take a walk around the square* of Wilber's 4 quadrants. Chapter 5 addresses the individual creator, the *I* as a filter or influence on the idea coming from the Great Thought. Chapter 6 explains the uses and abuses of ego, a self-awareness that both supports and blocks creativity. Chapters 7–8 turn from the singular to the plural. Chapter 7 explains how feeling part of a creative dyad can nurture invention, whether you are pursuing scientific discovery or discussing aesthetic ideas. Chapter 8 applies these ideas to larger groups.

Chapters 9–11 turn from process to product with a focus on the *it*. Key themes are the criteria for establishing greatness and the question of which characteristics are universal and which, domain-specific. As in other chapters, examples will be furnished from many fields.

Chapters 12–13 apply systems theory to the creative process. A system, the objective plural, can be supportive or toxic in its influence. In Chapter 12 we will look at "Great Groups" and other institutional teams. In Chapter 13 we will look at systemic forms of support for creativity, such as patronage.

Finally, Chapter 14 will establish common themes and make suggestions while appendices will offer supplementary material such as charts, alternative exercises, and a bibliography.

How to Use This Book

If you are a student, your instructor will probably want to assign some of the exercises for journaling and class discussion. This book may be heavy on theory in some chapters, but you are probably taking this course because you want to apply what you are learning. The exercises

---

3 Ken Wilber, "The Integral Operating System, What Type?" (February 19, 2012), retrieved from http://integrallife.com/integral-post/integral-operating-system, 4.

are a way to do that.

If you are an instructor in a public U.S. college, you will be concerned about separation of church and state. Accordingly, you will notice that parts of this book deal with spirituality—not to endorse any particular religion but to deal with universal patterns that inspire creativity. If you are hesitant to deal with issues involving transcendence or states of consciousness, you may wish to read the Astins' study of spirituality in entering college students, summarized at the beginning of Chapter 5. Young people report that they are involved with questions about ultimate concerns and values. In addition, many artists, writers, and musicians feel that their ideas are coming from an "idea-space"[4] larger than they are. This theory is called the "idealist" or "causal" view and has commonalities with the Unified Field theories emerging from quantum mechanics and cosmology.

If you are curious about the subject, you may wish to skip the exercises and focus on the chapter explanations. You may also wish to consult some of the additional sources in the bibliography.

If you are a creator looking for inspiration, you will definitely want to practice the ten-step method in Chapter 3. You may also find Chapter 1 interesting in its description of the creative process and Chapter 14 useful in its summary of suggestions. You may wish to study the chapters that pertain most to your field of interest and skim or skip the others. You are also encouraged to try some of the exercises.

For whatever reason you are using this book, I encourage you to contact me. I'd like to hear about your breakthroughs, suggestions, complaints, and ideas.

---

4 Richard Ogle's term as explained in his book *Smart World: Breakthrough Creativity and the New Science of Ideas* (Boston: Harvard Business School Press, 2007).

Introduction

"Imagination is more important
than knowledge."
—Albert Einstein[5]

Why Study Creativity?

The International Center for
Studies in Creativity at Buffalo State,
State University of New York, lists
"12 solid reasons."[6] Here they are, in
bold. (The explanations are mine.)

1. Development of "Your Potential"

The Human Potential Movement,
which blossomed in the 1960s, has
taught us that being fully human is
not just about eliminating pathology
but also about reaching our highest potential. As the old army recruiting poster said, "Be the Best that You Can Be." According to Abraham
Maslow's famous hierarchy, we fulfill our needs in this order: physiological, safety, belonging, esteem, and self-actualization. We must first
have air, water, and food; then we need to have a safe place to live;
then we need to have friends and/or a group; next we need to feel
good about our accomplishments; and at last we need to experience
actualization of our full potential. In his later years Maslow added an
even higher need: "transcendence," the need to transcend our narrow

---

5 Quoted in W. Isaacson, *Einstein: His Life and Universe* (New York: Simon and Schuster,
2007), 7.
6 "Why Study Creativity?" The International Center for Studies in Creativity, Buffalo State,
State University of New York, 2005, http://www.buffalostate.edu/orgs/cbir/readingroom/html/
Why_study.html.

identities and expand our awareness. It is with these last two needs in mind that I wanted to write this book. In order to achieve self-actualization and transcendence, we need to maximize our creativity.

2. "Rapid Growth of Competition in Business and Industry"

Thomas L. Friedman sums up this idea succinctly:

If Americans and Europeans want to benefit from the flattening of the world and the interconnecting of all the markets and knowledge centers, they will all have to run at least as fast as the fastest lion—and I suspect that lion will be China, and I suspect that will be pretty darn fast.[7]

Friedman calls our new world "flat" because technology has connected us and eliminated many hierarchies. Bloggers are competing with standard news outlets. Megacorporations are now competing all over the world, and one entrepreneur with a computer and an idea can compete as well. Friedman says that since the demolition of the Berlin Wall on November 9, 1989, and the mid–nineties proliferation of the Windows PC, followed by the explosion of the World Wide Web, we are all in competition with one another, and the best ideas will win. (This idea is developed further in Chapter 14, Conclusion.)

3. "Effective Use of Human Resources"

Because of the "flat world" mentioned above, we will have to learn to use our human resources wisely. Outsourcing and offshoring mean that jobs in the developed world are moving—to India, to Indonesia, and anywhere that the same job can be done more cheaply and efficiently. How can we compete in the new global economy?

Peter D. Hart Research Associates asked this question of US employers. In 2006 the firm interviewed 305 employers with a staff of at least

---

7 Thomas L. Friedman, *The World Is Flat: A Brief History of the Twenty-First Century*, rev. ed. (New York: Farrar, Straus, and Giroux, 2006), 150.

twenty-five and conducted focus groups with executives in Milwaukee, Wisconsin; Fairfax, Virginia; and Atlanta, Georgia. Overwhelmingly, these employers said that they wanted to hire new workers who had the "soft skills" provided by a liberal education: among them, teamwork (76%), oral and written communication skills (73%), critical thinking and analytical skills (70%), *the ability to be innovative and think creatively (70%)*, and the ability to solve complex problems (64%). In addition, employers felt that colleges did not place enough emphasis on the same above-mentioned skills.[8] [Author's emphasis] I got a similar message from the industry advisory board of Cal State Maritime in January 2001. Using the material in this book in a classroom or workshop setting will access all of these skills; simply reading the book will, obviously, help with creativity skills.

4. Discovery of "New and Better Ways to Solve Problems"

See the survey listed above. With critical thinking you can break problems into parts and critique them; with creative thinking you can synthesize ideas and have the "aha" moment that leaps beyond logic. Richard Ogle says that imagination isn't just another form of thinking. It is a discontinuous leap based upon what he calls "idea–spaces"—nodes of influence where "the extended mind" shares ideas with others. For more, see Chapters 7–8 and 12–13.

5. "Development of Society"

Here's what Daniel Pink has to say:

> For nearly a century, Western society in general, and American society in particular, has been dominated by a form of thinking and an approach to life that is narrowly reductive and deeply analytical . . . But that is changing. Thanks to an array of forces—material abundance that

---

8 P.D. Hart Research Associates, *It Takes More Than a Major: An Online Survey among Employers Conducted by the Association of American College and Universities*, (April 10, 2013), retrieved from www.aacu..org/leap/index.cfm, 1, 2, 8. This important report is also summarized in Rick Reis' *Tomorrow's Professor* listserv, post # 832. *Tomorrow's Professor*, housed at Stanford, is free to anyone who wishes to subscribe: https://mailman.stanford.edu/mailman/listinfo/tomorrows-professor.

is deepening our nonmaterial yearnings, globalization that is shipping white-collar work overseas, and powerful technologies that are eliminating certain kinds of work altogether—we are entering a new age ... [While] "left-brain" capabilities powered the Information Age. . . the capabilities we once thought of as frivolous—the "right-brain" qualities of inventiveness, empathy, joyfulness, and meaning—increasingly will determine who flourishes and who flounders. [9]

In other words, the new global culture demands creativity. Walter Isaacson says that in this new global economy, "A society's competitive advantage will come not from how well its schools teach the multiplication and periodic table, but from how well they stimulated imagination and creativity."[10]

6. Enhancement of your "Knowledge" Base

Some of the chapters in this book are heavily philosophical and will expose you to ideas from many disciplines. When you study the notebooks of Leonardo, the design of Brunelleschi's dome, the specifics of Newton's experiment with prisms, or the process used by Einstein or Feynman to generate ideas, you will have a bag of tools that you can apply to your own life. (Chapter 1 includes a 5-stage process; Chapter 3, a 10-stage process; and the chapter exercises include many other ideas.) In addition, you will enrich your mind by being exposed to some great art and thinking.

7. Part of Being Human

You may think that you are not creative, but you are. Most psychologists believe that like any other skill, creativity operates on a continuum, from the "Creativity with a capital C" that denotes the thinkers listed above to the "everyday creativity" you can apply to cooking or amateur art. By studying some processes and procedures, you can learn how to enhance the creativity you have.

---

9 Daniel Pink, *A Whole New Mind: Moving from the Information Age to the Conceptual Age* (New York: Riverhead Books/Penguin, 2005), 2-3.
10 Isaacson, *Einstein*, 6-7.

8. Augmentation of your "Mental Health"

If we are prevented from exercising our full potential, we can feel depressed or even ill. Seligman and Peterson, who call creativity one of the basic human virtues, narrate this moving example (italics theirs):

At age 68, Elizabeth Layton was a retired homemaker and aging grandmother, living out her final years in a small prairie town in Kansas . . . There was really nothing outstanding about her except for one fact: she frequently suffered profound depression. Indeed, for more than three decades she had undergone all kinds of therapy, including drugs and electroshock. Nothing really helped, but she managed to persevere. And then disaster struck. Her youngest son died after a prolonged illness, plunging her into the darkest despair ever. On several occasions she contemplated suicide as the only exit from her seemingly insurmountable depression. Yet following up her sister's wise suggestion, she enrolled in a drawing class. Elizabeth's art teacher recognized her elderly student's talent even before the course was completed. Elizabeth just loved to draw and draw and draw, creating one sketch after another with great facility and expressiveness. Besides allowing her to release pent-up feelings and beliefs—about death, sadness, AIDS, racism, nuclear war, American commercialism, and other personal and social issues—painting gave Elizabeth something to look forward to each day. She found her mission in life. Her works began to be displayed in art museums and galleries, first locally and then in a traveling exhibit that toured the nation. By the time she died in 1993, she had produced nearly a thousand drawings that made a deep impression on admirers all over the United States. To be sure, Elizabeth will not go down in history as a Michelangelo or a Picasso. But that was never her intention . . . The significant fact is that creativity allowed her to live out her final 15 years with a joy and a sense of purpose that she had been denied all the previous decades of her life. Moreover, while pursuing her vision, she managed to bring happiness and meaning to others.[11]

---

11 Martin Seligman and Christopher Peterson, *Character Strengths and Virtues: A Handbook and Classification* (Oxford, New York: Oxford University Press, in conjunction with the American Psychological Association, 2004), 110.

Creativity, however we practice it, is part of our higher need for self–actualization. Industrial engineers have come to realize that the old assembly line jobs, with their mind–numbing monotony, have an adverse effect on workers.

9. "Growing Body of Interest"

Since John Guilford addressed the American Psychological Association in 1950 to recommend a study of creativity, there has been a growing interest in the area. Psychologists now study both the process and the product. They conduct experiments, review case studies, and are defining what creativity is and how it functions.

A rich diversity of materials is now available on creativity, from the popular to the academic or the pragmatic to the theoretical. Specialized approaches also abound. Biographies of scientists like Barbara McClintock and artists like Michelangelo illuminate their creative processes. The business community regularly comments on what it calls "innovation," and in 2006 the academic liberal arts association AAC&U released an entire issue on creativity as one of its *Peer Review* magazines. Between 1920 and 1950, "out of the 121,000 titles listed in *Psychological Abstracts . . .* only 186 dealt with creativity . . . From the late 1960's until 1991, almost 9,000 references have been added to the creativity literature." [12] See the bibliography at the end of this book for many examples.

10. Application to "All Disciplines"

One of my colleagues, upon being told of creativity in science, engineering, math, business, and maritime transportation, exclaimed, "And I thought creativity was just an artsy–fartsy thing!"

Not at all! Creativity is all around us, even in the everyday objects we use. For instance, Daniel Pink alludes to an aesthetically remarkable toi-

---

12 These statistics are quoted in Gregory J. Feist and Mark A. Runco, "Trends in Creativity Literature: An Analysis of Research in the *Journal of Creative Behavior* (1967-1989)," *Creativity Research Journal 6 (*1993): 272, as cited in Robert S. Albert and Mark A. Runco, "A History of Research on Creativity," in *Handbook of Creativity,* ed. Robert J. Sternberg, (Cambridge, MA: University Press, 1999), 17.

let brush, to be had at Target for $5.99 and "designed by Michael Graves, a Princeton University architecture professor and one of the most renowned architects and product designers in the world."[13] Pink says, "We may not all be Dali or Degas. But today we must all be designers."[14]

11. Contribution to "Effective Leadership"

A leader today must know how to be creative and to inspire creativity in others. A good example is US Captain Michael D. Abrashoff, who commanded what he called "The Best Damn Ship in the Navy." He states his philosophy as follows: "I worked hard to create a climate that encouraged quixotic pursuits and celebrated the freedom to fail. I never once reprimanded a sailor for attempting to solve a problem or reach a goal. I wanted my people to feel empowered, so they could think autonomously."[15] In the modern maritime world, the empowerment that supports both creativity and leadership occurs in the system of Bridge Resource Management. (See the discussion by Professors Messer–Bookman, Hayes, and Buckley, interviewed for Chapter 12 of this book.)

12. Enhancement of the "Learning" "Process"

Thomas L. Friedman says that in our fast–changing global economy, "Average Joe has to become special, specialized, synthesizing, or adaptable Joe."[16] The world of the future belongs to the lifelong learner— someone willing to explore new ideas.

In US colleges the learning process can seem fragmented. You take one course, do a final and paper; take another course, do a final and project. It can seem that all you're doing is accumulating credits, checking off the boxes on a list. But when you think creatively, you transfer ideas from one course to another, synthesizing knowledge and creating new knowledge from it. This sort of skill that will make you happy, productive, and successful all your life. Daniel Pink says,

---

13 Pink, *A Whole New Mind*, 34.
14 Ibid., 69.
15 D. Michael Abrashoff, *It's Your Ship: Management Techniques from the Best Damn Ship in the Navy* (New York: Time Warner, 2002), 34.
16 Pink, *A Whole New Mind*, 367.

The last few decades have belonged to a certain kind of person with a certain kind of mind—computer programmers who could crank code, lawyers who could craft contracts, MBAs who could crunch numbers. But the keys to the kingdom are changing hands. The future belongs to a very different kind of person with a very different kind of mind—creators and empathizers, pattern recognizers, and meaning makers. These people—artists, inventors, designers, storytellers, caregivers, consolers, big picture thinkers—will now reap society's richest rewards and share its greatest joys.[17]

So here are "12 solid reasons" to study creativity. Can you think of any others?

---

17 Pink, *A Whole New Mind*, 1.

Exercises

1. Which of the reasons in this introduction appeals most to you? Why?
2. What can you add to this list, or how would you react to it in general?
3. What has been your experience with creativity so far? Do you feel you are a creative person? In what fields and in what ways?
4. How can you exercise your creativity now or in the future?
5. What creative people do you admire? Which of their characteristics would you like to imitate? (Try imitating them.)

THEORY:
BASIC ASSUMPTIONS
AND CONCEPTS

Synergistic Interlude

"The Golden Key,"
Jacob and Wilhelm Grimm, #200

"Once in the wintertime when the snow was very deep, a poor boy had to go out and fetch wood on a sled. After he had gathered it together and loaded it, he did not want to go straight home, because he was so frozen, but instead to make a little fire and warm himself first. So he scraped the snow away, and while he was thus cleaning the ground he found a small golden key. Now he believed that where there was a key, there must also be a lock, so he dug in the ground and found a little iron chest. 'If only the key fits!' he thought. 'Certainly there are valuable things in the chest.' He looked, but there was no keyhole. Finally he found one, but so small that it could scarcely be seen. He tried the key and fortunately it fitted. Then he turned it once, and now we must wait until he has finished unlocking it and has opened the lid. Then we shall find out what kind of wonderful things there were in the little chest."[18]

---

18 D.L. Ashliman, ed., *Folklore and Mythology: Electronic Texts*, accessed on April 3, 2014, http://www.pitt.edu/~dash/folkexts.html.

Questions to Ponder

1. What do you think the key is?

2. What are the combinations of opposites in this fairy tale?

3. What does this fairy tale have to say about spirituality and/or creativity?

4. What metaphor would you use instead of a key?

5. Of what other stories or fairy tales does this tale remind you?

1

What is Creativity?

A Trick Quiz

Circle all the statements that are true about creativity.

Creativity can be studied as a process.

Creativity is dependent on the individual will.

There is such a thing as the creative personality.

Creativity is the same in all domains.

Creativity results from inspiration.

Creativity is mysterious.

Creativity can be evaluated in a product.

Creativity is dependent on the environment.

Everyone is creative.

Creativity is different in different fields.

Creativity results from hard work.

Creativity has been studied and defined.

CALVIN AND HOBBES © 1995 Watterson.

If you circled all of the answers, you are correct.

The Process of Creativity

Like using the key, creativity is a process. You may have seen it listed as four, five, or six steps.[19] The usual description is of five stages:

Preparation. The creator becomes immersed in the formulas and rules of the craft. Often quoted is Pasteur's dictum: "Chance favors the prepared mind." Edison tested thousands of filaments to find one that would work in his incandescent electric light.[20] The often-cited "ten-year rule" is that a successful artist must practice the craft at least ten years before success.[21]

Concentration. The creator becomes obsessed. Flaubert spent whole nights searching for a single adjective and forced his mistress to live away from him, in Paris, lest he become distracted. Gauguin abandoned his family in France to find his artistic subjects in Tahiti. Edison spent days in his lab without going home;[22] and Einstein was the "icon" of the "absent-minded professor." On a journey, he sometimes forgot some of his clothes or even his suitcase.[23]

Incubation. The creator hits a wall, runs into a problem. Meanwhile, unconscious processes work on a solution. Poincaré, a mathematician, said, "Often when one is working at a hard question, nothing good is accomplished at the first attack. Then one takes a rest, shorter or longer, and sets down anew to the work."[24]

Illumination. The eureka moment arrives. Poincaré called it "a

---

19 See, for example, Rosanoff and Campbell.

20 I have seen the number mentioned as both ten thousand and forty-three thousand.

21 See, for example, Simonton, "Creativity as a Constrained Stochastic Process," 91-92; Weisberg.

22 Randall Stross, *The Wizard of Menlo Park: How Thomas Alva Edison Invented the Modern World* (New York: Crown, 2007), 66.

23 Isaacson, *Einstein*, 39.

24 Henri Poincaré, "Mathematic Creation," in *The Creative Process: Reflections on the Invention in the Arts and Sciences,* ed. Brewster Ghiselin (New York: Mentor Books, New American Library, 1952), 38. The three facets, based on his triarchic theory of intelligence, are "its relation to the internal world of the individual, its relation to experience, and its relation to the external world of the individual." (p. 132)

manifestation of long, unconscious prior work."[25] Nobel Prize winner Barbara McClintock called it "integration." She claimed that although the solution came suddenly, it was not a lightning bolt of intuition but in the words of her biographer Nathaniel Comfort, a sudden "synthesis of many bits of knowledge."[26] Comfort believes that this sort of thinking is common in math and physics: "The most famous integrator of all was Albert Einstein." His eureka moments came in pictures, such as when he conceived the relativity theory by imagining himself riding a beam of light. McClintock's illuminations came too fast for pictures.[27]

Verification. The creator must test the work to identify its usefulness in the field, defined by Csikszentmihalyi as "all the individuals who act as gatekeepers."[28] A poet like Emily Dickinson or a painter like Vincent van Gogh may eschew this step or make light of it; an engineer considers this phase crucial.[29] Verification was a problem for Edison—creative in the realm of ideas yet unable to grasp the pragmatics of marketing. He insisted that his phonograph should be used for office dictation rather than for music. When forced to produce records, he disdained the popular songs for which the public clamored, such as "Throw Him Down, McCloskey" and "One of His Legs is Longer Than It Really Ought to Be." He ignored the popularity of the cheap AC current and fought a losing battle for DC. He took an adamant stand against movie projection systems in favor of kinetoscopes into which people stooped to stare. His friend Henry Ford called Edison "'the world's greatest inventor and world's worst businessman.'"[30]

The Aspects of Creativity

Creativity can be evaluated in a product. Like the judge who claimed to know pornography when he saw it, most of us know creativity when

25 Poincaré, "Mathematical Creation," 38.

26 Nathaniel C. Comfort, *The Tangled Field: Barbara McClintock's Search for the Patterns of Genetic Control* (Cambridge, MA: Harvard University Press, 2003), 68.

27 Ibid., 67.

28 Mihaly Csikszentmihalyi, *Creativity: Flow and the Psychology of Discovery and Invention* (New York: HarperCollins, 1996), 28.

29 On the importance of the validation phase to engineers, see Petroski.

30 Stross, *The Wizard of Menlo Park,* 194, 199, 181, 197-198, 253.

we see it, especially in its highest manifestations. The criteria, of course, are different in different fields. Harold Bloom's test of literary greatness is the effect of the work:

> **The question we need to put to any writer must be: does she or he augment our consciousness, and how is it done? I find this a rough but effectual test: however I have been entertained, has my awareness been intensified, my consciousness widened and clarified? If not, then I have encountered talent, not genius. What is best and oldest in myself has not been activated.[31]**

The three criteria he cites are "aesthetic splendor, cognitive power, wisdom."[32] In contrast, scientists speak of the "beautiful experiment," one that embodies "unexpectedness, inevitability, and economy" as well as "depth."[33] One example is Newton's dispersion of light through prisms to prove the revolutionary hypothesis that white light is composed of colors.[34] (See Chapters 10–11 for aesthetic criteria.)

Creativity is dependent on the individual will. Robert Sternberg claims "the key attribute" of "creative people" is that they make a "decision to be creative."[35] In psychological terms, they are intrinsically motivated: interested in the task for its own sake. As a child, Nobel laureate Richard Feynman fixed radios for fun. Einstein's sister reported that as a boy, he had eschewed ordinary play for math: "'For days on end he sat alone, immersed in the search for a solution, not giving up before he had found it.'"[36]

---

31 Harold Bloom, *Genius: A Mosaic of One Hundred Exemplary Minds* (New York: Warner, 2002), 12.

32 Harold Bloom, *20th Anniversary Edition: Dramatists and Dramas* (New York: Readers Subscription Book Club, 2006), ix.

33 G. H. Hardy, "A Mathematician's Apology," cited in Robert P. Crease, *The Prism and the Pendulum: The Ten Most Beautiful Experiments in Science* (New York: Random House, 2003), xxvi.

34 Paul Strathern, *The Big Idea Collected: 6 Revolutionary Ideas That Changed the World* (New York: Quality Paperback Book Club, 1999), 54-56; Crease, *The Prism and the Pendulum*, 64-76.

35 Robert J. Sternberg, "Creativity as a Decision." *American Psychologist* 57, no. 5 (May 2002): 376.

36 Quoted in Isaacson, *Einstein*, 17.

Teresa Amabile has done many studies of intrinsic motivation. In one of her experiments, children were divided into two groups. Some were told they could play with crayons if they used colored markers first. Others were told the reverse: they had to play with crayons in order to use the markers. In both cases, children who could select their own art materials later were inclined to reject the tools that had been imposed on them as required. Instead both played with the ones that had been promised as rewards.[37]

Amabile has conducted many versions of this experiment, and she has found that extrinsic motivation—the anticipation of a reward—tends to extinguish intrinsic motivation—the inner willingness to perform a task. Occasionally intrinsic motivation remains when it was high originally and the subject is engaged in a heuristic task (one not following a formula by rote).[38] Her Intrinsic Motivation Principle of Creativity reads as follows: "Intrinsic motivation is conducive to creativity; controlling extrinsic motivation is detrimental to creativity, but informational or enabling extrinsic motivation can be conducive, particularly if initial levels of intrinsic motivation are high."[39] If we enjoy a pastime for its own sake, we are more likely to be creative. "Controlling" factors such as deadlines and external authorities can dampen creativity unless we perceive their feedback as helpful during an intrinsically interesting task. For example, students who enjoy writing will tend to react favorably to instructor feedback on a rough draft. They will see it as "informational" and "enabling," helping them to improve. On the other hand, those outer-directed students who dislike writing and are performing for a grade may be inclined to say, in exasperation, "Just tell me what you want." In one study undergraduates with an internal locus of control (inner-directed rather than outer-directed) scored higher on creativity tests.[40]

The following cartoon reveals the failure of most extrinsic motivation.

---

37 *Discovering Psychology,* Annenburg/CPB Collection featuring Philip Zimbardo, video 4, program 20: Constructing social reality (WGBH, Boston: PBS Educational video in association with the APA, 1989), VHS tape.

38 Teresa M. Amabile, *Creativity in Context* (Boulder, CO: Westview Press, 1996), 117-19.

39 Amabile, *Creativity in Context*, 119.

40 Ibid., 132-33.

CALVIN AND HOBBES © 1995 Watterson.
Reprinted with permission of UNIVERSAL PRESS SYNDICATE. All rights reserved.

Creativity is dependent on the environment. Csikszentmihalyi stresses the importance of the field in supporting or rejecting creative work. In the art world of the twentieth century, New York gallery owners determined who was hot and who was not.[41] In literary studies, the fads of the day determine what work is canonical. Blake, rarely taught in graduate school in the 1950s, became one of the most popular Romantic poets a few decades later; Milton was out by then, and Donne was in. Csikszentmihalyi goes so far as to say that a work is not creative unless it is endorsed by the field and changes it![42] At the extreme of such a position, Emily Dickinson's work did not become "creative" until after her death.

The Creative Personality

There is such a thing as the creative personality. There is some debate about whether a "creative personality" exists, but this chart summarizes the views of six prominent theorists. In some cases the descriptors may overlap because of varying definitions.

---

41 Csikszentmihalyi, *Creativity: Flow and the Psychology of Discovery and Invention*, 55.

42 See Howard Gardner's discussion of this theory in *Intelligence Reframed: Multiple Intelligences for the 21st Century* (New York: Basic Books, 1999), 117-19.

Sternberg (1988) From "A Three-Factor Model of Creativity," 146.	Maisel (2007) From *Creativity for Life*, 17.	Campbell (1977) From *Take the Road to Creativity . . .*, 43-71.	Andreason (2006) From *The Creative Brain*, 30-31.	Simonton (1999) From *Origins of Genius*, 90-92.
"Lack of conventionality": "one makes up rules as one goes along; has a free spirit; is unorthodox"	"Non-conformity"		"rebelliousness," "individualism," "adventuresomeness"	independence, autonomy, unconventionality, iconoclastism
"Integration and intellectuality": one "makes connections and distinctions between ideas and things; has the ability to recognize similarities and differences; is able to put old information, theories, etc., together in a new way"; *"Aesthetic taste and imagination"*: one has an appreciation of art, music, etc.; can write, draw, compose music; has good taste	"Intelligence"	"Playfulness," "Convergent Thinking," "Divergent Thinking," "Intellectual Curiosity" "playfulness," "curiosity"	"playfulness," "curiosity"	"an impressive array of intellectual, cultural, and aesthetic interests" "defocused attention" on more than one domain

Sternberg (1988) From "A Three-Factor Model of Creativity," 146.	Maisel (2007) From Creativity for Life, 17.	Campbell (1977) From Take the Road to Creativity . . ., 43-71.	Andreason (2006) From The Creative Brain, 30-31.	Simonton (1999) From Origins of Genius, 90-92.
"Decisional skill and flexibility": one "follows gut feelings in making decisions after weighing the pros and cons; has the ability to change directions and use another procedure"	"Self-centeredness," "Self-direction,"	"Avoidance of Early Self-Criticism of Ideas," "Independent Judgment"	"openness," "tolerance of ambiguity"	"openness to "novel, complex, and ambiguous stimuli," flexibility "both cognitively and behaviorally"
"Perspicacity": one questions societal norms, truisms, assumptions; is willing to take a stand"; "Drive for accomplishment and recognition": one "is motivated by goals; likes to be complimented on work; is energetic"	"Assertiveness," "Resiliency"	"Independent Judgment"	"persistence," "simplicity" in "singleness of vision" and "dedication" to the "work" [Intrinsic Motivation]	independence, autonomy
	"Introspective stance"			introversion
	"Honesty"			
	"Empathy"		"sensitivity"	

Can you think of anyone who has all or most of these traits? John Lennon comes to my mind.

He was unorthodox in his behavior, especially after meeting Yoko Ono, with whom he staged a "Bed–in–for Peace" during his honeymoon in Amsterdam and Montreal. The two of them sat in bed while journalists interviewed them about peace and Hare Krishnas chanted in the background. A still–famous song came out of this happening: "Give Peace a Chance." Lennon was also highly intellectual and integrative in his ideas. His dialogues, as recorded, roam from profanity to Eastern philosophy to cynical observation to bizarre symbolism to music history, and more. He drew highly original cartoons, wrote cryptic symbolism, and played the guitar and piano. He changed directions, after founding the Beatles as a pop band, when he grew bored with perpetuating the same moptop show; he wanted to explore new styles and grow as an artist. After he began living with Yoko in New York, he took so many stands for his radical ideas that the FBI was tailing him and efforts were made to eject him from the country. He was goal–oriented, especially in the beginning. He was often quoted as saying something like, "I always knew I was going to be famous someday but wasn't sure how. Maybe music, maybe crime." While the Beatles were still learning their craft and playing in dives, he would ask them, "Where are we going, boys?" And they would have to answer, "To the toppermost of the poppermost, Johnny!"

Francis Ford Coppola is the poster child for *Drive, Resilience, Independent Judgment, Self-Confidence, and Perspicacity*. His wife's documentary *Hearts of Darkness* (1991) shows the obstacles he overcame in making *Apocalypse Now* (1979): a typhoon, creative blocks, cast problems, equipment problems, and even struggles with his own mental well–being. Yet he said, "It's not in the cards that we're not going to make this film." When he finally finished, over budget and over schedule, he wanted to show it at Cannes. He was told that he had to enter it, even though he protested that it was unedited. He entered it—and won the *Palm D'or*.

He also works by intuition. *Hearts of Darkness* (1991) captured his creative process: his *openness* to using whatever happened, including Marty Sheen's drunken rage and a typhoon in the Philippines; his improvisational method of working with the actors' inspiration and giving them cards that said, just before shooting, "Dialogue to be determined." He had *decisional skill*. When he saw the rushes the first day, he was *flexible* enough to replace his leading man. When he didn't like a "plantation" subplot on which he had spent much time and money, he cut the whole sequence.

Additional Characteristics of Creativity

David Campbell lists additional characteristics. Here are some of the most notable of them.[43] (The concepts are his, and the bold type and explanations are mine.)

1. **"Convergent thinking"—"the ability to scan many relevant facts, then zero in on those facts most likely to result in the correct solution to a particular problem."**
For instance, cross out six letters below to leave a common English word.

B S A I N X L E A T N T E A R S

(The answer is at the end of this chapter.)

I personally loathe this sort of test, but early studies of creativity in the 1950s and 1960s used it. The idea is that most people get stuck in one mode of thought and creative people consider unusual and original alternatives. I prefer the more recent studies of creativity that do experiments or case studies of people actually creating in their fields.

Amabile, one of the most respected psychologists in the field today, might say that problems like the above are not true creativity: they are "algorithmic," dependent on coming up with the one correct formula, rather than "heuristic," defining original procedures. She adds that many views of creativity mention *defining the problem* as an important part of the process.[44] This would certainly be true in math, science, and engineering. (See Chapter 10.)

43David Campbell, *Take the Road to Creativity*, (Allen, TX: Argus, 1977), 43-71.
44 Amabile, *Creativity in Context*, 35, 36.

2. "Divergent thinking"—"the ability to fan out in all directions from an idea."

John Guildford and other earlier theorists about creativity liked to use this method.

An example was, "List the uses of a brick." The idea was that the creative person could concoct a longer list with more unusual examples.

3. "Independent Judgment"—the ability to have faith in one's ideas, no matter what others say.

A classic example is Emily Dickinson, who wrote quixotic poetry. She used startling word choices, capitalized all important words, and punctuated with dashes. She sought advice from an editor, Thomas Higginson, who warned her that she would have to regularize her verse in order to be published. So instead she put her verse in a drawer. Now her original choices are praised as highly creative, and the first editions of her poetry, which regularized punctuation and diction, are considered inferior.

4. "Intellectual curiosity"—the penchant to wonder "What?" Why?" and "How?"

The supreme example is Leonardo da Vinci, who wondered about almost everything he saw. He filled his notebooks with drawings of possible inventions and anatomical observations. (See Chapter 10 for examples.) Gelb, who calls *"Curiosità"* one of the main principles to follow in order to think like Leonardo da Vinci,[45] quotes this example from Leonardo's notebooks:

> I roamed the countryside searching for things I did not understand. Why shells existed on the tops of mountains along with the imprints of coral and plants and sea weed usually found in the sea. Why the thunder lasts a longer time than that which causes it, and why immediately on its creation the lightning becomes visible to the eye while thunder re-

---

45 Michael J. Gelb, *How to Think Like Leonardo da Vinci: Seven Steps to Genius Every Day* (New York: Delacorte, 1998), 48-75.

quires time to travel. How the various circles of water form around the spot which has been struck by a stone, and why a bird sustains itself in the air. These questions and other strange phenomena engage my thought throughout my life.[46]

5. Playfulness—the possession of "a strong sense of humor and rich fantasy life."

Richard Feynman, who shared the Nobel Prize for physics in 1965, characterizes himself as "a bit of a clown."[47] While he was working on the Manhattan Project to build the atomic bomb, he amused himself by figuring out ways to crack the locks on safes and filing cabinets in offices at the Los Alamos compound. He narrates his adventures in a delightfully humorous tone: "I had just opened two safes cold. I was getting good. Now I was professional." After he'd cracked a drawer or safe, he often left a note like: "'This one was no harder to open than the other one—Wise Guy.'" His colleagues were alarmed, suspecting an outside job, until they realized it was just Feynman goofing around again. The goofing could be productive, though. Once as he watched someone in the Cornell cafeteria throwing a plate into the air, he began to calculate the parameters of motion involved. Eventually he derived a complicated equation. He showed it to a colleague, who proclaimed it "' interesting'" but asked, "'What's the importance of it? Why are you doing it?'" "'Ha!'" said Feynman. "'There's no importance whatsoever; I'm just doing it for the fun of it.'" The calculations were to win him the Nobel Prize.[48]

6. Avoidance of "early self–criticism of their ideas"—the ability to play with an idea instead of rejecting it outright as flawed.

The example of Edison and the light bulb is listed above. He is said to have remarked that all his earlier trials were useful because they showed him ways in which the filament would *not* work! (See Chapter

---

46 Quoted in Gelb, *How to Think Like Leonardo da Vinci*, 50.

47 Richard Feynman, *Classic Feynman: All the Adventures of a Curious Character*, ed. Ralph Leighton (New York, London: Norton, 2006), 5.

48 The quote is from *Classic Feynman*, 168; the safecracking episodes are narrated in 154-71, with the quoted note on 165; the plate spinning episode on 190-91.

10 for this process of reworking ideas in engineering.)

Albert Rothenberg defines creative thinking another way: the ability to hold tensions of opposites together as true.[49] Einstein had this "ability to hold two thoughts in his mind simultaneously, to be puzzled when they conflicted, and to marvel when he could smell an underlying unity."[50] This sort of thinking, common in the East, is expressed in the famous saying, "Truth is one; many are the names." There is a truth of literary representation, a truth of scientific experimentation, and a truth of spiritual experience; we need not say *either-or* because we can say *both-and*. This sort of thinking creates powerful literary effects like irony and complexity: Luke Skywalker in *Star Wars* is both disciple of Yoda and son of Darth Vader; Frodo in *Lord of the Rings* sets out to destroy the ring but also succumbs at times to its seductions. In their use of arresting metaphors, poets draw upon this sort of thinking: the moon or the rose can convey many meanings, all simultaneously true. Arieti termed this kind of metaphorical thinking the ability to find "the similar in the dissimilar."[51] (For more examples, see Chapters 9 and 11.)

Amabile's Componential Model identifies a set of "dispositional, cognitive, and social factors" interacting to produce various degrees of creativity: "Domain–Relevant Skills," "Creativity–Relevant Skills," and "Task Motivation." [52] A "dispositional" factor would have to do with your temperament, as defined above: for example, your degree of flexibility, persistence, curiosity, playfulness, and perspicacity. A "cognitive" factor has to do with your thinking (such as unorthodox, convergent, divergent, synthetic, or integrative). A "social" factor might connote how well you are supported by a network or system (See Chapters 12 and 13, also "Creativity is dependent on the environment," above.) If you are in a band, you may well be able to play better than artists who are famous, but the social environment controls, to some extent, whether you get the breaks. (See the Conclusion to read how getting around gatekeepers may be easier now than it was a few decades ago.)

49 Albert Rothenberg, "The Process of Janusian Thinking in Creativity," *Archives of General Psychiatry 24* (1971): 195.

50 Isaacson, *Einstein*, 15.

51 Silvano Arieti, *Creativity: The Magic Synthesis* (New York: Basic Books, Harper Colophon, 1976), 136.

52 Amabile, *Creativity in Context*, 82-83, 77.

You must also be knowledgeable in your domain. A "domain," as defined by Csikszentmihalyi, is "a set of symbolic rules and procedures" such as "number theory"[53] or the rules of composition in painting. "Creativity–Relevant Skills" would entail effectiveness in the process, such as immersing yourself in the task and allowing time for incubation. "Task Motivation" refers to the drive or will to create: Sternberg's "decision to be creative." While all of these factors may not be present in all creators, there is a positive correlation between them and creative success in general. (See the Exercises for applications of these ideas.)

Creativity results from inspiration. We usually think of creativity as the Stage 4 "Aha" or Illumination: the "Eureka! I've got it!" of Archimedes in the bathtub. What he got, allegedly, was how to use water displacement in determining whether a gold crown had been adulterated with baser metal.

The British Romantic poets conceived inspiration as a divine wind, coming and going of its own will. In his poem "Dejection" Coleridge, who had an Aeolian harp set in his hallway to catch the drafts, yearns to be set quivering like his harp. In "The Eolian Harp" (1795–1817), Coleridge wonders whether there is a cosmic principle of creativity blowing through all of us like the wind:

> . . . what if all of animated nature
> Be but organic harps diversely framed,
> That tremble into thought, as o'er them sweeps
> Plastic and vast, one intellectual breeze,
> At once the Soul of each, and God of all? (ll. 44-48)

The problem with the "Wind Theory of Creativity" is the same as the problem with wind turbines as a source of alternative energy. The winds don't always blow. When they don't, you need another form of energy!

Creativity results from hard work. In contrast to the "Wind Theory" is the "Sweat Theory." Edison said that creativity is "one percent inspiration

---

53 Csikszentmihalyi, *Creativity*, 27-28.

and ninety–nine percent perspiration." The artists and thinkers before the Romantics would have agreed with him. The great painter Sir Joshua Reynolds (1769–1790) instructed his pupils at the Academy of Art to work not on inspiration but on technique.[54] Similarly, the great artists of the Italian Renaissance worked for commissions and learned their craft through guild apprenticeships. While building the great dome in Florence, Brunelleschi engaged in hard work. He created an ox–driven cogwheel with a reverse gear to hoist 1,700–pound stones "several hundred feet" to the "cupola." He invented sandstone–embedded chains to hold the gigantic structure in place without "centering" devices.[55] He was not waiting for the winds of inspiration to blow. (For more on the geniuses of the Florentine Renaissance, see Chapters 11 and 13.) Sweat Theorists focus on Stage 1, Preparation, and Stage 2, Concentration.

There is something to be said for both wind and sweat in the exercise of creativity. I received many mini–inspirations while writing this book, but I found that they came from daily writing and thinking about the project. I also found that the more often I wrote, the more easily the words would flow.

Creativity is mysterious. Many artists feel that their products are a gift from something greater than themselves. The ancients spoke of the *Daimon*, the creator's genius or Muse, the supernatural entity that allowed him to access higher realms and translate their eternal truths into reality.[56] Harold Bloom calls this "genius" "the god within."[57] Director Federico Fellini reports,

From the moment I begin to work . . . someone takes over, a mysterious invader, an invader that I don't know, takes over the whole show.

---

54 Dean Keith Simonton, "Creativity as a Constrained Stochastic Process," in *Creativity: From Potential to Realization,* ed. Robert J. Sternberg, Elena L. Grigorenko, and Jerome L. Singer, (Washington, D.C.: APA, 2004), 84.

55 Ross King, *Brunelleschi's Dome: How a Renaissance Genius Reinvented Architecture* (New York: Walker, 2000), 57-62, 70-75.

56 Albert and Runco, 1999; Sternberg, 1999; Simonton, 2004. Sheldrake, 310-16, has a good overview of the mechanistic philosophy of the seventeenth century. See also Bunny Paine-Clemes, "*The Yugas:* Divine Agents of Change," *Joy: The Journal of Yoga,* 4, No. 3 (Summer 2005) . (Posted July, 2005, at www.journalofyoga.org/).

57 Bloom, *Genius,* 11.

He directs everything for me. I just put my voice at his disposal, and my know-how, my attempts at being seductive, or borrowing ideas, or being authoritarian. But it's someone else, not me, with whom I co-exist, but who I don't know, or know only by hearsay.[58]

Bloom cites a passage from Emerson's *Journals* about the shock of recognition we find in a creative work that echoes our deepest feelings: "'It is a God in you that responds to God without, or affirms his own words trembling on the lips of another.'"[59] This view focuses on Stage 4, Illumination.

Creativity has been studied and defined. In a 1950 address to the American Psychological Association, John Guildford recommended more study of creativity. Since then the books, articles, and studies have proliferated. Between 1920 and 1950, "out of the 121,000 titles listed in *Psychological Abstracts* . . . only 186 dealt with creativity . . . From the late 1960s until 1991, almost 9,000 references have been added to the creativity literature." [60]

If you're interested in a summary of how major psychologists have studied creativity, a thorough overview is provided in Amabile.[61] From an initial focus on mechanical tasks, such as listing the uses of a brick or solving a problem with only one correct answer, psychologists have fanned out in many directions, doing experiments and studying famous creators.

What is Creativity?

So what is creativity? The working definition you will see in many sources is that it is the creation of something both novel and useful.[62]

For instance, John Lennon is known as a major creative artist. The group he assembled, the Beatles, wrote and performed music that

---

58 Federico Fellini, *Fellini: I'm a Born Liar*, (First Look Media: 2003), documentary movie.

59 Emerson's *Journals*: October 27, 1831, quoted in Bloom, *Genius*, 3.

60 These statistics are quoted in Feist and Runco, 1993, 272, as cited in Albert and Runco, 1999, 17.

61 Amabile, *Creativity in Context*, 3-41.

62 For instance, see Seligman, 110; Sternberg, "What is the Common Thread of Creativity?" 360.

revolutionized the taste of his era and is still enjoyed by listeners today. With succeeding albums, especially *Sergeant Pepper's Lonely Hearts Club Band* (1967), the Beatles experimented, pushed the boundaries of music, and provided delight with their lyrics and melodies.

Here is something that John Lennon did that was *not* so creative.

After talking with Yoko Ono all night their first time together, he made love to her as the dawn rose, and then they recorded an album celebrating their union. Called *Two Virgins*, it featured their naked bodies on the cover and consisted of electronic noises and caterwauling screeches. The album was undoubtedly meaningful to *them*—but others were not amused. The record sold only to diehard fans, and the cover photo was blanked out by what looked like a brown paper bag, except for the two heads of the lovers.

This was novelty, but it didn't have much use. (It may have some use now; the original covers without the brown bags are now worth a small fortune.) In this case Lennon forgot Stages 3, Incubation, and 5, Verification.

The Paradox of Creativity

So creativity is a paradox. It is both person and product, inspiration and perspiration, will and receptivity. It must also be novel yet acceptable. Jacques Barzun comments on the paradox often facing creators: "Most often their work has been hampered and ignored by the very society that now keeps boosting innovation. This paradox takes the form of saying, in words or by actions, 'We want what is new and wonderful, not the strange and repellent thing you offer.'"[63] Something must be new—but not *too new*. If it is, the audience walks out of the performance or the critic savages the poem or art exhibit. If you could call up some great creative artists of the past, you could ask them how their iconoclastic new work was received at first. Ask Nijinski about the simulated masturbation in his ballet *Afternoon of a Faun*; ask Stravinsky about his revolutionary chords in *Firebird*. Ask Melville how *Moby Dick* was first received; Coleridge, Wordsworth, and Keats, how Romantic

---

63 Jacques Barzun, "The Paradoxes of Creativity," *American Scholar* 58, no. 3 (Summer 1989): 341.

poetry was first received; the Impressionists, how their art was received. Ask Galileo how the church liked his refutation of Ptolemy. Ask John Lennon about the strong language in "The Ballad of John and Yoko": "The way things are going, they're gonna crucify me!"

Sternberg notes that creative people "often feel attacked for their ideas"—for good reason, "since their crowd–defying ideas are incompatible with conventional ways of thinking and vested interests." What they don't understand is that by presenting an idea in opposition, they themselves are generating the attack! "An antithesis is, by its nature, oppositional."[64] Hence the need for such creators to have courage and stand by their independent judgment, which may be vindicated after their death. Vera John–Steiner, perhaps quoting Rollo May, speaks of "'the courage to create'":[65] to persist despite lack of support or inspiration.

In the next chapter I will present an idea that may seem oppositional. However, I believe that rather than an antithesis, it is a synthesis: a theory that can coexist with traditional views of creativity.

The letters that are bolded and underlined have been crossed out:

B S A I N X L E A T N T E A R S.

Yes, if you cross out "SIX LETTERS," you get "BANANA"! (Ugh!)

---

64 Sternberg, "What is the Common Thread of Creativity?", 361.

65 Vera John-Steiner, *Notebooks of the Mind: Explorations of Thinking*, rev. ed. (1985; New York Oxford University Press, 1997), 79.

Exercises

1. Explain the ways in which the opening "Interlude" relates to the material in this chapter.

2. Read over the five-step process of creativity (pp. 2-3). How have you experienced it yourself, either while working on class assignments or creating for fun? Are the stages different for you? For instance, do you sometimes return to an earlier stage such as incubation when you have already had some "eureka moment"?

3. In your experience, when has extrinsic motivation (such as working for a grade) interfered with intrinsic motivation (creating for the sheer pleasure)? Is it different in different courses? Is it different in school than in other contexts? How would you advise teachers to draw on intrinsic motivation while still being required to provide a grade?

4. Read over the discussion of the "creative personality" (pp. 9-10). How would you apply these characteristics to yourself and/or someone else you know or know about?

5. How does the "Wind Theory" of creativity apply to you? How does the "Sweat Theory" apply? Explain examples.

6. Have you ever felt vulnerable to attack while expressing your creativity? If so, describe an example or two.

7. List some of the puzzling or unclear ideas in Chapter 1. Ask questions about them.

8. Explain what you think is most important in Chapter 1.

9. React to some of the ideas in Chapter 1. Debate, support, analyze, and/or reflect.

10. Give evidence from your own life or background experience about the ideas in Chapter 1. (Don't repeat what you have written in another exercise.)

11. Watch the film *Hearts of Darkness,* and analyze Francis Ford Coppola's creative process as he made *Apocalypse Now.* How did he use the stages of creativity? How did he exemplify the creative personality?

Synergistic Interlude

Alice in Wonderland Chapter I: "Down the Rabbit Hole"

"Alice was beginning to get very tired of sitting by her sister on the bank, and of having nothing to do . . .

"So she was considering in her own mind (as well as she could, for the hot day made her feel very sleepy and stupid), whether the pleasure of making a daisy-chain would be worth the trouble of getting up and picking the daisies, when suddenly a White Rabbit with pink eyes ran close by her.

"There was nothing so VERY remarkable in that; nor did Alice think it so VERY much out of the way to hear the Rabbit say to itself, `Oh dear! Oh dear! I shall be late!' (when she thought it over afterwards, it occurred to her that she ought to have wondered at this, but at the time it all seemed quite natural); but when the Rabbit actually TOOK A WATCH OUT OF ITS WAISTCOAT-POCKET, and looked at it, and then hurried on, Alice started to her feet, for it flashed across her mind that she had never before seen a rabbit with either a waistcoat-pocket, or a watch to take out of it, and burning with curiosity, she ran across the field after it, and fortunately was just in time to see it pop down a large rabbit hole under the hedge.

"In another moment down went Alice after it, never once considering how in the world she was to get out again.

"The rabbit hole went straight on like a tunnel for some way, and then dipped suddenly down, so suddenly that Alice had not a moment to think about stopping herself before she found herself falling down a very deep well.

"Either the well was very deep, or she fell very slowly, for she had plenty of time as she went down to look about her and to wonder what was going to happen next. . .

"Down, down, down. Would the fall NEVER come to an end! . . .

"Down, down, down. . . when suddenly, thump! thump! down she came upon a heap of sticks and dry leaves, and the fall was over. . .

"Suddenly she came upon a little three-legged table, all made of solid glass; there was nothing on it except a tiny golden key, and Alice's first thought was that it might belong to one of the doors of the hall; but, alas! either the locks were too large, or the key was too small, but at any rate it would not open any of them. However, on the second time round, she came upon a low curtain she had not noticed before, and behind it was a little door about fifteen inches high: she tried the little golden key in the lock, and to her great delight it fitted!"[66]

Courtesy of Lenny's Alice in Wonderland Site, http://www.alice-in-wonderland.net/

---

66 For all of the excerpts and pictures from the Alice stories, I am grateful to Lenny's Alice-in-Wonderland site.

Questions to Ponder

1. Jonathan Young of the Center for Story and Symbol says that falling down the rabbit hole represents a journey into the unconscious.[67] What elements of the story have a dreamlike or hallucinogenic feel to them? (At the end we discover that Alice has been dreaming.)

2. How is this story like the Grimms' tale of "The Golden Key"?

3. Do you have any theory about why Alice sees a rabbit with a watch before she begins her journey? (Young[68] would call this a threshold experience, like the fragmentary hypnogogic images we experience before we fall asleep.)

---

67 Jonathan Young, "The Psychology of Creativity" (workshop, sponsored by The Center for Story and Symbol, www.folkstory.com. Sacramento, CA, May 16, 2006).

68 Young, "The Psychology of Creativity" workshop in Sacramento, May 16, 2006.

2

A New Paradigm
for Creativity?

The Issue with Paradigms

A paradigm, of course, is "a set of associations, concepts, values, and practices that constitutes a way of viewing reality for the community that shares them, especially in an intellectual discipline."[69] Business professors define successful writing as succinct: the one-page memo and the executive summary. English professors want everything spelled out in depth: their mantra is "be specific."

What's more, even professors in the same field disagree about paradigms. Sternberg observes, "In general, scientists who are not well trained in one another's techniques are likely to be suspicious of other's techniques and of the conclusions drawn from them. These scientists probably will continue to do research within their own paradigm, which keeps supporting their views and thereby reinforces their confidence that they are right and that those who adhere to a paradigm from some other field are misguided . . . The history of psychology may be viewed as a history of failed paradigms."[70]

Our paradigms influence our view of reality. Jurors may hear the

---

69 Unless otherwise stated, all definitions in this book are drawn from the *American Heritage Dictionary of the* English Language, 4th ed. (Boston: Houghton Mifflin, 2000).

70 Robert J. Sternberg and Elena A. Grigorenko, "Unified Psychology," *American Psychologist* 56, no.12 (December 2001): 1075.

same evidence yet argue about what it means. One believes that police plant evidence; another believes that they are guardians of the public good. One has experience as a homemaker; another, as an electrician. All of them have different assumptions based on different backgrounds and experience. They view reality through different paradigms. Richard Ogle reminds us that such paradigms are used in "framing" reality but "can't be constructed" "linearly, step by step." [71] They may be implicit assumptions rather than conscious thoughts.

Paradigms for Creativity

Our paradigms determine how we view creativity. Hence Amit Go-swami says that creativity theories "are as diverse as the worldviews in which they are wrapped."[72] He identifies three major categories. In the "mechanistic" or "materialist–realist" views, the mind operates as a "Newtonian" "machine" to create logical innovations based on past models and experiences. These theories view creativity as "continuity in human behavior," with "only one domain of reality in the worldview underlying these theories—matter moving in space–time." Such "mate-rialist–realist" theories would include problem-solving techniques and emphasize Preparation and Concentration. Barbara McClintock, for instance, testified that her "aha" moments consisted of lightning–fast integration of previous facts. (See Chapter 1.) The "materialist–realist" theory, then, views creativity as thinking based on practice and tech-nique.

In contrast, says Goswami, "organismic theories" stress "becoming" and "development," with a focus on "a creative unfolding of purposive-ness of the universe and of the individual." [73] Vera John–Steiner traces, in *Notebooks of the Mind*, the way that early childhood interests develop

---

71 Ogle, *Smart World*, 66.

72 Amit Goswami, "Creativity and the Quantum: A Unified Theory of Creativity," *Creativity Research Journal* 9 (1996): 47. By 2014, Goswami had reduced creativity to "two basic categories one that is closer to problem solving (akin to technological innovation), and another that involves the discovery of deeper truth. [Amit Goswami, *Quantum Creativity* (Carlsbad, California: Hay House, 2014), xi.] Now he pokes gentle fun at "Dr. John Problemsolver," who cannot see beyond the materialist paradigm. (p.59)

73 Ibid.

"through multiple apprenticeships."[74] When Einstein was a child, he was given a compass. He testified later to the way in which this gift unfolded the "purposiveness" of his talent by inspiring him with the wonders of science.

> The fact that the magnetic needle behaved as if influenced by some hidden force field, rather than through the more mechanical method involving touch or contact, produced a sense of wonder that motivated him throughout his life. "I can still remember—or at least I believe I can remember—that this experience made a deep and lasting impression on me," he wrote on one of the many occasions he recounted the incident. "Something deeply hidden had to be behind things."[75]

More than simply solving problems based on past experience, he was fired by what Sternberg calls the "decision to be creative." His "development" unfolded as a result.

Finally, says Goswami, "In the idealist worldview, consciousness, not matter, is assumed to be the ground of being. There is transcendence in creativity because consciousness is transcendent."[76] In certain types of creativity, inspiration seems to come from beyond past experience; it is "discontinuous" with past knowledge and practice and seems a gift from the universe. The same idea may be coming to many different artists and thinkers, but its expression will be different, depending on the individual artist, the unique filter through which it emerges. There seems to be a Unified Field, the equivalent of a radio station, beaming information to receivers on its bandwidth.

All of these explanations are complementary rather than exclusive. Like the blind men touching different parts of the elephant, they explain different aspects of the same beast.

For instance, Einstein said, "'A new idea comes suddenly in a rather intuitive way . . . But . . . intuition is nothing but the outcome of earlier intellectual experience.'"[77] Each theory of creativity would have

---

74 John-Steiner, *Notebooks of the Mind*, 220.

75 Isaacson, *Einstein*, 13.

76 Goswami, "Creativity and the Quantum," 47-48.

77 Quoted in Isaacson, *Einstein*, 113.

a different explanation for why the "earlier experience" is necessary. The "materialist" would say that practice is necessary to lay down neural patterns and habits. The "organismic" view would say that each experience contributed to Einstein's development, based on the "purposiveness" created upon receiving the compass. The "causal" or "idealist" view, while not disagreeing with these explanations, would add that practice fine-tunes an individual mind or talent to a portion of the Unified Field. Like the phenomenon of non-locality in quantum physics, creative people need not be physically close to one another to resonate to the same ideas. What is necessary is resonance to the same universal, acquired by empathy with a particular domain or part of the Unified Field. The "materialist" and "organismic" views would claim that Mozart's genius arose from his childhood experience, hard work, and family background. The "idealist" view would add that Mozart was attuned to musical ideas, so he got symphonies easily. Einstein, attuned to a different part of the Field, received insights about physics

Goswami distinguishes between his "idealist" view, which he calls *"fundamental creativity,"* and every day *"situational creativity"* that entails "creating a new product or solving a problem" in a new way. He establishes a theoretical groundwork for this "idealist" view by explaining how new discoveries of quantum physics echo ancient East Indian philosophy.[78] In quantum physics, particles become "entangled" and communicate with one another even when they are separated in space, a phenomenon known as non-locality. In ancient Indian philosophy, "monistic idealism" says that everything in the universe is based on the same interconnected consciousness.

This unity of physics and monistic idealism appears also in new theories of cosmology that seem to be echoing ancient Eastern texts such as the Bhagavad Gita. It is possible that we may soon integrate diverse fields such as science, mysticism, and art in a "Unified Field theory" that explains phenomena of nature and art and the connection of universal patterns with individual efforts. By doing so, we will examine the deep structure of theories about the creative personality, process, and product. We will learn to see patterns and follow heuristics that will enrich our understanding and practice of creativity.

---

78 Goswami, "Creativity and the Quantum," 50, 47, 51.

A case in point is that concentration techniques developed in other traditions enhance creativity. This book contains some suggestions on how to use them but is by no means the only source. The text for a Stanford course, *Creativity in Business*, abounds with yogic exercises and concentration techniques. It supplements anecdotes from businessmen with philosophy from the conjunction of Eastern thought and science. Those who integrate the best of many traditions are being practical in this era of globalization.

The fact is, we are now in the midst of an integrative paradigm shift.

A History Lesson: The Paradigm Shift

Thomas Kuhn explains that in "normal science" paradigms guide research by establishing implicit rules that govern goals and procedures. Occasionally, however, some "new and unsuspected phenomena" appear. Then debate begins.[79] Resistance can be fierce until "an anomaly comes to seem more than just another puzzle of normal science." Then "More and more attention is devoted to it by more and more of the field's most eminent men," and the attacks become inconsistent or irrelevant. "When the transition is complete, the profession will have changed its view of the field, its methods, and its goals."[80]

Basil Willey explains how such shifts occur:

> A general demand for restatement or explanation seems to have arisen from time to time . . . Such a demand presumably indicates a disharmony between traditional explanations and current needs. It does not necessarily imply the "falsehood" of the earlier statement; it may simply mean that men now wish to live and act according to a different formula . . . The newer explanation may be said, not so much to contain "more" truth than the older, as to supply the *kind* of truth now demanded.[81]

---

79 Thomas Kuhn, *The Structure of Scientific Revolutions.* 2nd ed. (1962: Chicago: University of Chicago Press, 1970), 47, 52.

80 Ibid., 82-83, 85.

81 Basil Willey, *The Seventeenth Century Background* (1934: Garden City, New York: Doubleday Anchor, 1953), 13.

Such a "demand for restatement" occurred in the scientific revolution of the seventeenth century. Amid the upheaval caused by scientists such as Galileo and inventions such as the telescope, philosopher René Descartes tried to make sense of how the new truths offered by science could coexist with the old truths of religion. He became famous for his solution: "I think; therefore I am." In other words, "I may not be able to prove my consciousness in the same way that a telescope can verify objects in the heavens, but I know that it exists because I know that I think." With this maxim, Descartes split mind and matter, declaring them fundamentally different and not accessible by the same means of knowing. Though his intent was to protect religion from science, this "Cartesian split" had the opposite effect. It ended by promoting logical positivism: the extreme view that only matter accessible through the senses is a valid reality. The universe, stripped of its mystery and wonder, became a great machine, powered by the laws of Newton.

By the end of the nineteenth century came the paradigm that Alvin Toffler calls "indust-reality" or the Second Wave: a *zeitgeist* dominated by the factory model with its belief in standardization, specialization, synchronization, concentration, maximization, and centralization.[82] This paradigm includes the belief in the scientific method as the only valid approach to knowledge, the view of the universe as a mechanical system composed of elementary building blocks, the view of life in society as a competitive struggle for existence, and the belief in unlimited material progress to be achieved through economic and technological growth.[83]

Many thinkers believe that we are now undergoing a shift away from this paradigm. The new definition is holistic rather than fragmented, systemic rather than atomistic. As long ago as 1981, Toffler predicted that "a new age of synthesis" was being born:

In all intellectual fields, from the hard sciences to sociology, psychology, and economics . . . we are likely to see a return to large-scale thinking, to general theory, to the putting of pieces back together again. For it is

---

82 Alvin Toffler, *The Third Wave* (New York: Bantam, 1981), 46-56. The first wave was agrarian.

83 Fritjof Capra, *The Turning Point*, (New York: Simon and Schuster, 1982), 30-31. See also Paine-Clemes, *"The Yugas*: Divine Agents of Change." Simonton, "Creativity as a Constrained Stochastic Process," 84.

> beginning to dawn on us that our obsessive emphasis on finer measure-
> ment of smaller and smaller problems, leaves us knowing more and
> more about less and less.[84]

Christopher Alexander also notes "wholeness" as "one of the main themes of contemporary thought."[85] Richard Ogle, who believes that creative thinking occurs in the "idea–spaces" between various fields, ponders, in language synonymous to "the Unified Field,"

> Suppose genius (or whatever term we want to use for the mental ca-
> pacities underlying creative leaps) turned out to be a very high level of
> navigational skill in surfing the networked idea-spaces of the extended
> mind and locating powerful forms of embedded intelligence.[86]

Parker Palmer claims this holistic model also includes cooperation: "This transformation of images of reality—from fragmentation and competition to community and collaboration—has gone on in virtually every academic discipline over the past fifty years."[87]

Specialization vs. the Interdisciplinary Approach

You may have noticed that this book is *interdisciplinary*. It draws on many of the fields that we are used to viewing as separate: science, spirituality, literature, the arts, engineering, psychology, sports, busi-ness, and philosophy—as well as traditions both Eastern and Western. It may seem bizarre to write one book uniting what, until now, have been streams of very different approaches. But the trend in higher education has also been moving away from fragmentation and toward integration.

Ernest Boyer's popular approach to scholarly work includes the

---

84 Toffler, *The Third Wave*, 130.

85 Christopher Alexander, *The Nature of Order: An Essay on the Art of Building and the Nature of the Universe*, vol. 3, *The Phenomenon of Life* (Berkeley: The Center for Environmental Structure, 2002), 80.

86 Ogle, *Smart World*, 67.

87 Parker J. Palmer, *The Courage to Teach: Exploring the Inner Landscape of a Teacher's Life* (San Francisco: Jossey-Bass, 1998), 96.

Scholarship of Integration: "serious, disciplined work that seeks to interpret, draw together, and bring new insight to bear on original research."[88] The Scholarship of Integration doesn't offer new data; it synthesizes available ideas in the hope that thinking across fields will cause us to create new solutions to problems.

A search on the Web site of the *Chronicle of Higher Education* yields a plethora of articles stressing "interdisciplinary" teaching or research. A typical comment is that "Creative research and teaching increasingly occur at the junction between traditional disciplines."[89] Jeffery N. Waserstrom says that "interdisciplinary" has become so trendy that it can now be called "the I-word," a term with increasingly fuzzy boundaries.[90] Jossey–Bass, a noted educational press, has published in its New Directions for Teaching and Learning series a volume called *Advancing Faculty Learning through Interdisciplinary Collaboration*. In *Peer Review*, a magazine of the American Association of Colleges and Universities, Huber and others explain the importance of "integrative learning" given the "fragmented" curriculum of required and elective courses: "To participate responsibly as local citizens . . . people must also be citizens of the world, aware of complex interdependencies and able to synthesize information from a wide array of sources, learn from experience, and make connections between theory and practice."[91]

Recent books on creativity have followed this trend of integration. David Edwards' *Artscience* contains case studies of creators who have combined two disciplines usually deemed separate to forge unique careers. He says that "to live at this intersection of the arts and sciences is the most meaningful work of all, more than the creation of a new business, the completion of a novel, or the startup of a cultural center."[92]

---

88 Ernest Boyer, *Scholarship Reconsidered: The Priorities of the Professoriate* (Carnegie Foundation, 1990), 19.

89 S.J. Pfirman, J.P. Collins, S. Lowes, and A.F. Michaels, "Collaborative Efforts: Promoting Interdisciplinary Scholars," *The Chronicle of Higher Education,* February 2, 2005, retrieved July 22, 2006, from www.chronicle.com.

90 Jeffery N. Waserstrom, "Expanding on the I-word," *The Chronicle of Higher Education,* (January 20, 2005): retrieved July 22, 2006, from www.chronicle.com.

91 Mary Taylor Huber, Pat Hutchings, and Richard Gale, "Integrative Learning for Liberal Education," *Peer Review,* 7, no. 4 (Summer/Fall 2005): 4, 5.

92 David Edwards, *Artscience: Creativity in the Post-Google Generation* (Cambridge, Massachusetts: Harvard University Press, 2008), 157.

Ken Robinson makes a similar point:

> The recognition of common processes in the arts and the sciences has led to a wide range of collaborative projects and to the early dawning of what may prove in our own times to be a new Renaissance. It is a Renaissance based on a more holistic understanding of human consciousness.[93]

Clearly, thinking within the boundaries of a discipline can yield important results. Yet after it has been done for a while, there is also value in making connections. Einstein put the idea in a dramatic way: "'It is a glorious feeling to discover the unity of a set of phenomena that seem at first to be completely separate.'"[94] In fact, Robert Sternberg criticizes the fragmentation in competing fields of psychology, with their "Narrow specialization . . . where one looks at a problem with tunnel vision and knows only a narrow range of techniques to apply in solving that problem. In broad specialization, one may look at a fairly specific problem but do so with open eyes and with the benefit of the many problem–solving techniques a multidisciplinary approach leaves at one's disposal."[95] He calls for a "unified psychology" that eschews "single operations in favor of multiple converging operations" and uses many modes of inquiry.[96] Csikszentmihalyi makes the same point but in different worlds: "what we need now is an effort to synthesize the various approaches of the past into an integrated theory."[97] This book is one response to this call. It attempts to unite many fields that we are used to separating into discrete disciplines.

The work of Ken Wilber has a name for this mode of thinking: *integral.*

---

93 Ken Robinson, *Out of Our Minds: Learning to be Creative* (Chichester, West Sussex: Capstone, 2011), 195.

94 Quoted in Isaacson, *Einstein*, 67.

95 Robert J. Sternberg and Elena A. Grigorenko, "Unified Psychology," 1076.

96 Ibid., 1073.

97 Mihaly Csikszentmihalyi, "Society, Culture, and Person: A Systems View of Creativity," in *The Nature of Creativity*, ed. Robert J. Sternberg (Cambridge, Massachusetts: University Press, 1988), 138.

Integral Creativity

Spirit and science have been split since Descartes, but Ken Wilber explains that the masters of the great mystical traditions have experiences that are universal and can be replicated, just like scientific experiments, by someone who can attain the same states of consciousness:

> . . . these claims are not dogmatic; they are not believed in merely because an authority proclaimed them, or because sociocentric tradition hands them down, or because salvation depends upon being a "true believer." Rather, the claims about these higher domains are a *conclusion* based on hundreds of years of experimental introspection and communal verification. False claims are *rejected* on the basis of *consensual evidence,* and further evidence is used to adjust and fine-tune the experimental conclusions.
>
> These spiritual endeavors, in other words, are scientific in any meaningful sense of the word, and the systematic presentations of these endeavors follow precisely those of any *reconstructive science.*[98]

In other words, the inner science of spirituality has the same rules as the outer science of logical positivism: experimentation and replication. Experts in both fields can replicate the same results, though laymen may not have the "domain–specific skills" to do so.

The Dalai Lama, who has met with many leaders of the scientific community, reports that he has "long been gripped with a fascination for the parallels between this form of empirical investigation and those I had learned in my Buddhist philosophical training and contemplative practice." Science observes "phenomena," generates hypotheses, and "validates" them through experiments that, if replicated, contribute to the field. "The Buddha advises" testing "the truth of what he has said through reasoned examination and personal experiment."[99] As Paramhansa Yogananda says, "'Meditation is to religion

---

98 Ken Wilber, *The Collected Works of Ken Wilber,* vol. 6, *Sex, Ecology, Spirituality* (Boston: Shambhala, 1999-2000), 273.

99 His Holiness Dalai Lama, *The Universe in a Single Atom: The Convergence of Science and Spirituality* (New York: Morgan Road Books, Random House, 2005), 23-24.

what the laboratory is to science.'"[100]

Mystical Creativity: "The Force"

This section is theoretical, with some ideas that are controversial. You may want to skip or skim it. I present it so that you will have access to some of what is said about higher creativity in the philosophical circles that are now seeing a merger of science and spirituality, such as the Institute of Noetic Sciences, established by astronaut Edgar Mitchell. Some of the ideas will be presented again in the discussion of universal principles, physics, and mathematics (Chapters 9 and 10).

Not controversial is the belief of some creators that their ideas come from a higher power. (See above, the "inspirational" theories of the *Daimon* and the wind; and Chapter 3, The Process.) In *Star Wars* it is called "The Force," and in *The Matrix* it is the ultimate reality. Some creators, like Einstein, Emerson, and Fellini, use the word "God." However, this word can be controversial because it comes with so much cultural baggage. (For this reason one writer calls this force G.O.D.: a higher intelligence that is Governing, Organizing and Designing.[101]) You can call this power what you like: Spirit, a higher part of yourself, the "Unified Field," "The Force," or "what is trying to happen."

Whatever you call it, the mystical view is that some creators feel a higher intelligence is helping and guiding their efforts. They believe that cooperating with this intelligence will help us, and trying to "go against the flow" will frustrate us.

This higher intelligence is said to dwell in a realm that has been given many names. Some mystical philosophers today call it the "Causal" realm because it holds the ideas that cause manifestation in our physical reality. A familiar version in philosophy courses comes from Plato, who called it the realm of the "Forms."

Ken Wilber explains that this realm literally "pulls" on us: a "*manifest omega pull* on each individual and finite thing."[102] Physicist David Bohm

---

100 Quoted in Swami Kriyananda, (J. Donald Walters), *Superconsciousness: A Guide to Meditation* (Nevada City, California: Crystal Clarity, 1996), 3.

101 Gary Schwartz. He emphasizes that he is not discussing the "Creative Design" hypothesis that has been proposed as an alternative to evolution.

102 Wilber, *CW*, vol. 6, *Sex, Ecology, Spirituality*, 655.

would say that forms are unfolded in the implicate order, where they exist in potentiality until they have become physical and explicate.[103] Goswami, drawing on quantum theory, says that "thoughts exist in consciousness as transcendent potentiality of many possible meanings; collapse manifests them in a form."[104] Einstein, who wanted to read the mind of God, sensed it as a Unified Field but was unable to prove it mathematically.

Journalist Lynne McTaggart explains that this "Unified Field" concept as it exists today is "not simply based on beliefs but based on science, on thousands of published scientific studies."[105] Scientists interviewed for her book *The Field* said that they had "discovered . . . that . . . there was a giant matrix, a field of fields called the Zero Point Field," a pulsating energy field "like an invisible web" connecting everything that exists.[106]

They also discovered that we were made of the same basic material. On our most fundamental level, living beings, including human beings, were packets of quantum energy constantly exchanging information with this inexhaustible energy sea.[107]

McTaggart's research has shown that cultures as far-flung as "the aborigines, the ancient Greeks, the Egyptians, Indians, the Eastern religions like Buddhism and Taoism . . . all share a description of the rise of matter from a non–physical energy field."[108]

The Bhagavad Gita (VII.7) describes this field as a great web of consciousness, a web of idea–beads, a consciousness that connects and embraces All That Is:

> *mayi sarvam idaṁ protaṁ*
> *sūtre maṇigaṇā iva.*
>
> **On Me all this is strung,**
> **Like rows of gems upon a string.**

---

103 David Bohm, *Wholeness and the Implicate Order* (London: Ark Paperbacks, 1983), 177.

104 Goswami, *Quantum Creativity*, 33.

105 Lynne McTaggart, *Living the Field* (Boulder, Colorado: Sounds True, 2006,) 4 CDs.

106 Ibid.

107 Lynne McTaggart, *The Field: The Quest for the Secret Force of the Universe* (New York: HarperCollins, 2002), xvii.

108 McTaggart, *Living the Field*.

Commentator Swami Chidbhavananda explains that "Pure consciousness" itself is a thread, "the string–like supporter of the manifest
worlds."[109] We are the beads upon it.

> **The pearls in the necklace are necessarily uniform and homogeneous,
> and its thread, which is generally unseen, passes through the central
> core of every pearl, and holds them all, the big and the small, into a
> harmonious ornament of beauty . . . the same conscious Principle works
> through all.** [110]

The cutting edge of mid–1990s science described this concept as
superstring theory:

> **In this picture, each subatomic particle corresponds to a distinct reso-
> nance that vibrates only at a distinct frequency . . . think of a violin string,
> which can vibrate at different frequencies, creating musical notes like
> A, B, and C . . . In principle, the string can vibrate at any of an infinite
> number of different frequencies . . . what is fundamental is the string
> itself . . . According to string theory, if we could somehow magnify a
> point particle, we would actually see a small vibrating string . . . The
> string can, in turn, break into smaller strings or collide with other strings
> to form longer strings.**[111]

McTaggart describes this idea in everyday terms: "We're a bit like
an antenna, beaming and receiving information with our environment."[112]

Another Eastern metaphor for this concept is *Indra's Net*:

---

109 Swami Chidbhavananda, Commentary accompanying verses and translation of *The Bhagavad
Gita,* VII.7 (Tamil Nadu, India: Sri Ramakishna Tapovanam, 1982), 421.

110 Swami Chinmayananda, Commentary accompanying verses and translation of *The Holy
Geeta* (Bombay, India: Central Chinmaya Mission Trust, n.d.)

111 Michio Kaku, *Hyperspace: A Scientific Odyssey through Parallel Universes, Time Warps,
and the 10th Dimension* (New York: Oxford University Press, 1994), 153-54. Roger Penrose is
troubled by the reliance of string theory on 10 dimensions but considers it feasible that, ultimately,
the problem may be resolved, as it is twistor theory. For the virtues and limitations and current
popularity of string theory, see Roger Penrose, *The Road to Reality: A Complete Guide to the
Laws of the Universe* (New York: Knopf, 2005), 869, 880-82, 887-93, 926-28, 1017, 1018,
1040, 1024, 1042; for twistor theory, see 962-67, 973, 991-92, 1003-1004. A resolution to the
problem may be M-Theory, which posits an 11th dimension. In this dimension the strings, seen
from a "mountaintop" view, have become membranes. Kaku and other string theorists have now
endorsed this view. See Chapter 9.

112 McTaggart, *Living the Field.*

> Far away in the heavenly abode of the Great God Indra, there is a
> wonderful net which has been hung by some cunning artificer in such
> a manner that it stretches out indefinitely in all directions. In accordance
> with the extravagant tastes of deities, the artificer has hung a single
> glittering jewel at the net's every node, and since the net itself is infinite
> in dimension, the jewels are infinite in number. There hang the jewels,
> glittering like stars of the first magnitude, a wonderful sight to behold.
> If we now arbitrarily select one of these jewels for inspection and look
> closely at it, we will discover that in its polished surface there are re-
> flected all the other jewels in the net, infinite in number. Not only that,
> but each of the jewels reflected in this one jewel is also reflecting all the
> other jewels, so that the process of reflection is infinite. [113]

Michael Talbot remarks, "This is the key to creativity, that every thought
is contained in every other thought like the pearls in Indra's net."[114]

P.M.H. Atwater stresses that this web is *real*: that survivors of near-
death experiences have *seen it*:

> microscopic "threads" of luminous, vibrating light they see connect-
> ing everything and everyone together in a giant "web." . . . They also
> say that once light pulsates harmoniously through any section of the
> webbing, regardless of distance or time span, synchronicity naturally
> results, signaling that one portion of the network now resonates with
> others of equal light.[115]

McTaggart describes this network as "the *plenum* of all energy in the
universe in a basic ground state . . . a vast information headquarters
. . . a recording mechanism . . . a vast telephone network with everything the universe constantly on the phone." [116] Like McTaggart, Atwater
says that stories about this field appear in traditions "across the globe,
and each describes the same basic type of invisible, interconnecting

---

113 Phil Servedio, "The Indra's Net: What Is It?" Heart Space: The Web Site of Phil Servedio, accessed April 5, 2014: http://www.heartspace.org/misc/IndraNet.html.

114 Michael Talbot, *Mysticism and the New Physics* (New York: Bantam, 1980), 60.

115 P.M.H. Atwater, *Future Memory* (Charlottesville, VA: Hampton Roads Publishing Company, 1999), 131.

116 McTaggart, *Living the Field*.

threads or energy webbing created by life-forms interacting with each other," an "entire fabric net existent throughout the universe since the beginnings of time and space."[117] In the Huna tradition of Hawaii, the vibrating strings are called Aka Threads.[118] In the Hopi tradition they are the web woven by Spider Grandmother.[119] Carlos Castaneda describes them as "an egglike cluster of luminous fibers" seen by sorcerers around the human body. [120]

David Bohm, discussing the microcosm in quantum physics, speaks in similar terms: "the interactions between different entities (i.e., electrons) constitute a single structure of indivisible links, so that the entire universe has to be thought of as an unbroken whole . . . Further, the non–local, non–causal nature of the relationships of elements distant from each other evidently violates the requirements of separateness and independence of fundamental constituents that is basic to any mechanistic approach."[121] Ervin Laszlo, who calls this network the "a–field," writes of "a universe that is made up neither of just vibrating strings, nor of separate particles and atoms, but is instead constituted in the embrace of continuous fields and forces that carry information as well as energy."[122]

In biological terms this "a–field," as described by Rupert Sheldrake, is a "morphic field" of "information"[123] that shapes the embryo in the womb and the plant in the garden. It is the reason that the apple tree knows not to grow peaches and the chameleon knows how to grow a new tail. This field of information is so creative and ever–evolving that once any member of a species has accomplished a task, it becomes easier for the others.

For instance, rats have been getting smarter at running laboratory

---

117 Atwater, *Future Memory*, 132.

118 Ibid.

119 Gregg Braden, *The Divine Matrix: Bridging Time, Space, Miracles, and Belief* (Carlsbad, California: Hay House, 2007), 32.

120 Carlos Castaneda, *Tales of Power* (New York: Simon and Schuster, 1974), 39.

121 Bohm, *Wholeness and the Implicate Order*, 175-76.

122 Ervin Laszlo, *Science and the Akashic Field: An Integral Theory of Everything* (Rochester, Vermont: Inner Traditions, 2004), 3.

123 Rupert Sheldrake, *The Presence of the Past: Morphic Resonance and the Habits of Nature* (New York: Random House, Vintage Books, 1989), 113.

mazes. In one experiment at Harvard the first generation of rats "made on average over 165 errors" before locating a "safe" exit from a tank of water. The thirtieth generation "made an average of only twenty errors." This continued learning is evident even in rats from differing genetic pools and in different locations. A replication of the experiment in Melbourne showed "the first generation tested far quicker" than those at Harvard. There was also "a progressive increase in the rate of learning" in fifty generations over twenty years, even "amongst rats not descended from trained parents." [124]

Plato spoke of the Forms, the Divine Ideas that structure physical reality. Roger Penrose (Oxford University) says that in mathematics, such an ideational realm "provides a blueprint" for scientific investigation. He explains, "Platonic existence, as I see it, refers to the existence of an objective external standard. . . Such 'existence' could also refer to things other than mathematics, such as to morality or aesthetics."[125] In fact, he posits the existence of three worlds: the Platonic realm of Truth–Morality–Beauty and the other worlds of Mentality and Physicality. Each, he believes, "possesses its own distinctive kind of existence, different from the other two." [126] There is also a "mysterious connection between the worlds," what Penrose calls "three profound mysteries."[127]

Rupert Sheldrake notes that the Platonic concept implies stasis: "All possible forms have always existed as timeless Forms, or as mathematical potentialities implicit in the eternal laws of nature."[128] In other words, "A Platonic interpretation of the forms of organisms in terms of archetypal Ideas implies a one-way influence from the Idea to the organism, and the Idea itself undergoes no change."[129] However, Sheldrake's hypothesis implies continuing change as the organism and field act in synergy: "By contrast, the hypothesis of formative causation postulates a two-way flow of influence: from fields to organisms and from organisms to fields."[130]

---

124 Sheldrake, *The Presence of the Past*, 175.

125 Penrose, *The Road to Reality*, 12, 13.

126 Ibid., 1029, 1030.

127 Ibid., 17-18.

128 Sheldrake, *The Presence of the Past,* 308-9.

129 Ibid., 110.

130 Ibid.

Physicist Fred Alan Wolf elaborates on this idea:

> A single event, wherever it occurs, in the brain or anywhere else in the universe, will not constitute an event of consciousness. You need two events. Consciousness is the relationship between two events via this offer-echo quantum-physical mechanism . . . Thus I suggest that the consciousness field is the product of these two quantum waves (U*U), and this product appears as a probability field that exists everywhere, not just in the brain, but everywhere.[131]

Rupert Sheldrake, as he summarizes the thinking of Terence McKenna, makes the same point:

> The Cosmic Mind contains all possible forms and archetypes that are way out there in the future, and it somehow interacts with what's going on now. . . The evolutionary imagination works by a kind of spark between the divine mind, or cosmic attractor, and present situations open to creativity.[132]

We could think of these two "principles" as "the Indian Tantric notion of Shakti as energy and Shiva as the formative principle working together to create the world."[133] Gregg Braden says "the energy that does the connecting is what [physicist Max] Planck described as the 'matrix' of everything."[134] Professor Thomas Görnitz of Goethe Universitat sums up this theory: there is "no need and no place for any kind of dualism." From atoms, to quanta, to strings, "the world is only spirit," built on structures.[135]

Edgar Cayce, called "the sleeping prophet" and "the father of holistic medicine," stresses the same idea in his readings: "An entity, or soul, is a spark—or a portion—of the Whole, the First Cause; and thus is a co-

---

131 Fred A Wolf, *The Dreaming Universe* (New York: Simon and Schuster, 1994), 164.

132 Rupert Sheldrake, Terence McKenna, and Ralph Abraham, *Chaos, Creativity, and Cosmic Consciousness* (Rochester, VT: Park Street, 1992), 8-9.

133 Ibid., 26.

134 Braden, *The Divine Matrix*, 34.

135 Professor Görnitz traces the origin of this idea to Democritus and Plato. See: Görnitz, Thomas. "The Contribution of Quantum Theory to the Phenomena of Creativity in Science." Keynote Address. International Centre for Innovation in Education. 3rd annual conference. Athens, Greece, June 10, 2010.

worker with the First Cause, or Purpose, which is the creative influence or force that is manifested in materiality." (2079–1)[136]

Though this view is still controversial rather than mainstream, it is becoming prevalent among some physicists and metaphysicians at "the cutting edge."

Creative Synergy

So what is "Creative Synergy"?

There is a synergistic reaction between the many and the One, the net and the gem, the field and the organism. Something is trying to happen, trying to make its way down from the realm of the causal to the solid matter of the manifest world. We can hear it as a humming along the resonant wires of the vibrating strings. We can feel it as a Form that is trying to take shape, trying to impress itself upon us, trying to clarify from fuzzy to sharp. As we open to receive it, as we work to make it clearer, we are shaping it with our own creative consciousness as well. As it resonates, it strikes harmonious chords with similar nodes of consciousness, until the whole net of strings vibrates with an idea whose time has come, an idea rippling across the net like the pattern cast by a stone in a pond. In the words of Fellini, "A creator always has something of Almighty God."[137] In a more secular vein Ken Wilber says, "Creativity is part of the basic ground of the universe."[138]

Michael Talbot explains, "Whether we call the collective consciousness of all things 'God,' or simply 'the consciousness of all things,' it doesn't change the situation. The universe is sustained by . . . an act of stupendous and ineffable creativity."[139] When we cooperate with what is becoming and trying to merge into being, we are participating in *Creative Synergy*.

---

136 Edgar Cayce's 14,306 readings are referenced by two numbers: the first represents the client; the second, the number of the reading. All readings are housed in the vault of the organization founded on his work, the Association of Search and Enlightenment (A.R.E.) and are also available on CD-ROM or in the members' section of the ARE Web site, www.edgarcayce.org.

137 Fellini, *Fellini: I'm a Born Liar.*

138 Wilber, *CW*, vol. 7, *A Brief History of Everything*, 25.

139 Michael Talbot, *The Holographic Universe* (New York: HarperCollins, 1991), 285. See the excellent description at http://www.heartspace.org/misc/IndraNet.html.

So the core meaning of *Creative Synergy* is cooperation with what *Star Wars* calls "The Force." But there are others. To explain them all, we will look at sources Eastern and Western, mystical and scientific. As a framework we will use the Integral Operating System of Ken Wilber, the brilliant philosopher who has devised a schema to measure and codify all things, from the objective world of object and systems to the subjective world of self and culture. We will also discover how to clarify our vision and cooperate more with the synergistic process. For an elucidation of this process, I am deeply indebted to the work of Swami Kriyananda (Donald Walters).

The point, made lyrically by Andrew Cohen, is,

> When spirit took the leap from formlessness to form, from nothing to something, from being to becoming, it emerged from emptiness as the creative impulse—the urge to become, the desire to exist. This creative impulse expresses itself at all levels of the human experience . . . at the gross physical level—as the sexual impulse. . . But at higher levels of being, humans are the only life forms we know of that are compelled to innovate and to create. We can see this especially in individuals who are pioneers in their fields, whether they are great philosophers, musicians, artists, politicians, or poets. Most individuals who are deeply talented are driven by a sense of urgency, an ecstatically urgent sense that "I must bring into life this potential that I see and experience in the depths of my own being. This must come through me . . . "It's the will to create and the will to evolve.[140]

---

140 Andrew Cohen and Ken Wilber, "The Guru and the Pandit: Dialogue XXI: The Interdynamics of Culture Consciousness." *What is Enlightenment?* 42 (December-February, 2008-2009), 44, 46.

Exercises

1. Describe a few other "paradigm shifts" you know about. Have any ever occurred in your own life? Explain.
2. What examples of "holism" can you think of in the world today? Specifically, in what areas do you see a concern for "wholes" replacing a concern for fragments or parts?
3. What other examples of interdisciplinary studies can you cite? Explain.
4. Have you ever read or heard anything about the connection between physics and consciousness before? Explain.
5. Have you ever read or heard anything about Plato before? Explain.
6. List some of the puzzling or unclear ideas in Chapter 2. Ask questions about them.
7. Explain what you think is most important in Chapter 2.
8. React to some of the ideas in Chapter 2. Debate, support, analyze, and/or reflect.
9. Give evidence from your own life or background experience about the ideas in Chapter 2. (Don't repeat what you have written in another exercise.)
10. When have you felt a connection to the Unified Field? Explain your experience.

Synergistic Interlude

"The Lost Coin" by Jonathan Young

"There is a parable in the Scriptures about a woman who has lost a valuable coin. It is one of only ten that she has. She lights a lamp and sweeps day and night until she finds it. When it is found, she invites her friends over to celebrate with her.

"In those days it was the custom for women to wear coins that had been something like a dowry. It is as if a person whose savings are all in the form of jewelry were to lose a piece. Even though the lost piece does not represent the whole of her wealth, it is a thing of considerable value to her. She devotes herself totally to finding the coin and when she succeeds, she wants her neighbors to share her relief and joy. We might imagine that she spent the value of the coin on the festivities.

"The story is a marvelous illustration of the idea of regaining a lost sense of soul. On a simple level, a precious piece of her feeling that she was valuable was gone. It had fallen into the dust. When some part of one's self-esteem falls away, the sense of loss is tangible. Since the coin had been sewn to her dress, its absence also represents a loss of face. She had suffered a diminished self-image. It is like how we feel when a setback in a cherished project deflates us or a thoughtless comment gets us down. It takes some work to return to the full feeling of worthiness we had before.

"The larger meaning of the lost item of value could be that it is the jewel of the soul, which in many lives goes missing until thorough searching finds it again. Loss of soul is more subtle than the loss of a prized object. When we devote too much of our attention to practical concerns, the deeper regions of the inner life turn to wasteland. Like in the landscape in the grail stories, the generative energy of creativity languishes. Nothing can grow in such neglected soil. We must search for the missing element. It is usually a lack of investment in that which the soul values. The searching can be in the form of devotional practice. Taking the time for beauty and reflection leads back to the soulful sense of connection.

"The way we look at stories is a clue to how to search for soul. The exploration plays on the meanings of words like worth, value, face, lost, and found. The symbolism in these and other key words open up the wisdom of this ancient tale. This is a mythic story in the sense that it is probably not historical fact about any particular event in a real person's life. It is a poetic summary of an emotional and spiritual experience that anyone could have. Opening up aspects of such a story to multiple figurative readings is good practice for seeing the deeper meanings of the events in our lives. Soul does not live on the surface, but in the hidden recesses of everyday moments.

"On a cultural level, we might consider that the lost possession was the valuing of story itself. For too long, the charm and elegance of mythology went undervalued in an era obsessed with hard facts and bottom lines. Fortunately, some folks have been sweeping diligently under beds and in every corner to find the lost treasure.

"Many other associations about the images in the parable are possible. Coins and stories are among the oldest surviving cultural artifacts. Precious metals and prized stories tend to last. Each is a medium of exchange, a means of transferring value from one person to another. The point is, that mythic stories carry wisdom and guidance down from the ancients. These great tales are just waiting to be rediscovered. By extension, they help us see the soulfulness in common experiences.

"The parallels between coins and stories offer a clue to the visual nature of the rediscovery of soul. Coins usually bear images while stories are full of symbolic imagery. Every scene in a myth is a collection of images that we can study for spiritual significance. The woman sweeping to find the lost treasure reminds us of all the reading and searching that goes into reconnecting with the sacred in daily life. When she finds the coin, she calls in her friends to rejoice. This is a scene of ritual celebration much like the practice of gathering for worship.

"Joseph Campbell was occasionally asked about his own devotional practices. People wanted to know if he prayed or meditated or followed some other tradition. He would reply 'I underline sentences.' The sacred, for Campbell, was in the stories. In particular, he felt we could gain access to the divine mysteries through studying the symbolic imagery in mythology. When we have this connection, we say we feel inspired, a word that means having the spirit within. When soul is rediscovered, there is often a great surge of energy.

"People have gotten very enthusiastic lately about the inspiring qualities of mythic stories. A long-lost coin has been found. The word enthusiasm also refers to being one with spirit or, more precisely, possessed by the divinities. The root of the word, theus, is related to theology. When soulfulness fills us with enthusiasm, sacred currents take hold.

"It makes sense that ancient stories, whether fables, myths, or folklore, really can open us to magical energies. Even though they seem simple, these stories are about eternal themes. It follows that meditating on large issues will enhance the sense of connection with things greater than ourselves. Seeing our lives as part of the dance of divine wisdom puts us into an experience of meaning.

"The story of the woman who lost the coin reminds us that we can regain the sense of oneness with soul if we take the appropriate steps. First, we must endure the separation without collapsing into self-pity. Then, the situation may require lighting a lamp. This image may mean developing clarity of purpose. We will have to do much careful searching. The process may require sweeping away old accumulations of dusty ideas that hide the gleaming radiance of the lost beauty. In the end, when we reconnect with the treasure of the soul, joy abounds.

"One of the marvelous aspects of parables, fables, and fairytales is that they come to us very easily. We do not have to turn to classic novels to find stories that mirror familiar events. The stories are everywhere. The heroes of the television adventure face challenges much like those the knights of the round table confronted when seeking the Holy Grail. The characters on soap operas deal with family conflicts like those among the Greek divinities.

"When we hear, read, or tell a story, we have a visual experience. We are watching a movie in our minds as the tale unfolds. This is part of why television and film are so powerful. They match the inner process of a series of pictures moving through our minds.

"The images in the coin story tumble out — from the face of the woman who has suffered the loss, to the lighting of the lamp and her earnest sweeping, to the festive conclusion. The tale is a visual experience. Any one of these symbols is worthy of a close look. The lighting of the lamp, for example, can have many meanings. It can suggest an openness to the guidance of a transcendent presence, which is often represented by light or flame in mythology.

"Our hope is in the images. If we can experience life more imaginally, not in the sense of illusion but in terms of vision and creativity, we can discover the powerful autonomy of the images. This is a new perspective on the image of the deities. We are talking about images as manifestations of the sacred. This means that the divine energy is available in our ability to perceive, create, and accept images.

"We see images in stories. We also see them in dreams and fantasy. That which we may have dismissed as idle daydreaming is really a very fertile creative process. It has an autonomy to it. It is not just that we come up with these images. These are living pictures, each with their own unique qualities. They come to us with their own agendas. Imagination in this sense is a form of revelation. This is soul showing itself to us.

"The simple teaching stories called parables, as well as the more complex creation stories of mythology, give us powerful imagery. Our imaginative responses to these pictures generate abundant additional images, all richly symbolic. This is one way soul speaks to us. The passkey is receptivity. If we can be open to this divine flow and reflect on the meanings it presents to us, the inner life is greatly enriched.

"It is then that we have found the lost coin. All the sweeping and searching is more than worth the prize. Let us call in the neighbors and rejoice.

Creative Thought Magazine—January 1996[141]

---

141 Jonathan Young, "The Lost Coin," Center for Story and Symbol, January 1996: retrieved November 3, 2007, from http://www.folkstory.com.

Questions to Ponder

1. What is Young saying about the power of mythic stories?

2. What connections is he making between spirituality and creativity?

3. What do the coin and the lighting of the lamp represent?

3

The Process: Synthesis+Energy= Synergy

Definitions

Creative: *adj.* 1. Having the ability or power to create: *Human beings are creative animals.* 2. Productive; creating. 3. Characterized by originality or expressiveness; creating: *creative writing.* [Middle English *createn* from Latin, *creare, creat-*; Indo-European root *ker-*, to grow]

Synthesis: *n.* 1.a. the combining of separate elements or substances to form a coherent whole. b. the complex whole so formed. [Latin, collection, from Greek *sunthesis*, from *sunthethenai*, to put together]

Energy: *n.* 1. The capacity for work or vigorous activity; vigor, power. See synonyms at **strength**. 2a. Exertion of vigor or power; *a project requiring a great deal of time and energy.* b. Vitality and intensity of expression: *a speech delivered with energy and emotion.* [French, *énergie*, from Late Latin *energia*, from *energeia*, from *energos*, active: *en-*in, at; *ergon*, work.]

Synergy: *n.* 1. The interaction of two or more agents or forces so that their combined effect is greater than the sum of their individual efforts. 2. Cooperative interaction among groups . . . that creates an enhanced combined effect. [From Greek *sunesis*, union, cooperation, from Greek *sunergos*, working together.]

Integral Creativity, the focus of this book, is based on Ken Wilber's AQAL system. But what does the title mean? What is *Creative Synergy*?

It is "the interaction of two or more agents or forces so that their combined effect is greater than the sum of their individual efforts" in creating something new that is "trying to happen" or "trying to express itself"[142] through you. In this chapter we will examine it as cooperation with "The Force." Later we will see that it can also be the cooperation of different parts of the self (Chapters 5–6), elements of the work (Chapters 9–11), or individuals with a group (Chapters 7–8, 12–13). It is also revealed in the operation of universal forces across domains (Chapter 9) and exemplifies field theory, which Einstein believed to be "'the greatest'" of all contributions to science.[143]

How did I get the name *Creative Synergy*? In the 1980s it came to me as the title of a book or consulting practice. In 1999 my new husband said it had come to him as the name for a consulting or publishing business. Later I stumbled upon Stephen Covey using the term. He applies it to the synergistic reaction of people cooperating in some endeavor.[144] In the course of writing this book, I found myself exploring this usage of the term as well (Chapters 7–8, 12–13). But I began by conceiving it as cooperation with "The Force": the gems vibrating in tune to the strings of *Indra's Net* in a synthesis that is more than the sum of its parts. By now in the twenty-first century, "synergy" has almost become a buzzword.

To activate a synergy with the web, you must concentrate. You are cooperating, synthesizing forces to create a whole greater than the sum of its parts. This cooperation is not passive but dynamic. Swami Kriyananda explains, "Will power is the key to awakening energy. Yogananda used to say, 'The greater the will, the greater the flow of energy.'"[145] Only with energetic concentration on the Unified Field of All Things can you bring into being what is trying to happen. What follows

---

142 Swami Kriyananda, *Crystal Clarity: The Artist as Channel* (Nevada City, California: Crystal Clarity, 1987), 59, 74-75.

143 Isaacson, *Einstein*, 14— quoting "science historian Gerald Holton."

144 Stephen Covey, *First Things First* (New York: Simon and Schuster, 1994), 210 and 215.

145 Swami Kriyananda, *Art as a Hidden Message: A Guide to Self-Realization* (Nevada City, CA: Crystal Clarity, 1997), 98.

is a ten-step method to facilitate the process.

A Ten-Step Process

1. Immerse yourself in the formulas of your craft.

You have to put in your apprenticeship. The Beatles practiced in tacky venues and sweated seven-hour nights in Hamburg before they burst onto the popular music scene. Mozart produced juvenilia before he created his masterpieces. Michelangelo apprenticed briefly to a sculptor with lesser talent.[146] You have to learn, even internalize, the formulas of your craft before you can let go of your ego, contact the Unified Field, and cooperate as a co-creator of some work. The process entails not passive surrender but alert receptivity, and the field uses your preparation to find the formulas for expression.

Weisberg cites a number of studies establishing the importance of knowledge and practice. Hayes, for instance, was interested in the amount of "preparation" necessary for a creative breakthrough. When he investigated the careers of seventy-six composers, he discovered that among five hundred masterworks, only three had been composed before the tenth year, and those had been created a year or two before.[147] Mozart himself, the archetype of the prodigy, composed his first significant work, Piano Concerto 9 (K.271), in 1777, more than ten years after he began composing.[148]

In his investigation of 131 painters, Hayes discovered a similar pattern. An apprenticeship of least six years preceded a sudden six-year spurt of productivity, followed by twenty-five years of solid work and then a slow falling-off.[149] Even prodigies such as Pablo Picasso, Toulouse-Lautrec, and Paul Klee had to learn their craft. Pariser's study of their juvenilia reveals that they struggled, as all children do, to translate concrete objects into recognizable and well-limned forms on

---

146 Bruno Nardini, *Michelangelo: Biography of a Genius* (Florence-Milan: Giunti, 1999), 11-13.

147 Cited in Robert W. Weisberg, "Creativity and Knowledge: A Challenge to Theories," in *Handbook of Creativity,* ed. Robert J. Sternberg (Cambridge, Massachusetts: University Press, 1999), 230-31.

148 Ibid.

149 Weisberg, "Creativity and Knowledge: A Challenge to Theories," 230-31.

paper or canvas.[150] Similar patterns appear in poets. Gruber found the same rule in the development of Darwin's work, and Gardner found it in the histories of eminent creators from seven major intelligences: Pablo Picasso (visual–spatial), Mahatma Gandhi (interpersonal), Albert Einstein (logical–mathematical), Sigmund Freud (intrapersonal), Martha Graham (bodily–kinesthetic), Igor Stravinsky (musical), and T.S. Eliot (linguistic).[151]

A major characteristic of world–class creators is that they engage in "deliberate practice."[152] Jazz musicians improvise so skillfully because their repertoire is full of formulas derived from imitating recordings.[153] Concert pianists repeat, hour after hour, the scales and exercises that most of us would abandon as tedious and boring. Olympic ice skaters begin as early as three or four years of age and clock so many hours on the ice that they often resort to tutors or home schooling to steal practice time from what would otherwise be seven or eight hours in a conventional classroom.

John Lennon used to become irritated when people expressed amazement at the speed of the Beatles' development. They didn't know, he said, of the many years spent assembling the band, doing practice sessions, earning their dues in out–of–the–way dives. In his study of the Beatles' creative development, Weisberg meticulously documents what all their fans know: that a long, hard apprenticeship preceded the first hit record. Weisberg estimates that between 1957 and 1962, the Beatles spent over two thousand hours on stage performing, including four hundred jobs besides their marathon sessions in Hamburg. The creativity of the Lennon–McCartney songwriting partnership also exemplifies the ten–year rule. Their most celebrated album was *Sergeant Pepper's Lonely Hearts Club Band*, recorded ten years after the formation of the original band, the Quarry Men. Their other greatest hits were composed in 1965–1966.[154]

---

150 Juvenile drawings, as cited in Weisberg, "Creativity and Knowledge: A Challenge to Theories," 231.

151 Howard Gardner, *Creating Minds* (New York: Basic Books, 1993), as summarized in Weisberg, 232.

152 Weisberg, "Creativity and Knowledge: A Challenge to Theories," 233.

153 Ibid., 236-37.

154 Ibid., 238-41.

2. Before beginning a session, cultivate the Flow State.

For centuries artists have been creating, often without knowing how. Paul McCartney says, "I've often felt it's not me doing it really."[155] Isabel Allende reports a similar experience: "It is as if I have this terrible confidence that something beyond myself knows why I am writing this book."[156]

These creators have contacted the "a–field," the realm of all possibilities. Isabel Allende does a good job of describing the idea simply:

> I think that we are all particles of some sort of universal spirit . . . It's everywhere. You're just a particle of something that's beyond you. Then you understand the legends, the myths. You understand why so many people at a certain point do the same thing or dream the same thing or hope for the same thing or fear the same thing. Because you're just part of the wholeness.[157]

Feeling "part of the wholeness" is what Mihaly Csikszentmihalyi would define as the *Flow State.* During "flow" you are so involved in an activity that nothing else seems to matter; the experience itself is so enjoyable that you will do it even at great cost, for the sheer sake of doing it."[158] Here are some of his thoughts about "flow":

- It creates happiness.
- It is achieved by focusing your attention on some task and staying in the present, without regard for future rewards. You have

---

155 Paul McCartney says that his best ideas come to him when he's not trying. He composed "Yesterday," in the Guinness Book of World Records as the most recorded song of all time, by rolling out of bed one morning with a tune in his head. The melody was so perfect he went around for days asking people if they hadn't heard it before. He couldn't believe it was his. In a 1977 interview with Melvin Bragg, preserved on a recording, McCartney explained his songwriting method as a process of opening up and allowing an outside energy to flow through him. He said, "It's like it comes in out of the blue. . . . I've always felt it's not me doing it really." McCartney made the same point in September of 1986, when he was inducted into the Guinness Hall of Fame, a special honor for those whose records are not likely to be surpassed in their lifetimes. I watched the ceremony on TV when I was in Liverpool (an interesting synchronicity).

156 Isabel Allende, "Isabel Allende," in *Writers Dreaming,* ed. Naomi Epel (New York: Carol Southern, 1993), 8.

157 Isabel Allende, "Isabel Allende," 21-22.

158 Mihaly Csikszentmihalyi, *Flow: The Psychology of Optimal Experience* (New York: Harper and Row, 1990), 4.

learned "to focus attention at will, to be oblivious to distractions, to concentrate for as long as it takes to achieve a goal, and not longer."[159]

The enjoyment created by "flow" occurs when

- your task is likely to be completed;
- you are concentrating;
- the task "has clear goals and provides immediate feedback";
- you are immersed in the task and removed from "the worries and frustrations of everyday life";
- you have a sense of control;
- "concern for the self disappears, yet paradoxically the sense of self emerges stronger" afterward;
- "duration of time is altered."[160]

The activity should be challenging but not frustrating. You have the sense of operating at the peak of your powers. Abraham Maslow might say you are having a peak experience: a blissful, joyous moment in which you feel most alive.[161]

We enter flow when we are mindful: when we place our awareness squarely in the present, detached from past memories and future hopes, detached from the ego, that persistent yammering voice in the head. It is ego that makes us worry whether we are good enough, whether the work will be good enough, whether it will satisfy the gatekeepers in our field or even ourselves.

Eckhart Tolle has written a profound and delightful exposé of the ego's machinations. One of its tricks is to resist the present moment:

> **To the ego, the present moment is, at best, only useful as a means to an end. It gets you to some future moment that is considered more important, even though the future never comes except as the present moment and is therefore never more than a thought in your head. In other words, you are never fully here because you are always busy trying to get elsewhere.**[162]

---

159 Csikszentmihalyi, *Flow*, 31.

160 Ibid., 49.

161 Abraham Maslow, *The Farther Reaches of Human Nature* (New York: Viking, 1971), 174-75.

162 Eckhart Tolle, *A New Earth: Awakening to Your Life's Purpose* (New York: Dutton, 2005), 202.

For the creator, the ego is an irritant that interrupts the flow state with thoughts of *me*. Is my work good enough? Will the boss like it? Will the art gallery buy it? Will the publisher give me a contract?

Amabile's research has shown that during complicated procedures, a focus on evaluation results in a less creative product for two reasons: it "can divert attention away from the task itself" and "make the individual reluctant to take risks."[163] The explanation is simple. When we are focused on ourselves, we cannot possibly be focused on the product. When we are focused on *me*, the separate and little *I*, we cannot possibly be focused on the universal field that is trying to help us shape the work. We must let go in order to create. We must identify with a voice and a flow that is bigger than ourselves.

But how?

One way is to practice mindfulness, or what Buddhist meditation calls "bare awareness."[164] Place yourself fully in the present. This may be the hardest thing for anyone to do. I once took a retreat with Ram Dass, and he had us do a walking meditation. I don't recall how long it was, but I do know that it seemed light years longer than it was. The practice was simple. We had to walk with excruciating slowness, taking as much as a minute simply to put one foot down and being totally aware of the foot in its slow descent. It is one of the hardest things that I have ever been asked to do. But at the end of the meditation, I was totally *there*. I had no chattering ego asking me what was coming next, ruminating over what had just happened, connecting my mind with everything separate from the here and now. I was simply *there*. The only other time when I have had such an experience has been during engaged writing or deep meditation.

In fact, practicing some form of meditation is the best way to make yourself receptive to the flow state. If you study with a Buddhist group, you may be asked to watch your thoughts, paying attention as they arise, noticing them while being aware that they are separate from

---

163 Amabile, *Creativity in Context*, 132. On p. 132 she distinguishes between such difficult heuristic tasks and the much easier algorithmic ones, which require a "clear and straightforward solution" and are not affected as much by the thought of evaluation.

164 See Mark Epstein's book *Thoughts without a Thinker: Psychotherapy from a Buddhist Perspective* for a full explanation.

you. The Chinmaya Mission, a Hindu group studying Vedanta, uses a similar method: watching your thoughts and thinking that you are not your thoughts, sensing your body and thinking that you are not your body. If you are not your thoughts, if you are not your body, what are you? You are that which watches the thoughts.[165] You are the Witness, the spark of the Unified Field internalized in a human body. When you identify with this part instead of the chattering ego, you are on the path to spiritual growth. You can also create.

Various spiritual traditions may cultivate receptivity in different ways. In Islam you are stopped from your routine five times a day to feel this connection. In the Christian tradition you may pray, do the rosary, or practice the presence of God as Brother Lawrence did. [166] You may wish to follow *The Way of a Pilgrim*, a Russian Christian who took St. Paul's advice to "pray without ceasing" and lived in a state of divine communion by repeating the Jesus prayer.[167] In one Tibetan meditation you watch your thoughts flowing down a stream like logs. In many traditions you watch the breath. Who is breathing? You are not what is breathing; you are watching the breath. A method taught by Paramhansa Yogananda associates a mantra with the ingoing and outgoing breath.[168] A secular method taught in a popular 1960s book was called *The Relaxation Response.*

Edgar Cayce's recommendations are explained by Mark Thurston. Within us is the divine spark ("individuality"). In meditation we seek to join it to the divine ("universal Christ consciousness") through techniques that raise the energy "through the spiritual centers, or chakras."[169] We prepare the body through bathing; we prepare the mind through "intoning" (chanting), music, breathing exercises (*pranayama*), and focus

165 For this method see also Swami Kriyananda's commentaries on *The Bhagavad Gita*, 4:27, 198-99.

166 See Brother Lawrence's letters in *The Practice of the Presence of God* (White Plains, New York: Peter Pauper Press, 1963).

167 One edition of this classic is translated by R.M. French. See *The Way of the Pilgrim and the Pilgrim Continues His Way* (New York: HarperCollins, 1954).

168 See Swami Kriyananda's commentaries on *The Bhagavad Gita*, 2:58, 102-8; 4:29, 199-205; 4:32, 207-8; and The Genesis of the Story, 22-27. For the precise method, take lessons from Yogananda's Self-Realization Fellowship or see Kriyananda, *Superconsciousness: A Guide to Meditation*, 190-97.

169 Mark Thurston, *The Essential Edgar Cayce* (New York: Tarcher/Putnam, 2004), 90.

on the third eye.[170] Cayce defines meditation as "emptying *self* of all that hinders the creative forces from rising along the natural channels of the physical man." He defines prayer as "the concerted effort of the physical consciousness to become attuned to the Consciousness of the Creator." [171]

Ken Wilber writes often about identification with the Witness. He defines it as "The self that depends upon the causal line of cognition . . . the Self supreme that prevents the three realms—gross, subtle, and causal—from flying apart."[172] He explains it as the point where "Your very self intersects the Self of the Kosmos at large:"[173] i.e., your gem upon the net.

Swami Kriyananda relates,

> **Often I have found, by meditation-induced concentration, that I can accomplish in an afternoon what others have required days or even weeks to complete . . . Before taking up meditation, I would sometimes stare at a page for days before I could write a single word. Even then, I doubted whether what I'd written was what I really wanted to say.[174]**

On a more mundane level, creativity teachers often tell you that you need to "get out of your own way."[175] Writing teachers have methods and exercises that will help their pupils let go. For some of these, see the Exercises. As with meditation, establishing a warming–up ritual or formula always helps. Stephen Covey might say you develop a habit; he recommends the athletic model of visualizing success.[176]

---

170 Thurston, *The Essential Edgar Cayce*, 98.

171 Ibid.

172 Wilber, *CW*, vol. 5 *Integral psychology*, 599.

173 Wilber, *CW*, vol. 7, *A Brief History of Everything*, 233.

174 Kriyananda, *Superconsciousness*, 1-2.

175 For instance, Larry Block, the famed mystery writer, toured the country in the 1980s giving workshops called Write for Your Life. He also marketed an audiotape of affirmations to "help you get out of your own way," as well as a book based on his workshop. Jonathan Young, a Jungian psychologist, made the same point in a workshop in Sacramento, California (2006), as does Clarissa Pinkola Estés in *The Creative Fire: Myths and Stories about the Cycles of Creativity*, The Jungian Storyteller Series, Boulder, CO: Sounds True, 1991, Audiotape.

176 Stephen R. Covey, *The 7 Habits of Highly Effective People* (New York: Simon and Schuster, 1989), 134-35. I have also used this method many times in creative writing classes and workshops. In the late 80s and early 90s I marketed privately produced audiotapes with various visualization exercises for writers, including one to help them enter the flow state.

When you feel that your ego is disengaged, you are ready for Step 3.

3. Center your awareness.

For this method I am deeply indebted to Swami Kriyananda, a.k.a. Donald Walters. He explains, "The most important thing at all times, when expressing oneself artistically, is to hold mentally before oneself the thought, or feeling, that one is trying to express." Then one "should refer back again and again to this concept" during the act of creation.[177]

The concentration must be complete, and the conception must be clear. Kriyananda says that thirteen Celtic songs came to him in two days and that if the process had taken longer, they wouldn't have been as good.[178] He took three days to write eighteen melodies for Shakespeare's poems and one day to write thirty-three melodies for his oratorio, *Christ Lives*.[179] In *Crystal Clarity: The Artist as Channel*, he says,

> **The relationship between a thing seen and the consciousness one experiences on seeing it cannot be a mental perception only. It must come from inner clarity, which involves one on deeper levels. The more *clearly* one's whole being enters into the experience, the more crystal clear will be his expression of it.**[180]

In *Writers Dreaming* Isabel Allende says, "Books don't happen in my mind, they happen somewhere in my belly."[181] We must become totally involved with what we want to express until we merge with it and at last become it, as Barbara McClintock did with her grain. She says that she identified so fully with her plants that she felt she had become one of their genes or chromosomes.[182]

---

177 Kriyananda, *Crystal Clarity*, 85.

178 Lecture given on 1996 in Toronto, reprinted in *Clarity* newsletter.

179 Kriyananda, *Superconsciousness*, 2.

180 Kriyananda, *Crystal Clarity*, 89.

181 Epel, *Writers Dreaming*, 8.

182 Robert Root-Bernstein and Michele Root-Bernstein, *Sparks of Genius: The 13 Thinking Tools of the World's Most Creative People* (Boston: Houghton Mifflin, 1999), 195.

4. Relate to the center of what is trying to happen through you.

In his lectures on creativity, Swami Kriyananda gives the following instructions: go to your center; then relate to the center of what you want to know or express. If the concentration is complete, the right answers will come.

He explains how he used this process to write a song about St. Francis. He held the thought of the saint in his mind and received the notes of a melody. He later discovered that the first several notes were like the theme song from Franco Zeffirelli's film about St. Francis, *Brother Sun, Sister Moon*. Kriyananda has also written Renaissance and Celtic tunes without knowing those types of music.[183] He testifies,

> I don't know where the melodies come from. But I do know when they are right. For example, I wanted to write a melody for The Rubaiyat of Omar Khayyam, which would, of course, need a Persian melody. I was thinking about it, and I woke up with a beautiful melody in my mind. A few years ago I sang it to somebody from Iran, and he said, "Oh, but that's Persian." I hadn't heard Persian music before, but I knew he was right. It's as though melodies are given to me—I don't create them, but I listen and hear them.[184]

Harpist Derek Bell says that Kriyananda's music is intuitive:

> He more or less hints at that when he makes that wonderful statement about "Deirdre of the Sorrows." He says, "I didn't know what I should write for her, so I sat down and let her sing it to me."[185]

Kriyananda also makes a remark applicable to engineers, scientists, and business executives:

> Clarity begins with asking the right questions. It comes with knowing

---

183 See Kriyananda, *Art as a Hidden Message*, 99-105 for several examples.

184 Kriyananda, "Creativity, Music, and the Mystical Experience," excerpted from a talk given March, 1996. Interview. *Clarity Magazine,* Number 2 (1999), 5.

185 Derek Bell, "The Divine Gift of Melody," interview, *Clarity Magazine,* Number 2 (1999), 10.

**exactly what the problem is, and then, offering that problem up into the
creative flow, in the full expectation of receiving a solution.[186]**

Watson and Crick kept "asking the right questions" until they codified the exact structure of the double helix, a problem they solved by
building a model and applying Watson's insight that the two strands
should be contrasting rather than identical.[187] Crick says the "key
questions" were, "What are genes made of? How are they copied exactly? And how do they control, or at least influence, the synthesis of
proteins?"[188] Charles Link invented a new type of paper clip by asking
what design would solve two problems: the sharp end digging into
papers and the large end required to face up for use.[189] The inventor
of McDonald's asked, "Where can I get a consistent hamburger on
the road?" Businessman Marc Stuer explains, "That's how he invented
McDonald's. Not by having the answer, but by keeping the question
open."[190] Ray and Myers comment, "Implicitly or explicitly, creativity
always begins with a question.[191]

5. Get out of the way and let the inspiration flow.
If you have practiced the first four steps, the next one should be
simple. Keep your ego out of the way, and be receptive to the flow.
Swami Kriyananda says, "Once this clarity comes, inspiration flows."[192]
He also warns, however,

**The ego is an energy-stopper for creative activity of all kinds. The simple
thought, "I am painting a *tree*," is enough to hinder the clear flow of in-**

186 Kriyananda, *Art as a Hidden Message,*108.

187 See Rothenberg, "The Process of Janusian Thinking in Creativity," 200.

188 Francis Crick, *What Mad Pursuit: A Personal View of Scientific Discovery,* Alfred P. Sloane
Foundation Series (New York: Basic Books, 1988), 33.

189 Quoted in Henry Petroski, *Invention by Design: How Engineers Get from Thought to Thing*
(Cambridge, MA: Harvard University Press, 1996), 34-36.

190 Quoted in Michael Ray and Michelle Myers, *Creativity in Business: Based on the Famed
Stanford University Course That Has Revolutionized the Art of Success* (New York: Doubleday,
1986), 93.

191 Ibid., 91.

192 Kriyananda, *Art as a Hidden Message,* 108.

spiration. The greater the flow of creative energy, moreover, the greater the stoppage of energy in the thought of "I." [193]

We will investigate this problem in Chapters 5 and 6 on the role of the self in creation. When artists become preoccupied with their own self-expression, they can lose the thread that binds them to the source of inspiration. When they are inspired like Kriyananda, works can come quickly.

Buddhist author Mark Epstein uses the metaphor of *Thoughts without a Thinker*: "'Thoughts exist without a thinker,' taught the psychoanalyst W.R. Bion. Insight arises best, he said, when the 'thinker's' existence is no longer necessary."[194]

6. If you lose the felt sense of what is trying to happen, repeat stage 3 and/or 4.

It is common, after you've been working awhile, to feel a loss of contact with the Unified Field. You will notice when it happens: the flow will sputter into spurts, and you yourself, the small ego or *I*, will intervene to help, making up the words, advising the forms or colors, suggesting an additional chord or note. When this happens, as it will, stop what you are doing. Close your eyes and reconnect with the form.

Swami Kriyananda relates an experience of revising a paragraph, again and again, without being able to get the words right. He stopped to meditate, and the correct words came in a flash to him: words entirely different from the ones he had been trying to manipulate when he was less connected.

In *Crystal Clarity: The Artist as Channel*, he explains how he has written music that expresses the spirit of a certain place, such as the Holy Land:

If my mental definition was sufficiently clear, the melody has come, usually instantly, and has seemed completely appropriate not only to

---

193 Kriyananda, *Crystal Clarity*, 61.

194 Mark Epstein, *Thoughts without a Thinker: Psychotherapy from a Buddhist Perspective* (New York: Basic Books, 1995), 222. Epstein is discussing meditation and psychotherapy, but his remark is applicable to the creative process as well.

me, but to others who had visited those places with me.

If, on the other hand, the melody wouldn't come to me, then instead of worrying at it from the musical end, I would work at clarifying my mental image. Once the image has been crystal clear, the melody has come of itself.

I have never known this method to fail. It is why I insist with so much faith that one tune in, artistically, to the reality to which one wants to relate, whatever that reality, and then give it meaningful expression.[195]

You "hold" your idea "mentally before" yourself and keep returning to it as your act of creation "progresses." [196] You ask yourself, "What is trying to happen here?" "What is trying to express itself here?" and "What is the center of it?"[197] You have *clarity* when you have "one-pointed concentration," but "Nothing can be accomplished in the arts without complete attention, any more than a camera will take clear pictures if the lens is out of focus."[198]

7. Take a break.

The value of incubation is touted in most theories of the creative process. Often cited is the observation by Poincaré that "sudden illumination" is "a manifest sign of long, unconscious prior work" and that it appears only "after some days of voluntary effort which has appeared absolutely fruitless."[199] He recommends taking a break to facilitate this process. Crick, who shared the Nobel Prize with his coworker Watson for deciphering the form of DNA, credits incubation as a major key to their success:

Neither Jim nor I felt any external pressure to get on with the problem. This meant we could approach it intensively for a period and then leave it alone for a bit.[200]

---

195 Kriyananda, *Crystal Clarity*, 78.

196 Ibid., 85.

197 Kriyananda, *Crystal Clarity*, 59, 74-75.

198 Kriyananda, *Art as a Hidden Message*, 108.

199 Poincaré, "Mathematic Creation," 38; also cited in my Chapter 1.

200 Crick, *What Mad Pursuit*, 70.

When Bertrand Russell tried to "push his creative work by sheer force of will, he discovered the necessity of waiting for it to find its own subconscious development."[201] Jonathan Young (2006) says that such forcing often results in a creative block.

Also common are reports of illuminative dreams. Kekulé, stumped about the structure of the benzene ring, fell asleep in exhaustion and dreamt of a snake swallowing its tail. Elias Howe solved the problem of the sewing machine needle when he dreamt of savages chasing him, their spears punctured with holes in the ends. Dmitry Mendeleyev dreamt the placement of elements in the periodic table. In 1963 Otto Loewi won the Nobel Prize for an experiment told him in a dream. He had to repeat the dream the next night because his notes from the first night were indecipherable![202] In each case the dreamer was actively engaged in solving a problem and fell asleep, stymied, after "voluntary effort" that had seemed "fruitless."

Harpist Derek Bell, when asked how to court inspiration, replied in an interview,

> **Buddha gave the correct answer to this question in my opinion. He said if you want to know anything, humbly sit down and ask the great void. Ask for help, ask for what you need, and maybe next morning, when the morning light comes in, something will be given to you if you are fit to have it . . . The less you are thinking about it, the better it comes.**[203]

8. Watch for synchronicity to help you.

Synchronicity is the message from the universe that you are not alone, that there are forces waiting to help you if you are focused enough, full of concentration and will power, engaged in a task that will benefit the whole. Synchronicity, as defined by Jung, is a meaningful coincidence: "'the simultaneous occurrence of two meaningfully but not causally connected events'; or alternatively as 'a coincidence

---

201 Brewster Ghiselin, "Introduction," in *The Creative Process,* ed. by Brewster Ghiselin, Mentor Books, (New York: New American Library, 1952), 26.

202 The Kekulé and Howe dreams appear regularly in creativity books. Delaney mentions them and provides many other examples, including Mendeleyev and Loewi, in her Introduction.

203 Bell, "The Divine Gift of Melody," 9.

in time of two or more causally unrelated events.'" Combs and Holland call such events

> . . . the uncanny intrusion of the unexpected into the flow of common-place happenstance, an intrusion that hints at an undisclosed realm of meaning, a disparate landscape of reality that momentarily intersects with our own.[204]

They add that, according to Joseph Campbell and Bill Moyers, when you follow your bliss, "there is often a sense of 'hidden hands,' of un-expected opportunities and unanticipated resources."[205] Sometimes they seem to be arranged by a trickster with a sense of humor,[206] such as the episode narrated by Shirley MacLaine in *Out on a Limb* when she entered a book store and the book she needed fell on her head. When we are cooperating with a greater energy, there exists "an attitude of synergy by which a state of cooperation exists between the individual and the world."[207] Look for such opportunities, and make use of them.

9. Try it out in the material world.

Take your project to someone you trust and ask for feedback. Try to get your ego out of the way and listen, dispassionately, for ways your work can be improved.

Lennon and McCartney did most of their best composing together. Sir Paul often discusses how they used each other as sounding boards, how his romantic tone was toughened by his partner's sardonic irony. A favorite example of his is quoted by Barry Miles: "I was sitting there doing 'Getting better all the time' and John just says in his laconic way, 'It couldn't get no worse.'"[208] Crick makes it clear that he and Watson cooperated in studying the double helix: "If either of us suggested a new idea the other, while taking it seriously, would attempt to demolish it in

---

204 Allan Combs and Mark Holland, *Synchronicity: Science, Myth and the Trickster* (New York: Paragon House, 1990), 81.

205 Ibid., 125.

206 Ibid., 81, 86-93. Combs and Holland identify this Trickster with the ancient God Hermes.

207 Ibid., 131-32.

208 Quoted in Barry Miles, *Paul McCartney: Many Years from Now* (New York: Henry Holt, 1997), 314.

a candid but nonhostile manner. This turned out to be quite crucial."[209] Like Lennon and McCartney during their great creative period, the DNA team all but lived together:

> Over a period of almost two years, we often discussed the problem, either in the laboratory or on our daily lunchtime walk . . . or at home, since Jim occasionally dropped in near dinnertime, with a hungry look in his eye. Sometimes, when the summer weather was particularly tempting, we would take the afternoon off and punt up the river.[210]

They also "tried it out" by building models. (See Chapter 7 for the value of creative pairs.)

Ghiselin advises that our first response to our work may not be an accurate measure of its quality:

> A work may seem valuable to its creator because of his sense of stirring life and fresh significance while he was producing it. After that excitement is dissipated, its intrinsic value is its only relevant one even to himself. He must find out if it will serve to organize experience in a fresh and full and useful way. To that end he tests it critically.[211]

In other words, the work must be valuable as well as novel. A sympathetic critic can help.

10. Make adjustments.

Despite the example of Kriyananda, few works are created whole in a single burst of inspiration. The development of the fax machine began with a patent in 1843. The technology engaged Edison for a while and utilized the telegraph infrastructure for many years because AT&T, a monopoly, wasn't interested. Widespread use of the fax couldn't occur until deregulation of the telephone industry.[212] The search to discover

---

209 Crick, *What Mad Pursuit*, 70.

210 Ibid., 68.   Crick believes that Rosalind Franklin's difficulties lay not with gender discrimination but with a chilly work environment. Of course, some would argue that the two problems could coexist.

211 Ghiselin, "Introduction," 30.

212 Petroski, *Invention by Design*, 105-10.

longitude spanned many years and engaged many seekers. Walt Whit-
man spent his period of creative maturity rewriting *Leaves of Grass*.

Edgar Cayce stresses "patience" as one of the three dimensions in
which The Divine works: "Time, Space, Patience!" (262–114). Ghiselin
says, "Among the conditions to which every inventor must submit is the
necessity for patience. The development desired may have to be waited
for, even though its character may be clearly intimated."[213] When you've
taken a break and received feedback, make the necessary adjustments
and begin again—either on this project or on another. You may have
to wait if the time is not yet right. The bikini was invented in 1946 but
didn't enter the mainstream until the freewheeling 1960s![214]

Conclusion

Repeat all steps as often as needed. This method is recursive, and
at any time you may need to return to an earlier step while you are
working on a later one. (Admittedly, such persistence is difficult to ac-
complish in today's hurry–up world.)

Rollo May says that creation takes courage,

> **But if you do not express your own original ideas, if you do not listen
> to your own being, you will have betrayed yourself. Also you will have
> betrayed our community in failing to make your contribution to the
> whole.**
>
> **A chief characteristic of this courage is that it requires a centered-
> ness within our own being, without which we would feel ourselves to
> be a vacuum.**[215]

Swami Kriyananda often quotes Paramhansa Yogananda's dictum
that the universe is "Center everywhere, circumference nowhere." The
center of creation is here, now, within you.

---

213 Ghiselin, "Introduction," 26.

214 Sylvia Rubin, "The Bikini at 60: Barely There," *San Francisco Chronicle*, July 2, 2006,
accessed April 5, 2014, http://www.sfgate.com/default/article/THE-BIKINI-AT-60-BARELY-
THERE-2516337.php.

215 Rollo May, *The Courage to Create* (New York: Bantam, 1976), 3.

Exercises

1. Have you ever felt that something outside of you (like "The Force") ever helped you, especially when you were creating? Explain an example or two.

2. Explain an experience or two when you have been in "the Flow State." How did you get there? Can you think of a personal ritual that will help you get there again?

3. Try some form of meditation, concentration, or visualization. Write a report of the results.

4. Use this method when you are creating something. Center yourself, and then relate to the center of "what is trying to happen though you." Report on the results.

5. Use the Jungian technique of Active Imagination to dialogue with parts of yourself, such as the Inner Critic, who seem to be blocking your creativity. Estés explains how:

> Preferably, sitting up, relaxed . . . [I] imagine. . . what the Critic might look like . . . Now I decide I have to ask him for some information . . . I'm going to ask him why he comes to me like this; what does it mean that he's dressed like this . . . The first thing that comes to my mind (and this is how active imagination works: the first thing that comes to your mind, even though your ego might try to negate it) . . . [is] 'You need to be more earthy.' So I say to him in return, 'Well, why do I need to be more earthy?' . . . He says, 'You've had some ideas lately that are really not in the direction where you're best.' . . . . . . He's saying, 'I really would like you to do what you're really good at.' . . . Okay, I have a piece of information now . . . When you do active imagination, you do the same thing. You start out with an idea, a question, an issue, and ask one of the inner characters that lives inside you to come to you and help you or talk to you . . . Ask a question like, 'Who are you? What is your name? That's a good place to start. What have you come to tell me?' If there's an adversarial relationship, you can say, 'Why are we enemies? Why are we not cooperating? Is there some history here that I don't know about?' And then the first thing that comes to your mind is the response. It's like a real, true conversation, only with yourself, parts of yourself that are autonomous . . . in and of themselves. Their value systems may be different than yours. Even their

way of speaking may be different than yours. The point is, that they are very rich in information, and this is how we make a transformation and an amalgamation of ourselves and our inner complexes. We do that by talking to them. Jung said that active imagination was even a more profound way of knowing the unconscious psyche than dreams because you're awake when you're doing it; you're conscious. . . . The only problem that people talk about, that they have with active imagination sometimes, is that they don't believe what they're seeing, thinking, or sensing. They say, 'I think I'm making it up; I think I'm making the answers up.' . . . They probably are not. The rules of thumb I have is, If the responses make sense to you and are enriching for you, then let them stand as is, regardless of where they might be coming from . . . Lots of times in active imagination, more than just dialogue occurs . . . It's not only information; it can be a sensation of rest, peace, and reconciliation.[216]

6. Have you ever experienced the value of incubation or dreams in creativity? Explain some examples. If you like, do a bit of research on the subject and summarize what you've found.
7. Start asking for creative help before you fall asleep, and keep a notebook of your dreams. Write a brief report on anything useful that may have come to you in this way.
8. Have you ever experienced or read about synchronicity? Explain specifically. The idea comes from Jung's psychology; if you like, do a bit of research on it and summarize what you've found.
9. If you're working on a creative project right now, ask for feedback from someone whose advice you trust. What adjustments will you make? Write a brief report on the results.
10. List some of the puzzling or unclear ideas in Chapter 3. Ask questions about them.
11. Explain what you think is most important in Chapter 3.
12. React to some of the ideas in Chapter 3. Debate, support, analyze, and/or reflect.
13. Give evidence from your own life or background experience about the ideas in Chapter 3. (Don't repeat what you have written in another exercise.)

---

216 Estés, *The Creative Fire.*

Synergistic Interlude

Through the Looking Glass
Chapter VI: "Humpty Dumpty"

"When I use a word," Humpty Dumpty said in a rather scornful tone, "it means just what I choose it to mean—neither more nor less."

"The question is," said Alice, "whether you can make words mean so many different things."

"The question is," said Humpty Dumpty, "which is to be master—that's all."

Courtesy of Lenny's Alice in Wonderland Site,
http://www.alice-in-wonderland.net/

The Power of Naming is associated with creativity in many stories,[217] from Adam and Eve naming the animals in the Garden of Eden to the Princess discovering Rumplestiltskin's true name in the fairy tale. Professor Ashliman's Web site on folktexts calls this pattern "The Name of the Helper" (Type 500).[218] In some primitive tribes, one's true, secret soul name is kept hidden so that no enemy can discover and use it. In the Old Testament, the name of God (Yahweh) was held to be a sacred secret; when Moses asked the burning bush for a name, the reply he received was the primal definition of consciousness: "I Am That I Am. Tell them 'I Am' hath sent thee." The Old Testament also says it was the "Word" that "went forth" to create.

Questions to Ponder:

1. What do you think Humpty Dumpty is saying about the power of naming?

2. How does Alice's view differ? How do their philosophies seem to differ?

3. How does the power of naming relate to creation or creativity?

4. What names can you think of that were powerful in signaling or creating the identity of a person, group, team, or corporation?

5. Can you think of any arguments or wars that have originated in naming?

---

217 For this insight I am indebted to Jonathan Young, Workshop, Sacramento, May 16, 2006.

218 Ashliman, *Folklore and Mythology*, 2.

4

Ken Wilber's *Integral Operating System*

The next chapter provides the theoretical framework for the book. You may wish to skim these ideas or return to them later.

To describe creativity at all, an author must have a framework: case studies, biographies, puzzles, lists of tips, or reports of experiments and observations. As with the Power of Naming, the framework itself determines, to some extent, the discoveries and insights we can have, just as the paradigm (Chapter 2) determines what we ignore or study.

The framework for this book is the *Integral Operating System* of Ken Wilber, a brilliant philosopher–psychologist whose twenty–six books have been translated into at least thirty foreign languages.[219] The next chapter summarizes important aspects of his work, but for the best overview, I recommend *The Integral Vision*, a book aimed at a popular audience. In this small paperback he distills his sometimes difficult and abstruse prose into accessible language.

The Integral Operating System: Five Aspects

The value of the *Integral Operating System* is that it can measure just about anything. Wilber constructed it "'by a cross–cultural comparison

219 Integral Life website, "Who is Ken Wilber?" http://integrallife.com/contributors/ken-wilber.

of most of the known forms of human inquiry.'"[220] While synthesizing philosophical and intellectual systems around the world, he clarified five aspects that provide a "comprehensive map of human capacities." [221] In other words, he constructed a grid or format based upon a synthesis of most major systems, and this grid can be used to talk about any particular domain. So this grid furnishes a new slant on creativity.

The First Aspect: The Quadrants[222]

	INTERIOR	EXTERIOR
INDIVIDUAL	UPPER LEFT I Intentional (subjective)	UPPER RIGHT IT Behavioral (objective)
COLLECTIVE	WE Cultural (intersubjective) LOWER LEFT	ITS Social (interobjective) LOWER RIGHT

Figure 2: The Four Quadrants of the *Integral Operating System*

In the upper left is the "I", the individual creator, experiencing his or her five-stage process and enjoying the "Eureka!" moments. But sometimes this creator has a sense of being part of a group, a "we": perhaps a band, a team, or a community. (The plural of "I" is "we" in most languages.) So Wilber puts the "we" in the Lower Left. Both of these quadrants are subjective; they express an idea of interior feeling or self.

---

220 Quoted in Leadership Development in Perth, Integral Theory, https://www.integral.org.au/about/integral-theory.

221 Ibid.

222 Chart posted on Integral Life, Overview of Integral Theory, http://www.integrallife.com/integral-post/overview-integral-theory.

By contrast, the right–hand side expresses the objective. I am using it to explain the creative product as a thing–in–itself: a painting, a bridge, an experiment. Here I diverge from Wilber, who reminds us that "Beauty is in the "I" of the Beholder" (his article title). In other words, you may appreciate Picasso, but I may think his work looks distorted or unpleasant. There is a good deal of truth in this observation, but I will advance the case that there is also a good deal of consensus, especially within a domain, about what is beautiful and what is not. So for our purposes I am sticking the product in the Upper Right—with the stipulation that it overlaps somewhat in the Upper Left.

The Lower Right ("its" or "they") is reserved for systems, viewed from without. So we can also investigate the external systems that support creativity: patronage or institutions of government, education, and business. Whereas the lower left, as a subjective quadrant, stresses the interior feeling of belonging or camaraderie, the lower right, as an objective view, looks at a system from outside, without any feeling of identification with it, like Congress looking at the educational system in the US.

An Educational Application. You may have begun thinking that this grid applies to thinking styles or college majors. If so, you're right, and an educator called Kolb has done the work—without, I presume, knowing anything about Wilber!

You can read Kolb's book, *Experiential Learning*,[223] or take his learning styles test for a small fee. You will also take it if you use Dave Ellis' *Master Student* textbook in a college success skills class. You can then chart your spot on the quadrant where you fall, based on two poles of opposites: concrete experience (feeling) vs. abstract conceptualization (thinking) and reflective observation (watching) vs. active experimentation (doing). If you like concrete experience, you will enjoy the parts of an engine or the lines in a budget. If you like abstract conceptualization, you may get impatient when someone focuses on facts to the exclusion of broad–based ideas. If you like to apply your knowledge by watching, you probably want to observe the professor demonstrate the computer software; if you like "hands–on," you prefer to plunge in and

---

223 David A. Kolb, *Experiential Learning: Experience as the Source of Learning and Development* (Englewood Cliffs, New Jersey: Prentice Hall, 1984), 89. A useful chart of his four quadrants, illustrating college majors, is on p. 89.

experiment with the program yourself. Using these pairs of opposites, Kolb arranges the squares in a different sequence from Wilber's, but the meanings are the same.

If you have an affinity for the arts, humanities, and social sciences, you will find Wilber's Upper Left, the expressive "I", the most congenial. (In fact, my doctorate is in English literature, and I found the Upper Left chapters to be the easiest to write.) In your classes you have probably been most comfortable with formats that use journals, essay tests, discussions, and projects.[224] Kolb calls this type of thinker a Diverger: someone comfortable with feeling and watching.

Like Wilber's Lower Left is Kolb's Accommodation, the style of those who like the social or helping professions: dieticians, elementary education teachers, occupational therapists. These thinkers are comfortable with the camaraderie of "we". In fact, as students they can be irritating to teachers. Accommodators learn by talking, so you may see them in the classroom, chattering away to one another. When they are asked what they are talking about, if they are true Accommodators, it is the idea that someone else has just presented in discussion or lecture. They are comfortable with active experimentation (doing) and thinking, so they like group work, field trips, and open-ended problems.

Equivalent to Wilber's Upper Right is Kolb's Assimilator, the scientist at home in the lab. The opposite of the convivial Accommodator, the Assimilator likes to work alone and prefers formal lectures, textbook reading, data gathering, and multiple choice exams. This style is objective and prefers both watching and thinking.

Like Wilber's Lower Right is Kolb's Converger, someone comfortable with accounting, engineering, and medicine. These thinkers like social applications of their ideas whereas the Assimilators are the pure scientists. A Converger likes thinking and active experimentation: homework problems, multiple-choice exams, computer simulations.

If you ever find yourself squirming in a class or presentation, your learning style is probably out of synch with the presenter's. Of course, some people are the exceptions and can operate comfortably in more than one style—sometimes even in all of them!

---

224 The remarks about class activities and assignments congenial to each type come from a *Master Student* training session on Kolb, July 26, 1997, in San Francisco. The textbook, published by Houghton Mifflin, goes into a new edition every year or two.

Kolb's schema is based on empirical evidence, like Wilber's, and it is fascinating to see their similarity. They are both describing the same four phenomena! I became so enraptured with the quadrants that I wrote a prose poem about them. (Skip it if you like.)

The upper–left–hand quadrant is the subjective singular, the "I," focused on interior reality. In philosophy it is Bishop Berkeley, with the mind of the observer creating what is real. In poetry it is the Romantic Movement, with the *lyrical ballads* of Coleridge and Wordsworth expressing their feelings and experiences. In psychology it is Freud and Jung, finding in the broad landscapes of their inner selves a universal map for humanity. At its worst it is solipsistic navel–gazing. At its best it is the self–transcendence noted by Abraham Maslow. In science it is quantum theory, the effect of the subjective observer on the movement of atoms; and the experiments of Barbara McClintock, who became the plants she was investigating. In religion it is the personal God; in music it is the dramatic soundscapes of Beethoven. In Kolb's learning styles it is Divergence, the learning of the humanities and social sciences.

The upper–right–hand quadrant is the objective singular, the "it," focused on the world of external objects. In philosophy it is Locke, who believed that all ideas were compounded from sense experiences or their combinations. In poetry it is the balanced couplets of Alexander Pope in *The Rape of the Lock*. In psychology it is the behaviorism of John Watson and B.F. Skinner, who taught that human beings are animals, conditioned by rewards and punishments, to be studied for observable behavior alone. At its worst it is reductionism, the belief that only the scientific–rational world view holds the key to truth. At its best it provides the wonders of modern medicine and technology. In science it is the gravitational theories of Newton and the experimental method applied to chemistry, physics, biology, and neurology. In religion it is the Deist's Great Clockmaker, Who set the universe in motion and stepped away, or the blank universe that evolved of its own accord. In music it is the intricately rational patterns of Bach. In Kolb's experiential learning it is Assimilation, the study of mathematics and natural sciences.

The lower–left–hand quadrant is the subjective plural, the inwardly felt sense of shared culture or community. In philosophy it is Thomas Kuhn, who recognized that in the structure of scientific revolutions, experts in a field realize from time to time a need for a reassessment of reality, a shift of the "paradigm" or lens through which they make sense of the world–such as that from the Ptolemaic to the Copernican universe. In poetry it is religious celebration, the Christian hymns or Vedic chants, the rituals that gave birth to Greek drama and the medieval mystery play. In psychology it uses the qualitative method to view the interactions between individuals and groups, especially as the individual perceives the group experience, such as the interviews held with women to discern their relationship to the educational experience[225] or the moral code (Gilligan, 1982).[226] It views the sense of "we-ness" from within, like Dian Fossey bonding with her troop of gorillas to understand their culture. At its worst it devolves into negative mass consciousness like Nazism. At its best it creates a sense of the sacred in cathedrals used for centuries by devout worshippers. In science it is the defense of the group paradigm, the heartfelt sense of what truth is and how to measure it. In music it is the communal love-fest of a rock concert or evangelical prayer meeting. In Kolb's experiential learning it is the Accommodation style, represented by social professions.

The lower–right–hand quadrant is the objective plural, focused on the world of systems viewed externally. In philosophy it is the economic analyses of Adam Smith and Karl Marx. In poetry it is Alexander Pope synthesizing philosophical systems in *An Essay on Man*. In psychology it charts statistics about the interactions of social groups and individuals. At its best it provides validity for theories. At its worst it is reductionism that denies the inner life. In science it is the accumulation of facts that build consensus. In religion it is the church hierarchy: the governing boards, archbishops, bishops, deacons, priests, and lay ministers who encompass the external systems of the church and enforce its doctrines. In music it is the performance of a symphony orchestra. In Kolb's experiential learning styles it is Convergence, characteristic of science–based professions.

Wilber's website says that the *quadrants* are derived from the pronoun systems of "all major human languages": first–person singular

---

225 Baxter Magolda; Belenky, Clinchy, Goldberg, & Tarule. (See Bibliography for their titles.)

226 Carol Gilligan, *In a Different Voice: Psychological Theory and Women's Development* (Cambridge, MA: Harvard University Press, 1993).

and plural, second person, and third-person singular and plural. These represent the "intentional, cultural, behavioral, and social dimensions of all human beings."[227] Though traditional grammar would parse "we" as first person plural, Wilber prefers to call it second person plural, a harmonious agreement of the "I" and "you" in the sense of Martin Buber's "I-Thou relationship": "That 'we' is mystic, it's magic."[228]

The quadrants are also aligned, in Wilber's system, with what he calls "The Big Three": "the Good, the Beautiful, and the True." Every culture has these categories, whether known as *"art, morals, and science"* or *"self, culture, and nature"*[229]

As you can see in Figure 3, Wilber aligns "Beauty" with the Upper Left ("I"). It is the "I", the individual person, who both creates and appreciates beauty. He aligns "Goodness" mainly with the collective "we" as it is a culture or community that decides what is moral, such as whether a woman should cover her hair in public. He aligns "Truth" mainly with the objective–I suppose, since we think of it as experiment and verification.

However, notice that there is some overlap: there are four quadrants and only three of "The Big Three." In fact, when I found myself writing about "The Big Three" during the aesthetics chapters of this book (9–11), I perceived them to be intertwined in various ways. It seemed to me that a work of art could be beautiful, espouse truth, and inspire morality. Mathematician Roger Penrose, who traces these ideas to Plato, suggests the interrelationship of truth and beauty, especially in the "aesthetic criteria . . . fundamental to the development of mathematical ideas for their own sake."[230] For the purposes of this book, it is not important to decide in what ways "The Big Three" and the quadrants overlap, though if you are of a philosophical bent, you might want to write about the problem in an exercise.

Wilber stresses that no one quadrant is better than any others; all are simply different ways of categorizing reality. He does, how-

---

227 Wilber, http://integrallife.com/integral-post/integral-operating-system?page=0,5.

228 Ken Wilber, *Integral Operating System* (Boulder, CO: Sounds True, 2005), DVD.

229 Wilber, *Integral Operating System*, booklet to accompany the DVD, explanation on p. 28 and figure on p. 29.

230 Penrose, *The Road to Reality*, 22.

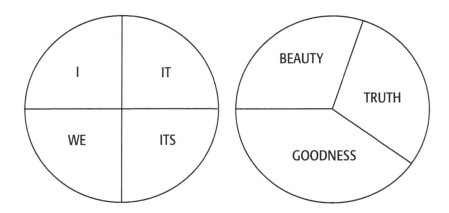

Figure 3: The Four Quadrants and Their Relationship to "The Big Three"

ever, point out a danger in scientific reductionism, the upper right, only because it has been overvalued in our culture.[231] Parker Palmer agrees: "The intuitive is derided as irrational, true feeling is dismissed as sentimental, the imagination is seen as chaotic and unruly, and storytelling is labeled as personal and pointless."[232] The Dalai Lama, however, believes that the objective need not be reductive: that in contemplative traditions, "subjective, first-person investigation of the nature and function of consciousness" occurs in "a disciplined way," "an empirical use of introspection, sustained by rigorous training in technique and robust testing of the validity of experience."[233]

The *integral* vision stresses that all these aspects work together as a whole:

Which of those approaches is right? All of them, according to Integral Theory.

> **The Integral approach simply points out that these dimensions of reality are present in all cultures, and therefore any truly comprehensive or integral approach would want to touch bases with all of those important dimensions,** *because they are in fact operating in people in any event,*

231 Wilber, *CW*, vol. 7: *A Brief History of Everything*: for example, 292-96.

232 Palmer, *The Courage to Teach*, 52.

233 Dalai Lama, "Contemplative Mind, Hard Science," 24.

> and if we do not include them in our analysis, we will have a partial,
> fragmented, and broken approach to any proposed solution.[234]

In *Integral Spirituality*, Wilber complicates the idea some more. He adds two zones to each quadrant, based on whether we are observing it from within or without. Thus in Quadrant 1, the Upper Left, I can observe my own creative process from within, or I can observe how you exercise your process. Don't worry too much about the zones; I'll be alluding to them later. In most cases the chapters will be observing a quadrant from outside (one zone) and the exercises will ask you to apply them in your own life (the other zone).

So these are the quadrants: the first aspect of the *Integral Operating System*. I am using this aspect to structure the book.

The Second Aspect: Lines

The next two aspects, *lines* and *levels*, are components of developmental stage theory. Human beings mature through various *lines* of development, some of the most famous of which are psychosexual (Freud), psychosocial (Erikson), cognitive (Piaget), and moral (Kohlberg and Gilligan). While progressing through these lines, people advance to various *levels* or *stages*. Because each *line* develops separately, maturation is uneven: someone with a highly developed intellect may have immature social skills. Figure 4 is an *integral psychograph*[235] demonstrating such an imbalance. In fact, as I focus on this example, I see that it could be the portrait of a scammer: someone clever, able to empathize enough to get the victim's compliance, but deficient in moral and spiritual values!

On the lines other than moral, Howard Gardner's theory of *multiple intelligences* suggests that there are at least 10 basic abilities: linguistic, musical, logical–mathematical, spatial, kinesthetic, naturalistic, interpersonal, intrapersonal, existential, and spiritual.[236] What is interesting is how some of these abilities combine in unusual ways. Einstein, for

---

234 Leadership Development in Perth, Integral Theory, https://www.integral.org.au/about/integral-theory.

235 Wilber, *CW*, vol. 4: *Integral Psychology*, 462.

236 Gardner, *Intelligence Reframed*, Chapter 4. Wilber also refers to Gardner's work in *Integral Operating System*, the booklet accompanying the DVD, 11.

example, had strong spatial–visual abilities but was less intuitive in math. Composers sometimes have mathematical abilities, but poets and novelists usually do not. The philosopher would have existential abilities (pondering the meaning of existence) but might not do well at interpersonal ones (dealing with politics and other people). Someone who works with art and music might not be so good at bodily–kinesthetic creativity like the dance. Someone who meditates might have intrapersonal intelligence, understanding of self from pondering it, and spiritual intelligence from feeling a connection with "The Force"—but this person might be weak in dealing with people (interpersonal) or using the body (kinesthetic).

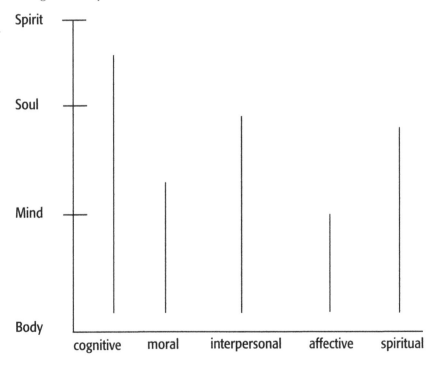

Figure 4: Psychograph Exemplifying One Person's Development

According to Wilber (and, in fact, many other theorists) the *line* of moral development contains three major levels.[237] As the child grows, it learns to expand its reality to include others, moving from selfishness to ever-wider circles of caring and empathy.[238] Don Beck, who writes and speaks about the research of Clare Graves, identifies these two principles as "express self" or "sacrifice self."[239]

The Third Aspect: Levels

The chart below codifies the three major levels. As an infant and toddler, the child is absorbed in body and self. Freud's first three psychosexual stages correlate here: the oral, in which the child feels

Stage	Age	Awareness	Identity
Preconventional/Egocentric	Infancy and early childhood	"largely self-absorbed": the *me* stage	Body, "gross physical reality"
Conventional/Ethnocentric	Older childhood to or through adulthood	Identified with the "group, tribe, clan, or nation"	Mind, expansion from the "isolated gross body" and focused on "relationships," especially those with "shared values, mutual interests, common ideals, or shared dreams'
Postconventional/Worldcentric	Adulthood for some people	Identified with "the wonderful diversity of humans and cultures" and perhaps even "the commonwealth of all beings"	Spirit

Figure 5: Three Levels of Moral Development

237 The information is drawn from *Integral Operating System*, booklet accompanying DVD, 8-9. The chart is my own.

238 Wilber, *Integral Operating System*, DVD.

239 Don Beck, *Spiral Dynamics Integral* (Boulder, Colorado: Sounds True, 2006), CD: Disc 1, Part 3.

pleasure from sucking (to 18 months); the anal, in which the child feels pleasure from withholding or releasing the feces (18 months to 3 years); and the phallic, in which the child becomes attached to the parent of the opposite sex (3 to 6 years). "The terrible twos," rightly named by our culture, occur just as the child gets a sense of his or her own autonomy and begins asserting a will independent from that of the caregiver/s. (One shopping catalog markets tiny T-shirts with the slogan, "*Warning: I Am Two.*")

Erikson's first three stages correlate with Freud's. Up through the first year, the child is learning the lesson of trust vs. mistrust: whether cries of discomfort will bring a loving response. Between the first and third years, the toddler learns to develop a sense of autonomy if the parents support curiosity and exploration; a sense of shame and doubt, if these assertions of independence are discouraged. In stage three (3 to 5 years), the child focuses on the challenge of initiative vs. guilt. Continued explorations of the environment result in more initiative unless they are discouraged.

In Piaget's cognitive model, the child is first in the sensorimotor stage (birth until age 2), learning to manage the body. Then between ages 2 and 7 (the preoperational stage), the child can pretend or engage in fantasy but still has mental limitations, such as egocentrism. At this level the child may believe that what he or she thinks is obvious to anyone else; there are no clear boundaries of selfhood. In all of these models the child is focused on *me*—on becoming at home in the body, self, or environment.

In the next major level of growth, the child learns to be less egocentric. With the beginning of school, the focus is now the group, community, or tribe—the *we*. Freud calls this the latency stage (from age 6 to puberty), a time when the child is focused on learning rather than on sex. (Woody Allen claims that he "never had a latency stage.") Erikson, who posits an age range of 5-12 years for his Stage 4, says that the child faces the challenge of industry vs. inferiority: of proving, in a new social environment, a capacity to learn and grow and fit in—or of feeling inferiority at an inability to do so. In Piaget's Stage 3, concrete operational (7-11 years), the child learns to understand the concrete objects of the environment better. In this stage, for instance, the child understands that if you pour a liquid from a tall to a short glass, the amount will stay the same, even though the level looks different.

Freud and Piaget posit one final stage, though Erikson has several more, tracing levels of growth through old age. Freud notes that in his last stage, the genital, an adolescent or adult forms healthy love relationships if as a child, he or she avoided getting hung up on a conflict in some earlier stage. (Reading Freud extensively will give you the feeling that pretty much everyone is hung up! He certainly was.) Piaget says that in his formal operational stage, beginning at age 12, the child learns at reason about abstractions such as truth or justice.

An important point is that some people never get beyond this last stage—or even to it. They never grow beyond identifications with the tribe; they never get unattached to Mommy or Daddy; they are never able to reason formally with great logical and precision. Wilber's scheme of moral development (Figure 5) acknowledges this unfortunate reality. In the highest level of moral development, the ability to empathize with all people and perhaps even all beings, we would find someone like Gandhi or Mother Teresa. In a like fashion, Wilber's charts of cognitive, social, and spiritual growth progress through many levels above Piaget's. As the human being attains these levels, identification and awareness grow.

In *Integral Spirituality* Wilber posits "10 major post-metaphysical levels of being and knowing." [240] In providing a summary of the most important levels, I will draw not only on Wilber's list but also on the classification of Spiral Dynamics, a system devised by Clare Graves and disseminated by Don Beck. The classifications are almost the same as Wilber's, though Beck's color scheme is different. Wilber's is drawn from an Eastern system called the *chakras*;[241] Beck's, originally used to avoid skin color problems during apartheid in South Africa, consists of "purely arbitrary colors" "for use as a shorthand."[242]

All these different modes of thinking are called *memes*. Here's Beck's definition of the term:

---

240 Ken Wilber, *Integral Spirituality,* Integral Books (Boston: Shambhala, 2006), 251.

241 The *chakras* are seven energy centers aligned from the anus to the top of the head along the spinal column. Some psychics can see them, and the colors appear to some meditators when the energy centers are stimulated. When fully activated, the *chakras* rotate clockwise.

242 Beck, *Spiral Dynamics Integral.*

A *meme* is at once a psychological structure, value system, and mode of adaptation, which can express itself in numerous ways, from wordviews to clothing styles to governmental forms.[243]

A meme is a sort of psychological or cultural identification unit, like the "gangsta" lifestyle in the late twentieth and early twenty–first century. Wilber and other thinkers use this term as well.

Beck cautions, "These aren't types of people; these are systems within people." We can be at different stages at different times or in different lines of the psychograph. Beck also says that, although these levels reflect historical development through the eons, "Every" mind set "that has ever appeared in history has reappeared right now" and "is on CNN."[244] Small wonder we have conflict!

It is important to note that Beck's system is not hypothetical. It is based on exhaustive data collection by Professor Clare Graves, who conducted interviews and surveys of thousands of people and "began to detect that certain patterns begin to surface." The theory came out of the data, not vice versa. "He did not design these; he uncovered them." Graves died before he was able to disseminate his ideas, so Beck took on his mission. He believes this system "may well hold the key" to solving "problems that are lethal."[245]

Level 1: Survivalist (first seen 100,000 years ago):[246] Wilber, who calls this stage "archaic" and gives it the color infrared, says this "sensorimotor" level consists of "what we're born with . . . Everybody's born at square 1."[247] Don Beck colors this "first level system, survivalist system" beige. He describes its prehistoric status in these terms: "The primary goal was to meet the physiological needs of the species: food, water, sex." We can find "residual evidence" of this level "in a fall–back

---

243 Wilber, *CW*, vol. 4: *Integral Psychology*, 479. Wilber cites David Beck and Clare Graves for these categories and insights.

244 Beck, *Spiral Dynamics Integral.*

245 Ibid.

246 All the estimates of when each state became available are given in Jessica Roemischer, "The Never-Ending Upward Quest: A *WIE* Editor Encounters the Practical and Spiritual Wisdom of Spiral Dynamics: An Interview with Dr. Don Beck," *What is Enlightenment?* 22 (Fall/Winter 2002), 108-9.

247 Ken Wilber, *The 1, 2, 3 of God* (Boulder, CO: Sounds True, 2006).

form," "in the case of tragedy, of crisis." After 9/11 some people "regressed" into "a temporary beige condition." Beck worked with FEMA to help such people, who were unable to handle insurance claims or make plane reservations. He warns, "If we don't insist on recovering quickly, we often lock people in a kind of beige–type existence."

Beck adds that today "beige in its healthy form" includes "newborn infants and senile elderly." However, "it can become a very unhealthy system in profound retardation and certain kinds of brain damage that means people are simply becoming helpless." [248]

Level 2: Magical (first seen 50,000 years ago): Wilber colors this stage "magenta" and gives it the tag "magical–animistic."[249] Beck, once again beginning with the historical perspective, says, "There was a shift in life conditions from Problems A, Basic Survival, to Problems B, safety and security."[250] What he calls the purple system emerged: "animistic, tribalistic, one for all, all for one; and for the first time, a pretty primitive cause–and–effect system emerged in the mind–brain. The cow died. The moon was full. The cow died because the moon was full." He augments, "American Indians that were purple would name their children after the elk or the eagle, with the belief that it would incur the spirit of the elk or the eagle . . . In this wonderful world of purple, spirits are everywhere . . . and events are caused when spirits are unhappy." There are taboos and rituals "almost like good luck charms" to get "safety and security" by "getting the spirits on one's side."

These days you can find this level "as a subsystem in the more complex first world environments." Beck, who has worked with professional athletes, says that many of them "are very superstitious." He adds that "when issues of safety and security" are involved, "we return to this particular system," as brides do with "Something old, something new, something borrowed, something blue."

---

248 Beck, *Spiral Dynamics Integral.*

249 Wilber, *The 1, 2, 3 of God; Integral Spirituality*, 251.

250 Beck, *Spiral Dynamics Integral.* The rest of the information in this section comes from the same source.

Level 3: Egocentric (first seen 10,000 years ago): Wilber and Beck agree in calling the third level "the egocentric" and assigning it the color red. Continuing his historical narrative, Beck says, "Once safety and security are no longer threatened, the youth, who don't remember the experiences of their grandparents, who had to band together to form the tribes, with all their rituals, and all the demands of rite of passage put onto children," find their spirit "wants to break free." He adds, "It's very upsetting to the traditional way of the elders, and all of a sudden, these young renegades will wish to go out on their own, and will draw with them others from the tribe."

He adds, "The egocentric system is neither good nor bad . . . This raw energy of red is necessary for humans to take on major risks and major tasks." However, there is "a heavy dominance of the red system" in prisons "in its negative form," lacking "discipline" and "sensitivity." Negative red occurs in *The Godfather*, Iraq, gangs, "mean girls"; positive red occurs in musicians, race car drivers, and women. "Egocentric" red, like "The Terrible Twos," says, "I want it all; I want it now." [251]

Level 4: Conformist (5,000 years ago): Wilber colors this system amber and calls it "ethnocentric" and "traditional:" [252] "the traditional fundamentalist orientation." [253] Beck, who colors it blue, says, "We see 'the transition from I-me-mine to we-us-our, the blue system . . . the purpose-driven, the absolutistic, the One Right Way'" that can "control the impulsivity of red." On this level "a sense of order and discipline begin to appear." We feel, "I'm part of something larger; I'm part of something permanent, and therefore I'm willing to conform . . . give up my quest for instant gratification and pleasure and live for something that's more permanent." Blue is often "triggered with an immense amount of zealotry . . . with the hearts burning with fire," as with "the spirit of the Crusade and the *jihad*, the Amish societies who can build a barn in a single day: you find a sense of purpose behind a religious system . . . or around a nationalistic system." Here, says Beck, enters the principle of "sacrifice self: to die for a cause, to work hard

251 Beck, *Spiral Dynamics Integral.*

252 Wilber, *Integral Spirituality*, 251.

253 Wilber, *Integral Spirituality*, 251; *The 1, 2, 3 of God.*

for a principle." In addition, "Law, justice, fairness, responsibility begin to appear."

Blue "obviously provides the foundation stone for any society. Without it anarchy and greed takes over." Nevertheless, it can create serious conflicts. Northern Ireland consists of "one blueism against another blueism." Beck adds, "Holy wars that demonize the other often become very, very vicious," as in Middle East conflicts. On the other hand, "Healthy blue becomes essential in the emergence of communities and of entire countries," including charity. With it "We begin to see a major quantum leap into nation–states" and "decency."[254]

Level 5: Rationalist (first seen 300 years ago): Wilber and Beck agree in coloring this level orange and styling it "rational." Wilber calls this level "worldcentric, pragmatic, modern" and finds it characteristic of Piaget's highest level: "formal operational cognition." He says it is the first level in which an "I" "can stand outside of my culture and reflect on my culture in general . . . Is my country always right?"[255]

Beck says it emerges after we tire of the authoritarian "do's" and don'ts." For instance, medieval Christianity, a blue system, yielded to the next level, orange, with the Enlightenment. With this shift "Society" changed from "a theocratic, divine fate control to a secular, pragmatic attempt to earn the secrets of the universe in order to control our own destiny." Martin Luther declared "the universal priesthood of each individual, and his partner Guttenberg put a Bible in the hand of everyone . . . It meant that each person could interpret the Bible on their own. It's a long way from dogma."

Along with the Reformation came the Enlightenment: "the age of science, the great breakthroughs in scientific investigation." It entailed "the shift from the sacred to the secular, from the acceptance of divine fate to the belief, . . . the breaking–out of fear–based kinds of dogma."

Says Beck, "Today orange is the dominant system on the planet: success–driven, profit–driven . . . a can–do philosophy." There are "dramatic, heroic acts in surgery," new medicines and "cures for diseases." He adds, "The orange memetic released us from the superstitions of the past

---

254 Beck, *Spiral Dynamics Integral.*
255 Wilber, *The 1, 2, 3 of God.*

. . . But if all we have is orange if the whole world is a casino" for "those
who are lucky" or have the right parents, "whether ethical or not," and
"determine the distribution of the resources, and they have little concern about the impact of the orange footprint upon the environment
. . . if orange is simply all there is, then we can see what damage it can
bring."[256]

Level 6: Pluralistic (first seen 150 years ago): Wilber and
Beck both color this level green. Wilber, who tags it "pluralistic, multicultural, postmodern,"[257] often cites movements such as Deep Ecology,
Feminism, and the Civil Rights Movement. Beck says "a major wave of
green" came from "the War in Viet Nam" and "big business, classicism,
and racism." We became more concerned with "our internal worlds." We
had "money in the bank or mom and dad's credit card." This fiduciary
backing was essential: "It was our affluence that produced the first expression of green." Beck says that there is no green in the Third World
or post–Katrina New Orleans. "You only find the green emergence in
the aftermath of orange success."

With green "we no longer worry where the next meal is coming
from; we have escaped the isms that contain us with guilt" and contained "the red threat" in "prisons." So the concern is for "human rights
and the demand for consensus: that each voice be heard and be heard
equally." The quest for meaning is in "the enrichments of the human"
and appreciation of the Goddess. There is "a deconstruction" of the
white male role in earlier stages. Beck cites Burt Bacharach: "What the
world needs now is love, sweet love." Green "releases all the energy of
the intelligences that have been trampled on or left behind."

Beck has identified "pockets of green" in San Francisco and Boulder,
with "the highest level of green in the Scandinavian countries." The
pockets are influenced "by life conditions, by the bio–region . . . and by
the migration of our DNA code to form little Petri dishes" of groupings.
Places occur "where these systems can begin to conform and to multi-
ply and to complexify." Beck says that the quarrel between blue vs. red

---

256 Beck, *Spiral Dynamics Integral.*

257 Wilber, *Integral Spirituality*, 251.

states in politics comes from the "differences" in "memetic codes." [258]

The Shift to Second Tier: Both Wilber and Beck find a qualitative difference after Level 6. They use the terms "staggering difference" and "quantum jump"[259] to explain a tier of levels still only emergent.

> This surge into the Second Tier involves a shift into a totally new dimension of thinking, a new conceptual order . . . For the first time man is able to face existence in all its dimensions, grounded in a value system rooted truly in knowledge and cosmic reality instead of delusions brought on by animal and social needs.[260]

The most significant difference is that at Level 7 and above, all earlier systems are felt to have value. All are felt to be part of the great evolutionary scheme of the universe. Wilber posits an additional four levels, from "beginning integral, high vision–logic, systemic" to "metamind and overmind."[261] Beck, who sketches two stages called yellow and turquoise, uses these terms: "integrative, systemic, ecological, authentic, real, natural, a bit more balanced." [262] Yellow, first seen 50 years ago, believes that

- Flexibility, spontaneity, and functionality have the highest priority.
- Differences can be integrated into independent, natural flows.[263]

Turquoise, first seen 30 years ago, believes that

- Self is both distinct and a blended part of a larger, compassionate whole.

258 Beck, *Spiral Dynamics Integral.*

259 Wilber, *The 1, 2, 3 of God;* Beck, *Spiral Dynamics Integral.*

260 Don Beck and Graham Linscott, quoted in Roemischer, "The Never-Ending Upward Quest,"125.

261 Wilber, *Integral Spirituality*, 251.

262 Beck, *Spiral Dynamics Integral.*

263 Roemischer, "The Never-Ending Upward Quest," 109.

- Holistic, intuitive thinking and cooperative actions are to be expected.[264]

The Second Tier understands that development is in waves, in stages . . . Each level, each meme code, adds something to the collective, which makes possible the emergence of the more complex codes . . . In Ken Wilber's language, "transcend and include."' . . . If we transcend [and exclude] the levels below us, we produce sink holes.[265]

In the First Tier, the memetic codes denigrate or disdain one another. Orange capitalistic enterprises "erode the indigenous" cultures. Green attacks blue as heavy "dogma" and orange as "materialism." Red fights orange and blue but forms an unhealthy coalition with green, which makes excuses for tribalism and lawlessness since all cultures are relative. Meanwhile, red lacks the guilt and moral structure of the blue and status of the orange. And green fails to credit orange with standing for "scientific thinking, quantification, the impulse to improve." At the same time "the nobility of the green" "often blocks the emergence of the blue." In Africa Nelson Mandela kept insisting that the children learn discipline while many of the consultants in education were trying to institute Montessori schools.[266] But we can't skip from red to green. All stage theorists—no matter whether they chart cognitive, moral, psychosocial, psychosexual, or spiritual stages—agree with two things: the stages are *qualitatively* different, and we can't skip one.

As I first wrote this section in 2007, the United States was mired in a conflict in Iraq. It began with the deposition of dictator Saddam Hussein and spiraled into a civil war, with local tribes of Shiites and Sunnis pursuing ancient hostilities stretching all the way back to the time of the Prophet Mohammed. The declared intent of the White House was to establish a representative democracy. If you have read the Spiral Dynamics material thus far, you will know why this mission was doomed to failure. Countries like Iraq are at red–blue/amber, fulminating civil wars and genocide to annihilate groups unlike themselves. The United

---

264 Roemischer, "The Never-Ending Upward Quest," 109.

265 Beck, *Spiral Dynamics Integral.*

266 Ibid.

States, along with much of Western Europe, is basically at amber/blue and orange. Wilber summarizes the amber/blue belief system in this way: "Cathedrals, the righteous man, chivalry, salvation, charity," with a view of "spirit as omniscient, omnipotent, omnipresent great other."[267] Orange is the rational–logical–scientific worldview left us by the Enlightenment. So during the Iraq War the amber/blue–orange United States wonders why the red–amber/blue tribes won't quit fighting each other and accept democracy! That is analogous to the seven–year–old child telling the three–year–old, "Look, this liquid is the same, even though the glasses may look different." The three–year–old isn't stupid—just in another mental space.

As Beck puts it, the challenge today is that "national boundaries have weakened, and people can go everywhere, but they bring with them their codes of living." Furthermore, "We've not yet produced the system to handle" the problem; "in fact, the systems that we are using have made the problem worse." [268] It will be the challenge of the Second Tier to work on these problems

By now you may have read more about levels than you ever care to know. Actually, these are only a few examples. The *Integral Operating System* is exhaustive in its classification of *levels* and *lines*.[269]

And why are these stages important in creativity? We'll explore that idea in Chapters 5 and 6. There we'll see that we can create only out of our own levels.

And our levels may be evolving now. In *Beyond Soul Growth,* Lynn Sparrow Christy argues that the universe exists so that all consciousness may evolve together: "We do not exist simply to transcend the manifest universe and exist in changeless, eternal bliss, but rather to express the outward movement of life as it expresses through us in this world of form. 'For the purpose is that each soul should be a co–creator with God'(4047–2), the Cayce readings tell us.'"[270] To become co–creators, we must apply our will and energy not just on the causal plane but on the

---

267 Wilber, *Integral Spirituality*, 259.

268 Beck, *Spiral Dynamics Integral.*

269 Wilber, *CW, vol. 7: A Brief History of Everything*; *CW*, vol. 4: *Integral Psychology: Consciousness, Spirit, Psychology, Therapy.*

270 Lynn Sparrow Christy, *Beyond Soul Growth* (Virginia Beach, VA: A.R.E. Press, 2013), 17.

denser plane of materiality, as "The Creative Forces" did. Christy explains this evolutionary process as realizing both "unity" and "individuality." "The process culminates in spirit that has learned perfectly both how to receive impressions and express through matter."[271] In other worlds, planet earth is not a prison for the unevolved; it is a "creative" "workshop."[272] Goswami calls such a "new theory of evolution" "the theme [of his 2014] book": "We create our own lives through the creative choices we make, which collapse new [quantum] potentiality into actuality . . . [and in this way] we are furthering the purpose of the evolutionary movement of consciousness."[273]

The Fourth Aspect: States

Two other aspects are *states* and *types*. As human beings we all fluctuate among various states of consciousness, the most familiar of which are waking, dreaming, and deep sleep. Western science identifies them with brain waves: alpha/beta (waking), delta (dreaming), and theta (deep sleep). The East Indian system of Vedanta identifies them with bodies:

State	Waking	Dreaming	Deep Sleep
Body	Gross	Subtle	Causal

Figure 6: The Three States and Bodies Identified by Vedanta

Beyond these bodies is the non–dual, which is ever present as the formless Witness.[274] The Witness is that part of you that stands aside when you are drunk or foolish and seems to be saying to you, "Wow, you're slurring your words" or "Oh, no, why did you say *that*?"

Wilber humorously asks,

I have 3 bodies? Are you kidding me? Isn't one body enough? But keep in mind a few things. For the wisdom traditions, a body simply means

---

271 Christy, *Beyond Soul Growth*, 97-98.

272 Ibid., 98.

273 Goswami, *Quantum Creativity*, 11.

274 Wilber, *Integral Operating System*, DVD.

a mode of experience or energetic feeling.[275]

These "bodies" represent states of consciousness, identification, or awareness.

Moving your identification from one body to another is like moving to a different city.[276]

Right now, assuming that you are awake, you are probably aware of the "gross" or physical body. Sri Aurobindo explains that this body-mind is limited and "can with difficulty respond to the higher forces":

> **Left to itself, it is sceptical [sic] of the existence of supraphysical things, of which it has no direct experience and to which it can find no clue; even when it has spiritual experiences, it forgets them easily, loses the impression and result and finds it difficult to believe.**[277]

Amit Goswami (cited in Chapter 2) might say that it is unaware of any "transcendental" influences. Svarupa Chaitanya is more optimistic in his reminder that even in this state, the subtle and causal levels "are also available for experience."[278]

> **But when you dream at night, you are no longer aware of this "gross" body. In the dream state you are identified with the "subtle" or astral body, and the mind projects a whole new objective world. . . . The waker dies entirely in order that the dreamer is born. These two states cannot exist simultaneously. . . The whole world is luminous with thoughts alone.**[279]

Wilber explains,

> **You are aware in the dream state, yet you don't have a gross body of**

---

275 Wilber, *Integral Spirituality*, 16.

276 Nilkanth Bhatt, lecture on Sankaracharya's *Tattva Bodha*, sponsored by Chinmaya Trust, Houston, TX, December 18, 1983.

277 Sri Aurobindo, *A Greater Psychology,* ed. A.S. Dalal (New York: Tarcher-Putnam, 2001), 46-47.

278 Commentary by Svarupa Chaitanya on IV.1, the waking state.

279 Commentary by Svarupa Chaitanya on IV.2, the dream state.

dense matter but a subtle body of light, energy, emotional feelings, fluid and flowing images. In the dream state, the mind and soul are set free to create as they please, to imagine vast worlds not tied to gross sensory realities but reaching out, almost magically, to touch other souls, other people and far-off places, wild and radiant images cascading to the rhythm of the heart's desire. So what kind of body do you have in the dream? Well, a subtle body of feelings, images, even light. That's what you feel like in the dream. And dreams are not "just illusion." When somebody like Martin Luther King, Jr., says "I have a dream," that is a good example of tapping into the great potential of visionary dreaming, where the subtle body and mind are set free to soar to their highest possibilities.[280]

This "great potential of visionary dreaming" can access the highest source of inspiration. For, as Cayce says, in dreams we access "the sixth sense," which "partakes of the *accompanying* entity that is ever on guard before the throne of the Creator itself." (5754-1)

Yet there is a state even more subtle than dreaming. In deep sleep, when you visit the causal, there is no awareness of body, mind, or intellect.[281] Sankaracharya's *Tattva Bodha* says of this state,

The sleeper does not know anything in this state, that is to say, he is ignorant. But he is also free from the limitations of the gross and subtle bodies and so he is in a state of bliss (Ananda). [282]

I follow Wilber here again:

As you pass from the dream state with its subtle body into the deep-sleep or formless state, even thoughts and images drop away, and there is only a vast emptiness, a formless expanse beyond any individual "I" or ego or self. The great wisdom traditions maintain that in this state—which may seem like a blank or nothingness—we are actually plunged into a great formless realm, a great Emptiness or Ground of

280 Wilber, *Integral Spirituality*, 16.

281 Nilkanth Bhatt, lecture on Sankaracharya's *Tattva Bodha.*

282 Commentary by Svarupa Chaitanya on IV.3, the deep sleep state.

Being, an expanse of consciousness that seems almost infinite. Along with this almost infinite expanse of consciousness there is an almost infinite body or energy—the causal body, the body of the finest, most subtle experience possible, a great formlessness out of which creative possibilities can arise.[283]

Wilber clarifies that "many people do not experience that deep state in such a full fashion." However, "the traditions are unanimous that this formless state and its causal body can be entered in full awareness, whereupon they, too, yield their extraordinary potentials for growth and awareness."[284]

Wilber stresses the difference between *stages* and *states*: a stage is earned; a state is not. Stages are reached through personal growth and effort, through introspection and experience: one learns to reason about justice or construct a moral code by having various epiphanies that show the limited range of earlier stages. States, however, are always available. In any stage we can be meditating and have a high experience, but we will interpret it through the level of our development.

Nevertheless, counters Wilber, when "you are plunged into a state that is bigger than you are," "it acts to dislodge" whatever stage you're at by providing "a micro-transformative event." No doubt meditation is so effective because it provides "an altered state once or twice a day." Still, cognitive development must accompany spiritual growth. "All of the great wisdom traditions suggest cognitive understanding" must accompany a higher state—or "it just doesn't stick very well." Then you have a framework and "can relate it to other areas."[285]

The stages of your cognitive, spiritual, emotional, and moral psychograph are crucial to your practice of creativity. The higher your stage, the more easily you can access the Unified Field and sense "what is trying to happen." If you are an artist or writer, your work will become more universal and uplifting. If you are a scientist or engineer, you will be able to solve problems more easily. In all cases you will be able to take on more perspectives other than your own.

---

283 Wilber, *Integral Spirituality*, 17.

284 Ibid.

285 Wilber, *Integral Operating System*, DVD.

The Fifth Aspect: Types

Also recognized have been "male and female orientations." [286] Wilber credits Deborah Tannen and Carol Gilligan with contrasting "the typical male orientation"—"agentic, autonomous, abstract, and independent, based on rights and justice"—with the typical "female orientation"—"more permeable, relational, and feelingful, based on care and responsibility." [287] In other words, the male is the yang; the female, the yin. As the book title goes, *Men Are from Mars, and Women Are from Venus.* These differences have become a staple of romantic comedy.

Another popular typology categorizes age cohorts in American culture. The Greatest Generation suffered through the Depression and World War II; the Silent Generation marched in lockstep to corporate jobs and look-alike bungalows in the fifties suburbs; the Baby Boomers wanted to make love and not war as they took to the streets in the cultural revolutions of the sixties; the "me" generation pursued material goals in the late seventies and eighties; Generation X of the 1990s seemed disaffected, disillusioned, and overloaded;[288] the Millennials have a "Net Gen" consciousness, with a learning style that favors "teamwork, experiential activities, structure, and the use of technology." Unlike Gen X, they are "close to their parents."[289]

Other typologies include the Jungian Meyers-Briggs inventory, which classifies personalities as Introvert vs. Extrovert, Intuitive vs. Sensing, Feeling vs. Thinking, and Judging vs. Perceiving; and learning styles classifications such as Kolb's Experiential Learning, Feldman's North Carolina inventory, and the VARK visual, aural, reflective, and kinesthetic modes.[290]

---

286 Ken Wilber, *A Theory of Everything* (Boston: Shambhala, 2000), 46.

287 Ibid.

288 A good summary of these typologies appears in Arthur Levine and Jeanette Cureton, *When Hope and Fear Collide: A Portrait of Today's College Student* (San Francisco: Jossey-Bass, 1998), 2-17. Most of the book describes Gen X.

289 Diana Oblinger, "Boomers, Gen-Xers, and Millennials: Understanding the New Students," *Educause* (July-August 2003): 38, accessed April 5, 2014, http://www.educause.edu/ero/article/boomers-gen-xers-and-millennials-understanding-new-students.

290 The best source for Kolb is his book *Experiential Learning.*

Learning Styles Models:

Dunn and Dunn	www.learningstyles.net
Felder	www.ncsu.edu/effective_teaching/Learning_Styles.html
Gregorc	www.gregorc.com
Kolb	www.infed.org/biblio/b-explrn.htm#learning%20style
VARK	http://www.vark-learn.com/english/index.asp

Figure 8: URLs for Learning Styles Models

The Root-Bernsteins characterize creativity by discussing "Thirteen Thinking Tools":

- Observing
- Imaging
- Abstracting
- Recognizing Patterns
- Forming Patterns
- Analogizing
- Body Thinking
- Empathizing
- Dimensional Thinking
- Modeling
- Playing
- Transforming
- Synthesizing.

This special typology crosses disciplines. Einstein excelled at imaging, synthesizing, and working with patterns. Watson and Crick used modeling, dimensional thinking, and playing, as well as working with patterns. Barbara McClintock relied on observing, abstracting, and synthesizing. All were scientists, yet all used slightly different skills. Some used skills also necessary for artists: observing, abstracting, dimensional thinking, modeling, and empathizing. So the type of creative thinking we do is not necessarily domain-dependent.

The Integral Operating System: AQAL

Wilber's system is complex, with spectrums of development for both individuals and civilizations. Because his system contains five aspects, it is nicknamed AQAL: "all quadrants, all levels, all lines, all states, all types."[291] He cautions that "the map isn't the territory," though he hopes his work will help to inaugurate a great new period in history, one in which "the first great new philosophy and religion" are being born.[292] Applying it to creativity may help us get a broad picture of all its aspects.

291 Wilber, *Integral Operating System*, booklet accompanying DVD, 27.

292 Wilber, *Integral Operating System*, DVD.

Exercises

1. Explain how the four quadrants relate to a domain with which you are familiar.
2. How do you think "The Big Three" relate to the four quadrants? Is Wilber's diagram accurate, or do "The Big Three" intertwine more closely?
3. Create a "psychograph" for yourself, identifying the major lines of development discussed in Chapter 4. Discuss.
4. Discuss and apply one of the systems of development in this chapter. How can the system help you understand your world or your life?
5. Check out the article and Advanced Resources at http://spiraldynamics.org. Apply the concepts to current events.
6. Narrate your experiences with the "three bodies" or states of awareness: "gross" physical, subtle, and/or causal. For instance, have you ever had an important or transformative dream? How is your dream reality different from your ordinary physical one? Do you ever get creative ideas in dreams? Have you ever experienced the "causal" state? Have you ever had a lucid dream, one in which you recognize you're dreaming?
7. Get online and investigate one of the generations or other types, such as male vs. female. Explain what you have found and how it relates to your own experience.
8. Take one of the "Learning Styles" quizzes. What did it reveal about you? Were you at all surprised, or did it vindicate what you already knew? If you have taken the Meyers-Briggs, you may wish to write about that. You can learn more about the Kolb Learning Styles by skimming his book, Experiential Learning, or by going to www.haygroup.com/ww/About/index.asp?id=495.
9. List some of the puzzling or unclear ideas in Chapter 4. Ask questions about them.
10. Explain what you think is most important in Chapter 4.
11. React to some of the ideas in Chapter 4. Debate, support, analyze, and/or reflect.
12. Give evidence from your own life or background experience about the ideas in Chapter 4. (Don't repeat what you have written in another exercise.)

Application Structured by Ken Wilber's Integral Operating System

The Creator (I)

Synergistic Interlude

Alice in Wonderland Chapter V: "Advice from a Caterpillar"

"'Who are YOU?' said the Caterpillar.

"This was not an encouraging opening for a conversation. Alice replied, rather shyly, 'I—I hardly know, sir, just at present—at least I know who I WAS when I got up this morning, but I think I must have been changed several times since then.'

"'What do you mean by that?' said the Caterpillar sternly. 'Explain yourself!'

"'I can't explain MYSELF, I'm afraid, sir' said Alice, 'because I'm not myself, you see.'

"'I don't see,' said the Caterpillar.

"'I'm afraid I can't put it more clearly,' Alice replied very politely, 'for I can't understand it myself to begin with; and being so many different sizes in a day is very confusing.'

"'It isn't,' said the Caterpillar.

"'Well, perhaps you haven't found it so yet,' said Alice; 'but when you have to turn into a chrysalis—you will someday, you know—and then after that into a butterfly, I should think you'll feel it a little queer, won't you?'

"'Not a bit,' said the Caterpillar.

"'Well, perhaps your feelings may be different,' said Alice; 'all I know is, it would feel very queer to ME.'

"'You!' said the Caterpillar contemptuously. 'Who are YOU?'

"Which brought them back again to the beginning of the conversation. Alice felt a little irritated at the Caterpillar's making such VERY short remarks, and she drew herself up and said, very gravely, 'I think, you ought to tell me who YOU are, first.'

"'Why?' said the Caterpillar.

"Here was another puzzling question; and as Alice could not think of any good reason, and as the Caterpillar seemed to be in a VERY unpleasant state of mind, she turned away.

"'Come back!' the Caterpillar called after her. 'I've something important to say!'

"This sounded promising, certainly: Alice turned and came back again.

"'Keep your temper,' said the Caterpillar.

"'Is that all?' said Alice, swallowing down her anger as well as she could.

"'No,' said the Caterpillar."

During the psychedelic era (late 1960s and early 1970s), the halluci-nogenic properties of Alice's adventures were celebrated. The goal of the counterculture during that era was to find one's identity by radical means, such as changing one's lifestyle or consciousness. (Many, like Ram Dass, found that the best way to change consciousness was not through LSD but through meditation.)

Questions to ponder:

1. Why do you think Alice in Wonderland appealed to the "Flower Children"?

2. The caterpillar is acting like a wise guru or Zen master, giving Alice advice on how to find her identity. What advice does he give her?

3. How might this advice apply to your daily life?

4. How does your identity or sense of who you are affect your creativity?

5

The Artist as "I": Creativity in the Upper Left, Part 1

The "Primary Imagination"

Artists quoted in Chapter 2 say that when they are creating a new and useful work, they are cooperating with something beyond themselves: what I am calling "the Unified Field" or "The Force." British Romantic poet Samuel Taylor Coleridge described this process as drawing on "The Primary Imagination."

According to Coleridge, this "esemplastic power" of "Primary Imagination" is analogous to the original act of creation. We might call this act the Big Bang, but he refers to it in biblical terms: "the eternal act of creation in the infinite I AM." He says that the gifted artist repeats this "eternal act" with his own "finite mind."[293] Dante (*The Divine Comedy*), Jonathan Swift (*Gulliver's Travels*), and Lewis Carroll (*Alice in Wonderland*) typify such "Primary Imagination" in their creation of whole worlds. Contemporary examples are J.R.R. Tolkien (*Lord of the Rings*) and George Lucas (*Star Wars*). In fact, on the Platinum Extended DVD collection of *The Lord of the Rings: The Fellowship of the Ring*, director Peter Jackson comments that he never viewed his Middle Earth as a movie set but as a real world. Artists who use the Primary Imagination, akin to "the infinite I AM," feel the power of what Cayce called "The Creative Forces": for "Each entity . . .is as a corpuscle

---

293 Samuel Taylor Coleridge, *Biographia Literaria*, Chapter 13, Project Gutenberg. Original work 1817. Retrieved from http://www.gutenberg.org/files/6081/6081-h/6081-h.htm.

in the body of that force called God." (2174–2)

In contrast to this replication of the act of "God" is the "Secondary Imagination," which Coleridge calls "an echo of the former, coexisting with the conscious will," an inferior form of playing with "counters" that are "essentially fixed and dead." [294] The less inspired artist moves "counters" in a too "conscious" way, using formulaic characters and metaphors. Such work may entertain us, but it is not "Creativity with a capital *C*."

An entire book could be written about the ways in which creators can prepare themselves to operate in harmony with "The Force." In this chapter we will explore only a few. In the process we will revisit principles from the first three chapters and conclude before introducing the crucial problem of ego, to be developed in Chapter 6.

First we will explore this question: who is the "I" that creates? Next we will ask, how do we optimize the "I" for creativity? Being as fully creative as we can is a dual process of self-awareness and letting go of self: being aware of our psychograph, with its levels and lines; cultivating the right states of consciousness; and then relaxing into what is trying to happen.

But first, we need a clarification.

A Clarification: Religion vs. Spirituality and its Relationship to Colleges

Chapters 5 and 6 draw on some spiritual traditions from both East and West. The intent is not to endorse any particular religion—only to highlight some universals in human psychology. The individual self or ego is an important part of creativity, but it is also an important component of spirituality, and some insightful commentators on the subject draw their terminology from the spiritual line.

If you are in a public college in the United States, your professors probably tiptoe around spirituality for fear of being accused of proselytizing. After all, Americans believe in the separation of church and state. It is a major reason their country was founded. Yet here is the paradox.

---

294 Samuel Taylor Coleridge, *Biographia Literaria*, Chapter 13, Project Gutenberg. Original work 1817. Retrieved from http://www.gutenberg.org/files/6081/6081-h/6081-h.htm.

A 2004 survey by the Higher Education Research Institute at U.C.L.A. found that "today's college students have very high levels of spiritual interest and involvement. Many are actively engaged in a spiritual quest and are exploring the meaning and purpose of life."[295]

The Higher Education Research Institute at U.C.L.A. is "widely regarded as one of the premier research and policy organizations on postsecondary education in the country."[296] One of the co-investigators of this report is Alexander Astin, famed for his books on the development of young adults in college. Assisting him was his wife, another Professor Emeritus at U.C.L.A. The data come from 112,232 entering students at 236 postsecondary institutions in the United States, supplemented by a "pilot" study of "3,680 third-year students at 46 colleges and universities." Data are now being analyzed from a spring 2007 survey to revisit the 2004 freshmen at the end of their second year in college.[297]

Here are a few of the findings. If you are interested in knowing more, you are encouraged to read the 28-page report, posted online.

> Four in five [of today's college students] indicate "having an interest in spirituality" and "believing in the sacredness of life," and nearly two-thirds say that "my spirituality is a source of joy." Many are also actively engaged in a spiritual quest, with nearly half reporting that they consider it "essential" or "very important" to seek opportunities to help them grow spiritually. Moreover, three-fourths of the students say that they are "searching for meaning/purpose in life," and similar numbers report that they have discussions about the meaning of life with friends. Additionally, more than three in five freshmen report having had a spiritual experience while "witnessing the beauty and harmony of nature," and over one-half say they have had such an experience while "listening to beautiful music."[298]

---

295 Alexander Astin and Helen Astin, *The Spiritual Life of College Students: A National Study of College Students' Search for Meaning and Purpose* (Higher Education Research Institute, U.C.L.A.), PDF file of Report, 2003-2005. Accessed April 3, 2014. http://spirituality.ucla.edu/, 3.

296 Ibid., 2.

297 Ibid.

298 Ibid., 4.

Claire Gaudiani, former president of Connecticut College and current fundraiser at New York University, states the importance of this report for postsecondary educators:

> **This research suggests that the newest generation expresses definite commitment to balancing material and spiritual interests—They hold challenging ideas for their boomer teachers, parents, and employers. We need to study the Astins' work and get ready for them.[299]**

There is some evidence, then, for James N. Gardner's belief that "the messy interface" among science, religion, and philosophy "is an incredibly fruitful cornucopia of creative ideas."[300] But if you're a public educator in the Unites States, you will need to tread carefully at this "interface" and confront what Parker Palmer calls your profession's "Culture of Fear."[301]

Unlike religions, though, spirituality is universal. It provides feelings of bliss, calmness, unity, centeredness, and self-transcendence. When you have a spiritual experience, you feel that there is something greater than yourself, whether you call it "Nature," "God," "The Force," "the Unified Field," "the Higher Mind," "the Moral Imperative," or something else. The HERI Report notes some commonalities between students who declare high levels of spirituality and those who proclaim themselves religiously engaged, but there are significant differences, as there are among the followers of various religions and Christian denominations and those who check the affiliation box as "None." Spiritual "questers," "strugglers," and "skeptics" receive a prominent place in the report. They are engaged with spiritual questions as well. I was a "struggler/quester/skeptic" during my undergraduate years, and I was deeply engaged in trying to figure out my own views about ultimate meanings. From this perspective, even atheists and agnostics are spiritual if they wrestling with ultimate questions as they try to live good lives and express compassion or charity. During my "struggler/quester/skeptic" years at

---

299 Quoted in Astin and Astin, *The Spiritual Life of College Students*, 22.

300 James N. Gardner, "Should Science Study Religion? Voices from the Edge: The Spirit of Science," *What is Enlightenment?* 36 (April-June 2007), 37.

301 Palmer, *The Courage of Fear*, part of the title of Chapter 2.

the University of Texas at Austin, I belonged to a Unitarian church that specialized in attracting atheists and agnostics.

"Spirituality," as a major line in the psychograph, is measured by degrees of identification with self or others. The HERI report measures degrees of these qualities: spirituality, ecumenical worldview, ethic of caring, religious skepticism, religious struggle, religious commitment, religious/social conservatism, spiritual quest, equanimity, compassionate self-concept, and charitable involvement.

Still, the terminology can be daunting. Einstein could mention "'the cosmic religious feeling'" as "'the strongest and noblest motive for scientific research,'"[302] and Newton wrote more about spirituality and alchemy than he did about mathematics and science,[303] but we live in more secular times. The vocabulary of science and spirituality seem so different that few terms work to describe them in common.

So the language in this chapter may be problematic at times. Also, depending on your learning style, heavy-duty theoretical concepts may cause you impatience or bewilderment. It is not important to understand everything in depth here—only to get the key concepts for application. And if you are tired of psychology and philosophy, hang on for Chapters 7 and 8, which are much more pragmatic and concrete. As an interdisciplinary work, this book includes the theoretical and the practical, the "artsy-fartsy" and the down-to-earth. In addition, the Exercises will give you a chance to go back to some of the more accessible and pragmatic concepts in the more theoretical chapters.

Who Is the "I" That Creates?

Swami Kriyananda (a.k.a. Donald Walters) says, "The universe, Yogananda stated, is 'center everywhere, circumference nowhere.' Every human being is, as far as he himself is concerned, the center of everything in existence!" [304] Each gem in the net sees the world from its unique center. Ken Wilber elaborates on the same idea: "there is no fixed point

---

302 Quoted in Isaacson, *Einstein*, 390.

303 *The Dark Secrets of Newton*. PBS. *Nova*. (Boston: WGBH, 2005).

304 Swami Kriyananda, *Revelations of Christ Proclaimed by Paramhansa Yogananda*, presented by his Disciple, Swami Kriyananda (Nevada City, California: Crystal Clarity, 2007), 376.

anywhere in the universe that can be considered center; each thing can be located only relative to each other."[305] The Dalai Lama says, "We ourself [sic], one individual: that is the center of the universe."[306] For this reason Ken Wilber calls creativity "part of the basic ground of the universe."[307]

In *Integral Spirituality* Wilber, refining his concept of the quadrants, says that each has two zones, depending on whether we view the interior or the exterior of the subject under question.[308] Hence in Zone 1 of Quadrant 1, we would experience ourselves as a unique and subjective center. The key word here is *feeling*. We would feel what it is like to be the individual center that is creating this world view of phenomena, moment by moment; or watching the stream of thoughts, feelings, and creative expression flowing through.

In Zone 2, we are still focused on the "I" of Quadrant 1, but we view it externally, as an object of study. The key word here is *looking*. We are looking at someone's contemplative or creative practice. We would describe the habits, temperament, or technique that someone brings to bear upon meditation or creative expression. The individual "I" is seen from outside.

Another way to answer the question of "I"–ness is to ask, "What do we mean by the ego?" Paramhansa Yogananda, using spiritual terms, defined it as "the soul attached to the body."[309] When we identify ourselves not with the net but with the individual gem, our awareness is focused on the idea of what ex–Beatle George Harrison once playfully termed "I-me-mine." We'll see how this problem stifles creation in Chapter 6.

Recall what Wilber and the most prominent stage theorists were cited as saying in Chapter 4: human development entails an ever-broadening sense of identification, from the separate self to the family and friends, then to the nation–state or ethnic group, and perhaps even at last to other beings, the planet, and the universe. Wilber cites three

---

305 Wilber, *Integral Spirituality*, 253.

306 *Wheel of Time*, directed by Werner Herzog (2003), Motion picture.

307 Wilber, *CW*, vol. 7, *A Brief History of Everything*, 25.

308 Wilber, *Integral Spirituality*, 35-40 and elsewhere in the book.

309 Swami Kriyananda, *The Essence of Self-Realization: The Wisdom of Paramhansa Yogananda* (Nevada City, California: Crystal Clarity, 1990), #7, 27.

broad levels of development: *preconventional* or *egocentric* (self–absorption in infancy); *conventional* or *ethnocentric* (identification with one's group, nation, or tribe); and *postconventional* or *worldcentric* ("a care and concern for all peoples").[310] Higher creativity means a broader identification.

Edgar Cayce has the same teaching. He reminds us, "The whole sin, ever, is selfishness" (1610–2) and "*selfishness* is the sin of man!" (3976–17) He recommends, "First know self and self's relationships to the Creative Forces in the universe, and applying those abilities day by day, in *whatsoever* way *or* manner as presents itself, will bring joy, peace, and understanding; for in service to others is the highest service as may be rendered . . ."(340–15)

How Do We Optimize the "I" for Creativity?

In *Integral Spirituality*, Wilber says that "perhaps the three most important facets of interior (or Upper–Left) awareness" are *Stages, States,* and *Shadow.* [311] Let's see what they are and how they integrate with the theory and practice of creativity.

A *stage* would indicate a level of developmental growth on the psychograph. To review, here are the characteristics of stages:

1.) Each is qualitatively different.
2.) We can't understand a stage we've never experienced.
3.) As stages advance, so does identification or awareness beyond the self.
4.) AQAL endorses all stages as necessary.
5.) We are probably at different stages in the different lines of our psychograph.

We have already looked at the spiritual stages described by Wilber and Beck (Chapter 4). In academia, for instance, the green *meme* proliferates among instructors, who value diversity and ecology. The administration is usually orange, focused on pragmatism and the bottom line. These two world views will never understand one another and,

310 Wilber, *Integral Spirituality*, 7.
311 Ibid., 140.

in fact, may even experience antipathy when they are thrown together on committees to set priorities and do strategic planning. Neither of them, however, would understand the trans-rational perspective of a yellow or turquoise, though at this stage someone sees the function of all the other stages.[312]

Here is another system that may prove useful.

Throughout the world, many religious systems describe the essentials of spirituality. Conventional sources include the Bible, the Tibetan Book of the Dead, the Talmud, the Book of Mormon, and the Quran; less mainstream are mystical writers such as the Jewish Kabbalists, the Islamic Sufis, and the Christian Gnostics. In the next section I will be drawing on some East Indian sources–only because I am familiar with them, not because I believe they contain more "Truth." The Hindus themselves acknowledge all religions with the cliché, "Truth is one; many are the names."

Swami Kriyananda says that the Indian caste system originated as a descriptor of different stages of "souls." In his discussion he describes levels that are reminiscent of the ones described by Wilber and Beck (Chapter 4). Equivalent to the infrared/beige stage is the Hindu *shudra,* or *slave,* interested only in material survival or the lower levels of existence. He is focused on the body and on survival. Kriyananda says, "His lack of creativity is a travesty of his divine potential, for he needs continual supervision in everything he does, lest he break things or misplace them."[313] You may have seen such people in K–12 schools or on the streets; they cannot create because they have no ambition. The next Indian stage, *vaishya,* or *merchant,* is interested in making money: what Spiral Dynamics and Ken Wilber's system would classify as orange, sometimes with a tinge of red egotistical authoritarianism or amber/blue "follow-the-rules" conformity. Of him Kriyananda says, "he defines 'getting ahead' as accumulating wealth." However,

> At higher levels of evolution, a *vaishya* sees himself as providing society with its practical needs. Where, first, he concentrated on fulfilling

---

312 Beck, *Spiral Dynamics Integral.*

313 Swami Kriyananda, *The Hindu Way of Awakening: Its Revelation, Its Symbols* (Nevada City, California: Crystal Clarity, 1998), 258-59.

> his selfish desires, at higher levels of development the *vaishya* caste produces musicians and artists. It leaves to a later stage, however, those attitudes of which the pure aim is, through the arts, to help people spiritually. . . .
>
> There are many merchants, of course, who derive great satisfaction from giving generously to others. In such persons, the bonds of selfishness have already begun to loosen. For them, to live only for the advantages that they can squeeze out of others is no longer attractive; they have more expansive uses for their creativity.[314]

The *kshatriya* is concerned with defending a society or making a contribution to it. In the systems of Ken Wilber and Spiral Dynamics, this is the level of green egalitarianism or turquoise–yellow integral cognition. Of this stage Kriyananda says,

> In contrast to the *vaishya's* typical question, "'What's in it for me?" the *kshatriya's* natural question is, 'What's in it for everyone?' His nature is epitomized by the selfless ruler, or by the warrior hero who willingly sacrifices his life for the good of others.

As his consciousness "becomes gradually refined, 'it becomes by nature scholarly, or philosophical, or priestly, and loses its penchant for directing other people's activities. If priestly in its inclinations, it feels called upon to dedicate itself to the spiritual welfare of all.'"[315] It reaches the last stage, the *brahmin*: turquoise–yellow and above.

In the systems of Wilber and Beck, there is a huge qualitative leap between this level and the other earlier ones. It is called Second Tier thinking in Spiral Dynamics or perhaps what Ken Wilber's chart of "Stages of Consciousness" sees as an emerging third tier.[316] Very few people in the history of the human race would qualify here, especially in the highest levels. Of this stage Kriyananda says, "the true *brahmin*, or spiritual guide [is] the teacher of others in the ways of truth . . . His

---

314 Kriyananda, *The Hindu Way of Awakening*, 259-60.

315 Ibid., 261-62.

316 Dialogue with Andrew Cohen, "The Guru and the Pandit: Dialogue XV: Creative Friction: Community and the Utopian Impulse in a Post-Modern World," *What is Enlightenment?* 36 (April-June 2007), 54; also Wilber, *Integral Spirituality*, slick insert between 68-69.

typical question of life is, 'What is true? And what, in everything, is the divine will?'"[317] Though we can't understand this stage if we haven't experienced it, history and literature have left some accounts of what it feels like, from inside, or looks like, from outside, when someone has no ego left and feels merged with All That Is.

So as mentioned in Chapter 1, creativity is a "continuum." Any level above *shudra* (infrared/beige) can exercise it, though the product will be informed by the contents of the artist's consciousness.

It is important to reiterate that AQAL stresses the importance of all lines, levels, and stages. All have a purpose in society. We need the *shudra* to do the manual labor, the *vaishya* to provide the wealth, the *kshatriya* to fight the good fight, and the *brahmin* to remind us of our mission or purpose. In fact, the *vaishya* and *kshatriya* probably furnish much of the creativity in developed societies. They are the business executives, the engineers, the entertainers, the artists, the teachers, and the inventors.

As we ponder these categories, our focal questions should be these: Who am I? What is my purpose? What am I trying to create? How does my personal expression relate to the greater good? How do my spiritual development and creative expression interact?

For our stage determines the level of creativity we can access and provides filters through which we can access it. Knowing where we are can help us critique our work and, perhaps, decide where we want to be and how to get there.

Ken Wilber defines cognitive growth as "the capacity to take per-spectives. . . .an increase in the number of others with whom you can identify and an increase in the number of perspectives you can take." He explains that cognitive development is a "necessary but not sufficient" [318] component of growth in other developmental lines: we have to "get it"–or "*grok* it," as Heinlein proposed in *Stranger in a Strange Land*: understand it totally and empathetically from within. The red–amber/blue tribes of Iraq, focused on their differences and absorbed in their fundamental codes, could not *grok* the orange–level

---

317 Kriyananda, *The Hindu Way of Awakening*, 262.

318 Wilber, *Integral Spirituality*, 113 and 113n. This is also the definition of spiritual growth espoused by Swami Kriyananda and the definition of cognitive maturity publicized by the Critical Thinking Foundation at Sonoma State University.

Enlightenment democracy that the United States government was so intent in foisting on the populace.

So stages are important. We can't grasp, can't access on a regular basis, the stages above us on the ladder. This is where *states* come in. All states are theoretically open to us at all times. Any one of us, given the right conditions, can have a high spiritual experience of self-transcendence; it's just that it won't stick without the cognitive framework to absorb it. It will also be interpreted through the stage the person has attained. Meditation or contemplation is valuable because it gives us a taste of those states and helps, consequently, to move us up the level of stages.[319] Hence it is important to cultivate the habits that will encourage stage development and invite higher states. As Hamlet says, "The readiness is all." (V.2.195)

And part of that readiness entails being aware of our shadow.

The *shadow* is a disowned part of ourselves that develops as we are growing up. Teachers and caregivers socialize us with strictures appropriate to our culture: be nice and share, cover up the parts that are "private," etc. Robert Bly humorously says that all of these impulses get stuffed into a big sack that we carry around behind us, and that by adulthood, we all have big sacks.[320] What is in the sack is not–us, something we would certainly never do or be. So no one in my family expressed anger, and I am nice, too, and don't express anger, and abhor violence in all its forms. I can't stand to watch violent movies or scenes of cruelty. I have a strong detestation of angry and violent people. Why can't they control their tempers?

So why am I in traffic, screaming and pounding the wheel because the cars won't move?

It is because I have stuffed everything to do with anger into the big sack. But it doesn't go away. Instead it pops out, like a goblin, and starts doing its thing in a way that seems totally separate from me. Or I dissociate from it and end up projecting it onto others, those people out there that I can't stand because *I'm Not Like That.* Ken Wilber explains,

---

319 Wilber, *Integral Spirituality*, 196-97.

320 Robert Bly, "The Long Bag We Drag Behind Us," in *Meeting the Shadow: The Hidden Power of the Dark Side of Human Nature*, ed. Connie Zweig and Jeremiah Abrams (Los Angeles: Tarcher, 1991), 6-7.

> The moment I push the anger away from me, the moment I push the anger on the other side of my I-boundary, it becomes a *2nd-person occasion* in my own 1st person . . . "Somebody else is angry, not me . . ."
>
> If I continue to deny my anger, it can be completely dissociated, or repressed into a *3rd-person occasion,* which means *I am no longer on speaking terms with it:* my anger has finally become an "it" or a complete stranger in my own awareness . . . It just comes over me.[321]

In *The Strange Case of Dr. Jekyll and Mr. Hyde*, the doctor's negative qualities have been split off in his consciousness and emerge as another being, a beastly character with whom he has no identification. In some movie versions of this story the split is exacerbated by showing the doctor as extra nice. The point is that we can't be extra nice all the time; there are other parts of us, and if we don't acknowledge them, they will pop out suddenly, like Mr. Hyde. It is interesting that after a while, the doctor *chooses* to drink the potion that will allow Mr. Hyde to come out. The pressure of being oh–so–good all the time is too much to take; unconsciously the doctor wants an excuse to go to the music hall, drink, and look at the girls kick their legs (a version of his evil impulses in one film). The good doctor can't keep his "Mr. Hyde" hidden forever.

The shadow is also depicted in "The Enemy Within," Episode 5 of the old *Star Trek* series. Captain Kirk, while going through the transporter, gets split into half: the "good" Kirk who is weak and indecisive and the "evil" Kirk who has energy, swills Saurian brandy, sexually harasses a pretty lieutenant, and plots to take over the ship. Confusion reigns as identical Kirks with opposite behavior patterns blunder about the ship. Each time the "evil" one commits a transgression, the "good" one is accused and says "It wasn't *me!*," dramatizing the split between acknowledged self and unacknowledged shadow. When the "good" Kirk realizes another form of himself stalks about the ship, he also realizes he must reunite with this dark side he disowns: "I can't survive without him. I don't want to take him back! He's brutal; he's an animal." After he climbs back into the transporter with his other half and the two are reunited in one body, he can again make decisions. Dr. McCoy says the

---

evil side is "half of who we are. Without the negative side you couldn't be the captain; he has your strength of command." [322]

So we don't get anywhere by imitating Dr. Jekyll and disowning the shadow. We have to acknowledge it, take it out of the sack, and work with it. But since it is unconscious, how do we see it? How do we get a glimpse of "Mr. Hyde"?

Zweig and Abrams, citing the work of "English psychoanalyst Molly Tuby," list six ways:

- In our exaggerated feelings about others ("I just can't believe he would do that!" "I don't know how she could wear that outfit!")
- In negative feedback from others who serve as our mirrors ("This is the third time you arrived late without calling me.")
- In those interactions in whch [sic] we continually have the same troubling effect on several different people ("Sam and I both feel that you have not been straightforward with us.")
- In our impulsive and inadvertent acts ("Oops, I didn't mean to say that.")
- In situations in which we are humiliated ("I'm so ashamed about how he treats me.")
- In our exaggerated anger about other people's faults ("She just can't seem to do her work on time!" "Boy, he really let his weight get out of control!")[323]

Clarissa Pinkola Estés, a Jungian psychologist, says,

> . . . probably the most important thing that you can do for your creativity is to realize that you have to reach into the dark, sometimes, to find it; and that the dark is not a horrible place: it's a place where lots of treasures are, lots of gifts—and, there is, I think, a natural inclination of the ego not to reach into the dark. . . but, you know, that's your only hope . . . to go after that which you've lost—in other words, to go into the underworld.[324]

---

322 Richard Matheson, "The Enemy Within," *Star Trek,* season 1, episode 5, directed by Leo Penn, aired October 6, 1966 (Hollywood, CA: Paramount, 1991). The original and uncut television series.

323 Connie Zweig and Jeremiah Abrams, "Introduction," in *Meeting the Shadow: The Hidden Power of the Dark Side of Human Nature*, ed. Connie Zweig and Jeremiah Abrams (Los Angeles: Tarcher, 1991), xviii-xix.

324 Estés, *The Creative Fire.*

Wilber says it is essential to do shadow work to reach the higher levels but that Quadrant 1, Zone 1 meditative practices ignore it. As far as creativity is concerned, being aware of the shadow is important if we want to create art that is uplifting or inspiring. Much "art" in theaters and museums today is both ugly and disgusting. One example is the Paris Hilton Autopsy statue. The naked body of the celebrity, crafted in resin, lies sprawled with a cell phone in one hand and drink glass in another, her innards spread out next to her. The art is interactive; the innards will fit back inside the body.[325]

Some movies seem to be a parade of the shadow: gore for no reason other than to horrify. On the other hand, Zweig and Abrams believe that in some "horror novels and movies," a cathartic purgation can occur: "Through a vicarious enactment of the shadow side, our evil impulses can be stimulated and perhaps relieved in the safety of the book or theater."[326] Perhaps this is why many of us enjoy *Star Wars* and *Lord of the Rings*.

Like the autopsy statue, which the artist claimed was to demonstrate the evils of drink, *Star Wars* and *Lord of the Rings* have spiritual purposes. Both movies show that we must fight the evil outside of us but be mindful that we are prey to its influences within. Both Luke Skywalker and Frodo manage to acknowledge and overcome their shadows. Luke refuses to hate, as the Emperor urges him to do, and accepts and acknowledges his fallen-angel father. Frodo accepts his role as the ring-bearer and manages to fend off the whispered seductions of the ring. While both movies demonstrate these psychological and spiritual truths, they also have uplifting, cathartic endings, like tragedy. There has been loss, but also increased knowledge and self-awareness, and good triumphs in the end.

Go with the Flow

To cooperate with "The Force," we must possess a unique combination of opposites. Like Luke Skywalker, we must have humility enough

---

325 Verena Dobnik, "Hilton Dead in Provocative NYC Statue," *San Francisco Chronicle*, May 9, 2007.

326 Zweig and Abrams, "Introduction," xx.

to let go and trust our feelings, but also confidence enough to summon the will to act. There must be a unique combination of receptivity and alertness, an ability to ask, "What is trying to happen here?" and to apply the totality of our concentration and energy into helping to make it happen. The balance is delicate. At times, what is trying to happen may not be what our individual wills would strive to create. Woody Allen has, for a long time, secretly yearned to write tragic scripts in the style of Ingmar Bergman and even laughs at himself in one film sequence, during which aliens land on earth and tell him, "We like your other films. The older, funnier ones." His *Interiors*, a Bergman imitation, has never achieved the popularity of quirky *Annie Hall*. Henry Fielding, an eighteenth-century novelist who achieved fame with his comic epic *Tom Jones*, always yearned to be a tragic dramatist, as did Miguel de Cervantes, who gave us the inimitable comic figures Don Quixote and Sancho Panza. These gifted artists were not comfortable "going with the flow" of their talent. They wanted to be someone else.

Of course, surrendering to the flow does not mean flopping down passively and wailing, "There's nothing I can do." It means using all our energy to understand not what we want but "what is trying to happen." The Cayce readings stress the importance of "the application of the will as respecting that held as the ideal, or the ideal's relationship to the Creative Energy as is One in All. As to whether the influences are used as exaltations of self, self's interest, self's influence, or affluence, depends upon the application of that as lies within each individual." (23–1)

For that, we need to watch the influence of the ego.

Exercises

1. Contrast some examples of Primary Imagination (Creativity with a capital C) and Secondary Imagination (work that is more formulaic and less inspired). What do you think makes the difference? Analyze a few examples. (Don't repeat what this book says about *Star Wars* and *Lord of the Rings*.)

2. Read the Astins' report *The Spiritual Life of College Students,* available at http://spirituality.ucla.edu/spirituality/reports/FINAL%20REPORT. pdf. Write a personal reaction to it.

3. Have you ever had a spiritual experience, perhaps in nature or out at sea? Explain.

4. Have you ever felt "The Force" flowing through you or supporting you? And/or have you ever experienced "going with the flow" or fighting it? Explain, with examples.

5. If you didn't construct a psychograph for yourself in Chapter 2, do so now. What levels do you think you are one in some of the major lines? How have these levels affected your life or creativity?

6. Write a reaction to one of the five points on page 115. Explain, analyzing examples from your life, experience, or reading.

7. Explain a conflict you witnessed, and speculate on how it may have been a conflict between two memes or stages of development.

8. Explain which of the East Indian categories you believe typify your stage and life purpose. (You may be straddling two categories.) How would awareness of your stage help with your life, your mission, and/or your creative work?

9. Scan the bullets on page 121. Use one or more items to explore your own shadow. For instance, what characteristics do you really hate in other people? Psychologists say these are repressed and disowned parts of yourself. If you didn't repress and disown them, they wouldn't bother you; you'd have a neutral reaction to them. For example, for many years I disliked being around children, and a psychologist told me I had disowned my inner child—no doubt true, as I have a tendency to be serious rather than playful.

10. Explain examples of "art" that seem to you to embody a low state of consciousness, like The Paris Hilton Autopsy Statue.

11. Swami Kriyananda (a.k.a. Donald Walters) discusses three states of consciousness: subconscious, conscious, and superconscious. When we are in the subconscious state, we are reacting rather than acting, feeling low in energy, and taking things personally. When we are in the conscious state, we are acting, feeling high or even nervous, and solving problems. When we are in the superconscious state, we see the big picture, ask what is trying to happen, and feel calm.

Here is an example: your car breaks down on the way to the airport.

Subconscious Reaction: Why me? Why now? Why does this always have to happen to me? I'll never make it to the airport on time!

Conscious Reaction: Hmm, my car has broken down. I'd better call my husband to pick me up and drive me to the airport. He can go back to my broken-down car and wait for Triple A.

Superconscious Reaction: Now, why did this happen? What's the lesson in it? Hmm.

Lesson 1: I should have checked the car out before the trip.
Lesson 2: I should express more appreciation to my husband for all he does for me.
Lesson 3: I should learn not to react so emotionally and personally to everything that happens.

As you may have guessed, this is a true example, and I did, in fact go through all three stages within about fifteen minutes. Now write an example from your own experience. What was the problem? What would be the subconscious reaction? The conscious reaction? The superconscious reaction? (You need not confess which reaction/s you actually had!)

Here's the application of this exercise to art: if you are creating from the subconscious level, you get something like the Paris Hilton Autopsy Doll. In my field, writing, I prefer to use the superconscious level for inspiration and the conscious level for revision and editing. The subconscious creeps in (oh, self-absorbed me!), but it detracts, and I try to catch it and weed it out.

12. This chapter is focused on the literary and visual arts. How would you apply one or more of its principles to science or engineering or to another domain in which you are interested? Be specific.

13. List some of the puzzling or unclear ideas in Chapter 5. Ask questions about them.
14. Explain what you think is most important in Chapter 5.
15. React to some of the ideas in Chapter 5. Debate, support, analyze, and/or reflect.
16. Give evidence from your own life or background experience about the ideas in Chapter 5. (Don't repeat what you have written in another exercise.)

Synergistic Interlude

Alice in Wonderland
Chapter I: "Down the Rabbit Hole"

"Down, down, down . . . when suddenly, thump! thump! down she came upon a heap of sticks and dry leaves, and the fall was over.

"Alice was not a bit hurt, and she jumped up on to her feet in a moment: she looked up, but it was all dark overhead; before her was another long passage, and the White Rabbit was still in sight, hurrying down it. There was not a moment to be lost: away went Alice like the wind, and was just in time to hear it say, as it turned a corner, `Oh my ears and whiskers, how late it's getting!' She was close behind it when she turned the corner, but the Rabbit was no longer to be seen: she found herself in a long, low hall, which was lit up by a row of lamps hanging from the roof.

"There were doors all around the hall, but they were all locked; and when Alice had been all the way down one side and up the other, trying every door, she walked sadly down the middle, wondering how she was ever to get out again.

'Suddenly she came upon a little three-legged table, all made of solid glass; there was nothing on it except a tiny golden key, and Alice's first thought was that it might belong to one of the doors of the hall; but, alas! either the locks were too large, or the key was too small, but at any rate it would not open any of them. However, on the second time round, she came upon a low curtain she had not noticed before, and behind it was a little door about fifteen inches high: she tried the little golden key in the lock, and to her great delight it fitted!

"Alice opened the door and found that it led into a small passage, not much larger than a rat-hole: she knelt down and looked along the passage into the loveliest garden you ever saw. How she longed to get out of that dark hall, and wander about among those beds of bright flowers and those cool fountains, but she could not even get her head though the doorway; 'and even if my head would go through,' thought poor Alice, 'it would be of very little use without

my shoulders. Oh, how I wish I could shut up like a telescope! I think I could, if I only know how to begin.' For, you see, so many out-of-the-way things had happened lately, that Alice had begun to think that very few things indeed were really impossible.

"There seemed to be no use in waiting by the little door, so she went back to the table, half hoping she might find another key on it, or at any rate a book of rules for shutting people up like telescopes: this time she found a little bottle on it, ('which certainly was not here before,' said Alice,) and round the neck of the bottle was a paper label, with the words 'DRINK ME' beautifully printed on it in large letters.

. . . she very soon finished it off . . .

'What a curious feeling!' said Alice; 'I must be shutting up like a telescope.'

And so it was indeed: she was now only ten inches high, and her face brightened up at the thought that she was now the right size for going through the little door into that lovely garden. First, however, she waited for a few minutes to see if she was going to shrink any further: she felt a little nervous about this; 'for it might end, you know,' said Alice to herself, 'in my going out altogether, like a candle. I wonder what I should be like then?' And she tried to fancy what the flame of a candle is like after the candle is blown out, for she could not remember ever having seen such a thing.

"After a while, finding that nothing more happened, she decided on going into the garden at once; but, alas for poor Alice! when she got to the door, she found she had forgotten the little golden key, and when she went back to the table for it, she found she could not possibly reach it: she could see it quite plainly through the glass, and she tried her best to climb up one of the legs of the table, but it was too slippery; and when she had tired herself out with trying, the poor little thing sat down and cried.

"'Come, there's no use in crying like that!' said Alice to herself, rather sharply; 'I advise you to leave off this minute!' She generally gave herself very good advice, (though she very seldom followed it), and sometimes she scolded herself so severely as to bring tears into her eyes; and once she remembered trying to box her own ears for having cheated herself in a game of croquet she was playing against herself, for this curious child was very fond of pretending to be two people. 'But it's no use now,' thought poor Alice, 'to pretend to be two people!

Why, there's hardly enough of me left to make ONE respectable person!'

"*Soon her eye fell on a little glass box that was lying under the table: she opened it, and found in it a very small cake, on which the words 'EAT ME' were beautifully marked in currants. 'Well, I'll eat it,' said Alice, 'and if it makes me grow larger, I can reach the key; and if it makes me grow smaller, I can creep under the door; so either way I'll get into the garden, and I don't care which happens!' . . .*

"*So she set to work, and very soon finished off the cake. . . .*

Chapter II: "The Pool of Tears"

"*. . . Just then her head struck against the roof of the hall: in fact she was now more than nine feet high, and she at once took up the little golden key and hurried off to the garden door.*

"*Poor Alice! It was as much as she could do, lying down on one side, to look through into the garden with one eye; but to get through was more hopeless than ever: she sat down and began to cry again.*"

The White Rabbit typifies those of us who are consumed with "busyness," running frantically from one appointment to another, thinking, I'm late! Alice, however, has fallen down the rabbit hole of the unconscious mind, so her reality is dreamlike, timeless, and illogical. (In fact, the conclusion of her tale is that she has been dreaming it all.)

Questions to ponder:

1. What do you think the golden key represents? (See the Grimm's tale at the beginning of Chapter 1.)

2. What does the beautiful garden represent?

3. Why is it so hard for her to get into the garden?

4. What relationship might this story have to spirituality or creativity?

5. What might this tale be saying about the ego and spirituality or creativity?

   A song by Jefferson Airplane, a 1960s–1970s counterculture band, relates this episode.

6

Creativity in the Upper Left, Part 2: The Paradox of Ego: Uses and Abuses

The Paradox

As with so many other facets of creativity, the ego is a paradox. We need a strong and healthy ego to create. Then we need to put it aside.

Uses of Ego

First, we need a strong and healthy ego to create. Without self–confidence, we will never be able to promote our work, perhaps not even create it.

Some geniuses show an early predisposition to self–confidence: an insistence on their own ideas, often with support from caretakers and mentors. Barbara McClintock, who won the Nobel prize for her experiments with maize, was not forced to go to school as a child and sometimes stayed at home "for as long as a semester or more." When a neighbor reprimanded the child for being tomboyish rather than ladylike in her interests, young Barbara's mother called the offending woman and remonstrated with her, "'Don't ever do that again!'"[327] Freud's mother gave him "special attention," and he had "a doting nurse." He ate alone in a room reserved for that purpose, and when he became irritated at his sister's piano playing, "the piano was removed

---

327 Evelyn Fox Keller, *A Feeling for the Organism* (New York: Henry Holt, 2003), 23, 24.

from the house."[328] Picasso had to be coaxed to attend school with the assurance that his father "was with him, remained nearby, or promised to return at a certain hour."[329] Martha Graham, diva of dance, is the subject of childhood anecdotes that suggest an independent streak. As a toddler bored in church, she is said "to have danced down a church aisle." In later childhood, when trapped on a train "that suddenly began to move," she announced, "'Man, I'm Doctor Graham's daughter and I want out of here.'"[330]

Suzanne Farrell,[331] a prima ballerina who danced for choreographer George Balanchine, achieved her dream with the help of her mother. A single mother of three daughters, Mrs. Farrell said, "I don't think they've got talent; I know they've got talent"—and vowed to do what she could to "make it happen for them." Daughter Suzanne said that she "had seen pictures of the New York City Ballet" with Balanchine and decided, "I was going to dance for him . . . I don't think anything or anyone could've stopped this destiny that was happening." So the family packed a U-Haul and left Cincinnati for New York. Said Mrs. Farrell, "I just didn't have one single doubt in my mind." Added daughter Suzanne, "We were living in a tiny one-room apartment. Mother worked almost 20 hours a day . . . I just knew at that time that I had to be there." Suzanne Farrell auditioned for the School of American Ballet on her sixteenth birthday and was on her way to fame.

Howard Gardner, who traces the life and work of creative geniuses representing six types of intelligence, says that creative "prodigies" may have been surrounded by admiring audiences in early childhood, but they have to be prepared for the "shock" of defending their position in a field or domain as they enter their twenties. [332] They must have what Sternberg defines as *"Perspicacity,"* be one who "questions societal norms, truisms, assumptions; is willing to take a stand."[333]

---

328 Gardner, *Creating Minds*, 51-52.

329 Ibid., 141.

330 Ibid., 268.

331 The information about Farrell comes from *Suzanne Farrell: Elusive Muse* (Seahorse Films, 2006).

332 Gardner, *Creating Minds*, 139-40.

333 Robert J. Sternberg, "A Three-Facet Model of Creativity," in *The Nature of Creativity,* ed. Robert J. Sternberg (Cambridge: Cambridge University Press, 1988), 146.

Man Ray's career epitomizes such self-confidence.[334] In the 1920s when New York critics "rejected his art," he joined "The Lost Generation" in Paris and became one of the Dada group, whose byword was "artistic anarchy." "His most famous object" was made from a flat iron, on which he glued a row of tacks, "'to make it useless.'" Everyone was invited to interpret the object differently and puzzle over the title: *Le Cadeau*, The Gift. Ray elaborated, "'I always wanted to be accepted, not understood.'" With the Dadaists, he achieved both objectives.

Ray made a name for himself photographing the most famous creative celebrities of the era in Paris: Sinclair Lewis, T.S. Eliot, Ernest Hemingway, James Joyce, Pablo Picasso, and Henri Matisse. He shot a picture of Marcel Proust on his deathbed. He photographed Arnold Schoenberg, dressed in a celluloid collar and sitting stiffly, and put a black scarf around him so just the face showed. Ray made most of his living from these photos but seems not to have been anxious about where his next franc was coming from or whether anyone would accept his art. He proclaimed, "'They say I am ahead of my time . . . It's the others who are behind the times.'"

Francis Ford Coppola had the same sort of courage when he filmed *Apocalypse Now*, though he admitted to moments of great anxiety. The film went considerably over budget and over schedule, and he had to pour his own money into the production. Early in the filming, he fired his leading man and hired another, who proceeded to have a heart attack. He had difficulty securing helicopters. A typhoon struck. Marlon Brando was shy and difficult to work with. Coppola himself didn't know where the film was going or how it would end. He liked to work intuitively, without a script, letting his characters improvise. Yet he persevered, and the film was completed, to great critical and popular acclaim. Basically, he refused to give up. He said, "It's not in the cards that we're not going to make this film."[335] Similarly Rodin, who faced heart-breaking difficulties in the field of sculpting, is said to have succeeded for three reasons: "he had genius, he was stubborn, and he had

---

334 The following information about Man Ray is drawn from *Man Ray: Prophet of the Avant Garde*, directed by Mel Stuart (PBS, American Masters series, 1999).

335 *Hearts of Darkness: A Filmmaker's Apocalypse*, directed by Francis Ford Coppola, narrated by Eleanor Coppola (American Zoetrope, 1991).

an enormous capacity for work."[336]

Terry Gilliam,[337] who started as an illustrator for *Mad Magazine* and went to England in 1967 to join the Monty Python group, also seems to have the self-confidence and courage that come with a strong ego. Robert J. Emery says, "Terry Gilliam is definitely a film-making rebel. He insists on following his own instincts, as his films will attest. His movies are not for everyone, nor does he want them to be." Gilliam himself breezily confesses, "'I never knew where I got the brain floating around in this skull; I just think I'm one of nature's mutants.'" On the other hand, Brad Pitt says, "The man has no ego," "and he's so aware of what he knows and so aware of what he doesn't know." Can we perhaps say that Gilliam has such self-confidence because he goes with the flow and doesn't worry whether everyone understands and appreciates his efforts?

How do we define the creative ego? Do we say that there must be a strong sense of self, a strong self-confidence, even a sense of purpose and destiny? If so, how does that balance with the need to step out of the way and let creativity happen?

There seems to be a delicate balance of yin and yang, of feminine receptivity and masculine force or will. Swami Kriyananda (a.k.a. Donald Walters) says,

> **The need for balancing outward, masculine creativity with inward, feminine inspiration is especially great in the present age, when creativity has become so generally associated with emotional extremes, stormy likes and dislikes, and so little control over one's reactions that creativity itself seems virtually equated with violent mood swings rather than with emotional balance and mental clarity.[338]**

Paramhansa Yogananda, who calls will "the cosmic energizer," describes the process not as balance but as union: "To attain mastery over cosmic energy, the missing link between consciousness and matter,

---

336 Odile Ayral-Clause, *Camille Claudel: A Life* (New York: Henry N. Abrams, 2002), 31.

337 The information about Gilliam all comes from *Terry Gilliam*, Directors series: written, produced, and directed by Robert J. Emery for the American Film Institute, 2000.

338 Kriyananda, *The Hindu Way of Awakening*, 183.

body and Spirit, is to realize the true nature of the Self—or everything in creation—and the oneness of all with the Creator."[339] Edgar Cayce says the same: "To make the will one with the Creative Energy should be the desire of *every* being." (78-3) How? The individual will should first be energized and applied. Kriyananda often quotes Yogananda as saying, "The greater the will, the greater the energy."[340] Then this will must be directed to align with the greater Will of what is trying to happen. During the process, says Yogananda, we must be "calmly active" and "actively calm."[341]

Abuses of Ego

Jane Loevinger, commenting on Freudian theory, says, "The problem of the ego is domination. It is menaced by reality, by instincts, and by conscience, and it must dominate the situation to defend itself."[342] In fact, Freud explained the many "defense mechanisms" the ego uses to fend off painful realities. (We will look at a few of these in the Exercises.)

When spiritually minded people first learn about the ego, they may believe it is their duty to crush it. They may oppose, vigorously and consciously, this selfish part of themselves that says "I-me–mine." They may want to say, "I shouldn't be like that." But, of course, they do no good by stuffing the ego into the sack. They will only watch it pop out at an unpleasant time, like a demon that has been shoved into a hamper. They may sit on the lid, but eventually the demon will pop out and send them hurtling skyward, wondering, *What was that?*

The myth of Adam and Eve may be a story of the ego. Originally the primal pair were innocent and naïve, totally identified with the nature around them, unaware of any sense of separateness. Then they ate the apple of knowledge. They became aware of themselves as individual entities in bodies and saw that they were naked. At that point they were

---

339 Paramahansa Yogananda, "The Missing Link between Consciousness and Matter," in *Man's Eternal Quest* (Los Angeles: Self-Realization Fellowship, 1975), 369.

340 For example, see *Superconsciousness*, 134.

341 Paramahansa Yogananda, "A New Look at the Origin and Nature of Cosmic Creation," in *The Divine Romance,* (Los Angeles: Self-Realization Fellowship, 1986), 29.

342 Jane Loevinger, *Ego Development: Conceptions and Theories*, The Jossey-Bass Behaviorial Science Series. (San Francisco: Jossey-Bass, 1976), 378-79.

expelled from the garden of unconscious bliss.

The twist, however, is that now they had to go out in the world and work. They had to grow and develop, as they never would have done in Eden. In the Middle Ages, this story was called the *felix culpa*, the "paradox of the fortunate fall."

If we wish we were back in Eden, unconsciously enjoying perfect unity with Creator and Creation—if we identify this state with the expansive union that being at the upper levels of Tier Two bring—then we are committing what Ken Wilber calls the "pre–trans fallacy." Original ignorance in an unaware state is *not* the same as waking up fully to cosmic awareness. To be enlightened, we must first have an ego to transcend.

The British Romantic poets had a hard time with this concept. Repeatedly they fell into the trap of the "pre–trans fallacy," characterized by Wilber as "the eulogizing of infancy . . . or the confusing of *pre*–rational states and *trans*–rational states simply because both are *non*–rational."[343] They believed that the infant must be in a high spiritual state because of what psychologists call "oceanic feeling," a blissful lack of boundaries between self and mother. Jane Loevinger says, "The primal unity between mother and child is gratifying, but the strong early tie to mother, and particularly regression to it from earlier stages, is also threatening, since it implies return to an earlier, less differentiated stage of ego development."[344] One example of this pre–trans confusion occurs in Wordsworth's "Ode: Intimations of Immortality from Recollections in Early Childhood":

> **Heaven lies about us in our infancy!**
> **Shades of the prison-house begin to close**
> **Upon the growing Boy,**
> **But He beholds the light, and whence it flows;**
> **He sees it in his joy;**
> **The Youth, who daily further from the east**
> **Must travel, still is nature's Priest,**

---

343 Wilber, *CW*, vol. 2: Introduction, 3. Here Wilber says that Phase 2 of his work was characterized by the clarification of this confusion "between *pre*-rational" and "*trans*-rational."

344 Loevinger, *Ego Development*, 380-81.

> And by the vision splendid
> Is on his way attended;
> At length the Man perceives it die away,
> And fade into the light of common day. (Part 5, II.66-76)

"The prison–house of the body" was a standard phrase used by Neoplatonists to describe the embodied soul. However, Plato himself, in the Allegory of the Cave[345] from *The Republic*, does not commit the "pre–trans fallacy." He stipulates that most of us are living a half–life, unaware, like prisoners shackled in a cave and watching shadows cast on the wall from a fire behind us. This allegory is parallel to the Hindu concept of *maya*, used in the popular film *The Matrix*: we are trapped in a virtual reality and unable to see that it is not real in the way we think it is. There is something beyond the dream–world creating it, like the fire creating the shadows on the wall. Paramhansa Yogananda likened this dream state to watching a movie, becoming involved in it, and not noticing that the pictures are created by the white light streaming from the projector: "In a movie, the action seems very real. If you look up to the projection booth, however, you will see that that whole story is being produced by a single beam of light." [346] Scientist Roger Penrose uses the same metaphor: "Our picture of reality is like the screen in a cinema theatre, where a particular point on the screen retains its identity no matter what kinds of vigorous movement might be projected on it."[347]

However, the true quest is to become aware of what is behind the shadows: to look at the white light from the projector. Plato says that a prisoner who is suddenly released will look around and see the fire, but that its brilliance will create a painful glare and he will be likely to affirm, still, the reflection of the shadows as the true reality. If he walks to the mouth of the cave, he will be almost blinded by the reality of

---

345 Plato, *The Republic*, beginning of Book 7.

346 Kriyananda, *The Essence of Self-Realization*, #5, 15. For three other instances of Yogananda's use of the movie metaphor, see Yogananda, "The Missing Link between Consciousness and Matter," 369; Kriyananda, *Conversations with Yogananda* (Nevada City, California: Crystal Clarity, 2004), #344, 372; Paramhansa Yogananda, *Autobiography of a Yogi* (Nevada City, CA: Crystal Clarity, 1994), Chapter 30, 269-71.

347 Penrose, *The Road to Reality*, 383.

actual sunlight. When his eyes finally adjust to this new reality, he will look first at shadows, next at reflections on the water, next at the moon and stars. At last his eyes will be accustomed to daylight, and he will look up at the sun itself. When he returns to the cave to report what he has seen, the other prisoners will scoff at him because his eyesight is no longer accustomed to the darkness. They will say that it was better not to leave the cave and that, if anyone tries to help another do so, the penalty should be death. As John Lennon once said, all too prophetically, "They always kill the messenger."

In fact, according to many spiritual traditions, the heroes who have seen the light and return to the cave are often killed. A common metaphor is that they are awake and come to tell us we are asleep and that we don't appreciate the message.

If you can't relate to spiritual examples, here is a secular one. Charles Tart, Professor Emeritus at the University of California at Davis, says that we walk around asleep like automatons in a "consensus trance" induced by enculturation. Though our potential is actually unlimited, "Each of us is born into a culture, a group of people with a shared belief system, a consensus about how things are and how they ought to be." From birth on, some ideas and impulses are encouraged and others, discouraged. The process is similar to hypnosis but more pervasive and effective: it lasts years instead of minutes and is accompanied by physical force, emotional force, rewards for conformity, and guilt. In addition, the child's mind is like that of someone in hypnosis: subject to suggestion and deeply trusting of parental guidance.[348] Waking up from this state has been compared to lucid dreaming, the state in which we realize suddenly that we are in a dream.

Yogananda explains,

> **In the Vedanta and Yoga philosophies the universe is spoken of as God's dream. Matter and mind—the cosmos with its stars and planets; the gross surface waves and the subtle undercurrents of the material creation; the human powers of feeling, will, and consciousness; and the states of life and death, day and night, health and disease, success and**

---

348 Charles Tart, *Waking Up: Overcoming the Obstacles to Human Potential*, New Science Library (Boston: Shambhala, 1987), 85-95.

failure—are realities according to the law of relativity governing this dream of God's . . . To escape from maya, illusion, the law of relativity, one must awaken from the dream into eternal God-wakefulness[349]

Identification seems to be a major component of *creation*. What we identify with, we create. We unconsciously identify with our shadow components, so we create them in our environment, either by projecting them onto someone else or by watching them hop out of us at inappropriate moments. We identify with the characteristics of our parents, and we find them in our bosses. (One of my friends changed jobs three times in two years because every boss he had was like his mother! At last he understood he had to deal with the "mother problems" in his shadow. When he did, he drew another sort of boss.) If I identify with red–level emotions, I create tribalistic warfare around me, and no amount of coaxing will help me see orange rationalism. (This is the problem with trying to force democracy on tribal countries like Iraq. Beck says that a culture can't leap from red to orange.)[350]

Charles Tart used to do an exercise in his workshops. He would bring a paper bag to class and ask the students to concentrate on the bag and project themselves into it, to identify with the bag and *become* the bag. After a few moments of this exercise, he would smash the bag! Students would react violently. They would become agitated and upset. This, Tart would tell them, is the problem of identification.[351] We project our psyche into something until it becomes an extension of *me*. Tart says that we can identify with anything:

Your name, your body, your possessions, your family, your job, the tools you use on your job, your community, 'the cause,' country, humanity, the planet, the universe, God, your fingernail, a victim in a newspaper story . . . The list of things people have identified with is endless.[352]

Wordsworth identified himself with his poetry. Then he associated

---

349 Paramhansa Yogananda, "Understanding the Unreality of Matter," in *Man's Eternal Quest*, (Los Angeles: Self-Realization Fellowship, 1975), 58.

350 Beck, *Spiral Dynamics Integral*, CD 2.

351 Tart, *Waking Up*, 109.

352 Ibid., 108.

his imaginative gifts with divine union, which he believed strongest in infancy. Not surprisingly, the older he grew, the less he felt the light.

> It is not now as it hath been of yore; —
>> Turn whereso'er I may,
>> By night or day,
> The things which I have seen I now can see no more. (Part 1, ll. 6-9)

His friend and colleague, Samuel Taylor Coleridge, bewailed the same loss of imagination.

He describes his depression:

> A grief without a pang, void, dark, and drear,
>> A stifled, drowsy, unimpassioned grief,
>> Which finds no natural outlet, no relief
>> In word, or sigh, or tear—("Dejection: An Ode" Part 2, ll. 21-24)

Both he and Wordsworth believed they needed inspiration to create; both felt that they were losing it; and both failed to write any memorable verse thereafter. They were too aware of trying to create while they were trying to create. They were too aware of the separate self: the "I" encased in a body, mind, and emotions.

Swami Kriyananda (a.k.a. Donald Walters) says, "The ego . . . can block the flow of creativity and inspiration by crying, "Wait a minute! The credit is all *mine.*"[353] He remarks,

> Many highly creative people rise to certain heights of creativity, then find it impossible to rise any farther. Why? Many of them actually begin, at a certain point, to lose their creativity. Again, why? Always, it seems to me, the loss follows an increase of egotism. Their thought "I'm doing it all" blocks the energy-flow to the superconscious, whence they derived their highest inspiration.[354]

He also cites the nineteenth century as an era in which egotism

---

353 Kriyananda, *Superconsciousness*, 205.
354 Ibid., 236.

seems to have blocked many creative talents and even created madness. He says, "It is as though the high energy required to create a master-piece, if that energy is blocked by a growing sense on the artist's part of his own importance in the scheme of things, resulted in disturbances to the brain."[355]

Clarissa Pinkola Estés remarks that nineteenth-century Romantics were slaves to excess. She explains that there is a dark side to the Muse: "possession." She describes not a forgetfulness of ego in service to what is trying to happen but an ecstatic possession by a dark god. Her words evoke the spirit of "Dark Romantics" such as the twentieth-century rock star and self-proclaimed shaman Jim Morrison:

> The Muse is a drug. It's a mind and body drug that enables you to go without food, without sleep, without companionship—actually alters your whole sense of time. The Muse is a hallucinogen that, in proper proportions, is meant to connect you with the imaginal world—but in improper and too large proportions, actually takes you away from your human life and makes you think, at least momentarily, that you are a god.[356]

To watch the self-implosion she is discussing, see Oliver Stone's film about Jim Morrison: *The Doors*. Morrison, convinced that he embodies the spirit of a dead Indian shaman, cultivates extremes of excess in drugs, alcohol, and daredevil experiences to "break on through to the other side." He ends up "breaking on through" by dying.

Estés explains that in the Greek myths,

> . . . sailors who are passing through the place of the clashing rocks, would tie themselves to the masts of the ships because there were Sirens there . . . like beautiful mermaids who sang beautifully, who lived under the sea, and they're so beautiful and so compelling . . . the sailors would suddenly believe that they could live underwater, too. . . that they could live under water with these beautiful women . . . This phenom-enon of the otherworldly Muse . . . who comes from a plane that is not

355 Kriyananda, *Superconsciousness*, 237.
356 Estés, *The Creative Fire*.

quite human, who lures the human being to some kind of destruction is also very, very ancient. [Many stories tell of those] who lose their senses and then return to their senses but have lost everything.[357]

Ken Wilber says that "Much (but not all) of the Romantic agenda was a colossal confusion of pre and trans."[358] Like Thomas Wolfe, Wordsworth and Coleridge couldn't go home again, so they felt they could go nowhere—at least creatively. Wilber remarks that "instead of going forward to a transpersonal tomorrow, the Romantics recommended a recapture of a prepersonal past."[359] They wanted to lose their egos in a great swoon, a primordial, orgiastic retreat to unconsciousness.

So while one abuse of ego is dumping it for a dark "possession," a more common is being focused on it, to the exclusion of what is trying to happen. If you are too absorbed in the Little "I" of the separate self, you will not be able to cooperate with the Big "I" of the "Unified Field."

Eckhart Tolle says that the "Little Me" is a self of "continuous contraction," with an "illusion of separateness," and the antidote is "that stillness" that provides "freedom" from "that self as the Little Me."[360] He adds,

It's the opposite of doing. . . .Internally align yourself with the form this moment takes . . . The moment you fight the form, the form of *me* gets strengthened . . . The illusion of *me* gets strengthened through fighting *what is*.[361]

You are the servant of not your own ego but of your art. Suzanne Farrell said it well when she told her students, "You are the servant of the dance."[362]

---

357 Estés, *The Creative Fire*.

358 Wilber, *CW*, vol. 2: Introduction, 3.

359 Ibid.

360 Eckhart Tolle, *Through the Open Door*, (Sounds True and Namaste Publishing, 2006), CD 1.

361 Ibid., CD 2.

362 *Suzanne Farrell: Elusive Muse.*

Acting without Concern for the Results

The Bhagavad Gita, an ancient Indian epic, is a story of the battle between good and evil, represented by a battle between the Pandavas and the Kurus on the field of Kurukshetra. As the two sides are drawn up in preparation for the fight, the warrior Arjuna sits in his chariot between the two armies, with Krishna as his charioteer. Arjuna's heart sinks because he recognizes family members in the opposing armies, and he tells Krishna, his spiritual teacher, that he *cannot* fight. Krishna, however, advises Arjuna that it is his duty to act because he is a warrior and his cause is righteous. The goal is to act as he must, with forthright determination, but with no emotional attachment to what he is doing or what its results might be:

> karmaṇy evā 'dhikāras te
> mā phaleṣu kadācana
> mā karmaphalahetur bhūr
> mā te saṅgo 'stv akarmani. (II.47)

"Seek to perform your duty; but lay not claim to its fruits. Be you not the producer of the fruits of karma; neither shall you lean towards inaction."[363]

If we are here on earth, we *must* act; even refusing to act is, paradoxically, a type of action. If we neglect to pay the mortgage, we lose the house. If we forget the electric bill, the lights go off.

However, the outcomes of most actions are uncertain. We can sculpt the statue, but we cannot control who will buy it. We can follow the protocols for the experiment, but we cannot make it prove the hypothesis. In fact, Amabile's work has shown that a focus on outcomes usually impairs creativity. (See Chapter 1.) Swami Kriyananda (a.k.a. Donald Walters) would say that when we are focused on the outcomes of creation, we are no longer able to see the product with "crystal clarity." (See Chapter 3.) Swami Chidbhavananda explains, "When duty is discharged untarnished by desire, clarity of understanding ensues. In

---

363 The original Sanskrit and translation are drawn from Swami Chidbhavananda's *Bhagavad Gita* (Tamil Nadu, India: Sri Ramakishna Tapovanam, 1982).

addition to it, efficiency increases."[364]

An anecdote narrated by Eckhart Tolle illuminates this paradox. The great spiritual teacher Krishnamurti once asked an audience, "'Do you want to know my secret?'" Tolle reports that

> Everyone became very alert. Many people in the audience had been coming to listen to him for twenty or thirty years and still failed to grasp the essence of his teaching. Finally, after all these years, the master would give them the key to understanding. "This is my secret," he said. "I don't mind what happens."

Tolle explains,

> When I don't mind what happens, what does that imply? It implies that internally I am in alignment with what happens . . . To be in alignment with *what is* means to be in a relationship of inner nonresistance with what happens. It means not to label it mentally as good or bad, but to let it be. Does this mean you can no longer take action to bring about change in your life? On the contrary. When the basis for your actions is inner alignment with the present moment, your actions become empowered by the Intelligence of Life itself.[365]

So we have the responsibility to act in a way suited to our destiny, but not the power to manipulate the outcomes. Perhaps artists with courage are aware that they are cooperating with "*what is*" and, in asserting what they feel they must do even in the face of resistance, are revealing a *lack* of selfishness, a *lack* of self-absorption.

Swami Kriyananda (a.k.a. Donald Walters) advises,

> If you are creating something, or even if you are seeking guidance in anything that you do, relax the consciousness in the medulla of personal "doership," and direct the flow of energy onward to the point between the eyebrows. Keep your thoughts uplifted while you work. Don't ac-

---

364 Swami Chidbhavananda's *Bhagavad Gita*, commentary on II.47,173.

365 Eckhart Tolle, *The Power of Now: A Guide to Spiritual Enlightenment* (Novato: New World Library, 1999), 198-99.

cept an initial inspiration, then snatch the ball from Higher Guidance and run with it yourself. [366]

Roman Catholic writer Thomas Moore says, "Creativity is not about self-expression." We should ask, "Does it contribute something? If not, it's not creative."[367] Madeleine L'Engle, author of *A Wrinkle in Time*, says that an elevator operator can be creative if he uses his job as an opportunity to greet people warmly and spread good feeling.[368]

How should you begin? In answering this question for someone without faith or self-confidence, Edgar Cayce advised,

> In considering such conditions for self, there is first the necessity of an individual taking stock *of* self, as it were; taking an *inventory* of self, self's abilities, self's desires, and self's will . . . Then, when self has taken this stock of self, and has outlined to self wherein the shortcomings may lie, in the direction—when this is taken as the criterion—that the desire of self should be to make self's will one with the Creative Energy (whatever one may desire or may in their own minds designate that Energy), and then when this is understood in self, then self may find that there is much reason for carrying on, much reason for the introspection of self. (78-3)

---

366 Kriyananda, *Superconsciousness*, 237.
367 *Creativity: Touching the Divine.*
368 Ibid.

Exercises

1. Explain how will power and a strong sense of self are important in creativity. Cite examples from your life, reading, and/or experience. (Don't summarize what is said in this book.)

2. What do you think it means to be "calmly active and actively calm"? Cite examples from your life, reading, and/or experience. (Don't summarize what is said in this book.) Can you create well in this way, or do you prefer the "adrenalin rush"?

3. Explain how the bliss an infant feels is different from the spiritual experience of an adult with a healthy ego and sense of boundaries.

4. Many of Freud's doctrines have come under scrutiny, but his itemizations of "defense mechanisms" are still held to be true. A "defense mechanism" is something the ego uses to defend itself against troubling or dangerous feelings. One of these is repression: pushing something into the unconscious so that we are not aware of it. For example, in the 1980s a rash of therapists believed that their clients had been sexually abused as children and then forgotten the incident because it was too painful. The incident may have been forgotten, but it would come out as symptoms, such as sexual promiscuity and nightmares. (For the record, this was a period of hysteria, and some of these cases were false memories, but others were found to be true because of corroborating facts.) Often operating in tandem with repression is projection: insisting that I myself am okay and that it is the other fellow over there who has the problem. If you are astute you may have realized that repression and projection are key factors in keeping the shadow hidden. For instance, during the Cold War, the Soviet Union celebrated the social good and repressed the rights of the individual into its shadow, which it then projected onto the United States. The US, said the Soviets, coddled the individual too much, respecting the rights of criminals, allowing crime and materialistic greed to run rampant. Of course, by the same token, the US projected its shadow onto the Soviets! The USSR, said Americans, crushed the rights of the individual for the good of the social welfare. (They would have made the same claim about Japan, a country that also cared about social norms and, at

the time, repressed individualism as shadow material.)

The purpose of this long explanation is twofold. First, when countries or people conflict, they are usually projecting their shadow onto one another. Second, in order to live or create consciously from the highest level, you need to be aware of how repression and projection work in you and in others.

So here's the exercise. Write about repression and projection in yourself, your everyday life, and/or in international conflicts, present or past. (During wars, this process often works with dehumanization, making the enemy less than human in order to be able to kill. For example, in World War I the Germans were called "huns," and posters were circulated with bestial-looking creatures grabbing women. In the Vietnam conflict the enemy were "gooks.")[369] Here's another alternative: write about repression and projection you see in art: perhaps movies, horror stories, or pictures of the enemy.

5. What are some things you identify with? Your car, your country, your neighborhood, your school, a sports team, your writing? Explain how this sort of identification can create conflict.

6. Have you ever found it difficult to take criticism of your writing or other creative work because you were too identified with it? Did any critique seem like a rejection of you, personally? (Just about everyone who writes has to wrestle with this problem at one point or another.) If you've managed to deal with the problem, what advice can you give to others?

7. List some of the puzzling or unclear ideas in Chapter 6. Ask questions about them.

8. Explain what you think is most important in Chapter 6.

9. React to some of the ideas in Chapter 6. Debate, support, analyze, and/or reflect.

10. Give evidence from your own life or background experience about the ideas in Chapter 6. (Don't repeat what you have written in another exercise.)

11. Write one or more of the exercises from Chapter 1 and/or 3, espe-

---

369 The material on projection and dehumanization during war comes from Sam Keen. Philip Zimbardo discusses dehumanization quite a bit in *The Lucifer Effect*. For instance, he mentions that forcing the prisoners in Abu Ghraib to be nude dehumanized them and made them easier to abuse.

cially those that have to do with the role of self in creation. (Don't repeat what you have written in another exercise.)

12. Write one or more exercises from another creativity book.

13. Watch a movie about dark Romantics, such as *Haunted Summer, Gothic,* or *The Doors.* How did they destroy themselves while trying to "break on through to the other side"?

The Support Group (We)

Synergistic Interlude

Through the Looking Glass
Chapter IV: "Tweedledum and Tweedledee"

"'You like poetry?' [asked Tweedledee].

"'Ye-es, pretty well—some poetry,' Alice said doubtfully. 'Would you tell me which road leads out of the wood?'

"'What shall I repeat to her?' said Tweedledee, looking round at Tweedledum with great solemn eyes, and not noticing Alice's question.

"'The Walrus and the Carpenter" is the longest,' Tweedledum replied, giving his brother an affectionate hug.

"Tweedledee began instantly . . .

*'The sun was shining on the sea,
Shining with all his might:
He did his very best to make
The billows smooth and bright—
And this was odd, because it was
The middle of the night.*

*'The moon was shining sulkily,
Because she thought the sun
Had got no business to be there
After the day was done—
"It's very rude of him," she said,
"To come and spoil the fun!"*

*'The sea was wet as wet could be,
The sands were dry as dry.*

You could not see a cloud, because
No cloud was in the sky:
No birds were flying overhead—
There were no birds to fly.

'The Walrus and the Carpenter
Were walking close at hand;
They wept like anything to see
Such quantities of sand:
"If this were only cleared away,"
They said, "it would be grand!"

'"If seven maids with seven mops
Swept it for half a year,
Do you suppose," the Walrus said,
'That they could get it clear?"
"I doubt it," said the Carpenter,
And shed a bitter tear.

'"O Oysters, come and walk with us!"
The Walrus did beseech.
'A pleasant walk, a pleasant talk,
Along the briny beach:
We cannot do with more than four,
To give a hand to each."

'The eldest Oyster looked at him.
But never a word he said:
The eldest Oyster winked his eye,
And shook his heavy head—
Meaning to say he did not choose
To leave the oyster-bed.

'But four young oysters hurried up,
All eager for the treat:
Their coats were brushed, their faces washed,
Their shoes were clean and neat—
And this was odd, because, you know,
They hadn't any feet.

'Four other Oysters followed them,
And yet another four;
And thick and fast they came at last,
And more, and more, and more—
All hopping through the frothy waves,
And scrambling to the shore.

'The Walrus and the Carpenter
Walked on a mile or so,
And then they rested on a rock
Conveniently low:
And all the little Oysters stood
And waited in a row.

'"The time has come," the Walrus said,
'To talk of many things:
Of shoes—and ships—and sealing-wax—
Of cabbages—and kings—
And why the sea is boiling hot—
And whether pigs have wings.'

'"But wait a bit,' the Oysters cried,
"Before we have our chat;
For some of us are out of breath,
And all of us are fat!"
"No hurry!" said the Carpenter.
They thanked him much for that.

'"A loaf of bread," the Walrus said,
'Is what we chiefly need:
Pepper and vinegar besides
Are very good indeed—
Now if you're ready, Oysters dear,
We can begin to feed.'

'"But not on us!' the Oysters cried,
Turning a little blue,
"After such kindness, that would be
A dismal thing to do!"
"The night is fine," the Walrus said

"Do you admire the view?

'"It was so kind of you to come!
And you are very nice!"
The Carpenter said nothing but
"Cut us another slice:
I wish you were not quite so deaf—
I've had to ask you twice!"

'"It seems a shame," the Walrus said,
"To play them such a trick,
After we've brought them out so far,
And made them trot so quick!"
The Carpenter said nothing but
"The butter's spread too thick!"

'"I weep for you," the Walrus said.
"I deeply sympathize."
With sobs and tears he sorted out
Those of the largest size.
Holding his pocket handkerchief
Before his streaming eyes.

'"O Oysters," said the Carpenter.
"You've had a pleasant run!
Shall we be trotting home again?"
But answer came there none—
And that was scarcely odd, because
They'd eaten every one.'

'"I like the Walrus best,' said Alice: 'because you see he was a little sorry for
the poor oysters.'

'"He ate more than the Carpenter, though,' said Tweedledee. 'You see he held
his handkerchief in front, so that the Carpenter couldn't count how many he
took: contrariwise.'

'"That was mean!' Alice said indignantly. 'Then I like the Carpenter best—if
he didn't eat so many as the Walrus.'

Courtesy of Lenny's Alice in Wonderland Site, http://www.alice-in-wonderland.net/

When we say that two people are "Tweedledee and Tweedledum," we mean that they are of one mind. They work together are a team or partnership, with similar goals, personalities, and interests. Hence it is appropriate that Tweedledee recites to Alice a poem about another partnership: that between the Walrus and the Carpenter. Acting together, the walrus and the carpenter manage to fool and eat the oysters, though the Walrus seems to be the leader. (It interesting that John Lennon, who loved the Alice stories, wrote a song that claimed, "I am the Walrus!") In Tweedledee's poem, the Walrus and the Carpenter look different and act different but still work together. Tweedledee and Tweedledum are brothers——perhaps identical twins——but have a silly mock fight, for which Alice arms them.

In this chapter we will see creative pairs who act in harmony, as one, but sometimes quarrel later.

Questions to ponder:

1. When have you acted harmoniously and creatively with someone close to you?

2. What did you create?

3. What part did each of you have in this creation?

4. Did you ever quarrel? How and why?

7

"The Two of Us": Creativity in the Lower Left, Part 1

The notion of the solitary thinker still appeals to those molded by the Western belief in individualism. However, a careful scrutiny of how knowledge is constructed and artistic forms are shaped reveals a different reality. Generative ideas emerge from joint thinking, from significant conversations, and from sustained, shared struggles to achieve new insights by partners in thought.

—Vera John-Steiner,
Creative Collaboration, 3

What Is the "We"?

Wilber speaks of "The Miracle of We,"[370] the magical conjunction of selves and wills focused on a common task. In this chapter we will explore the "we" as a dyad or collaboration of partners. In the next chapter we will focus on larger groups or teams.

As with the Upper Left, which focuses on the individual *holon*, a sense of community can be felt from within or studied from without.[371] The Exercises will stress how you feel inside to be a part of a group (Zone 3),

---

370 Wilber, *Integral Spirituality*, 147.
371 Ibid., 148.

and the chapter will analyze such groups from the outside (Zone 4).

What the "We" Is Not.

Wilber stresses that *"the we is not a super-I."* [372] An "I" is an indivisible unit with a *"dominant monad,"* "an organizing or governing capacity that all of its subcomponents follow." For instance, when his dog Isaac moves, *"all* of his cells, molecules, and atoms get up and go with him."[373] By contrast, the "we" has individual *holons* that can make separate choices and movements. As a "social *holon,"* it operates by a *"dominant mode of discourse,"* a *predominant mode of mutual resonance."* Members of the "we" "resonate with the basic communication that the group is using."[374] They speak the same language. Lovers and twins finish each other's sentences, families laugh at private jokes, and members of a profession signal their solidarity with jargon and acronyms: the alphabet soup of belonging. Those ignorant of the argot are outsiders, and the "we" is reinforced by knowledge of the special language. Wilber provides the example of migrating geese that operate "on the same wavelength."[375] Edgar Cayce says, "All souls were made as companions, as a portion of the Whole." (1230–1)

But what happens when the "we"-members no longer resonate on the same note? The couple divorces, the team breaks up, the gestalt is gone; and something that *was* no longer *is*. This is as true of a football team as it is of the creative collaborators we'll examine below. Something real is lost when the magical synergy of the humming "we" is gone. The parts can go on to create alone, or in tandem with another group, but the results will be different—not only because of the diversity of individual contributions but even more, because of the synergy of the whole, the group energy that created a separate identity, a super-"I" that actually did the creating.

All "we's" eventually dissolve. Heraclitus speaks of a stream that is ever-changing; Hegel speaks of history as the opposition of thesis and

---

372 Wilber, *Integral Spirituality*, 149.

373 Ibid., 145.

374 Ibid., 149.

375 Ibid.

antithesis and their reconciliation in a new synthesis. East Indian philosophy speaks of Shiva, who breaks up old patterns so that Brahma can create the new that Vishnu will, for a certain time, preserve.

John–Steiner, speaking of the complicated dynamics between Thomas Mann and his brother, speaks of a cycle "starting with mutual influence, then moving to opposition, and ending in reconciliation."[376] The editors of *Creative Couples in the Sciences* trace four patterns: a "complementary" relationship, an initial relationship of student and mentor, "a spectrum of mutually supportive couples," and relationships "devolving from creative potential to dissonance."[377]

Some collaborations grow unstable because of personality or power dynamics; others last until death or the end of a career. In Chapter 8 we will see that some groups end after a project is finished and others continue but reflect changes in group membership.

Collaborative Pairs: "Joined Lives and Shared Work"

While discussing *Creative Collaboration*, Vera John–Steiner identifies one pattern as "Joined Lives and Shared Work."[378] The partners give one another "the gift of confidence" to counteract "periods of self–doubt and rejection by those in power" and to establish "a safety zone within which both support and constructive criticism are effectively practiced."

Simone de Beauvoir and Jean–Paul Sartre (writers and philosophers). Simone de Beauvoir characterizes this pattern as she describes her relationship with Jean–Paul Sartre:

> We have a common store of memories, knowledge and images behind us; our attempts to grasp the world are undertaken with the same tools, set within the same framework, guided by the same touchstones. Very often one of us begins a sentence and the other finishes it; if someone asks us a question, we have been known to produce identical answers. The stimulus of a word, a sensation, a shadow sends us traveling along

---

376 Vera John-Steiner, *Creative Collaboration* (New York: Oxford University Press, 2000), 31.

377 Helena M. Pycior, Nancy G. Slack, and Pnina G. Abird-Am, "Introduction," in *Creative Couples in the Sciences,* ed. Helena M. Pycior, Nancy G. Slack, and Pnina G. Abir-Am (New Brunswick, NJ: Rutgers University Press, 1996), 3-20.

378 John-Steiner, *Creative Collaboration*, Chapter 1.

the same inner path, and we arrive simultaneously at a conclusion, a memory, an association completely inexplicable to a third person.[379]

Like the Lennon–McCartney song "The Two of Us," the description above celebrates what is best in creative partnerships, the sense of two minds working together in harmony. While the harmony exists, the pair can critique and evaluate one another's ideas without disgruntlement and, in fact, depend upon one another's judgment and draw on their differences as strengths.[380] While Sartre and de Beauvoir never created the same work together, their collaboration was responsible for the ideas that fed both of their individual works. John–Steiner explains the interrelationship of their creative efforts:

From the very beginning of their relationship, de Beauvoir was able and willing to support Sartre when he was formulating novel ideas. She was also a consistent and thoughtful critic, one whom Sartre trusted. Some of his key ideas, such as the concepts of freedom and action, ethics and praxis, and the pursuit of meaning were developed in his philosophical essays. They were given concrete shape in their shared political activities and in fiction and drama written by both of them.[381]

Like the modern–day pair of John and Yoko, these two developed different works but found creative sustenance in their relationship and common philosophy. Their ideas helped to shape Existentialism and feminism in the early to mid–twentieth century.

Pierre and Marie Curie (science). Pierre and Marie Curie, who shared a 1905 Nobel Prize for their work with radium, achieved a similar harmony in their work and relationship. John–Steiner says, "They supported each other's extraordinary devotion to scientific research, they worked together in a laboratory with limited facilities, and they jointly published reports of their findings."[382] Helena M. Pycior calls

---

379 Simone de Beauvoir, *Hard Times: Force of Circumstances, 1952-1962* (*Autobiography of Simone de Beauvoir*) (Harmondsworth: Penguin Books, 1963), 659, as quoted in John-Steiner, *Creative Collaboration*, 11.

380 John-Steiner, *Creative Collaboration*, 16-25, 32-35, 39.

381 Ibid., 16.

382 Ibid., 32-33.

them "complementary partners" whose differences meshed to create a successful whole: Pierre, dreamy and abstracted, a slow and deliberate thinker who did not rush to publication; and Marie, active and dynamic, a quick thinker whose eye was on public recognition. Their lives and work so merged that Marie saw radium as "her third child, the offspring of the Curies' interlocking intimacy and creativity."[383] So deeply did this family structure impress itself on their daughter Iréne that she recreated it in her own marriage with Frédéric Joliet, with whom she received the Nobel Prize in 1935.[384]

William Wordsworth and Samuel Taylor Coleridge (poetry). Another pair who, for a while, experienced "Joint Lives and Shared Work" helped to create the romantic movement in English poetry with their first edition of *Lyrical Ballads* (1798). J.R. Watson, reviewing a book by Lucy Newlynn, summarizes their synergistic collaboration:

> In the early stages of the friendship, the 'Golden time' as it is called here, we can observe the bouncing back and forth of ideas, the equipoise of theme and expression, the catching of echoes, the fusion of theory and practice: so that the childhood of Hartley Coleridge, for example, is 'an ideal childhood in which Wordsworth's actual experience and Coleridge's theoretical beliefs are fused' (p.38) . . . Wordsworth's friendship with Coleridge does, in its early stage, lend itself to a mythology of great creative minds striking sparks off one another.[385]

Paul Magnusen says that, given new editions of their work issued by Princeton and Cornell, we have the opportunity "'of developing a new methodology of reading their poetry as an interconnected whole, of reading their works as a joint canon, and of understanding the generation of their greatest poetry.'"[386]

---

383 Helena M. Pycior, "Pierre Curie and 'His Eminent Collaborator Mme Curie': Complementary Partners," in *Creative Couples in the Sciences*, ed. Helena M. Pycior, Nancy G. Slack, and Pnina G. Abir-Am (New Brunswick, NJ: Rutgers University Press, 1996), 42-47, 48.

384 Bernadette Bensaude-Vincent, "Star Scientists in a Nobelist Family: Iréne and Frédéric Joliot-Cure," in *Creative Couples in the Sciences*, ed. by Helena M. Pycior, Nancy G. Slack, and Pnina G. Abir-Am (New Brunswick, NJ: Rutgers University Press, 1996), 65.

385 J.R. Watson, Review, *"Coleridge, Wordsworth, and the Language of Allusion* by Lucy Newlyn." *The Review of English Studies*, New Series, 38, no. 152 (November 1987): 570.

386 Quoted in Christopher Salvesen, Review, *"Coleridge and Wordsworth: A Lyrical Dialogue* by Paul Magnuson. " *The Review of English Studies*, New Series, 41, no. 162 (May 1990): 266.

Eventually they split. Coleridge seems to have felt intimidated by Wordsworth, whom he saw as living a happier and more fulfilled life. Wordsworth, for his part, seems to have underrated his partner's contribution to the *Lyrical Ballads*. A philosophical disagreement created an ever-larger rift: Wordsworth wanted to create dramatic monologues in which the speakers, often lower-class rustics, used the language of ordinary people; Coleridge decried this diction as non-poetic. He believed that the poet himself should be the speaker and that the language should be rich, evocative, and metaphorical. He was also attracted to supernatural ballads instead of the natural homilies preferred by Wordsworth. Gradually the pair drifted apart, divided by these personal, philosophical, and stylistic differences.[387] The "Golden Time" was no more, though we still have the poems it generated.

William and Dorothy Wordsworth (poetry). Wordsworth's other collaborator was his sister Dorothy, whose sensitive perceptions furnished the inspiration for much of his poetry. Separated during childhood, the pair chose to live together in young adulthood and became especially close before his "late marriage." Her journals helped to form his ideas and recollections; they shared the same values, and he trusted her "sensibility and judgment."[388] John-Steiner explains,

> They shared a love of nature and a belief in the communicative power of poetry based on observations drawn from daily life. They not only cultivated their intimacy by their common pursuits, but they celebrated it in their writings.[389]

Auguste Rodin and Camille Claudel (sculpture). Camille Claudel was an arrestingly beautiful and highly talented young woman, determined to make her way in the difficult field of nineteenth century French sculpture. As a child she busied herself not with dolls but with modeling clay dug from the road. As a young adult she insisted upon setting up her own studio and practicing her art, in defiance of the

---

387 See Stephen Maxfield Parrish, "The Wordsworth-Coleridge Controversy," *PMLA,* 73, no. 4 (September 1958): 367-74.

388 John-Steiner, *Creative Collaboration,* 27-28.

389 Ibid., 36.

mores of the time and sullen objections of her mother. Though she was forbidden to study in official academies, partially because they taught the nude (an unacceptable model for women to view), Claudel began by educating herself, managed to find an art class with her father's support, set up a studio with another female artist from Great Britain, and at last attracted the attention and support of the great sculptor Auguste Rodin, twenty-four years her senior.

For a while their collaboration was fruitful on both sides. She modeled for him. He taught her technique. Both worked together in the same studio and influenced one another's style and subjects. After they became lovers, their synergistic energy heightened, and both created astonishing sculptures, vibrating with motion and life, their styles similar and yet different. As the relationship deepened, she got referrals and financial support from him, and he got emotional support from her. At its height the creative synergy produced a golden period, during which both worked happily together and his influence with the establishment secured commissions for her despite her youth, inexperience, and gender.

But eternal resonance was not to be. Rodin, though dependent on her emotionally, could never commit to the marriage he had promised her. He was bound to Rose Beuret, with whom he had lived in a fashion of marriage for many years. He was bound likewise by his thoughts that a sculptor must stay free of the influence of women.

Claudel, on the other hand, though in many ways defying nineteenth-century conventions, seemed to have been bound by the sexual mores of the time. She was aware of her family's disapproval. She was aware of being a mistress instead of a wife. The relationship began to sour for her, and the turning point was probably an abortion. The couple parted, and Claudel grew steadily more delusional, sinking into paranoia, believing that Rodin and his "gang" were persecuting her and stealing all her ideas. After the death of her father, her mother had her committed to an asylum, where she lived the last thirty years of her life, until 1943.[390]

Anne Higonnet believes that despite Rodin's support, Claudel never

---

390 This account is taken from Ayral-Clause. A feature film, *Camille Claudel*, follows most details of the relationship with relative accuracy, though it portrays Rodin as a bit more callous and aloof than is evidenced here.

had a chance at commercial success. The frank sexuality of her sculpture outraged contemporary mores: Rodin could sculpt a headless vulva to great acclaim, but Claudel must cover a waltzing couple with drapery. Rodin received expensive commissions; Claudel received what he could beg for her. Rodin and Claudel executed complementary pieces on common themes; she must be imitating him. Higgonet believes that Claudel herself never quite understood her situation. Naïve about the politics of the art world, she thought that her talent was a sufficient entrée and never understood that the public viewed her as a sexual toy rather than as a serious artist. Ironically, now her art is appreciated, and her fame has been secured with the 1989 film starring Isabelle Adjani.[391] The question still remains, though, how much she was collaborator and how much victim.[392]

Camille Claudel, *Mature Age*, featuring a version of herself pulling on Rodin, who is held by his long-term mistress, Rose Beuret.

Kathleen Cohen's collection at the California State University Image Project, http://worldart. sjsu.edu or http://image.calstate.edu

Courtesy of Kathleen Cohen, WorldImages,
http://worldimages.sjsu.edu/

391 *Camille Claudel* (1989).

392 Anne Higonnet, "Myths of Creation: Camille Claudel and Auguste Rodin," in *Significant Others: Creativity & Intimate Partnership*, ed. Whitney Chadwick and Isabelle De Courtivron (New York: Thames and Hudson, 1993), 28, 29.

Camille Claudel, *The Waltz,* originally dancing nudes on which she was forced to sculpt drapery–from Kathleen Cohen's collection at the California State University Image Project, http://worldart.sjsu.edu or http://image.calstate.edu

Rodin, *The Thought,* with a strangely decapitated version of Claudel portrayed as less than a whole person–possibly just one of his thoughts–from Kathleen Cohen's collection at the California State University Image Project, http://worldart.sjsu.edu or http://image.calstate.edu

Courtesy of Kathleen Cohen, WorldImages, http://worldimages.sjsu.edu/

Rodin, *The Kiss:* nudity not a problem here
http://www.mam.org/images/collections_19th_rodin.jpg

Courtesy of Kathleen Cohen,
WorldImages, http://worldimages.sjsu.edu/

Frida Kahlo and Diego Rivera (art). Also depicted in a contemporary movie,[393] this couple exemplifies a similar pattern, that of artists in an intimate partnership doing separate but interrelated work. In the beginning Diego Rivera was the known genius, the famous muralist who celebrated Mexican culture in flamboyant and intricate detail on a mammoth scale. Frida painted small and intimate portraits in the Surrealist style. Injured by a freak accident, she spent much of her time in bed and insisted she created only because she was bored.[394] According to Amy Stechlo, "Where Diego's work was grand and symbolic, Frida's was intimate and personal. Its natural scale grew smaller and smaller" until it was "less than a square foot." Rather than epic portrayals of Mexican history, she focused on "impressions of her childhood, Mexican folk art, and tiny tin" portraits of the saved in churches, the "pain and blood" of church portraits reminiscent of her sufferings.[395]

Herrera, who believes that Frida was in Diego's shadow, cites their wedding portrait as evidence. In it Frida depicts her outsized husband in a domineering pose, staring straight ahead, huge feet planted firmly on the ground; her diminutive figure has doll-like feet and a head angled in his direction. He holds the paintbrushes; she holds his hand. Herrera concludes, "Both of them have become myths. Rivera was world famous in his lifetime; thanks largely to feminism and multiculturalism, Kahlo has recently become a cult figure."[396]

However, Herrera might be trying too hard to make the case of the neglected artist discovered by feminist and multicultural sensibilities. For one thing, the wedding portrait is a realistic portrayal of their physical disparities. When they married August 21, 1929, according to Stechlo, "Diego was over six feet tall and weighed over three hundred pounds. Frida was five-foot-three and weighed less than one hundred." Her mother, according to Frida, "said it was the marriage between an elephant and a dove." In addition, both seem to have operated with a certain amount of independence and recognition, both having multiple

---

393 *Frida* (2002), based on a book by Herrera.

394 This account follows Herrera. "Beauty to his Beast: Frida Kahlo and Diego Rivera," in *Significant Others: Creativity & Intimate Partnership*, ed. Whitney Chadwick and Isabelle De Courtivron (New York: Thames and Hudson, 1993), 119-35.

395 *The Life and Times of Frida Kahlo*, produced by Amy Stechlo, PBS/WETA, 2004.

396 Herrera, *Significant* Others, 119.

affairs and being feted with shows and commissions in major cities around the world.[397]

Frida Kahlo, wedding portrait with Diego Rivera, SF MOMA

SF MOMA, © 2014 Banco de México Diego Rivera Frida Kahlo Museums Trust, Mexico, D.F./Artists Rights Society (ARS), New York

John Lennon and Paul McCartney (music). The magic of the Lennon–McCartney songwriting team is unequaled. During their golden period, which spanned most of the sixties and climaxed in 1966–67, Lennon and McCartney worked so well together because they appreciated one another's differences and blended their talents into a harmonious whole. It is a truism that John was the cynical one, the poet with the gift of words, creating cryptic imagery in "Strawberry Fields" or "I Am the Walrus"; Paul was the melodist, the hymnist of pretty love songs like "Yesterday." In some ways this myth is an oversimpli-

---

397 *The Life and Times of Frida Kahlo.*

fication; John could write lyrical ballads like "Beautiful Boy," and Paul was capable of raucous rockers like "Why Don't We Do It in the Road" and "Get Back." Still, the major difference held; in most cases the ironic cynicism of Lennon tempered the saccharine sweetness of McCartney. Lennon once said, "'You could say that [Paul] provided a lightness, an optimism, while I would always go for the sadness, the discord, the bluesy edge.'"[398]

In their early collaboration as adolescents, they would skip school and compose together, facing each other, guitars in hand. Tony Bramwell, a long–time friend and employee, sums up the power of their working relationship:

> Although John and Paul very seldom tackled a songwriting project as a team of two equal contributors, each needed the other as a catalyst. Neither would admit dependence upon his partner in terms of creative abilities, but it's quite clear now with the benefit of hindsight that the duo's best work was done within the context of the Beatles.
>
> Of the two, Paul McCartney always appeared more confident to the extent that he did occasionally believe that he had yet another new hit when it wasn't good enough, something common to most songwriters. That's where the basic benefit of working in collaboration with a pal who was also a rival talent took on a great value. Paul might get carried away over the strength of a tune he'd just penned. John might be full of satisfaction about a set of intricate lyrics he'd just worked out. In each case, the second opinion balanced truth against emotion and sensible compromises were struck.[399]

Their musical producer George Martin explains,

> They did love each other very much throughout the time I knew them in the studio. But the tension was there mostly because they never really collaborated. They were never Rodgers and Hart. They were always songwriters who helped each other with little bits and pieces.

---

398 Quoted in Geoffrey Giuliano, *Two of Us: John Lennon and Paul McCartney, Behind the Myth* (New York: Penguin, 1999), 151.

399 Quoted in Giuliano, *Two of Us*, 148-49.

One would have most of a song finished, play it to the other, and he'd say, "Well, why don't you do this?" That was just about the way their collaboration worked.[400]

By the time of their trip to India, this system had unraveled. Lennon claims that in *The White Album* (1969), "Every track is an individual track—there isn't any Beatle music on it . . . It was John and the Band, Paul and the Band, George and the Band, like that."[401]

John Lennon and Yoko Ono (music, art, social reform). After the Beatles broke up, John claimed that Yoko was his Muse. Right before his untimely death in 1980, he said, "She inspired *all* this creation in me. It wasn't that she inspired the songs; she inspired *me*."[402] The two of them outraged mainstream values by posing nude for an album cover, inviting journalists to participate in a "bed–in for peace" during their honeymoon, and sponsoring dubious artistic projects like "baggism," which consisted of crawling into bags. She converted him from a pop star to a revolutionary, much to the disgust of fans and the general public. Though certain commentators report rifts in their later relationship, John always held steady to the myth of their solidarity as creative collaborators. His attitude is summed up in a 1971 interview with Jan Wenner: "There is nothing more important than our relationship, nothing."[403]

Van Gogh and Gauguin (art). In one sense Van Gogh's collaborator was his brother Theo, who provided the financial support that kept the art and artist alive.[404] But during nine weeks in Southern France, Van Gogh had another collaborator: Gauguin, with whom he lived in a yellow house. Though the two painters labored separately on their art, their cohabitation produced a creative synergy for both of them. The idea of cooperative living and working had been Van Gogh's:

---

400 Quoted in Giuliano, *Two of Us*, vii.

401 Quoted in Editors of *Rolling Stone*, *The Ballad of John and Yoko*, Dolphin Books (Garden City, New York: Doubleday, 1982), 88.

402 *John Lennon and Yoko Ono: The Final Testament . . . Interviews by David Sheff*, ed. G. Barry Golson (New York: Berkeley Books, 1982), 197.

403 Quoted in Editors of the *Rolling Stone*, *The Ballad of John and Yoko*, 109.

404 John-Steiner, *Creative Collaboration*, 74.

By *collaboration,*" he informed Émile Bernard, he did not necessarily mean several painters working on the same picture. He meant a pooling of thoughts and techniques, so that the community of artists would create "paintings that differ from one another yet go together and complement one another." More and more paintings would "probably be created by groups of men combining to execute an idea held in common.[405]

As well as executing paintings on the same subjects, the pair experimented with materials, not buying canvases ready-made but cutting "jute sackcloth" and applying "liquid barium sulphate, which was thinner and browner" than the usual "smooth, white gesso" for a more roughly textured effect.[406] Van Gogh dreamed of "a cooperative community of painters," "a peaceful monastery of artists, cooperating at the birth of a new art."[407] His belief that such art would begin in warmer climes helped to inspire Gauguin to leave for the tropics.[408]

Watson and Crick (science). An understanding of DNA has changed the world, from the "cold hits" of criminal databases that identify perpetrators of crimes long past to the innovative medical research that is exploring how to cure cancer and modify food. Would the secret have been discovered without the collaboration of this famous pair?

Like Lennon and McCartney, this pair thrived because of their equal status and complementary personalities. The American Watson paints a fond but condescending picture of the British Crick at the age of thirty-five:

Although some of his closest colleagues realized the value of his quick, penetrating mind and frequently sought his advice, he was often not appreciated, and most people thought he talked too much . . . [At the Cavendish Laboratory in Cambridge] he talked louder and faster than anyone else, and when he laughed, his location within the Cavendish was obvious. Almost everyone enjoyed these manic moments, espe-

---

405 Martin Gayford, *The Yellow House: Van Gogh, Gauguin, and Nine Turbulent Weeks in Arles* (New York: Little, Brown, 2006), 72.

406 Ibid., 121.

407 Ibid., 80, 81.

408 Ibid., 81.

cially when we had the time to listen attentively and to tell him bluntly when we lost the train of his argument . . . Anything important would attract him . . . Almost immediately he would suggest a rash of new experiments . . . As a result, there existed an unspoken yet real fear of Crick . . . The quick manner in which he seized their facts and tried to reduce them to current patterns frequently made his friends' stomachs sink with the apprehension that . . . he . . . should expose to the world the fuzziness of minds hidden from direct view . . . [Though] he was a delightful dinner companion . . . a stray remark over sherry might bring Francis smack into your life.[409]

Crick says that the "difference" between them was in their "background knowledge" but that they "hit it off immediately" because of a similarity in interests and attitudes: "partly, I suspect, because of a certain youthful arrogance, a ruthlessness, and an impatience with sloppy thinking that came naturally to both of us." Amusingly, given the portrait drawn of him above, Crick reports that "Jim was distinctly more outspoken than I was."[410] Perhaps he means that this brash American voiced judgments openly and ignored some of the niceties of British etiquette. Watson, commenting on Crick's polite deference to rival Maurice Wilkins, seems aggravated by "England's coziness—all the important people, if not related by marriage, seemed to know one another—plus the English sense of fair play would not allow Francis to move in on Maurice's problem."[411] More recently, in 2007, Watson's brashness and bluntness got him in trouble. After he suggested that those of African extraction are genetically inferior, he was forced to resign from his job supervising the lab at Cold Spring Harbor.

Richard Ogle thinks that Crick's contribution entailed connecting "idea–spaces" from different disciplines:

. . . weaving back and forth between the genetic and the molecular, the informational and the physical, letting each play against the other

---

409 James D. Watson, *The Double Helix: A Personal Account of the Discovery of the Structure of DNA*, A Mentor Book (New York: New American Library, 1969), 15-17.

410 Crick, *What Mad Pursuit*, 64.

411 Watson, *The Double Helix*, 19.

until the twin end results, code and double helix, finally emerged in a harmonious unity. Even a maverick mind like Watson's couldn't match Crick's ability to move with ease between multiple idea-spaces—physical chemistry, biochemistry, X-ray crystallography, mathematics, and genetics—but also, on a higher level, to constantly allow the informational and physical dimensions of the problem to act as mutual frames for one another . . . [O]nce key ideas from idea-spaces that otherwise had little contact with one another were connected, they began, quasi-autonomously, leading to the emergence of a whole that was more than the sum of its parts.[412]

Here is *Creative Synergy* operating in the "idea–spaces" between disciplines, like the Scholarship of Integration—making meaning out of the new connections of various domains. Arthur Koestler, who calls this process "'bisociation,'" finds it characteristic of scientific creativity: "'each new synthesis leads to the emergence of new patterns of relations.'"[413]

The toxic "we." In some collaborations, the "we" can become toxic. Though based on the communion of at least two people who seem to function as partners, "the toxic we" denies the contribution of one group member or draws on the energy of this person, usually with the victim's complicity. I am calling this problem "The *Middlemarch* Syndrome" because it was depicted in George Eliot's famous novel. In a common version of this syndrome, a woman with creative gifts abjures her art or science in order to be a handmaid to her male partner's talent.

The Einsteins (science). In some cases it is clear that the handmaid's talent is lesser. Mileva Mariæ, Mrs. Einstein, could do physics herself but was not a genius like her husband. Their early letters reveal "a dream of common interests and scientific collaboration," though as the relationship developed "her scientific voice became less clear," especially after she failed her qualifying exams and bore his child out of wedlock. Current biographers are uncertain what her role may have been in the development and support of his genius.[414]

Gardner says that Einstein

---

412 Ogle, *Smart World*, 49.

413 Quoted in John-Steiner, *Notebooks of the Mind*, 186.

414 John-Steiner, *Creative Collaboration*, 21.

appreciated the opportunity to try out his ideas on others—such as members of the Olympiad, Besso, and his physicist-wife Mileva—and to benefit from their feedback. One might even go so far as to say that, without the kind of stimulation and critique offered by a trusted friend or lover, [Einstein as well as Freud] might never have completed their innovative work.[415]

Isaacson agrees with the "sounding board" idea. He also thinks, based on the preponderance of the evidence, that Mileva "helped to check [the] math" but was not responsible for formulating any of the theory. He adds, with a touch of humor, "In addition, she encouraged him and (what at times was more difficult) put up with him."[416]

Stachel calls the relationship of the Einsteins "a collaboration that failed to develop." Perhaps it never could have, given the gulf between their intellects. In their letters, according to Stachel, "Einstein's [comments] show a young man passionately engaged with his subject," conveying "the distinct impression of an original mind at work. Mariæ's comments display an eager, hardworking student, but without a spark of . . . scientific originality."[417]

John Johnson, describing letters recently published by the California Institute of Technology and Princeton University, says that Mileva was delighted as her husband's groundbreaking publications began in 1905, but that the relationship had soured by 1914, at which point he was telling her "to forgo intimacy, serve his meals in his room, 'desist immediately from addressing me if I request it . . . leave my bedroom or office immediately without protest if I so request.'"[418] Mileva lost two dreams: romance and collaboration. Her situation is not uncommon in the art, science, and history of the Modernist world. One example is depicted in a masterpiece of nineteenth-century fiction.

---

415 Gardner, *Creating Minds*, 102-3.

416 Isaacson, *Einstein*, 136.

417 John Stachel, "Albert Einstein and Mileva Mariæ: A Collaboration that Failed to Develop," in *Creative Couples in the Sciences,* ed. Helena M. Pycior, Nancy G. Slack, and Pnina G. Abir-Am (New Brunswick, NJ: Rutgers University Press, 1996), 212-13.

418 John Johnson, Jr., "A Glimpse at Personal Side of Einstein: Notes and Letters from a Troubled Man," *San Francisco Chronicle,* February 4, 2007, B-1, accessed April 5, 2014: http://www. sfgate.com/default/article/A-glimpse-at-personal-side-of-Einstein-Note-and-2619536.php.

The Middlemarch Syndrome (literature). In George Eliot's *Middlemarch* (1871–1872) Dorothea Brooke, like any other middle- or upper-class Victorian woman who has been well socialized, wants to dedicate herself to a great cause. As the novel progresses, we see that she has ethics, intellect, and sensibility. What she does not have is a clear means to exercise them for the benefit of society. She does some good by helping to construct homes for poor factory workers, but she wants to do more.

Pursuing this goal, Dorothea decides to marry an elderly scholar, Casaubon, who seems to have embarked upon the colossal task of itemizing all knowledge in what will be a monumental tome—a history and philosophy of everything. This will be her mission: to help him organize his notes, to be midwife to the great work he is writing. She seems to have conceived roles that proved productive for Will and Ariel Durant in *The Story of Civilization*: a partnership of writer and secretary that ended with an equal collaboration.[419]

However, there are early signs that Dorothea's plan is doomed to failure. On their Italian honeymoon Casaubon will not take her to the great libraries and museums with him; he brushes her off as if she were an aggravating fly and tells her he must do his work alone. Then, when they return home and she offers, repeatedly, to help him organize his notes, he shoos her away. He is especially troubled whenever she asks him when he is going to begin writing. At last she realizes that the work will never be written. Casaubon has the peculiar sort of writers' block common to the would-be authors of dissertations: the accumulation of notes to the exclusion of constructing any sort of original expository narrative of them. She realizes that he will never have enough notes to begin the actual composition. When he dies, he controls her from beyond the grave, stipulating that she will lose the inherited estate if she marries the young man with whom she has meanwhile fallen in love, his nephew.

So Dorothea has thrown a large part of her life away on a toxic and pejorative "we." Eliot contrives a happy ending for her, but the endings of other women in nineteenth and twentieth century Europe were not so happy.

---

419 John-Steiner, *Creative Collaboration*, 13-15.

Gustave and Alma Mahler (music). An archetype of this situation appears in the film *Bride of the Wind*, in which Gustave Mahler tells his future wife something to the effect that "When we marry, your music will be mine." This statement seems cryptic until the marriage unfolds on film and we see her copy out his music and bear and nurture his children while he becomes famous and her own composing is forgotten. Arguably, she was helping a greater talent reach his goals by providing support—but who will ever know whether she might have made a contribution as well?

Rosalind Franklin and the Search for DNA (science). Another example is Rosalind Franklin. Though not involved in an intimate relationship with her coworkers, she suffered on the cross of the "toxic we." Both Watson and Crick acknowledge that her work was hampered by a lack of support from her male collaborator while they themselves forged a close and productive partnership. Crick says, "Unfortunately, Rosalind and Maurice found it difficult to work together," whereas "Jim and I hit it off immediately."[420] Watson's description of her creates the impression of a serious scientist unable to play the game of "good old boy." While giving a lecture, he says, she "spoke . . . in a quick, nervous style," with no "trace of warmth or frivolity." Outrageously, while observing her, Watson "wondered how she would look if she took off her glasses and did something novel with her hair." He then observes, critically, "The years of careful, unemotional crystallographic training had left their mark. She had not had the advantage of a rigid Cambridge education only to be so foolish as to misuse it." Well, of course. A no-nonsense scientist, meticulous about her data, "Rosy" (as the American Watson dismissingly terms her) did not dare to play with models like Pauling, Watson, and Crick: "The idea of using tinker-toy-like models to solve biological structures was clearly a last resort."[421]

The British Crick is more polite. He observes that "Rosalind's experimental work was first class . . . Everything she did was sound enough—almost too sound." Huh? Crick continues, "And I believe that one reason for this . . . was because she felt that a woman must show herself to be fully professional." No doubt. Crick contrasts her to Watson,

420 Crick, *What Mad Pursuit*, 64.

421 Watson, *The Double Helix*, 51.

who—as his previous comments suggest—"had no such anxieties about his abilities." Nevertheless, Crick does not "believe the facts support" the feminist charges of sexism![422]

John–Steiner says that "Collaboration has been widely recognized in the sciences, from the founding of quantum mechanics by Bohr and Heisenberg to the joint discovery of DNA structure by Crick and Watson, to the work of an increasingly long list of researchers in the physical and biological sciences."[423] If Watson's attitude is any indication, Rosalind Franklin never had a chance at real collaboration. He complains that she "would not think of herself as Maurice's assistant" and, moreover, an "inspection" of her physical attributes suggested "that she would not easily bend":

> **By choice she did not emphasize her feminine qualities. Though her features were strong, she was not unattractive and might have been quite stunning had she taken even a mild interest in clothes. This she did not. There was never lipstick to contrast with her straight black hair, while at the age of thirty-one her dresses showed all the imagination of English blue-stocking adolescents . . . Clearly, Rosy had to go or be put in her place.[424]**

In the end, Rosy went. She died in 1958, just before Watson, Crick, and her partner Maurice Wilkins shared the 1962 Nobel Prize for discovering the structure of DNA. [425]

Conclusion

John–Steiner believes that especially today, "in our changing world," the "historical and technological context promotes collaboration in science, artistic endeavors, universities, industrial settings, and schools."[426] The *"dynamics of mutuality are not restricted to artists and scientists, but are*

---

422 Crick, *What Mad Pursuit*, 69.
423 John-Steiner, *Creative Collaboration*, 4.
424 Watson, *The Double Helix*, 20.
425 Crick, *What Mad Pursuit*, 52.
426 John-Steiner, *Creative Collaboration*, 3.

relevant to people in every walk of life.[427] Cayce says that "the purposes for which each soul enters materiality are that it may become aware of its relationships to the Creative Forces or God; by the material manifestation of the things thought, said, *done*, in relation to its fellow man!" (1567–2) In Chapter 8 we will see how artists create as a group or get support from an extended network. In Chapters 12 and 13 we will see how teams can transform an organizational chart into a humming synergy of community.

---

427 John-Steiner, *Creative Collaboration*, 3.

Exercises

1. When have you collaborated successfully with a partner? What pattern did your collaboration take? Did you serve as "sounding boards" for one another like Lennon and McCartney? Did you inspire one another but do separate work like be Beauvoir and Sartre or Wordsworth and Coleridge? Did you work on the same product like Watson and Crick? How and why did your collaboration end? Did it ever grow "toxic" or end because of a personality conflict?
2. What other collaborative pairs do you know of? What pattern did their collaborations take?
3. How might you use collaboration with a partner in your future life and/or career?
4. Select a partner, and collaborate with him or her on some creative project. Write about the results. (Note: if this partnership is for a class project, get permission from your professor to make sure that the form of your "collaboration" won't be called plagiarism or cheating.)
5. What is the value of creating as part of a pair? Be specific.
6. What are the problems in creating as a part of a pair? Be specific.
7. List some of the puzzling or unclear ideas in Chapter 7. Ask questions about them.
8. Explain what you think is most important in Chapter 7.
9. React to some of the ideas in Chapter 7. Debate, support, analyze, and/or reflect.
10. Give evidence from your own life or background experience about the ideas in Chapter 7. (Don't repeat what you have written in another exercise.)
11. Watch a movie about a collaborative creative pair. Write a report on the results.

Synergistic Interlude

Through the Looking Glass Chapter III:
"A Caucus Race and a Long Tale"

"[After emerging from the pool of Alice's salt tears,] they were indeed a queer-looking party that assembled on the bank—the birds with draggled feathers, the animals with their fur clinging close to them, and all dripping wet, cross, and uncomfortable. . . .

[The Dodo said,] ' [T]he best thing to get us dry would be a Caucus-race.'

"'What IS a Caucus-race?' said Alice; not that she wanted much to know, but the Dodo had paused as if it thought that SOMEBODY ought to speak, and no one else seemed inclined to say anything.

"'Why,' said the Dodo, 'the best way to explain it is to do it.' (And, as you might like to try the thing yourself, some winter day, I will tell you how the Dodo managed it.)

"First it marked out a race-course, in a sort of circle, ('the exact shape doesn't matter,' it said,) and then all the party were placed along the course, here and there. There was no 'One, two, three, and away,' but they began running when they liked, and left off when they liked, so that it was not easy to know when the race was over. However, when they had been running half an hour or so, and were quite dry again, the Dodo suddenly called out 'The race is over!' and they all crowded round it, panting, and asking, 'But who has won?'

"This question the Dodo could not answer without a great deal of thought, and it sat for a long time with one finger pressed upon its forehead (the position in which you usually see Shakespeare, in the pictures of him), while the rest waited in silence. At last the Dodo said, 'EVERYBODY has won, and all must have prizes.'

Courtesy of Lenny's Alice in Wonderland Site, http://www.alice-in-wonderland.net/

Lewis Carroll, author of the Alice stories, says he chose the word "caucus" because it sounded funny to him. However, the word actually has meaning in this situation. In a caucus, politicians who may have differences decide to band together for a common purpose: the Democratic Women's caucus, The Log Cabin Republicans' caucus, and so forth. Here the very different creatures band together to devise a way to get dry.

Questions to ponder:

1. What elements of the race by the seashore remind you of the political process?

2. What elements remind you of other groups experiencing camaraderie?

3. What does it mean that all start and stop when they wish?

4. What does it mean that all get prizes?

Courtesy of Lenny's Alice in Wonderland Site, http://www.alice-in-wonderland.net/

8

"We" as a Larger Group: Creativity in the Lower Left, Part 2

"Throughout history, groups of people, often without conscious design, have successfully blended individual and collective effort to create something new and wonderful. The Bauhaus School, the Manhattan Project, the Guarneri Quartet, the young filmmakers who coalesced around Francis Ford Coppola and George Lucas, the youthful scientists and hackers who invented a computer that was personal as well as powerful, the creators of the Internet—these are a few of the Great Groups that have reshaped the world in very different but enduring ways." —Bennis and Biederman[428]

The Scope of Chapter 8

You know you have something special when your band gels, improvising harmoniously, the saxophone and trumpet coming in to the beat set by the drum, each player sensing without words what the other is feeling, all of you resonating together on a magical wave. You

---

428 Warren Bennis and Patricia Ward Biederman, *Organizing Genius: The Secrets of Creative Collaboration* (Reading, MA: Addison-Wesley, 1997), 2.

183

know you have something special when your girls' basketball team, like Duke University's in 2000, operates as one, all of you anticipating one another's moves and passing the ball in synchrony, moving without thinking.[429] If you have been in that sort of group, you have felt the "we" from within. Ken Wilber explains,

> **Whenever you are together with a friend and you experience a shared feeling, or you believe that you understand each other, or see eye to eye, or share an emotion, the actual texture of those experiences, thoughts, shared insights, emotions, feelings—the actual felt texture of that shared space—is an example of the inside of a we.**[430]

In Chapter 7 we saw Simone de Beauvoir explaining her relationship with Jean–Paul Sartre in such terms. However, as readers learning about her experience, we cannot *feel* it inside as she does. We can only *observe* it from outside. Wilber explains that "the inside view is how it *feels*," but "The outside view is how it *looks*." He adds,

> **The inside of a we can be felt, but the outside of a we has to be seen from a distance, and then over time, in order to grasp its full significance and structure. The same thing that makes zone #2 hard to grasp makes zone #4 hard to grasp. It cannot be seen with introspection, contemplation, feelings, or meditations, no matter how long you look.**[431]

In this chapter we will continue our exploration of Zone 4, an external view of the Lower Left (LL): interiority, a sense of feeling one with a particular community. Similarly, most of the Exercises will stress partly how we feel inside to be a part of a group (Zone 3).

To some degree the division of these chapters and sections is arbitrary. A dyad like Lennon and McCartney (Chapter 7) supports a creative group (Chapter 8). A support group like Bloomsbury (Chapter 8) is similar to a "Great Group" that generates ideas in an institution (Chapter 12).

---

429 Lee G. Bolman and Terence E. Deal, *Reframing Organizations: Artistry, Choice, and Leadership*, 3rd ed. (San Francisco: Jossey-Bass, 2003), 103.

430 Wilber, *Integral Spirituality*, 155-56.

431 Wilber, *Integral Spirituality*, 154, 162-63.

In addition, in Chapter 7 we have not explored distinctions between work created together, as with Watson and Crick, and cross-fertilization of ideas, as with Van Gogh and Gauguin, Sartre and de Beauvoir, and John and Yoko. In these cases and others the joint philosophy and shared experience of what begins as mutual support can spill over into one another's work. Finally, the division into pairs (Chapter 7) and larger groups (Chapter 8) is arbitrary, as is the selection of pairs and groups for discussion. As I wrote, I was aware of how many creative "we's" I was *not* mentioning: the Impressionists, the Cubists, the Pre–Raphaelites, and partners in ballet, to name a few. Certainly as you write the exercises, you will write more of what needs to be said in the book!

Groups Not Assembled by Institutions

Monty Python (comic actors, directors, and writers). Mad, zany, endearing, obstreperous, outrageous—cross–dressing and fish–slapping—equal offenders of all classes, playing dull ditch–diggers with handkerchiefs on their heads, bourgeois housewives with a penguin on the telly, and "upper–class twits" competing to be shot—impersonating housewives in drag, lumberjacks in plaid, and majors in uniform—this comedy team operated as a synergy. Whether in the series *Monty Python's Flying Circus* or the films *Monty Python and the Holy Grail* (1975) and *Monty Python's Life of Brian* (1979), this troupe delighted and amazed audiences in Britain and the U.S.A. in the 1970s, and it still delights many of us today.

Why did the group split? It stopped resonating. Terry Gilliam[432] explains that by 1983, *Monty Python's The Meaning of Life* was "a tired attempt to keep the group together." The Pythons made a movie because it takes less time than a series, but the film itself, he says, was a pastiche of "sketches," "uneven" and "independently written."

Gilliam's contribution was an old animated cartoon idea about accounting clerks who set out on the seas and become pirates. Originally it was supposed to be "about ⅔ of the way through the movie," but he testifies that "my rhythms and the group's rhythms" had become "different": they wanted "laugh, laugh, laugh." So the others pulled his car-

---

432 All of the information about Gilliam, as well as the quotes, comes from *Terry Gilliam*.

toon out of the film and made it "a featurette attacking the main film."

Afterward he went his own way and wrote the screenplay for *Brazil* (1985). Dedicated Python fans will notice the difference. Katherine Helmond says people don't appreciate *Brazil* because of "the density of it," the richness and complexity: "it's impossible to see it all the first time through."[433] The same qualities are apparent in his next films: *Adventures of Baron Munchausen* (1989), *The Fisher King* (1991), and *12 Monkeys* (1995). The Pythons together, as Gilliam testifies, went for the "laugh, laugh, laugh" of antic comedy.

Shelley's Circle (poetry and fiction). Mary Shelley's *Frankenstein* was created from a dark and stormy night and a group challenge. Mary was sojourning with her husband–to–be the poet and her stepsister Claire Claremont on Lake Geneva. They frequently visited the nearby Villa Diodati, occupied by the poet Lord Byron and his companion Dr. Polidori.[434] Mary reports, "It proved a wet, ungenial summer, and incessant rain often confined us for days to the house."[435] To entertain themselves, the group read ghost stories. Then Lord Byron issued a challenge: "We will each write a ghost story." Mary says she "busied myself *to think of a story* . . . I thought and pondered—vainly . . . *Have you thought of a story?* I was asked each morning, and each morning I was forced to reply with a mortifying negative."[436]

On one particular night, which may have been June 16,[437] Byron and Shelley fell into a philosophical discourse about "the nature of the principle of life, and whether there was any probability of its ever being discovered and communicated." Their discussion turned to a rumored experiment about "a piece of vermicelli in a glass case" that "by some extraordinary means . . . began to move with voluntary motion."[438] Polidori was familiar with Galvani, who claimed to have electrified corpses so that they could "sit up, raise their arms, clench their fists, and blow

---

433 *Terry Gilliam.*

434 Dorothy Hoobler and Thomas Hoobler, *The Monsters: Mary Shelley and the Curse of Frankenstein* (New York: Little, Brown, 2006), 139-41.

435 Mary Shelley, "Introduction to *Frankenstein,*" 1831, accessed April 5, 2014. http://www.rc.umd.edu/editions/frankenstein/1831v1/intro.

436 Ibid.

437 The Hooblers give this conventional date; Rieger believes it to be approximate.

438 Shelley, "Introduction to *Frankenstein.*"

out candles placed before their mouths."[439]

Byron and Shelley speculated, "Perhaps a corpse would be re-animated; galvanism had given token of such things: perhaps the component parts of a creature might be manufactured, brought together, and endured with vital warmth."[440] At bedtime Mary found herself unable to sleep. Perhaps she entered the hypnogogic state, that period of fragmentary imagery that comprises Stage 1 of sleep, for she reports a "waking dream":

> My imagination, unbidden, possessed and guided me, gifting the successive images that arose in my mind with a vividness far beyond the usual bounds of reverie. I saw—with shut eyes, but acute mental vision,—I saw the pale student of unhallowed arts kneeling beside the thing he had put together. I saw the hideous phantasm of a man stretched out, and then, on the working of some powerful engine, show signs of life, and stir with an uneasy, half vital motion. Frightful must it be; for supremely frightful would be the effect of any human endeavour to mock the stupendous mechanism of the Creator of the world. His success would terrify the artist; he would rush away from his odious handywork [sic], horror-stricken.

She opened her eyes "in terror." She had found her story:

> The idea so possessed my mind, that a thrill of fear ran through me . . . Swift as light and as cheering was the idea that broke in upon me. "I have found it! What terrified me will terrify others; and I need only describe the spectre which had haunted my midnight pillow." On the morrow I announced that I had *thought of a story.* I began that day . . .

She intended to write only "a short tale," but Shelley encouraged her "to develope [sic] the idea at greater length." She testifies that, "but for his incitement, it would never have taken the form in which it was presented to the world."[441] So Mary was supported not only by a group but also by her intimate partner.

---

439 Hoobler, *The Monsters*, 142.

440 Shelley, "Introduction to *Frankenstein.*"

441 Ibid.

Though minor details of this story have been questioned,[442] the results are undeniable: that evening produced two classics of horror fiction still influential today. Mary Shelley wrote *Frankenstein*, and Dr. Polidori wrote *The Vampyre*, which inspired Bram Stoker's *Dracula*. By coincidence (if there is such a thing), two movie production companies were filming versions of this creative summer interlude at the same time in the same Lake Geneva setting.[443]

The Brontës (novelists and poets, with one painter). The Yorkshire town of Haworth is smaller than you would expect, a parsonage and an inn and a few other stone buildings clustered along a dirt path in a cold moorland haunted with barren beauty. To visit it is to understand how isolated the Brontës were—how, if they were to be creative, these miraculous siblings had to depend upon one another.

As children the Brontës first reinforced one another's creativity in interlocking tales about the kingdom of Gondal. This early sense of community helped to inspire the later masterpieces of Charlotte's *Jane Eyre* (1857) and Emily's *Wuthering Heights* (1847), as well as the underrated and still quite readable Anne's *The Tenant of Wildfell Hall* (1848). It is also a truism that brother Branwell, though damaged early by dissipation, had talent that inspired the girls. He may have furnished the model for Heathcliff in *Wuthering Heights*, and his portrait of his sisters remains an important contribution to literary history. John–Steiner, who notes that creative collaboration is not uncommon among English siblings, also mentions the experiences of Jessica Mitford, Margaret Drabble, and Charles and Mary Lamb.[444] She adds that "parental unavailability," also experienced by the Brontës, can lead to such collaboration among siblings.[445]

Edgar Cayce's Circle (soul group helping to precipitate a paradigm shift). As mentioned in a Chapter 2 footnote, 14,306 of Edgar Cayce's readings have been transcribed and made available. After he loosened his tie, reclined on a couch, and put himself into a

---

442 See James Rieger, "Dr. Polidori and the Genesis of Frankenstein," *Studies in English Literature, 1500-1900*, 3, no. 4 (Autumn 1963), *Nineteenth Century*: 461-72.

443 *Gothic* (1986) and *Haunted Summer* (1988).

444 John-Steiner, *Creative Collaboration*, 25-27.

445 Ibid., 26.

trance, Cayce could read any medical condition by seeing inside the person. "Yes, we have the body," he would say. He would prescribe arcane treatments, often unknown to the doctors of the time. Once when he prescribed a nostrum that no one could find, he did another reading and said in what druggist's shop it was to be found, on what dusty shelf way in the back. His cures were so remarkable that doctors began sending him their hopeless cases. In some instances Cayce drew on the Akashic records, the psychic imprint of all that has ever happened. When Arthur Lammers, one of his associates, asked what kinds of information the readings could produce, he got an answer he wasn't expecting. Cayce's Source replied, among other things, that it could provide details of subjects' past incarnations on earth. When told about this answer, the devout Christian Cayce was initially troubled, but at last accepting.

Sidney Kirkpatrick, author of the biography *Edgar Cayce: An American Prophet*, makes it clear[446] how important Cayce's work was and how it was supported by a "soul group" that came in with him for that purpose. While Cayce was still a child, when some of these helpers were not yet born, he could see them. After he told his father Leslie how important these "imaginary playmates" were to him, Leslie started lecturing him about reality and illusion. The playmates lined up behind Leslie, mimicking him, and little Edgar dissolved into laughter. The Source later said in a reading, "They appeared to you as children because that was the only way you'd look at them. They've been with you a very long time."

"This is the soul group," said Kirkpatrick—"Gertrude, Gladys, Blumenthal; they hadn't yet incarnated." Gertrude would question him during the readings; Gladys would transcribe them; Blumenthal would provide financial support. Kirkpatrick stressed that the result was not the work of one man but of a group. Edgar Cayce "did not beat his own drum," but still famous people came for readings: Woodrow Wilson, George Gershwin, Gloria Swanson, Thomas Edison, Nicola Tesla, Ernest Hemingway and his mother (who "was having trouble with little Ernest"), and the DuPont family. Kirkpatrick continued, "We don't think of

---

446 The following information in the next two paragraphs comes from lectures Sidney Kirkpatrick gave on July 20, 2013, at the A.R.E. Northern California Conference at Asilomar, Pacific Grove, California.

him as a pivotal figure in US history now, but that's changing." Stanford is now working on Cayce's perpetual motion machine. Over thirty percent of the American public believes in reincarnation. Holistic medicine has become part of the mainstream. Cayce's work, in brief, helped to inaugurate the great paradigm shift mentioned in Chapter 2.

The Beatles (music). They were the voice of the sixties, from boyish moptops altering the sound of rock and roll to psychedelic messengers of the Summer of Love. Yoko Ono once said, "[T]hey were like mediums. They weren't conscious of all they were saying, but it was coming through them." John Lennon clarified: "We tuned in to the message. That's all."[447] In this way they exemplified Paramhansa Yogananda's statement that "Thoughts are universally and not individually rooted; a truth cannot be created, but only perceived."[448] They had a universal impact. Fans born well after their era still love their music, and it is not too outrageous to claim that the current connection between India and the West is partly a result of their influence.

The Beatles played random gigs in cheap music halls at first, then formed their unique sound after months of pulling all–night performances on the Reeperbahn in Hamburg. They took their act to the Cavern Club in Liverpool and achieved worldwide fame after they found a manager who put them in suits and marketed them. At the height of Beatlemania, as they lived and worked together, they bonded because no one else could have possibly understood what they were going through. McCartney says, "We lived out of each other's pockets for a long time. That was one of the strengths of the band, that was why we were a tight little band. We could read each other very well through having gone through all these experiences." [449]

But the group reflected the principle that everything changes. By the *Let it Be* recording session in 1969, the dissolution of the band is there for all to see, the cameras rolling to record Paul bossing people around, trying to recreate the old group energy, while Ringo sits listlessly by his drums, George looks resentful, and John waltzes apart with Yoko. Their

---

447 *John Lennon and Yoko Ono*, 106.

448 Yogananda, *Autobiography of a Yogi*, Ch. 15: p. 154 in the Ananda reprint of the First Edition.

449 Quoted in Miles, *Paul McCartney*, 582-83.

differences had become a source of discord, and after the death of their manager Brian Epstein, their collaboration unraveled.

Lennon and McCartney themselves, interviewed at different times, gave different reasons why. What is clear is that several factors were involved. Both of them were competing for the A–side of each 45–rpm record; George Harrison's writing began to compete for additional spots in both singles and albums; the tours ceased because the music became too complex to play outside of the studio and the screaming drowned it out anyway; the cessation of tours dissolved their intimacy. At one point McCartney said their eventual break–up was natural, the result of boys growing up and finding spouses with whom they preferred to collaborate: "Wedding bells are breaking up that old gang of mine." Lennon would add that he got tired of repeating himself: that he wanted to grow as an artist while the fans wanted more of the same moptop show. The boys had grown up and apart and become men who wanted to strike out on their own.

The Bloomsbury Group (artists, writers, social revolutionaries). First came Leslie Stephen, that eminent Victorian who had edited the *Dictionary of National Biography* and who roared about his home like a wounded lion, taking the privilege of genius to be irascible.[450] Next came a quiver full of his gifted children, including Vanessa the painter and Virginia the famous writer. In 1904 at his death, Vanessa moved the family from Hyde Park Gate to Gordon Square, near the British Museum. Here they were free to live bohemian lives "distant from prying relatives": a distinct advantage for "two women in their twenties living unchaperoned with their brothers."[451] One of the brothers, Thoby, decided to hold Thursday "at–homes" for his friends from Cambridge, and thus the core of the group began, one devoted to "open intellectual inquiry and tolerance."[452]

As the group grew, it attracted a plethora of talent: Lytton Strachey,

---

450 The portrait of Stephen comes from Louise De Salvo, "'Tinder-and-Flint': Virginia Woolf & Vita Sackville-West," in *Significant Others: Creativity & Intimate Partnership*, edited by Whitney Chadwick and Isabelle De Courtivron (New York: Thames and Hudson, 1993), 92.

451 Lisa Tickner, "The 'Left-Handed Marriage': Vanessa Bell and Duncan Grant," in *Significant Others: Creativity & Intimate Partnership*, ed. Whitney Chadwick and Isabelle De Courtivron (New York: Thames and Hudson, 1993), 70.

452 Ibid.

who shocked the mores of the public with his exposé, *Eminent Victorians*, and whose relationship with painter Dora Carrington is the subject of a contemporary film;[453] Clive Bell, who married Vanessa, and, along with E.M. Forster, wrote anti–colonial pieces critical of the Empire; Maynard Keynes, who revolutionized economics;[454] Duncan Grant, who collaborated with Vanessa on painting and fathered her child Angelica;[455] Roger Fry, who organized the scandalous London Post–Impressionist exhibition;[456] Leonard Woolf, who wed Virginia[457] and founded Hogarth Press; and others. Nine of the ten men had been at Cambridge, chiefly at Trinity and King's colleges.[458] Though apolitical, they saw themselves as cultural iconoclasts. Virginia Woolf signaled the end of an era not with the death of King Edward VII but with the Post–Impressionist exhibition seven months later: "'On or about December 1910 human character changed.'"[459]

The intimate relationships of the group read like the script of a soap opera. Cross–gender and same–gender relationships were common. Vanessa Bell had always wanted a child with her painting partner, the openly homosexual Duncan Grant, and he obliged her.[460] She also indulged in a fling with Roger Fry, whereas Duncan Grant enjoyed affairs with her brother Adrian Stephen as well as Lytton Strachey and Maynard Keynes.[461] Writers Virginia Woolf and Vita Sackville-West had a passionate affair, but both depended on the emotional support of their

---

453 *Carrington*, directed by Christopher Hampton, Freeway Films, 1995.

454 For some of the information about group membership I am indebted to the *Wikipedia* article, Bloomsbury Group.

455 Lisa Tickner, "The 'Left-Handed Marriage': Vanessa Bell and Duncan Grant," in *Significant Others: Creativity & Intimate Partnership*, ed. Whitney Chadwick and Isabelle De Courtivron (New York: Thames and Hudson, 1993), 77-78.

456 Susan Joyce, "On or about 1901 [sic]: The Bloomsbury Group Looks Back at the Victorians," *Victorian Studies* 4, no. 6 (2004):632.

457 Leonard and Virginia also appear in a contemporary film, *The Hours*, directed by Stephen Daldry, Paramount Pictures, 2002.

458 Joyce, "On or about 1901 …," 640.

459 From "Mr. Bennett and Mrs. Brown," quoted in Joyce, "On or about 1901 …," 632.

460 Tickner, "The 'Left-Handed Marriage': Vanessa Bell and Duncan Grant," 77-78.

461 Ibid., 77.

long–suffering husbands.[462] Within the supportive circle of the group, members were free to be who they were, in defiance of Victorianism, and to advocate free love, social reform, and feminism. Leonard Woolf said that "'we were in the van of the builders of a new society which should be free.'"[463]

Emerson and his Circle (essayists, poets, social re–formers, and authors of fiction). Harold Bloom credits Emerson with an immense influence on American culture and letters:

> Emerson is the mind of our climate, the principal source of the American difference in poetry, criticism, and pragmatic post-philosophy . . . From his moment to ours, American authors are either in his tradition, or else in a counter-tradition originating in opposition to him.[464]

During his own time in the early and mid–nineteenth century, Emerson bestrode the land like a colossus. We know that he founded the movement of Transcendentalism, an optimistic and spiritual philosophy based on his reading of the Bhagavad Gita. We know that he wrote gnomic, gem–like sentences that coalesced into essays surpassingly memorable. We know that many writers of the time deferred to him as the Yankee Plato, the Sage of Concord, the *paterfamilias* of American literature. What we may not know is how Emerson created and sustained a place where creativity could flower: Concord, Massachusetts, which Henry James had once called "the biggest little place in America."[465]

At this crossroads of the Cambridge Turnpike and Lexington Road, a colony of writers and thinkers dwelt, leading entangled lives, discussing heady ideas, and promoting social reform. Emerson was the financial or emotional support for most of them. Bronson Alcott, the dreamy

---

462 Summary of Louise De Salvo, "Tinder-and-Flint': Virginia Woolf & Vita Sackville-West," in *Significant Others: Creativity & Intimate Partnership*, ed. Whitney Chadwick and Isabelle De Courtivron (New York: Thames and Hudson, 1993), 83-95.

463 Leonard Woolf, *Sowing*, (London: Hogarth Press, 1961), 161, quoted in Joyce, "On or about 1901 …,"639.

464 Harold Bloom, *20ᵗʰAnniversary Edition: Essayists and Prophets* (New York: Readers Subscription Book Club, 2005), 97.

465 Quoted in Susan Cheever, *American Bloomsbury: Louisa May Alcott, Ralph Waldo Emerson, Margaret Fuller, Nathaniel Hawthorne, and Henry David Thoreau: Their Lives, Their Loves, Their Work* (New York: Simon and Schuster, 2006), 5.

and impractical intellectual, could not stoop to the sordid business of making a living. His most famous social experiment was Brook Farm, a failed utopian community that his daughter Louisa May nicknamed "Apple Slump." This daughter, whom he discounted because she was not fair-haired and blue-eyed, sold stories that brought in money and became famous for her novel *Little Women*. She also wrote *Moods*, a novel that described her conflicting affections for both Emerson and Thoreau. Henry James used her as the model for strong-willed Isabel Archer in *Portrait of a Lady*.

As well as supporting Alcott, Emerson provided the property on which Thoreau wrote his famous diary *Walden Pond*. The philanthropic "Yankee Plato" also owned the Old Manse (at which Nathaniel Hawthorne and his young wife lived for a time) and sent Thoreau to start their vegetable garden. Hawthorne, whose most famous work is *The Scarlet Letter*, also wrote many fine short stories and other novels. He had an intense friendship with Melville, whose greatest work is *Moby Dick*. Margaret Fuller, feminist editor of the *Dial*, helped to spread Transcendental and reformist ideas. Serenaded by Thoreau on the flute, courted by both Emerson and Hawthorne, she lived for a while in Emerson's home, to the chagrin of his wife. Even Edgar Allan Poe was friendly with the group. [466] Cheever calls this creative community "the mothers and fathers of our literature."[467] She also marvels at the confluence of talent in this time and place:

> Since ancient Rome, theories have been offered to explain why geniuses seem to be grouped together in specific times and locations . . . Modern research on genius clusters has shown that circumstances, political conditions, landscape, and community forces sometimes come together to create an unusual concentration of talent.[468]

In some instances, as we will see in Chapters 12 and 13, the talent is nurtured by a system of patronage or institutional support. In many other instances it is not. The expatriates in twentieth-century Paris lived

---

466 All of the information about Emerson's circle is taken from Cheever.

467 Cheever, *American Bloomsbury*, 5.

468 Ibid.

hand to mouth by their own wits. The Dada movement, the Impression-ists, the fiction of Hemingway and Fitzgerald suddenly appeared, as did the art of the Pre-Raphaelites before them. How or why? Is the "Unified Field" involved? Do creative people receive hunches about where to go? Bennis and Biederman have a colorful explanation:

> **The talented smell out places that are full of promise and energy, the places where the future is being made. The gifted often catch the zeit-geist and ride it to a common shore. Certain schools and academic de-partments are lodestones for talent. Certain cities attract it as well.**[469]

It is also true that places have a definite feeling or magnetism. Enter a Gothic cathedral where worshippers have heard the *kyrie* for a thousand years, and you will feel peace and transcendence. Enter a prison or other place where people feel desperate, and you will sense that the place itself has absorbed the feeling and emanates a negative magnetism.

Artists go to certain places to create because of the feeling as well as the sight. A whole colony of them has grown up around Mt. Shasta, California, because something about the place inspires transcendental and ethereal art. Other such places are Sedona, Arizona, and Glaston-bury, England. If you have the chance to visit any such place, close your eyes and examine what you are feeling.

Burning Man (art, social performance). San Francisco, the quintessential land of the Happening, home of the 1967 Human Be-In and Summer of Love,[470] the place where singer Scott Mackenzie said you should wear flowers in your hair, was also the birthplace of what may be the largest communal and temporary art happening in the world: the Burning Man festival. Each year over Labor Day weekend, thousands[471] of artists, performers, and revelers from all over the country assemble on a barren desert in Nevada to erect temporary art structures, dance all night to ear-splitting technopop, and watch a crowd of costumed iconoclasts locomote on specially crafted machines. The festival was

---

469 Bennis and Biederman, *Organizing Genius*, 201.

470 The *San Francisco Chronicle* ran a special series on The Summer of Love, May 19-23, 2007. During the final installment on May 23, one commentator said that this famous hippie be-in prefigured and inspired the communal consciousness of Burning Man. See www.sfgate.com.

471 Almost 40,000 celebrants watched the effigy burn in 2006.

inspired by a few San Franciscans who watched a bonfire on a beach and decided fire would be a good idea for a festival. Now thousands come each year to the same location. It must be awesome to watch the climax of the event, the burning of a mammoth statue: rather like a hippie Guy Fawkes Day. It is arguable whether the Summer of Love in the Haight could be considered a creative group, but the art produced at this festival is truly spectacular: mammoth in scale and disassembled or set ablaze the last night.[472] In this era of the instant party or rave, with text messaging or Twitter spreading the word, it could be that eventually, Be-Ins will themselves become an art form.

Burning Man 1 *(The Man)*

---

472 For pictures, articles, and an anniversary special, see www.sfgate.com/burning man.

Burning Man 2 *(The Man Burning)*

(Group Affirmation)

2013 Burning Man festival photos by permission of Burning Man,
leeanna@burningman.com, and photographer, Frank Roberto

In fact, it may be that the leading edge of evolution will involve human beings cooperating in a group mind. John–Steiner says,

> **Contemplentarity is a consequence of a basic and often ignored reality. Each individual realizes only a subset of the human potential that can be achieved at a particular historical period.**[473]

Andrew Cohen describes the phenomenon as already active amongst his students. When some of them resonating in high states create a "superholon," it can be sensed by other members of the group leading a seminar in a distant city:

> **. . when the superholon is coming together elsewhere in this extraordinary way, they'll *know* that the event they're leading will be very powerful, almost automatically. Whereas at other times, without that "nonlocal support," they would have to work very hard to achieve the same effect.**[474]

Wilber responds to this example of non–locality with the analogy of "morphic fields" (see Chapter 2):

> **. . . for example, one laboratory trying to crystallize a complex molecule for years and years and years, and then as soon as they succeed, a dozen other labs do it in the next month without even knowing about one another!**[475]

Wilber says that the feature of such a "social holon" is "mutual resonance." [476] Your string vibrates with my string. Keith Sawyer, who first experienced this phenomenon in jazz improvisations, describes it as "an invisible collaborative web."[477] Parker Palmer defines it this way:

---

473 John-Steiner, *Creative Collaboration*, 40.

474 Andrew Cohen and Ken Wilber, "The Guru and the Pandit: Dialogue XIV: A Living Experiment in Conscious Evolution," *What is Enlightenment?* 35 (January-March 2007), 50.

475 Cohen and Wilber, "The Guru and the Pandit," 50.

476 Wilber, *Integral Spirituality*, 150.

477 Keith Sawyer, *Group Genius: The Creative Power of Collaboration* (New York: Basic Books, 2007), x-xi.

"reality is a web of communal relationships, and we can know reality only by being in community with it."[478]

An earlier architect of the "social holon" is Swami Kriyananda, who took to heart his guru Yogananda's injunction to create spiritual communities for like–minded people to engage in high–minded principles and right living. A favorite injunction of Yogananda's was, "Environment is stronger than will power."[479] If we operate in a supportive environment with like–minded people, we are more likely to achieve our goals. Hence Kriyananda has established "colonies" or communities in which people committed to the same spiritual path can support one another and create the synergistic power of a superholon. These colonies, part of the Ananda spiritual fellowship, exist all over the world, from Italy to India, with important centers on the West Coast of the US, especially in northern California.[480] Kriyananda says, "People who do things together, instead of each one battling alone, can move mountains . . . An Ananda saying puts it well: 'Many hands make a miracle.'"[481]

Like John–Steiner, Bennis and Biederman forecast the importance of groups in the coming age:

> The myth of the triumphant individual is deeply ingrained in the American psyche. Whether it is midnight rider Paul Revere or basketball's Michael Jordan in the 1990s, we are a nation enamored of heroes—rugged self-starters who meet challenges and overcome adversity . . . And yet we all know that cooperation and collaboration grow more important every day. A shrinking world in which technological and political complexity increase at an accelerating rate offers fewer and fewer arenas in which individual action suffices.[482]

Alan Combs reminds us that "communal consciousness" is "not new," having been part of "hunting–and–gathering" societies "twelve or fifteen thousand years ago and beyond." However, individuals in these primi-

---

478 Palmer, *The Courage to Teach*, 95.

479 For instance, see Kriyananda, *The Essence of Self-Realization*, 182.

480 See www.ananda.org.

481 Swami Kriyananda, *Cities of Light: A Plan for this Age* (Nevada City, California: Crystal Clarity, 1987), 24.

482 Bennis and Biederman, *Organizing Genius*, 1.

tive groups had not developed a firm ego or sense of self, "so individual identity was submerged in the identity of the group." The difference with groups like Andrew Cohen's is that they experience "a kind of shared intelligence that develops around problem–solving situations" without any "loss of individuality." Everyone contributes as a "unique" mind or consciousness "to the ongoing problem–solving process."[483] So if we say that the two kinds of group awareness are the same, we are committing *the pre-trans fallacy* (Chapter 6). Communal awareness without a sense of self is *not* the same as communal cooperation amongst individual selves.

Combs explains the importance of this new group spirit:

> **This kind of shared consciousness seems to be a form of intersubjectivity that penetrates deep into the inner dimension of lower-left-quadrant shared experience. The fact that it is emerging in today's world suggests that it may indeed be the cutting edge of the evolution of consciousness.[484]**

Napoleon Hill calls this "Co–operation" "the Law of the Master Mind": the Co–operation [sic] between people who group themselves together or form alliances for the purpose of attaining a given end."[485] He also notes a second principle: "the Co–operation between the conscious and the subconscious [sic] minds, which forms a reasonable hypothesis of man's ability to contact, communicate with and draw upon *infinite intelligence*."[486]

These principles form the energy spiral that I am calling *Creative Synergy*. Individuals in partnerships (Chapters 7–8) or systems (Chapters 12–13) interact "for the purpose of" creative work (Chapters 9–11). The self applies "domain–relevant skills" and creative formulas to draw "what is trying to happen" from "*infinite intelligence*" (Chapters 1–3). This process is aided by self-awareness (Chapters 5–6), and its parts may be mapped on the 4 Quadrants of the Integral Operating System.

---

483 Allan Combs, "Horizontal Evolution and Collective Intelligence. Integral Ideas," *What is Enlightenment?* 36 (April-June 2007), 42.

484 Ibid.

485 Napoleon Hill, *Law of Success*, 4th ed. (Chicago, IL: Success Unlimited, 1979), Lesson 13, 81.

486 Ibid.

Exercises

1. Explain another group (or two or three) that has achieved power through communal consciousness. What form did this consciousness take—mutual support like Emerson's Transcendentalists or communal creativity like the Beatles? (Remember to focus on the feeling of "we," the Lower Left. The external system is the Lower Right.)
2. When have you experienced this power of the "we" in a group? For example, was it at church, at a rock concert, or during a sports event? Did you feel a shared consciousness, a group mind? Explain.
3. Form a collaborative team, such as a study group or band. Or create a project as a team. Report on the results. Did you ever feel a communal consciousness? (Note: if this team is for a class project, get permission from your professor to make sure that the form of your "collaboration" won't be called plagiarism or cheating.)
4. Go to the www.sfgate.com website, and look up Burning Man or the Summer of Love. How did these events create the communal consciousness of "we"?
5. Watch Oliver Stone's movie *The Doors*. How does Jim Morrison create a communal consciousness in his fans? How does this movie exemplify other principles elucidated in this book?
6. List some of the puzzling or unclear ideas in Chapter 8. Ask questions about them.
7. Explain what you think is most important in Chapter 8.
8. React to some of the ideas in Chapter 8. Debate, support, analyze, and/or reflect.
9. Give evidence from your own life or background experience about the ideas in Chapter 8. (Don't repeat what you have written in another exercise.)

The Product (It): Aesthetics and the "Big Three"

Synergistic Interlude

Through the Looking Glass Chapter IV: "Tweedledum and Tweedledee (The Red King's Dream)"

"[Alice] checked herself in some alarm, at hearing something that sounded to her like the puffing of a large steam-engine in the wood near them, thought she feared it was more likely to be a wild beast. 'Are there any lions or tigers about here?' she asked timidly.

"'It's only the Red King snoring,' said Tweedledee.

"'Come and look at him!' the brothers cried, and they each took one of Alice's hands, and led her up to where the King was sleeping.

"'Isn't he a lovely sight?' said Tweedledum . . .

"'He's dreaming now,' said Tweedledee: 'and what do you think he's dreaming about?'

"Alice said `Nobody can guess that.'

"'Why, about you!' Tweedledee exclaimed, clapping his hands triumphantly. 'And if he left off dreaming about you, where do you suppose you'd be?'

"'Where I am now, of course,' said Alice.

"'Not you!' Tweedledee retorted contemptuously. 'You'd be nowhere. Why, you're only a sort of thing in his dream!'

"'If that there King was to wake,' added Tweedledum, 'you'd go out—bang!—just like a candle!'

"'I shouldn't!' Alice exclaimed indignantly. 'Besides, if I'M only a sort of thing in his dream, what are you, I should like to know?'

"'Ditto' said Tweedledum.

"'Ditto, ditto' cried Tweedledee.

Courtesy of Lenny's Alice in Wonderland Site, http://www.alice-in-wonderland.net/

This strange episode evokes the perennial theological or metaphysical question: If we're all characters in the vast dream of the universe, Who is the Dreamer, and what happens if It/He/She awakens?

That we are moving about in a dreamlike, unconscious state is a truism in many philosophical, psychological, and spiritual traditions. (The Australian aborigines speak of the "Dream-Time" as a world of surreal reality.) If we are like characters in a dream, though, how do we become aware of the Dreamer? Ellen Langer of Harvard talks of mindfulness, and Charles Tart talks of "waking up."

We can wake up after a dream and analyze the patterns in it, to discern the deeper meanings. In the same way, it may be possible to analyze patterns that run through science, art, and nature to discern the characteristics of the "dream" that creates our world.

Questions to ponder:

1. Have you ever had a dream that, in some way, reflected or forecasted reality?

2. What patterns have you noticed in nature that seem to be reflected in mathematics, music, or art?

9

The Aesthetic Object or "Thing in Itself": Creativity in the Upper Right, Part 1: Universal Principles

"Beauty is truth, truth beauty,"—that is all
Ye know on earth, and all ye need to know.

—John Keats,
"Ode on a Grecian Urn" (1820)

Questions to Consider

Are beauty and truth synonymous? Or is one subjective and the other, objective? What is their relationship to the Good? How might this "Big Three," as Wilber calls them (Chapter 4), relate to nature, art, science, and mathematics? Are there universal characteristics that indicate some sort of blueprint organizing the world?

The Ideational Realm—or, The Unified Field

To get a perspective on these questions, let's review an idea from Chapter 2. There we saw that Plato spoke of the Forms, the Divine Ideas that structure physical reality. We also heard from Nobel prize winner Roger Penrose of Oxford University, who explains, "Platonic existence, as I see it, refers to the existence of an objective external standard . . . Such 'existence' could also refer to things other than mathematics, such as to morality or aesthetics."[487] In fact, he posits the existence of three worlds: the Platonic realm of Truth–Morality–Beauty and the other worlds of Mentality and Physicality. Each, he believes, "possesses its own distinctive kind of existence, different from the other two."[488] There is also a "mysterious connection between the worlds," what Penrose calls "three profound mysteries":[489] how the two immaterial worlds connect to the third of physical reality.

You may recall that in Chapter 2, we saw Penrose remarking that

> The mathematical assertions that can belong to Plato's world are pre-cisely those that are objectively true . . . To my way of thinking, Platonic existence is simply a matter of objectivity and, accordingly, should cer-tainly not be viewed as something "mystical" or "unscientific," despite the fact that some people regard it that way.[490]

We also saw Rupert Sheldrake summarizing the thinking of Terence McKenna:

> The Cosmic Mind contains all possible forms and archetypes that are way out there in the future, and it somehow interacts with what's go-ing on now. . . The evolutionary imagination works by a kind of spark between the divine mind, or cosmic attractor, and present situations open to creativity.[491]

In this model, there is a two-way interaction between the field and the individual, the net and the gem: the process I am calling *Creative Synergy*. Edgar Cayce would call it cooperation or co-creation with "the Creative Forces": ". . . the entity, the soul, is a portion—an effort of the Creative influence to make aware in manifested form in the earth or

---

487 Penrose, *The Road to Reality*, 12, 13.

488 Ibid., 1029, 1030.

489 Ibid., 17, 18.

490 Ibid., 15.

491 Sheldrake et al, *Chaos, Creativity, and Cosmic Consciousness*, 8-9.

material world of *what* creative forces *are!*" (274-3)

If we follow Penrose's idea that "Platonic existence is simply a matter of objectivity," then we would place his "first mystery" in the Upper Right quadrant. Though the "mystery" begins with an invisible blueprint, it eventually appears as repeating patterns in the world. It is a "mystery" because the patterns can be defined by mathematics; and, as we shall see, even sensed by artists (aesthetics, "the second mystery"). Yet, as Penrose says, we still don't know what all of these connections mean.

The Upper Right

The upper right quadrant is the objective singular, the fact, the empirically verifiable object accessible to the senses. Wilber says,

> **In the Upper-Right Quadrant, we can see the evolution of exterior or "material" or "physical" forms, as disclosed by modern science. These exterior forms include, in order of increasing evolutionary complexity, items such as: atoms, molecules, early or prokaryotic cells, true or eukaryotic cells, organisms with a neuronal net, organisms with a neural cord (e.g., shrimp), a reptilian brain stem (e.g., lizard), a limbic system (e.g., horse), a neurocortex or triune brain (e.g., humans, with several higher "structure-functions" also listed).**
>
> **Those are all "exterior" or "material" forms, in that you can see them in the exterior, sensorimotor world.**[492]

In this chapter we will ponder how such forms in nature find an echo in the aesthetics of various domains. We will look for universal qualities, criteria of excellence in the arts (visual, performing, and literary), mathematics, and the sciences. Then in Chapters 10 and 11, we will note how criteria can differ by domain.

Einstein said that his main objective was to read the mind of God: "I want to know how God created this world. I am not interested in this or that phenomenon, in the spectrum of this or that element. I

---

492 Wilber, *Integral Spirituality*, 220-21.

want to know his thoughts. The rest are details."[493] The principles in this chapter may be one step in that direction. They seem to hold true across domains. Many are also reducible to mathematics, which Professor James Gates notes as "central" in "empowering . . . creativity"[494] by providing as a special language in which the human imagination can be expressed.

Ideational Blueprints

This chapter deals with Penrose's "first" and "second" "mysteries," the relation of an ideational realm to mathematics and aesthetics (the True and the Beautiful). It is not necessary to understand this chapter in depth to be a creator. In fact, I wrestled with Penrose's ideas for months during a sabbatical before I began to grasp what he was talking about, and his mathematical proofs always eluded me. Still, if we are positing a Unified Field from which creators draw, these ideas seem an important part of the puzzle. You can treat them as a philosophical background that may or may not be interesting to you.

Some artists are aware they are working with one or both of the "mysteries." Sculptor Anton Nemeth, who creates delicate porcelain objects from clay, explains how he uses ideational blueprints in his art (interview, January 30, 2007). "The clay is an unknown, kind of a crack in the world, you might say; it's an idea from Carlos Castaneda. Because of its plasticity it's an opportunity to feel into a realm that's invisible . . . and bring back expressions of harmony, rhythm, beauty" from a realm "which ultimately is all-encompassing and in which we are visitors by the grace of our awareness."

Nemeth's sculptures look like shells, leaves, and flowers. As he works with the clay, he feels "what the clay wants to become." He says, "What that phrase means most likely is that there's a gift present of awareness, of invisible structures that wants to express itself in some manner or form." His exquisite ceramic objects often take the shapes

---

493 Quoted in *The Expanded Quotable Einstein*, collected and edited by Alice Calaprice and Freeman Dyson (Princeton and Oxford: Princeton University Press, 2000), 202.

494 S. James Gates, Jr., "Lecture 1, The Macro/Micro/Mathematical Connection," *Superstring Theory: The DNA of Reality*, 24 DVDs (Chantilly, Virginia: The Teaching Company, 2006).

of nature—flowers and leaves, whirls and spirals in symmetrical curves of beauty. Samuel Taylor Coleridge would say that he is sensing the "organic form," which "shapes as it develops itself from within" (*Lectures on Shakespeare*).

Qan Yin Lilly by Anton Nemeth

Blushing Flame by Anton Nemeth

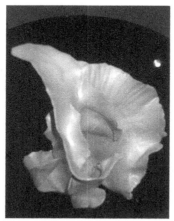

Flowering Conch

Art work and photos courtesy of Anton Nemeth: Blossoming Lily, Blushing Flame (his names), Flowering Conch (mine)

Michelangelo worked the same way. From Ficino he had first heard the idea that form is encased in stone and waiting to be released:

> **"If a sculptor should remove little by little, with knowing skill, everything that is 'too much,' there would emerge from it, there would be freed from it, a marvelous statute. It is not with the hands . . . that we paint or sculpt, but with the intellect."**[495]

Michelangelo applied this idea to a block of marble that had been spoiled and abandoned by an earlier artist. When a council of experts first gazed on the results,

> **. . . rivalry and jealousy had to yield to admiration. Knowing all about the spoiled block of marble, the committee unanimously declared that Michelangelo had overcome difficulties thought to be insuperable, and in creating such a beautiful statue had worked a greater miracle than if he had brought a dead man back to life.**[496]

The result was the *David*.

One Blueprint: Circles and Curves

Nemeth's work, which he feels is drawn from "a realm that's invisible," often assumes the form of spirals and curves. In nature this pattern occurs often. Hurricanes and typhoons rotate like water spiraling down a drain, their direction determined by their position above or below the equator. The same spiral appears in black holes depicted on television science programs. "Land artist" Andy Goldsworthy mimics these patterns in his ephemeral art, constructed from bracken, stones, and branches near rivers and oceans.[497] For a commission in Nova Scotia, he made a circular sculpture from a nest of branches. Spiraling outward from a central hole, it rotated as the currents caught it. "It has the sense of a whirlpool," said one bystander. Goldsworthy mused, "It feels as if

---

495 Quoted in Nardini, *Michelangelo*, 17.

496 Nardini, *Michelangelo*, 56-57.

497 *Rivers and Tides*, documentary by Thomas Reidelsheimer (Mediopolis, Skyline, 2003).

it's been taken off into another plane, another world."[498]

See the "whirlpool" image below being built in *Rivers and Tides* at http://www.youtube.com/watch?v=iBcdL8uO71E&feature=related.

Stick dome hole
made next to a turning pool
a meeting between river and sea
carried upstream
turning
10 February 1999
Printed by Permission

The same pattern appears to meditators. It is a universal experience of those who concentrate deeply enough at the spot between the eyebrows: a spiral rotating clockwise, its deep central core like a white cloud that wavers into a five-pointed star, its background the star-studded deep blue or black of space, bounded by a golden ring. The same sort of energy

---

498 *Rivers and Tides*, documentary by Thomas Reidelsheimer (Mediopolis, Skyline, 2003).

swirls in Van Gogh's *Starry Night*, with dark blue spirals of paint over a sur-realistic view distorted by waves of power; and in the earthwork sculpture *Spiral Jetty*, built by Robert Smithson near the Salt Lake in 1970.

Spiral Jetty, Areal View, 1970, Art © Estate of Robert Smithson/Licensed by VAGA, New York, NY, 111 Broadway • Suite 1006 • New York, NY 10006, License 21760

Above: Smithson's Spiral Jetty

The picture below illustrates Leonardo's theory that hair should be portrayed in natural swirls around the head, to imitate the swirling movements of nature: "The free play of tousled, wind–blown hair resembles, in Leonardo's theory, the representation of flows of currents of water. The lines of force of whirlpools in their spiraling motion are designed like wavy, curly locks of hair."[499]

Leonardo, La Scapigliata

Leonardo, p. 173 *La Scapigliata and Star of Bethlehem*, Wikimedia Commons

---

499 Carlo Pedretti, *Leonardo da Vinci: Artist, Scientist, Inventor* (Florence-Milan: Giunti, 2005), 202.

Van Gogh, Starry Night

24, p. 173, Courtesy of Wikimedia Commons

When Swami Kriyananda designed his retreat home in Northern California, he eschewed the hard angles and boxes of the traditional Western European or American home for the shape of the geodesic dome, conceived by Buckminster Fuller. Citing the peace he felt in a planetarium and in an Arizona home with rounded corners, he says, "Roundness in some form spoke meaningfully to me." He later discovered that Sioux Indians "believe that roundness in a building helps one to feel in tune with the earth and the universe. Square corners, according to them, capture evil spirits. I suppose that's a way of saying corners reduce the sense of harmony in a home."[500]

McTaggart says that this preference for the circle abounds in "native" and "indigenous" cultures. "Native American cultures" use the "medicine wheel" to "depict," among other things, the "circular" movement of time: "the cyclical nature of life, the regeneration of all things, with birth, growth, maturity, and death." "Native cultures" also sense "the rhythms of life" as marked by "circularity in the movement of the planets" and "the rising and setting of the sun."[501]

In mathematics a remarkable instance of this curvilinear energy is the Mandelbrot set. Given the right set of equations, points plotted on a graph assume shapes of curves and swirls, now visible graphically to us because of advanced computing techniques.[502] They look like pieces of ink blots or shattered snowflakes, with feathers and spirals emerging in near–symmetry from various circles. Once again, this relationship of mathematics and shapes in the natural world is something that Nobel–Prize–winning mathematician Roger Penrose calls "the first mystery," the relationship of a Platonic realm of mathematics to the real world.

Of the Mandelbrot Set, he observes,

> **Remarkably, this structure is defined by a mathematical rule of particular simplicity . . . The Mandelbrot set was certainly no invention of any human mind . . . Nor can its existence lie within the multitude of computer printouts that begin to capture some of its incredible sophis-**

500 Swami Kriyananda, *Space, Light, and Harmony: The Story of Crystal Hermitage* (Nevada City, California: Crystal Clarity, 2005), 10.

501 McTaggart, *Living the Field.*

502 Gregg Braden, *Awakening to Zero Point: The Collective Initiation*, rev. ed., A Sacred Spaces/Ancient Wisdom Book (Bellevue, Washington: Radio Bookstore Press, 1997), 31.

tication and detail, for at best these printouts capture but a shadow of an approximation to the set itself. . . Its existence can only be within the Platonic world of mathematical form.[503]

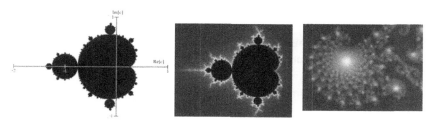

Above: details of a single Mandelbrot set,

Courtesy of Wikimedia Commons, Image 3 is a picture by Lars H. Rohwedde

An associated "mystery" is a Mandelbrot crop circle photographed near Cambridge, England, in 1991.[504] Though it is difficult to confirm what crop circles mean, especially since pranksters claim to have created some of them, the image is certainly striking. At the very least, the pranksters were replicating a natural and mathematical pattern.

Another Blueprint: Symmetry

According to Roger Penrose, the "notion" of symmetry is important "in modern physical theory," such as "relativity theory" and "quantum theory." In fact, "it seems to be a tenet of many of the modern approaches to particle physics to take symmetry as being" "fundamental to Nature's ways." He adds, "as a related point of interest, there are circumstances where an exact symmetry group can come about even with structures where no symmetry is initially imposed."[505]

One example found in both art and nature is the Fibonacci Sequence: a sequence of integers in which each is the sum of the two preceding it. The following table and explanation are excerpted from Braden:

---

503 Penrose, *The Road to Reality*, 16-17.
504 Photograph in Braden, *Awakening to Zero Point*, 129.
505 Penrose, *The Road to Reality*, 1036-37.

1	1	2	3	5	8	13
21	34	55	89	144	233	377
610	987	1597	2584	4181	6765	10946 ...

Beginning with the integer 1 and adding 1 to itself, a pattern is developed as any one term results from the sum of the two previous terms. One plus one equals two. Two plus one equals three. Three plus two equals five and so on.[506]

Artist and philosopher Harry Paine wrote a note about this series: "These numbers, when applied to a graphic display, using measurements from a ruler," create "a sequence which results in a spiral like that found in nature: chambered nautilus, the spiral at the crown of the human head, and many others" (personal communication, March 2007). Braden cites the following applications:

- Relative proportions of the human body
- Ratios of males to females in an uncontrolled population
- Branching patterns of trees, plants, shrubs (without pruning)
- Dendritic branching patterns of lightning and root systems.[507]

Braden also explains how this sequence has a relationship to the Golden Ratio, sometimes known as *phi*:

The actual ratio may be determined in the division of any term in this series by the next higher term, producing an interesting phenomenon:
$$21/34=.6176 \qquad 89/144=.6180$$
Though the terms vary, the ratio of the terms is relatively constant! Used in ancient Greece to describe the most pleasing proportions of human anatomy, as well as classical Greek architecture, the ratio is known today as the golden Mean or the Golden Ratio; the fractional value of .618. This code is . . . fundamental to "life" on earth.[508]

---

506 Braden, *Awakening to Zero Point*, 31.
507 Ibid.
508 Ibid.

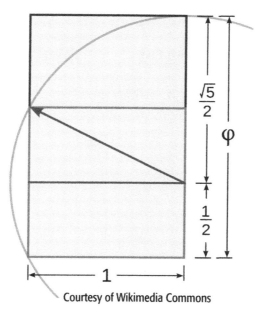

Courtesy of Wikimedia Commons

According to *Wikipedia*,[509] this ratio has been tremendously influential, from the first mention of it by Euclid to present–day applications by Roger Penrose. Renaissance artists such as Leonardo drew consciously upon it, especially after the 1509 publication of Pacioli's *De Divina Proportione*. The most famous application is "Vitruvian Man," Leonardo's drawing sent into space to represent humanity to alien beings. It was based on the idea of the Greek author Vitruvius that

> If a man be placed flat on his back, with his hands and feet extended, and a pair of compasses centered at his navel . . . the fingers and toes of his two hands and feet will touch the circumference of the circle therefrom. And just as the human body yields a circular outline, so too a square figure may be found from it. For if we measure the distance from the soles of the feet to the top of the head, and then apply that measure to the outstretched arms, the breadth will be found to be the same as the height. [510]

---

509 Quoted in *Wikipedia*, "Golden Ratio," accessed May 12, 2014, http://en.wikipedia.org/wiki/Golden_ratio.

510 Quoted in Richard Stemp, *The Secret Language of the Renaissance: Decoding the Hidden Symbolism of Italian Art* (London: Duncan Baird, 2006), 56.

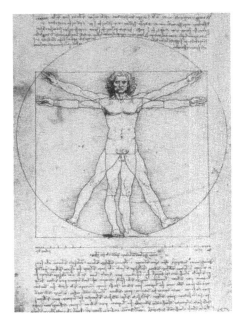

Leonardo, Vitruvian Man

The Golden Ratio has been found in parts of the Acropolis, Parthenon, and the Great Mosque of Kairouan. It greatly influenced the architecture of Le Corbusier and the art of Mondrian and furnished the design for Salvador Dali's *The Sacrament of the Last Supper*. In music it has influenced harmonic chord progressions and sequences of keys. In botany, according to Adolf Zeising, it governs the relationship of branches to stems and veins to leaves; in biology, the arrangement of bones, veins, and nerves; in geology, the design of crystals.[511] In a passage written in 1854 he deemed it a universal law

> **in which is contained the ground-principle of all formative striving for beauty and completeness in the realm of both nature and art, and which permeates, as a paramount spiritual ideal, all structures, forms,**

and proportions, whether cosmic or individual, organic or inorganic, acoustic or optical; which finds its fullest realization, however, in the human form. [512]

Renaissance artists believed that this "sacred geometry" was created by God, Who, according to the Book of Proverbs, "'set a compass on his creation." [513] William Blake portrayed this idea in his engraving, *Ancient of Days*, reproduced in the beginning of this book.

Anton Nemeth would say that these patterns, found in nature and in art, give us glimpses into "a realm that's invisible." He admits that working with this realm can be a challenge: "Working with any medium is kind of like going from unconscious incompetence to or through conscious incompetence to conscious competence to unconscious competence. Each one sows the seed for the next. That's dialectic. It's a spiral, not a line." Working with the Unified Field, like any other work, takes practice and technique. It takes a feeling for what is trying to happen and how it is trying to express its universality. The same idea may be coming to many different artists and thinkers, but its expression will be different, depending on the individual artist, the unique filter through which it emerges.

Science professor Lloyd Kitazono,[514] who notes the prevalence of "symmetry in biology," relates the principle to "evolution" or "natural selection." He explains, "Symmetry in animals is related to lifestyles and position on the phylogenetic tree of animals," then cites concepts similar to Wilber's discussion of the Upper Right at the beginning of this chapter:

No symmetry—[arrangement] common among sessile or slowing animals and/or simple animals such as protozoa.

Radial symmetry—symmetric arrangement about a central point or axis; common among sessile but more advanced animals such as sea anemones, sea urchins, and sea stars.

Bilateral symmetry—[arrangement in which] one plane, called the

---

512 Quoted in *Wikipedia*, "Golden Ratio," accessed May 12, 2014, http://en.wikipedia.org/wiki/Golden_ratio.

513 Stemp, *The Secret Language of the Renaissance*, 58.

514 Lloyd Kitazono, personal communication with author, March 3 and 4, 2007.

sagittal plane, will divide an organism into external, mirror images; common among actively mobile animals and more complex animals, such as annelids, arthropods, mollusks, and vertebrates.

He adds that symmetry also appears in "flowering plants."

Science professor Jim Wheeler[515] remarks,

> In "nature" or in our known universal existence, symmetry plays an even more profound role than one might initially think. We mostly think of symmetry as being a recognizable, but mostly passive element in our reality. However, especially the enlightened chemist, biochemist, biologist, ocean scientist, etc., realizes that symmetry is a **controlling** agent in much of how our universe plays out.

Fibonacci sequences also operate in botanical systems, such as tree branches, pineapples, ferns, and pine cones.[516]

Such an "enlightened" experimenter is Masaru Emoto, who photographs ice crystals in different conditions. The crystals exposed to classical music grow intricate, symmetrical patterns; those "exposed to violent, heavy-metal rock music" are asymmetrical and malformed. The phrase "Thank you" in various languages creates beautiful, symmetrical crystals. "The word 'Fool' produces crystals similar to the water exposed to heavy-metal music, malformed and fragmented." [517]

According to Roger Penrose,

> Spaces that are symmetrical have a fundamental importance in modern physics . . . Although a symmetrical object, such as a square or sphere, has a precise existence as an idealized . . . 'Platonic' . . . mathematical structure, any *physical* realization of such a thing would ordinarily be regarded as merely some kind of approximate representation of this Platonic ideal, therefore possessing no actual symmetry that can be regarded as exact. Yet, remarkably, according to the highly successful physical theories of the 20th century, all physical interactions (including

---

515 Jim Wheeler, personal communication with author, March 3 and 4, 2007.

516 See *Wikipedia*, http://en.wikipedia.org/wiki/Fibonacci_number.

517 Masaru Emoto, *The Hidden Messages in Water*, trans. David A. Thayne (Hillsboro, Oregon: Beyond Words, 2001), xxiv-xxv.

gravity) act in accordance with an idea which, strictly speaking, depends crucially upon certain physical structures possessing a symmetry that, at a fundamental level of description, is indeed necessarily exact![518]

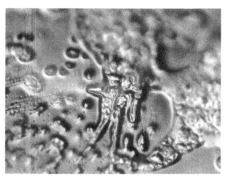

Water exposed to "Thank You"
http://www.adhikara.com/art_kunst/
emoto/water-16.htm

Water exposed to "You make me sick.
I want to kill you."
http://www.adhikara.com/art_kunst/emoto/
water-17.htm

Courtesy of Office Masaru Emoto, LLC, Tokyo, Japan

Symmetry governs other domains as well. In a 1480 Italian publication based on Pythagorean harmonics, the ratio 1:2 depicts an octave; 2:3, a fifth; 3–4, a fourth.[519] In Europe between about 1660 and 1780, symmetry was the preferred mode of artistic expression. The fugues of Bach and Mozart are built on symmetrical balance: repetition with a difference, like Emoto's pictures of water crystals. Formal gardens of the time were laid out in rows, and the heroic couplet was built on a principle known as balance, in which one half of a line echoed the structure of the other. Alexander Pope mastered this artistic form. Here is his description of how the sylphs, invisible fairy–like creatures, assist the coquette Belinda at her toilette:

---

518 Penrose, *The Road to Reality*, 247.

519 Stemp, *The Secret Language of the Renaissance*, 58.

> These set the head, and those divide the hair,
> Some fold the sleeve, while others plait the gown.
> *(Rape of the Lock* (1712), Canto I, ll.146-147)

Notice the symmetry of the grammatical phrases (called parallelism):

these	those	some	others
set the head	divide the hair	fold the sleeve	plait the gown.

Composition teachers drill their students on the power of sentence parallelism and balance in style. A more contemporary example is Martin Luther King's famous "I Have a Dream" speech, spoken before the Lincoln Memorial on the hundredth anniversary of the Emancipation Proclamation. The oration is so powerful because of balanced phrases like these: "One hundred years later, the life of the Negro is still sadly crippled by the manacles of segregation and the chains of discrimination." Like the couplet from Pope, this sentence balances items that are grammatically parallel:

the manacles	the chains
of segregation	of discrimination.

So here is Penrose's "second mystery," the relationship of an Ideational blueprint to the realm of aesthetics (The Beautiful).

Another Blueprint: Unity

Roger Penrose says,

> Those who have worked long and hard on some collection of mathematical ideas can be in a better position to appreciate the subtle and often unexpected unity that may lie within some particular scheme. Those who come to such a scheme from the outside, on the other hand, may view it more with bewilderment, and may find it hard to appreciate why such-and-such a property should have any particular merit, or why some things in the theory should be regarded as more surprising—and,

perhaps, therefore more beautiful—than others. Yet again, there may well be circumstances in which it is those from the outside who can better form objective judgments; for perhaps spending many years on a narrowly focused collection of mathematical problems arising within some particular approach results in distorted judgments![520]

He adds that "mathematical beauty and coherence are indeed closely related. It seems to me that the need for such coherence, in any proposed physical model, is unarguable. Moreover, unlike many aesthetic criteria, mathematical coherence has the advantage that it is fairly clearly something objective." [521]

Unity is an aesthetic principle of Formalist literary criticism, which investigates how the parts of a piece of literature combine to form the whole. To the Formalist, the best fiction is what Henry James called the "well-made" story, with every part essential to the impact. Called "The New Criticism" during its heyday in the 1920s and '30s, Formalist theory hailed the form of the work most important and celebrated "close reading" to show how binary opposites, ironies, and parts coalesce into a whole.

Let's take a work of literature with which you may be familiar as an example: the films of J.R.R. Tolkien's *Lord of the Rings*, directed by Peter Jackson. A formalist might say that, despite its length and division into three parts, this trilogy has a unity dependent on its universal theme: the struggle between good and evil. This struggle is reflected not only in the external conflict between the Fellowship of the Ring and the dark lord of Mordor, but also in the internal struggle endured by the ring-bearer, Frodo. Ironically, Frodo bears within himself the seeds of darkness and the essence of goodness. The reflection of external and internal struggle contributes to the unity of the whole.

Christopher Alexander, who writes about buildings that observers agree possess or lack the quality of "life," says that in architecture, wholeness makes the difference (i.e., *holons*):

It is not an isolated fragment in itself, but part of the world which in-

---

520 Penrose, *The Road to Reality*, 1014-15.
521 Ibid., 1014.

cludes the gardens, walls, trees, streets beyond its boundaries, and other
buildings beyond those. And it contains many wholes within it—also
unbounded and continuous in their connections. Above all, the whole
is unbroken and undivided.[522]

In Jungian psychology, wholeness is represented by the circle, or
the mandala, which is supposed to represent the soul. If you take a
workshop with a Jungian psychologist, you may be asked to draw one
of your own. Buddhist sand paintings, constructed with elaborate detail
and color, are created only to be destroyed—as a representation of the
transience of life.

Conclusion

At the turn of the new millennium, there is a debate raging between
the adherents of evolutionary theory and the proponents of an idea
called creationism. The first theory, supported by the scientific community in general, adheres to the empirical facts assembled by Darwin and
endorsed by later geological discoveries. The second theory, supported
by some of the religious community, postulates that the created world
shows signs of intelligent design.

In fact, forms of both theories may be partially true. The basic facts
of evolution, as we understand them today, seem beyond dispute. But
given universal principles such as the Fibonacci Series and the Golden
Ratio, I would say that there is *some* kind of design principle beyond
natural selection operating.

Of course, there are many possible theories of what it might be.
Richard Ogle, for instance, cites Stuart Kauffman's notion of "order
for free." This idea stipulates that, at a certain tipping point, a random
condition organizes itself.

The emerging sciences of complexity begin to suggest that the order
[of the natural world] is not all accidental, that vast veins of spontaneous
order lie at hand. Laws of complexity spontaneously generate much of
the order of the natural world. It is only then that selection comes into

---

522 Alexander, *The Nature of Order*, vol. 3, 80.

> play . . . the range of spontaneous order is enormously greater than we have supposed.[523]

To Ogle "the central fact [is] that *breakthrough creativity is inherently an emergent process governed by network dynamics.*"[524] However, it may be that "network dynamics," after "the tipping point," organize themselves by prearranged types of Platonic Forms. Or the Forms may be there from the beginning. To reiterate Michael Talbot's statement, quoted in Chapter 2: "Whether we call the collective consciousness of all things 'God,' or simply 'the consciousness of all things,' it doesn't change the situation. The universe is sustained by . . . an act of stupendous and ineffable creativity."[525]

---

523 Quoted in Ogle, *Smart World,* 128.

524 Ogle, *Smart World*, 116.

525 Talbot, *The Holographic Universe*, 285.

Exercises

1. Can you add anything to the discussion of swirls and curvilinear movements in nature?
2. Can you help out the author and explain some of the mathematical ideas in this chapter?
3. Can you add anything to the discussion of symmetry in art or nature?
4. Can you say anything else about the Golden Ratio?
5. Can you add anything to the discussion of unity in art, mathematics, and nature?
6. What television programs have you seen that deal with principles in this chapter?
7. List some of the puzzling or unclear ideas in Chapter 9. Ask questions about them.
8. Explain what you think is most important in Chapter 9.
9. React to some of the ideas in Chapter 9. Debate, support, analyze, and/or reflect.
10. Give evidence from your own life or background experience about the ideas in Chapter 9. (Don't repeat what you have written in another exercise.)
15. Create some art that expresses the principles in Chapter 9. Be prepared to explain it.

Synergistic Interlude

Through the Looking Glass Chapter VIII: "It's My Own Invention."

"[The White Knight] was dressed in tin armour, which seemed to fit him very badly, and he had a queer-shaped little deal box fastened across his shoulder, upside-down, and with the lid hanging open. Alice looked at it with great curiosity.

"'I see you're admiring my little box,' the Knight said in a friendly tone. 'It's my own invention—to keep clothes and sandwiches in. You see I carry it upside-down, so that the rain can't get in.'

"'But the things can get out,' Alice gently remarked. 'Do you know the lid's open?'

"'I didn't know it,' the Knight said, a shade of vexation passing over his face. 'Then all the things must have fallen out! And the box is no use without them.' He unfastened it as he spoke, and was just going to throw it into the bushes, when a sudden thought seemed to strike him, and he hung it carefully on a tree. 'Can you guess why I did that?' he said to Alice.

"Alice shook her head.

"'In hopes some bees may make a nest in it—then I should get the honey.'

"'But you've got a bee-hive—or something like one—fastened to the saddle,' said Alice.

"'Yes, it's a very good bee-hive,' the Knight said in a discontented tone, 'one of the best kind. But not a single bee has come near it yet. And the other thing is a mouse-trap. I suppose the mice keep the bees out—or the bees keep the mice out, I don't know which.'

"'I was wondering what the mouse-trap was for,' said Alice. 'It isn't very likely there would be any mice on the horse's back.'

"'Not very likely, perhaps,' said the Knight: 'but if they do come, I don't choose to have them running all about.'

"'You see,' he went on after a pause, 'it's as well to be provided for everything. That's the reason the horse has all those anklets round his feet.'

"'But what are they for?' Alice asked in a tone of great curiosity.

"'To guard against the bites of sharks,' the Knight replied. 'It's an invention of my own.'"

The rest of the chapter continues in the same vein. The White Knight is innovative, but he seems to be unaware that his products must be useful. He wouldn't be successful as an inventor or engineer.

Questions to ponder:

1. What are some inventions that seem both innovative and useful to you?

2. What inventions seem silly or impractical?

3. How do your verify that something you have made is both innovative and useful?

10

The Aesthetic Object or "Thing in Itself": Creativity in the Upper Right, Part 2: Science vs. Engineering

"Beauty is truth, truth beauty,"—that is all
Ye know on earth, and all ye need to know.

—John Keats,
"Ode on a Grecian Urn" (1820)

Beauty and Truth

Are *beauty* and truth synonymous? Or is one subjective and the other, objective? What is their relationship to the Good? We will continue our exploration of these questions by pondering how truth and beauty are exemplified in various domains. But first, let's review a few definitions.[526]

Beauty: "The quality that gives pleasure to the mind or senses and is associated with such properties as harmony of form or color, excellence of artistry, truthfulness, and originality."

Truth: "1. Conformity to fact or actuality. 2. A statement proven to

---

526 All of these definitions come from *The American Heritage Dictionary*, fourth edition.

be or accepted as true. 3. Sincerity; integrity. 4. Fidelity to an original or standard. 5 a. Reality; actuality. b. That which is considered to be the supreme reality and to have the ultimate meaning or value of existence."

Huh? It seems that truth can be just about what you say it is. What is "fact or actuality"? Is it the empirically verifiable, like the result of a DNA test or a replicated experiment? Or is it "the supreme reality," verified by meditation experiments conducted in the Upper Left quadrant? Is it what people have "accepted to be true"? That could be either empirical *or* supreme reality—or any number of no longer tenable hypotheses, such as a flat earth. All or any of these have been held by people with "sincerity" and "integrity." And what is "fidelity to an original or standard"? Does it mean that "truth" is one thing to the literary critic and another to the scientist?

In search of this elusive "truth," I looked up a few more definitions of troublesome terms, and here is what I found.

Reality. "1. The quality or state of being actual or true. 2. One, such as a person, entity, or event, that is actual: *the weight of history and political realities*" (Benno C. Schmidt, Jr.). 3. The totality of all things possessing actuality, existence, or essence. 4. That which exists objectively and in fact: *Your observations do not seem to be about reality.*
Fact. 1. Knowledge or information based on real occurrences: *an account based on fact; a blur of fact and fancy.* 2. a. Something demonstrated to exist or known to have existed: *genetic engineering is now a fact. That Chaucer was a real person is an undisputed fact.* 2. b. A real occurrence; an event: *had to prove the facts of the case.* c. Something believed to be true or real: *a document laced with mistaken facts.*"

Hmm. How can "the totality of all things possessing actuality, existence, or essence" be said to exist "objectively"? "Essence" belongs to the realm of being, as in "It is his essence to be optimistic." Essence is *subjective*. And *fact* can be based on subjective analyses as well: "Something believed to be true or real." I am reminded of Shirley MacLaine's statement in the 1980s when she was faced with people who denied the actuality or fact of her past-life or out-of-body experiences: "That's *your* reality." In fact, everyone's reality *is* different. Past experiences and cognitive associations *make* our realities. I hear someone trying to break into the house; you hear a twig scraping the window.

On the other hand, Plato saw truth and beauty as timeless absolutes, perfect Forms in a immaterial realm. Goswami also sees truth as an "archetype": " . . . the whole truth is transcendent; no perfect description of it here, on earth, is possible . . . "[527] He quotes Rabinath Tagore: "'Beauty is truth's smile when she beholds her own face in a mirror.'"[528]

So what does this philosophical discourse have to do with creativity?

It shows that while the domains have commonalities (see Chapters 3 and 9), they also have significant differences. Their values and assumptions can be quite different, as I keep being reminded when a group of professors get together. One of the funniest stories I ever heard was about an assessment plan: a strategy to measure whether students were learning anything. Instructors from all departments in a university were tasked with putting together such a plan. They couldn't do it. They disbanded after a year because they couldn't agree what a "fact" was.

I have several other such stories about professors, but you get the point. They are aligned with different disciplines because they believe in different ways of finding "Truth" or because they have *learned* these different ways in their training or both. In our continued examination of the Upper Right, the thing in itself, let's see what various disciplines have to say about the creative product and its relationship to beauty and truth. We'll begin with science and engineering.

Beauty and Truth in Science

The Ten Most Beautiful Scientific Experiments. In his book with the preceding title, Robert Crease asks, "What does it mean for experiments, if they can be beautiful? And what does it mean for beauty,

---

527 Goswami, *Quantum Creativity*, 50.
528 Ibid., 52.

if experiments can possess it?"[529]

He acknowledges that scientists rarely talk about such issues to lay-persons. "The social convention for researchers is to appear as objective observers of nature, and to downplay the subjective and the personal."[530] Nonetheless, amongst themselves, mathematicians and scientists talk of the "beautiful" experiment, theory, or equation. One scientist in a study said of his successful experiment,

> **It was elegant, it was simple, it was straightforward, it was pretty. The esthetics were there. I could sit down and explain how this stuff works in 1 or 2 pages. Five years ago we had 10 or 12 pages that couldn't explain it nearly as well.[531]**

Following G.H. Hardy in *A Mathematician's Apology*, Crease cites "the essential criteria for beauty in his field" as "unexpectedness, inevitability, and economy—and also depth, or how fundamental a proof is." Though a mathematical proof can qualify by these rules, a chess move cannot, says Hardy. No chess move can change the fundamentals of the exercise, but a mathematical proof can change the rules of the domain itself. [532]

During a talk in London, "nineteenth-century British physicist Michael Faraday" described candles as "'beautiful.'" He hastened to add that he meant not their aesthetic qualities but their function: "'not the best-looking thing, but the best-*acting* thing.'" Wax, wick, and flame interact "with economy" in an "intricate play of scientific principles."[533] Similarly, says Crease, "The beauty of an experiment lies in *how* it makes its elements speak . . . a beautiful experiment is one that shows something deep about the world in a way that transforms our understanding about it."[534]

---

529 Crease, *The Prism and the Pendulum*, xv.

530 Crease, *The Prism and the Pendulum*, xv.

531 Quoted in Melvin P. Shaw, "Affective Components of Scientific Creativity," in *Creativity and Affect*, ed. Melvin P. Shaw and Mark A. Runco, Creativity Research Series (Norwood, New Jersey: Ablex, 1994), 27.

532 Crease, *The Prism and the Pendulum*, xvii.

533 Ibid., xvii-xviii.

534 Ibid., xviii.

He conducted a poll in the international magazine *Physics World* to determine the ten most beautiful experiments in science. His poll was also replicated in "Weblogs and Internet discussion groups." He received about three hundred candidates and selected "the ten most frequently mentioned."[535] You may have heard of many of them, such as Eratosthenes measuring the earth's circumference, Galileo (supposedly) dropping a ball from the Leaning Tower of Pisa, and Newton breaking white light into colors by sending it through a prism. I'll summarize my favorite, the one that affected me most dramatically: Foucault's pendulum to show the rotation of the earth.

Crease narrates his boyhood experience of watching with excitement a Foucault pendulum "at the Franklin Institute in Philadelphia."

The pendulum hung—and still hangs—in the well of a main stairway. Its thin wire cable, he recalls, descended "four stories," while the "bob" at the end "glided silently back and forth over a compass dial (which has recently been replaced by a backlit globe) embedded in the floor." As the "bob swung back and forth in a straight line silently and ponderously," the line of its "swing slowly shifted to the left (clockwise) at an unchanging rate throughout the day: 9.6 degrees per hour." Crease explains the importance of this sight:

> The sign informed me that although the pendulum seemed to be changing direction, this was false . . . Instead, what the museum visitor was really seeing was the earth—and along with it the floor of the Institute building and the compass dial on the floor—turning underneath the pendulum.[536]

About "every twenty minutes or so," this pendulum "signaled its change of direction by knocking down" "one of the set of four-inch steel pegs that stood in two semicircles on the floor, tracing the outside of the dial." Crease reports his excitement as "the bob would begin to creep toward the next peg" and knock it down, "*plink!*" He adds, "Sometimes I'd just stare at the pendulum itself, trying to obey the sign and make myself see that it was *I*—and the solid floor beneath my feet—that was

---

535 Crease, *The Prism and the Pendulum*, xxi-xxii.
536 Ibid., 125-26.

moving." He never quite succeeded.[537]

The nineteenth-century French scientist Jean-Bernard-Léon Foucault first devised this experiment in his laboratory. Foucault wrote about the emotional effect of this experiment:[538]

> **Everyone who is in its presence . . . grows thoughtful and silent for a few seconds, and generally takes away a more pressing and intense feeling of our ceaseless mobility in space.**[539]

The pendulum creates a sense of wonder. Crease sums up the power of this experiment: "With Foucault's pendulum, the earth's rotation seems to become visible."[540] He adds that the pendulum reveals "a sublime beauty": "In the sublime, we feel our existence as puny and insignificant, and nature as incomprehensible and overwhelming: nature as an alien power."[541]

Beauty and Miracles. According to Penrose, these two concepts "are not unconnected." The "undoubted mathematical beauty" of "Euclidean geometry," "the extraordinary elegance of Newtonian dynamics," "the exquisite" "mathematical form of Maxwell's electromagnetism," "the supreme mathematical beauty of Einstein's general relativity" and "the structure of quantum mechanics," especially "the extraordinary mathematical elegance of the quantum-mechanical spin" seem miraculous because "they accord so well with the workings of our universe."[542]

However, Penrose warns that most aesthetic considerations are "subtle" and which mathematical trail to follow can rely on individual preference.

> **Occasionally, however, something can arise, in research into mathematical theories of the physical world, which has a much more powerful impact on such choices than mere mathematical elegance, and this is**

---

537 Crease, *The Prism and the Pendulum*, 126.

538 Ibid., 127-30.

539 Quoted in Crease, *The Prism and the Pendulum*, 130.

540 Ibid., 131.

541 Ibid., 140.

542 Penrose, *The Road to Reality*, 1038.

> what I refer to as a "miracle." [One example is] "the ' theory . . . I am
> sure that string theory and M-theory have themselves been guided by
> a great many such miracles.[543]

M–Theory does indeed seem to be both beautiful and miraculous, though in a sublime and haunting way that touches on the core of Truth. Let's look at a simpler explanation of it from a television program that contains both narrative explanation and expert testimony.[544]

According to this program, "the fervent desire of physicists" from Einstein onward has been to find "a single elegant theory which would sum up everything in the universe." In the early 1990s the explanation seemed to be *string theory*: that "matter emanated from these strings like music." Michio Kaku (City University of New York) gives a poetic explanation: "All of a sudden we realized, the universe is a symphony, and the laws of physics are harmonies of a superstring." Here is Py–thagoras' "music of the spheres"! This "string theory" seemed like the "theory of everything." Burt Ovrut (University of Pennsylvania) testifies, "It certainly did sweep us by storm. It's a beautiful, elegant, and simple theory."

But there were two problems.

First, if string theory were to explain "everything," "it would have to explain" the origin of the universe in the Big Bang. Second, there were five versions of string theory! Kaku reports, with a touch of humor, "Cynics began to say . . . It's not the theory of everything; it's the theory of nothing."

The second problem was solved by returning to an old idea that had been rejected in the 1980s: supergravity. The only difference was that string theory posited ten dimensions and supergravity, nine. With the addition of the eleventh dimension, says Ovrut, "These five string theories turned out simply to be five different manifestations of the same fundamental theory." Kaku says, "Looking down from the mountaintop . . . you could see string theory as being part of a much larger reality, the reality of the eleventh dimension."

---

543 Penrose, *The Road to Reality*, 1040-41.

544 The following explanation comes from the documentary *Parallel Universes*, including the quotes from Kaku and Ovrut and other physicists. *Parallel Universes*, documentary series, *The Universe*, 7 seasons: season 3, episode 3 (TLC/BBC, 2008).

However, with the addition of the eleventh dimension, the strings "stretched . . . and combined. The astonishing conclusion was that all the matter in the universe was connected to one vast structure: a membrane. In effect, our entire universe *is* a membrane."

This "Membrane Theory or M-Theory" appeared "so enigmatic and profound" that some physicists" believed the M should "stand for other things: *Magic—Mystery—Mother, the Mother of all strings—The Majesty of a comprehensive theory of the universe—Magical—Mystical—Madness."*

To discover whether this theory was true or not, "The scientists needed to know more about this eleventh dimension. It quickly became clear that this was a place where all the normal rules of common sense had been abandoned. For one thing, it was infinitely long but only a very small distance across." "It exists only one trillionth of a millimeter from every point in our three-dimensional world. It's closer than the clothes to your body. And yet we can't sense it." "In this mysterious membrane . . . our universe is floating."

Scientists "dived in" and tried to solve other problems by going into the eleventh dimension, and each time, they found "more and more universes. From every corner of the eleventh dimension, parallel universes came crawling out of the woodwork. . . .Some took the form of three-dimensional universes," like our own. "Others were merely sheets of energy. Then there were cylindrical and even looped membranes. In no time at all, the eleventh dimension seemed to be jam packed full of membranes."

Kaku says, "We began to ask ourselves the question, who lives in the eleventh dimension? We have intersecting membranes, we have membranes with holes in them, we have membranes that look like doughnuts or have many different kinds of doughnut holes. We're just littered with many different kinds of membranes."

"Each of these membranes was a possible other universe." Kaku explains, "In another universe, the proton may be unstable, in which case atoms would dissolve and DNA cannot form and therefore there's no intelligent life in these universes . . . Perhaps it's a universe of lightning bolts and nutrinos but no stable matter." Explains Michael Duff (University of Michigan), early advocate of supergravity, "The other universes are parallel to ours and may be quite close to ours."

No wonder that the "M" can stand for "*Magical—Mystical—Madness!"*

Could such a startling idea really be a "theory of everything"? If it were, it would have to explain the thorniest problem in cosmology, the problem called "the singularity": What caused the Big Bang?

The problem was solved during a conference in England. Neil Turok (Cambridge University), Paul Steinhardt (Princeton University), and Burt Ovrut "decided to take time out" and hop a train to London to see a play about physics: *Cophenhagen*. Ovrut explains, "We had whatever it was, an hour or so, to sit on a train and talk about these ideas."

Steinhardt makes an important point: "I think people get the wrong impression about scientists, in that they think in an orderly, rigid way, from Step 1, Step 2, to Step 3. What really happens is that often you make an imaginative leap which at the time may seem nonsensical." Turok says they "were just sitting on the train and free associating." Steinhardt says, "We had this conversation, one of us completing the sentences of the other, in which we kind of just let our imaginations go." (A scientist in another study makes the same point: "I think anyone who has ever done it will tell you that you just don't sit down and follow the scientific method."[545])

During this freewheeling conversation, Ovrut says he began to understand how the "membranes" of the parallel universes could collide to produce the Big Bang. Turok clarifies, "People tended to think of 'Branes as being flat perfect sheets, geometrical planes, but I think to us it was clear" that description of the surface was not true: "It has to ripple." Steinhardt adds that when the rippling surfaces come together, "they don't hit at exactly the same time, the same place." Ovrut adds, "So when the collision takes place, it imparts those ripples into real matter." "Parallel universes move through the eleventh dimension like waves . . . It was the ripple that went on to cause the clumps of matter after the Big Bang."

Is that why ripples and swirls form in nature? Do science and mysticism join hands at last in M-Theory?

In saying the eleventh dimension is like a "view from the mountaintop," Kaku uses a metaphor common among mystics: i.e., Moses going to the mountaintop to speak with the burning bush. He also uses a metaphor common among yogis: "Big Bangs probably take place

---

545Quoted in Shaw, "Affective Components of Scientific Creativity," 13.

all of the time . . . Our universe could be just one bubble, floating in an ocean of other bubbles." So familiar is this imagery in the East that Paramhansa Yogananda wrote a song that repeats, "I am the bubble; make me the sea."

Penrose sums up the effect of these new and controversial theories:

I am sure that string theory and M–Theory have themselves been guided by a great many

> . . . miracles. Surely one of the most important was the discovery of mirror symmetries whereby the puzzling collection of apparently quite different string theories . . . received strong indications that they could be united into one grand scheme referred to as "M" theory. These mirror symmetries acted like magic, and numbers that had previously seemed to have little to do with one another were found to be the same . . . This certainly qualifies as a miracle, in the sense that I am us- ing the term here . . . Are such apparent miracles really good guides to the correctness of an approach to physical theory? This is a deep and difficult question. I can imagine that sometimes they are, but one must be exceedingly cautious about such things.[546]

If true, however, this new theory could illuminate many ideas about how the universe acts in creative synergy with the individual will . . . how we're all connected in the membrane of strings, in Indra's Net: what Edgar Cayce calls "the Law of One." (1497–1)

In the documentary *Parallel Universes*, summarized above, a pictorial representation of the eleventh dimension looks like the long blue tun- nel that opens up in the center of the forehead when one meditates deeply! Let's reread the description of the eleventh dimension in the film: "infinitely long but only a very small distance across . . . It exists only one trillionth of a millimeter from every point in our three–dimen- sional world. It's closer than the clothes to your body. And yet we can't sense it. In this mysterious membrane . . . our universe is floating."

Mark H. Gaffney, who has studied the Gnostics (early mystical fol- lowers of Jesus), has identified imagery that exists both in their teach-

---

546 Penrose, *The Road to Reality*, 1040-41.

ings and in those of the East. He connects biblical teachings about "the gate of heaven" with the Eastern idea of the "blue bindu," the third eye that opens in the center of the forehead in deep meditation. (See Chapter 9, including the art of Goldsworthy.) Gaffney sounds as if he is referencing the eleventh dimension of the physicists when he discusses this "point of maximum focus and concentration in which duality is compressed into a singularity":

> **Although the bindu has no size, no dimensionality, and no mass, it is quite real and in the East is considered the threshold between the physical world and the spiritual domains . . . The bindu is associated with a spiritual center, located between the eyebrows, the *ajna* chakra . . . As one-pointed meditation deepens . . . the disciple begins to experience unitive states.**[547]

"Infinitely long but only a very small distance across . . . only one trillionth of a millimeter from every point in our three-dimensional world . . . closer than the clothes to your body—and yet we can't sense it." Like the swirl of a black hole or a Goldsworthy sculpture, it spirals and rotates. It is, in the words of Yogananda, "Center everywhere—circumference nowhere."

Indeed, as Penrose says, the eleventh dimension of M-Theory is a beautiful miracle. Like the Force of *Star Wars*, it surrounds us; like the "Infinite I-AM" of Coleridge, it is constantly creating new worlds. And yet we can discover it in equations! Small wonder that British physicist Sir James Jeans asked, "'Is God a mathematician?'"[548]

In fact, though physicists enjoy flashes of illumination, they testify to the burden of having to work out the mathematics. Here is what two of them said in a study: "It's a euphoria that will carry on." "Then, in doing that, you run into mathematical, technical problems that you need to solve or go crazy."[549] The documentary *Parallel Universes* depicts physicists trying again and again to make the mathematics support the vision of

---

547 Mark H. Gaffney, *Gnostic Secrets of the Naassenes: The Initiatory Teachings of the Last Supper* (Rochester, VT: Inner Traditions, 2004), 158-59.

548 Quoted in Gary E. Schwartz with William L. Simon, *The G.O.D. Experiments: How Science is Discovering God in Everything, including Us* (New York: Atria Books, 2006), 114.

549 Quoted in Shaw, "Affective Components of Scientific Creativity," 21.

five or ten universes—and succeeding, at last with eleven. Einstein was bedeviled by the math in trying to extend his special theory of relativity to a general one.

"And now," as Monty Python would say, "for something completely different."

Engineering

Engineering vs. Science. Henry Petroski claims that science describes "the world as it is" while engineering focuses on "design and development."[550] Physicists write equations and ponder whether "M-theory" is the "theory of everything." Engineers design for use.

Creativity in Engineering. Petroski describes many engaging examples of how creativity functions in engineering. One of my favorites is the lowly paper clip.

Petroski explains, "The paper clip works because its loops can be spread apart just enough to get around some papers and, when released, can spring back to grab the papers and hold them. This springing action, more than its shape per se, is what makes the paper clip work."[551]

The "springing action" was first contemplated by Greeks in the fourth century BC and gained the attention of scientist Robert Hooke, "contemporary of Newton," who as "an early advocate of the microscope" was able "to articulate the essential elements of elasticity."[552] He "discovered" that up to a point, the more we pull on something elastic like a rubber band, the more it will stretch. "Conversely, the more we stretch something elastic, the more resistance it offers to being further stretched." It is these "springing phenomena," which form the basis of "Hooke's Law:"

Heavy wire cables that support elevators in skyscrapers have a springiness that is exaggerated by the extreme length of the cable, and the

---

550 Petroski, *Invention by Design*, 2. The rest of the discussion of the paper clip follows this source.

551 Ibid., 9.

552 Ibid., 10.

bounce it produces can be unsettling to passengers if not properly taken into account in designing the elevator system.[553]

From the science of Hooke's law to the engineering of the paper clip took a few centuries. The straight pin served to keep papers together "well into the twentieth century." It took engineering creativity to furnish a more effective design.

Folding wires was not the problem; the Romans had done so to create "safety pins." The real advancement came after "American inventor John Howe" designed "a pin–making machine." The stumbling block to further development lay in the familiarity that people had with the pin and their consequent inability to imagine a different form for wire that would attach papers. Petroski explains the importance of creativity in such a situation: "the very fact that long–existing artifacts have become so familiar also means that people have adapted to any inconveniences or problems associated with their use. In fact, it is at first only the inventor or engineer, effectively acting as technological critic, who even sees anything wrong with things the way they are."[554] Then the problems become "obvious to everyone."[555]

"The problems" of using a straight pin to fasten paper were noticeable by the nineteenth century. The pin "was difficult to thread through more than a few sheets of paper; it left holes in the paper; its point could prick one's finger; it could catch extraneous papers; it bulked up piles of papers." A flurry of "paper clip patents" appeared around the turn of the century, but none have survived. Petroski observes, "This is not surprising, since as each new artifact comes on the scene it becomes an object of criticism, especially by inventors who imagine how this or that shortcoming (which, at first, only they see) can be removed, first by giving this or that leg of a paper clip a slightly different bend, turn, or twist."[556]

Ironically, the Gem design, "the one that has virtually become synonymous with 'paper clip,'" was never patented. The first known patent was "for a machine . . . for *making* paper clips." The origin of the Gem

---

553 Petroski, *Invention by Design*, 11.

554 Ibid., 15.

555 Ibid.

556 Ibid., 16.

is "believed" to have been late nineteenth–century England. Numerous attempts to revamp it, such as "the plastic–coated variety," have never been quite successful, though many inventors have tried. [557]

This is not to say that the design is perfect. Petroski says that when many documents are stacked, the paper clips add unattractive and dysfunctional bulk to one corner. Also, when the structure clips the papers, "the gem can look curiously incomplete and misaligned, with its straight end not on target to meet the loop disappearing behind the sheets." He makes an important point about creativity in engineering:

> Engineers and inventors are not so easily pleased with the object in the abstract. While they are not averse to designing things that look attractive, that is not the only criterion for elegance and beauty, which can be only skin deep. How a thing functions is where engineers begin their quest, and no object that fails to function properly can be considered truly beautiful or perfected. [558]

For instance, bridges collapse. *Time* Magazine has done a photojournalist study of "The Worst Bridge Collapses in the Past 100 Years."[559] Another example of design foiled in reality occurred with the reconstruction of the Bay Bridge connecting Oakland and San Francisco. The original structure, which had collapsed during the Loma Prieta Earthquake in 1989, had been shored up and was at last replaced, a process culminating in early 2013. Soon, however, mistakes appeared. By March the rods had begun cracking because they "had been made brittle by hydrogen" after a faulty galvanization process with zinc from a spray. "The rods were supposed to be blasted only with grit, to avoid having hydrogen contaminate the steel before it was dipped in molten zinc."[560] The next failure was bolts, welded too "firmly" to allow for "a natural

---

557 Petroski, *Invention by Design*, 18-24.

558 Ibid., 29.

559 "The Worst Bridge Collapses in the Past 100 Years," (n.d.) *Time* Photos, retrieved from http://content.time.com/time/photogallery/0,29307,1649646,00.html.

560 Jaxon Van Derberken, "Caltrans Documents Tell of Bay Bridge Woes," *San Francisco Chronicle*, June 22, 2013, http://www.sfgate.com/default/article/Caltrans-documents-tell-of-Bay-Bridge-woes-4615826.php.

expansion of the bicycle path that happens in hot weather."[561] Finally, by February 2014 the bridge began to leak. "'That's a problem, a big problem,' said Lisa Thomas, a metallurgical engineer who studies material failure at a laboratory in Berkeley and analyzed bridge rods that snapped last year. 'They want it to last 150 years, but with water coming in, something is going to corrode until it's too thin and weak.'"[562]

The pure scientist can speculate on the origin and results of the Big Bang; the engineer is concerned about use. For this reason ideas can succeed or fail because of socio–cultural factors. Petroski gives the example of the fax machine,[563] which began with an 1843 patent and caught the interest of Edison himself. Other patents between 1902 and 1940 refined the first crude idea. By the 1950s Western Union was selling "Desk–Fax units" that could send and receive telegrams. By the 1970s this technology had combined with a Telex that could send and receive messages over phone lines.

So why did the fax machine, such a ubiquitous instrument today, take so long to become popular? The answer lies with AT&T, which owned the phone lines and was disinterested in this new technology. "Social and cultural" factors had to arise to make the public interested: the growth of Fed–Ex, the use of photocopiers, the rise of personal computers, and the subsequent dissatisfaction with "snail mail." In addition, Japanese research and development completed the picture by devising new and better equipment at an affordable cost. The fax machines needed to have one universal design to function in an exchange of information.

Petroski observes that universality of design is rarely an outcome in engineering:

> **Unlike problems in mathematics, which practically always have a unique answer, a single problem in engineering can have many different solu-**

---

561 Jaxon Van Derberken, "Bolts along Bay Bridge Bike Path Fail," *San Francisco Chronicle*, May 29, 2013, http://www.sfgate.com/default/article/Bolts-along-Bay-Bridge-bike-path-fail-4555354.php.

562 Jaxon Van Derberken, "Bay Bridge's New Problem: Leaks," *San Francisco Chronicle*, February 8, 2014, http://www.sfgate.com/default/article/Bay-Bridge-s-new-problem-leaks-5217783.php.

563 The discussion of the fax machine appears in Petroski, *Invention by Design*, 104-19.

tions. Thus, there are many different ways of providing portable power for electronic devices, and hence we have a plethora of batteries with different physical sizes and configurations, not to mention voltage output. Though this can be a great annoyance when trying to buy replacement batteries for a portable calculator, it is unlikely that the situation could be remedied, for it is unreasonable to require the various successful calculator companies to redesign their products around a single battery.[564]

So creativity in engineering depends on the optimum design for use. While not averse to beauty, the engineer seeks truth: "conformity to fact or actuality,"[565] with design and development adjusted to the social context as well as to the ultimate function. A design may work theoretically, yet Petroski observes that "real materials and structures seldom occur in conditions as pure as mathematics. Real materials have variations and imperfections that make strength meaningful only in some statistical sense."[566]

The engineer also seeks truth as "fidelity to an original or standard,"[567] adhering to time-honored principles and correcting errors by learning from mistakes in the past. Petroski remarks,

Everyone makes mistakes, even geniuses like Galileo. Engineers must always be alert for what they may be oversimplifying and overlooking or to what conclusions they may be jumping. Because errors in engineering can have disastrous consequences, it is especially important for engineers to be reflective and alert in their design and analysis. One way of being better prepared for catching one's own errors is to be familiar with the kinds of mistakes that have been made by others, whether three centuries ago or yesterday.[568]

Also important is " the human factor" or "ergonomics, endeavors to make the interface between a person and a piece of technology as

564 Petroski, *Invention by Design*, 112.

565 *The American Heritage Dictionary*, fourth edition.

566 Petroski, *Invention by Design*, 63.

567 *The American Heritage Dictionary*, fourth edition.

568 Petroski, *Invention by Design*, 63.

logical, safe, comfortable, and friendly as possible."[569] In "the cockpit of an airplane," "the dials, switches, levers, buttons, and other meters and controls have distinctly different looks and feels" so that the pilot will not become confused and flip the wrong switch. In the first nuclear power plants, operator mistakes resulted because "the components on a control console" had been designed to match rather than "to have distinguishing features."[570]

Engineering: The True, the Beautiful, the Good? Can engineering be beautiful as well? To answer this question, we need only look at the Golden Gate Bridge.

Courtesy of Wikimedia Commons, photo by Rich Niewiroski Jr.
http://www.projectrich.com/gallery

---

569 Petroski, *Invention by Design*, 137.
570 Ibid.

A breathtaking span of 1.7 miles, towering 726 feet above the water,[571] serving 40 million crossings a year,[572] it is the icon of San Francisco, its orange vermillion[573] arch arising from cold mists above a sapphire bay dotted with white sails.[574] Herb Caen rhapsodized about it thus in May 1958: "The mystical structure, with its perfect amalgam of delicacy and power, exerts an uncanny effect. Its efficiency cannot conceal the art-istry. There is heart there, and soul. It is an object to be contemplated for hours"[575] Carl Nolte said, in commemoration of its 75th anniversary in May 2012,

> The Golden Gate Bridge has everything: good looks, a gorgeous setting, a distinct color, a famous city on one side and steep, rolling hills on the other. It has style and sweeping curves. It appears and disappears in the fog, it has myths and legends and, sometimes, a fatal attraction.[576]

People go there to die.
Edward Guthman writes about this "lethal beauty"[577] in lyrical prose:

> On those halcyon days when fog threads the bridge's harp strings and suspension cables, when clouds settle over the East Bay hills and the sun catches diamonds in the bay, this greatest of vistas exhibits itself proudly: tawny hills of Marin, shimmering bulk of Angel Island, raw beacon of Alcatraz and the lazy, Mediterranean contours of San Francisco.
>
> This is the view, on a good day, that greets the suicide before he jumps—a panorama enthralling in its harmony of land, sea, and sky. Even when the cooling fog blunts the view, the vast majority of jumpers take

---

571 "Construction Data," accessed May 12, 2014, http://goldengatebridge.org/research/factsGGBDesign.php, 1-2.

572 Golden Gate Bridge—Facts—Figures, accessed May 12, 2014, http://gocalifornia.about.com/cs/sanfrancisco/a/ggbridge_3.htm.

573 Ibid.

574 Celia Kuppersmith, General Director for the Golden Gate Bridge District, pronounced it "'truly known around the world as an icon of grace and beauty'" (quoted in Nolte "Golden Gate Bridge: Monument, Work of Art, Star").

575 In other words: Great quotes on the gate.

576 Nolte, "Golden Gate Bridge: Monument, Work of Art, Star."

577 *Lethal Beauty*, a descriptor of the bridge, is the name of a 7-part series in the *San Francisco Chronicle*, in October-November 2005, available at www.sfgate.com.

their last step facing east instead of west toward the Pacific.

The Golden Gate Bridge is the world's No. 1 suicide magnet, in part because it makes suicide so easy. People jump and kill themselves there, an average of 19 a year.[578]

It is a sublime death, they imagine—jumping, bracketed by views of azure sky and sea, tumbling like Icarus from heaven when his wings melted too close to the sun. Guthman speculates, "Some dive expecting not obscurity or oblivion but a kind of grace—a welcoming body of water that inducts the jumper into nature."[579]

It is, in fact, a terrible death.

Guthman describes it:

Once a person dives, depending on where he or she jumps, the body plummets 240 to 250 feet in four seconds, traveling about 75 mph, and hits the water with the force of a speeding truck meeting a concrete building. Some die instantly from extensive internal injuries; others drown in their own blood.

The jump is fatal 98 percent of the time.[580]

More than 1,250 perished between statistics gathered in 2005 and the opening of the bridge in 1937.[581] Those who survive remain paralyzed and broken.

So here is the paradox: a bridge designed for use and beauty, the longest span in the world at its completion and the seventh-longest today,[582] an "engineering marvel"[583] built to sustain winds of 60 mph,[584] known all over the world, has become a "fatal attraction." Over a thousand people have

---

578 *Lethal Beauty*: The Allure, part 1, paragraphs 1-3.

579 Ibid., part 1, paragraph 4.

580 Ibid., part 1, paragraphs 6-7.

581 Carolyne Zinko, "Three Options Offered for Suicide Barrier," *San Francisco Chronicle*, May 24, 2007. Retrieved from http://www.sfgate.com/default/article/Three-options-offered-for-bridge-suicide-barrier-2592326.php.

582 Golden Gate Bridge——Facts——Figures, accessed May 12, 2014, http://gocalifornia.about.com/cs/sanfrancisco/a/ggbridge_3.htm. The bridge opened in 1937 and was the longest until the construction of the Verrazano Narrows Bridge in New York in 1964.

583 Golden gate bridge——facts——figures, http://gocalifornia.about.com/cs/sanfrancisco/a/ggbridge _4htm.

584 Ibid.

jumped already, and more will do so unless a suicide barrier stops them.

But what is the optimum design for such a barrier? John King calls the engineering challenge of such a structure "daunting": it would need to "be formidable enough to stop or slow down people who want to leap off the edge–but not so formidable that it adds dangerous stress to a structure that on three occasions was closed because of high winds." In 1951 the most dramatic incident occurred when "the deck whipped up and down erratically" in 70–mph winds and "swayed 12 feet in either direction." Since then "trusses below the deck" were added to "stiffen" it, and "a planned $160 million retrofit . . . includes design features, such as alterations to the western railing, that will allow wind to flow through the structure more fully."[585] Any creative solution to thwarting the jumpers would need to address the problem of high winds.

Other concerns exist as well: cost, effectiveness, and aesthetics.[586] A barrier "would cost between $15 million and $25 million," and the feasibility study would cost "$2 million." The barrier must be high enough to discourage suicides yet low enough not to block the sightlines of pedestrians and motorists. It must address the sentiments of "preservationists" concerned with beauty: "the quality that gives pleasure to the mind or senses and is associated with such properties as harmony of form or color, excellence of artistry."[587] By May 27, 2007, three possible designs had been chosen.[588] In October 2008 it was announced that voters in a bridge district poll had chosen, by 49.9%, the design of a net twenty feet below the bridge. Such a design could break the fall of a jumper before death but not spoil the beauty of the span.[589] In May 2010 the net design was approved.[590] However, as of February 25, 2014,

---

585 John King, "Lethal Beauty: The Engineering Challenge: A Suicide Barrier Must Be Effective and Safe," Part 6 of a 7-part series, "Lethal Beauty," *San Francisco Chronicle*, November 4, 2005, A-1, accessed April 5, 2014, http://www.sfgate.com/default/article/LETHAL-BEAUTY-THE-ENGINEERING-CHALLENGE-A-2562115.php, paragraphs 5-7.

586 The rest of the information in this paragraph comes from J. King.

587 *The American Heritage Dictionary*, fourth edition.

588 Zinko, "Three Options Offered for Suicide Barrier," A-14.

589 Michael Cabanatuan, "Net Seems Likelier for Bridge Suicide Barrier," *San Francisco Chronicle*, October 4, 2008, B-1.

590 Janet Frishberg, "Suicide Net Needed on Gold Gate Bridge," *San Francisco Chronicle*, June 7, 2013. http://www.sfgate.com/default/article/Suicide-net-needed-on-Golden-Gate-Bridge-3584667.php.

funding had yet to be found for the safety net. The death count at this point was over 1600, with forty-six perishing in 2013.[591]

So as of this writing in March 2014, the Golden Gate Bridge, designed for the True and the Beautiful, has still not been redesigned for the Good: deterring suicides.

Pure Engineering as an Example of Genius. The sublime example of creativity in engineering is, of course, Leonardo da Vinci, who filled his notebooks with ideas. Some of those included are

> *"A braking device applied to a wheel"* (1478);
> A *"device for stretching a bow and belt for conveying buckets"* (1478);
> *"Studies for a flying machine and other mechanisms"* (c. 1480);
> *"Technological studies,"* including a *"device similar to a drill and device for making screws* (c. 1489–1490);
> A *"bellows-operated machine for raising water and man drawing an armillary sphere with perspectograph"* (c. 1480);
> A *sheet of studies on artificial flight* with a *sketch of a parachute* (1480);
> *Systems of locks for river navigation* (c. 1480–1482);
> *Devices for fabricating concave mirrors* (c. 1478–1480);
> *System of physiological printing* (sage leaf), (1508–1510);
> *Machine gun* (1480–1482);
> *Machine for excavating a channel* (c. 1503).[592]

Some of his inventions included machines for parties hosted by his patron, Ludovico ("The Moor") Sforza, Grand Duke of Milan. Others were centuries ahead of their time: inventions that could not be built by the materials of the fifteenth century. As well as being fascinated by the dynamic swirls of energy common in nature (Chapter 9), he was also interested in the anatomy of movement, whether the joints of horses or the circulation of arteries into the heart. His notebooks contain many studies for the mammoth horse designed to honor Francesco Sforza,[593] father of Ludovico. For over ten years Leonardo drew anatomy studies

---

591 Vivian Ho, "Golden Gate Suicides Hit Record High——46," *San Francisco Chronicle*, February 25, 2014, http://www.sfgate.com/default/article/Golden-Gate-Bridge-suicides-hit-record-high-46-5263870.php.

592 Pedretti, *Leonardo da Vinci*, 266-70, 290-91, 354-63. These are just **some** examples!

593 Some of the drawings are reproduced in Pedretti, *Leonardo da Vinci*, 284-87.

and planned the statue. Gelb describes the eventual model, "twenty-four feet high":

> Vasari wrote that "there was never a more beautiful thing or more superb." Leonardo calculated that casting this masterpiece would require more than eighty tons of melted bronze. The bronze, unfortunately, was not forthcoming, as Ludovico needed it to build cannons to stave off invaders. He failed, and in 1499 the French overwhelmed Milan and drove Sforza into exile. In a historical act of bad taste and barbarism that ranks with the Ottoman army's blowing the nose off the Sphinx, and the Venetian fleet's landing a mortar projectile on the Pantheon, the French archers destroyed the model horse by using it for target practice.[594]

Like his flying machines, another great project of Leonardo's came to nothing. Yet he remains the example of the universal genius, master of science and engineering, art and philosophy. Endlessly curious, he pondered nature and experimented with art. His notebooks show that he learned by drawing. In him *Creative Synergy* means a fusion of all the talents and disciplines: anatomy studies furnishing the core of art, sketched faces divided with the Golden Ratio, flowers exploding with the swirls of natural energy.

Science vs. Art. Crease ponders the difference between science and art with "the Beethoven–Newton comparison."

> The usual argument contrasts the two, claiming that the products of science are inevitable but that those of the arts are not. The underlying assumption is that the structure of the world investigated by science is prefigured, and scientists work toward uncovering that already-existing structure . . . Artists, on the hand, are fully responsible for the overall structure of their works . . . While scientists can teach their work to others, artists produce *original* works, the secret of whose creation is unknown and unknowable.[595]

---

594 Michael J. Gelb, *How to Think Like Leonardo da Vinci: Seven Steps to Genius Every Day* (New York: Delacorte, 1998), 30-31.

595 Crease, *The Prism and the Pendulum*, 54-55.

However, Owen Gingerich has challenged this view. He argues that the structure of a scientific theory, rather than being inevitable, is a creative construct that might have been assembled more than one way. Crease explains this viewpoint:

> The Newtonian world system is not inevitable, he argued, for alternative explanations for celestial phenomena, in the form of Kepler's laws, can be derived from other sources, such as conservation laws. Gingerich's assertion of an alternative highlights the role of imagination and creativity in, and thus the singularity of, Newton's achievement. "Newton's *Principia* is a personal achievement that places him in the same creative class as Beethoven or Shakespeare," he concluded.[596]

Beethoven and Newton: is their creativity similar—or different? These musings are so complex that we will need to continue them in another chapter as we follow the Good, the Beautiful, and the True into the arts.

---

596 Crease, *The Prism and the Pendulum*, 54.

Exercises

1. Explain a "beautiful" experiment not summarized in this book. What makes it beautiful?
2. Have you ever seen a Foucault pendulum? If so, explain the experience.
3. Have you heard of "string theory" or "M-Theory" before? Explain what you have heard, or do a bit more research on it.
4. Explain an engineering problem not mentioned in this book.
5. Read more about the Golden Gate Bridge and/or the proposed suicide barrier. (Go to www.sfgate.com, search with the term, "Golden Gate Bridge.") A full report on the barriers is posted at http://www.ggbsuicidebarrier.org/.) Write a report on what you have read. If you are an engineer, provide your special expertise in analyzing and evaluating some of this material.
6. What else do you know about Leonardo? Explain.
7. List some of the puzzling or unclear ideas in Chapter 10. Ask questions about them.
8. Explain what you think is most important in Chapter 10.
9. React to some of the ideas in Chapter 10. Debate, support, analyze, and/or reflect.
10. Give evidence from your own life or background experience about the ideas in Chapter 10. (Don't repeat what you have written in another exercise.)

Synergistic Interlude: "Prometheus"

Courtesy of Wikimedia Commons,
photo by Rich Niewiroski Jr.
http://www.projectrich.com/gallery

The Titan Prometheus enraged Zeus by giving fire to mankind. Now humanity had the means of warmth, but also the means of invention, with a creative fire that could cause many products of invention, from breastplates and weapons to the arts of sculpture, painting, and music.

As a result of sharing the creativity and fire known only to the gods, Prometheus was chained to a rock, where each day an eagle gnawed his liver. At night the liver grew back so the torment could begin the following dawn.

Prometheus was not unchained until Hercules came to aid him, many decades later.

Questions to Ponder

1. What are the combinations of opposites in this myth?

2. What does this myth have to say about the heights and depths of creativity?

3. What do you think the fire stolen from Zeus represents?

4. What do you think the gnawing of the liver represents?

5. How does this story depict the myth of the tortured or suffering artist?

11

The Aesthetic Object or "Thing in Itself": Creativity in the Upper Right, Part 3: The Arts

Beauty

So we have seen that beauty can reside in math, science, and engineering. In all of these domains the Beautiful dwells with the True. What is simple and elegant must also express what is fundamentally true about the nature of the universe, whether we are discussing M–Theory or Foucault's pendulum. In engineering the Beautiful is subordinated to the Good and True. The orange vermillion arch of the Golden Gate Bridge is known throughout the world, but an engineer would not be impressed with its sweeping vistas if it were closed to cars and pedestrians. Its Truth lies in its adherence to engineering principles; its Goodness lies both in its aesthetic sublimity, which uplifts the spirit, and in its redesign to avoid the lure of suicides.

How do the "Big Three" manifest differently in the arts? We now turn to the domain of aesthetics.[597]

---

597 Definition provided, as usually, by the fourth edition of *The American Heritage Dictionary*.

Aesthetics

Aesthetics: "1. the branch of philosophy that deals with the nature and expression of beauty, as in the fine arts." "2. The study of the psychological responses to beauty and artistic experiences." "3. A conception of what is artistically valid or beautiful." "4. An artistically beautiful or pleasing experience."

What *is* beauty? Swami Kriyananda relates an anecdote that increases the mystery rather than answering the question:

> The great Indian mystic, Sri Ramakrishna, had his first experience of ecstasy when, as a young man, he was watching a flight of geese fly against the background of a grey sky. The beauty of the scene moved him so deeply that he lost all sense of outer reality, and his mind soared into a heaven of inner bliss.[598]

What moved him? Was it the contrast of colors? The contrast of stasis and movement? The sense of soaring into realms above?

Is "beauty" a universal? The author of a prominent text in *Introduction to Psychology* reminds us that the concept is culture–specific: in Niger, Africa, a woman is beautiful if she is fat enough![599] *The American Heritage Dictionary*, fourth edition, defines *beauty* as "The quality that gives pleasure to the mind or senses and is associated with such properties as harmony of form or color, excellence of artistry, truthfulness, and originality." Such a description seems subjective; and, in fact, Wilber relates beauty to the Upper Left quadrant as one of "The Big Three." He says that "Beauty is in the "I" of the Beholder": what is beautiful to me may not be to you. One of us may stand rapt in front of Renaissance art; another may get lost, transfixed, in the geometric swirls of modernist or postmodernist painting. Each of us has a different "psychological response" or "artistically pleasing experience."

The following diagram is reproduced from Chapter 4:

---

598 Kriyananda, *Art as a Hidden Message: A Guide to Self-Realization*, 86.

599 Rod Plotnik, *Introduction to Psychology*, 6th ed. (Pacific Grove, California: Wadsworth-Thomson, 2002), 603.

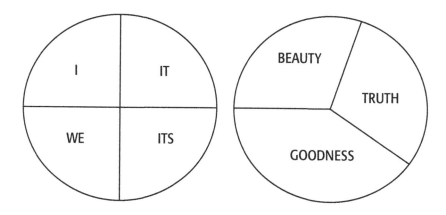

Figure 3: The Four Quadrants and Their Relationship to "The Big Three"

As demonstrated in this figure, then, beauty would be a subjective response rather than objective thing–in–itself. *Are* some of us more susceptible to beauty than others? According to Seligman and Peterson of the Positive Psychology Movement, those of us prone to "peak experiences" are more likely to feel the awe, wonder, or transcendence associated with an appreciation of beauty. The peak experience, as defined by Abraham Maslow, is the exultation or joy we feel when we are actualizing our potential and feel oneness with something greater than ourselves. It happens to people who have had their deficiency needs met (physiological, safety, belongingness, and esteem). (See the Introduction.)[600] Edgar Cayce attributes a susceptibility to beauty to interlife sojourns in the vicinity of Venus.[601] In these two cases the response to beauty is subjective, as Wilber implies.

However, Penrose seems to believe beauty is in some sense objective. He first remarks on what Wilber calls "The Big Three": "Mathematics is crucially concerned with the particular ideal of *Truth*. Plato himself would have insisted that there are two other fundamental ideals, namely that of the *Beautiful* and that of the *Good*."[602] However, unlike

---

600 Seligman and Peterson, *Character Strengths and Virtues*, 543-44.

601 See, for example, Reading 255-5.

602 Penrose, *The Road to Reality*, 22.

Wilber, who posits Truth as a function of the Upper Right and Beauty as a function of the Upper Left, Penrose views Beauty as allied with Truth in the higher realms of math and science. He says, "It is my opinion that there is no denying the value of such aesthetic considerations, and they play a fundamentally important role in the selection of plausible proposals for new theories of fundamental physics." However, he admits, "The difficulty with aesthetic judgments, in general, is that they tend to be very subjective."[603] He adds a cautionary note: "We can see many examples throughout history, where a beautiful mathematical scheme has seemed, at first, to provide a revolutionary new way to discover Nature's secrets, yet where these initial hopes have not been realized—at least, not in the way originally anticipated."[604] He gives a specific example: "What makes string theory so difficult to assess dispassionately is that it gains its support and chooses its directions of development almost entirely from aesthetic judgments guided by mathematical desiderata."[605]

Does beauty in math and the sciences differ from beauty in art? Do mathematicians and scientists have something more universal and objective in mind than the dictionary definition would suggest? If so, why does Penrose say that "aesthetic judgments" are "subjective"?

It is my contention that, to some degree, aesthetic principles are universal.

Jackson Pollock, painted by walking around a canvas and splattering paint, so why do so many of us find his works beautiful? They have been found to contain precise mathematical ratios.[606] In the arts, while tastes differ, the greatest works have universal appeal.

While in Florence, I saw a work that causes all who view it fall under its spell.

If you go to see it yourself, you will walk down a long corridor. Along the wall as you approach, you will view photographs of others who have seen it earlier. You will see wondering faces: children's mouths rounding to an *O*, mothers pointing to direct their gaze.

---

603 Penrose, *The Road to Reality*, 1014.

604 Ibid., 1015.

605 Ibid., 888.

606 The Golden Rectangle and Number 5, 1948, Jackson Pollock.

At last you will enter a circle under a high cupola. If you are like me, you will draw a sharp breath.

No photograph can do him justice.

He dominates his space. Each muscle and vein delineated, he gazes fiercely ahead, poised, ready to meet the challenge of Goliath. He is the spirit of Florence and the Spirit of all times. No *David* by any other sculptor can compare to him for beauty, for energy, for power.

Courtesy of Wikimedia Commons

Why is Michelangelo's *David* universally acknowledged as a great statue? Following are a few principles that I consider universal, principles that may help us answer that question.

A Universal Principle: Energy

Swami Kriyananda says, "The *sine qua non* of greatness in every form, whether artistic or human, is energy . . . For a strong flow of energy, like the flow of electricity in a copper wire, creates a magnetic field that actually attracts inspiration to itself."[607]

Think of a favorite movie, a favorite book, a favorite song or singer, a favorite performance or work of art. Chances are, you are responding to the energy. One of my favorites is Shakespeare's inimitable Falstaff, with his "continuous high spirits," his "charisma," a character who is "not only witty in himself but the cause of wit in other men."[608] Falstaff, inimitable Falstaff, equipped for war with a bottle of sack in his holster, evading an actual encounter by falling down and pretending to be dead! Bloom calls him "sublime": "sublime pathos, potential, the drive for life, more life, at every and any cost."[609] Shakespeare's plays are alive with such characters, brimming over with life and energy. Even his greatest villains, like Iago, captivate us because of their mythic diabolism, the power of their hatred and evil. Swami Kriyananda, no friend to evil, remarks, "The villainy of Shakespeare's Iago suggests an almost primal force."[610]

For energy in music, we can't get any better than Beethoven's *Fifth Symphony* and that perennial Fourth of July staple, Tchaikovsky's *1812 Overture*, which ends with the explosion of cannons. In the music of the Beatles or the Doors there is a charisma, a magnetism lacking in the performances of other musicians. Quieter music such as that of Enya also has its own captivating power. Swami Kriyananda sums up the main point: "In every case, it is *energy* that makes possible vital expression in the arts."[611] In fact, he says, "It takes energy to produce good work of any kind."[612]

---

607 Kriyananda, *Art as a Hidden Message*, 147-48.

608 Bloom, *Genius*, 22.

609 Ibid.

610 Kriyananda, *Art as a Hidden Message*, 149.

611 Ibid.

612 Kriyananda, *Space, Light, and Harmony*, 133.

A Universal Principle: Juxtaposition and Contrast

Throughout the arts, juxtaposition and contrast provide aesthetic experiences that are pleasing. With juxtaposition, two similar cases or instances are presented together; with contrast, their differences are made apparent. The effect differs, depending on the intent of the artist. In some cases the symmetry is pleasing; in others, the similarity–within–a–difference provides irony.

Michelangelo's *David* embodies such contrasts. His hands are enormous, the hands of a Maker, yet one of them grasps the sling that reminds us of his vulnerability. He now is a giant who once faced a giant. He is a man—every vein standing out in definition—yet his gaze is godly. He knows his task; no one can deter him. Unlike the *Davids* of other masters, he is caught at the moment of decision. No head of Goliath is at his feet; he rests, in stasis about to take motion, in strength along with calmness, every muscle flexed, his face calm and determined, his stance relaxed but sure, his fate given up to God and his every lineament prepared to let that force flow through him and use his form as it will. He abides in the presence of his fate while he yet is about to determine it. He is perfect rest and action, receptivity and will.

For another example, let's return to the couplet[613] quoted in Chapter 9:

> **These set the head, and those divide the hair,**
> **Some fold the sleeve, while others plait the gown.**
> **(*Rape of the Lock* (1712), Canto I, ll.146-147)**

We have already noted the symmetry of the grammatical phrases (called parallelism):

these	those	some	others
set the head	divide the hair	fold the sleeve	plait the gown.

This couplet attains its power not only through balance but also

---

613 The heroic couplet, a staple of eighteenth-century poetry, consists of two lines of rhymed iambic pentameter.

through contrast. Note that the two halves of the line contrast as well as balance: "these" are doing one thing, and "those" are doing another. Balance and contrast around the central pause of the line (called the *caesura*) was a principle of eighteenth-century poetry.

The master of contrasts (as in other things) is, of course, Shakespeare, who gives us the gravedigger's maudlin and gruesome humor in *Hamlet* and the drunken porter answering the door in *Macbeth*. In both cases the genre is tragedy and the mood is somber; some deaths have occurred and more are to come; evil is ascendant in a vulnerable society; yet the tragic action pauses for a bit of vulgar humor voiced by lower-class characters. Such oppositions convey the bittersweet mixture of vales and peaks that make up our experience.

This principle is also crucial to film editing. Director Martin Scorsese talks about "creating an emotional impact in the audience by intercutting two shots that are not related to each other." [614] A famous example of this principle, usually called cross-cutting, is the baptism scene near the end of Francis Ford Coppola's *The Godfather*. While Michael Corleone stands at the baptismal font and promises to abjure Satan and all his ways, the scene cross-cuts several times to violent and bloody murders being executed at Michael's command.

All the greatest art carries such a tension of opposites. It looks two ways at once like Janus, the god of the doorways.[615] It is a magical synthesis, a manifestation of the primary process operating in dreams to fuse unlikely images into surprising unities.[616]

A Universal Principle: Pattern Recognition

Another universal aesthetic principle is pattern recognition. The artist includes patterns; the work is enriched by them; the audience recognizes them and feels pleasure. Some of this process is unconscious. The artist may *feel* that a certain line, chord, or word is right without being able to articulate why. The audience may *feel* that the structure

---

614 *The Cutting Edge: The Magic of Movie Editing*, directed by Wendy Apple, Starz Encore Entertainment, ATCEP, Inc., Production, in association with ACE, produced by NHK and the BBC, 2004.

615 Rothenberg, "The Process of Janusian Thinking in Creativity."

616 Arieti, *Creativity.*

of a work gives pleasure without being able to explain the underlying pattern that provides awe or closure.

Howard Gardner says that some mathematicians are interested in music because both domains depend upon patterns.[617] An example would be the fugue, a mathematically inclined form popular during the baroque period. In this type of music an exposition or basic melody is stated, and then the composer plays with it, transposing it to other keys, answering it in a voice that is similar but different. Again we have juxtaposition and contrast, here called point and counterpoint. In fact, the mathematics–music analogy was popular during the baroque period, especially in the notion of "the music of the spheres," the idea that as the planets turn in space, they form a sweet and harmonious choir of notes.

This analogy is less than perfect, though. One musician who read this manuscript said that in music, a feeling for harmony is more important than an enjoyment of mathematical–logical patterning.[618] Gardner, qualifying the connection between the two domains, says that the attraction doesn't work both ways: musicians don't regularly feel an affinity for mathematics.[619] He also believes that the connection appears chiefly in mathematicians who like classical music,[620] such as Einstein with his violin.

In discussing Gödel's announcement of his Incompleteness Theorem, Rebecca Goldstein draws an analogy between math and painting. His theory, she says, "was the mathematical analogue to a painting representing the nature of beauty itself."[621] What on earth does she mean? She means that it is simple and fundamental, a sort of Platonic Form—yet it has far-ranging implications.

The Incompleteness Theorem merely states that "'propositions . . . may be really contextually [materially] true but unprovable in the formal system of classical mathematics.'"[622] Goldstein calls this statement

---

617 Gardner, *Intelligence Reframed*, 103.

618 Harry Paine, personal communication, April, 2007.

619 Gardner, *Intelligence Reframed*, 103.

620 Ibid., 104.

621 Rebecca Goldstein, *Incompleteness: The Proof and Paradox of Kurt Gödel*, Great Discoveries Series (New York: Norton, 2005), 157, 156.

622 Quoted in Goldstein, *Incompleteness*, 155-56.

"one of the most astounding pieces of mathematical reasoning ever produced, astounding both in the simplicity of its main strategy and in the complexity of its details." She then compares it to music, "a thoroughly ordered blending of several layers of 'voices', both mathematical and metamathematical, counterpoint merging into harmonic chords never before heard." She cites Ernest Nagel and James R. Newman, who call the proof "'an amazing intellectual symphony.'" She adds, "It must have been an extraordinarily exhilarating experience to have produced such mathematical music, especially since it is mathematics that sings, at least in the ear of its composer, of his beloved Platonism."[623]

There are other commonalities between mathematics and painting. We have discussed the Golden Ratio (Chapter 9). In the new science of stylometrics, painting can be reduced to fractals, repeating patterns of parts and wholes that can then be reduced to mathematical ratios. Richard Taylor (University of Oregon) identified the style of Jackson Pollock, famous for his technique of dashing around a canvas and dripping paint, as a fractal ratio of 1.4 in his early work and 1.7 in his later work. By contrast, fractals in nature include the "pulmonary system" at 1.6 and fern leaves at 1.8. During a phone interview Taylor made this observation about mathematics and art:

People often ask me, 'Why would you bring mathematics in to look at art?' My response is, 'Well, why not?' When I got into it, I didn't realize how close math and art are, but in retrospect, it's pretty clear. Both mathematics and art are all about pattern. I mean, it would be unusual that you would not apply mathematical analysis to the question.[624]

Here, again, is transposition between mathematics and art. But the map, as we hear so often, is not the territory. And the analogy is not the reality. The arts may share a common creative base with the sciences (see Chapters 3 and 9), but there are significant differences in the rules of the domains. Let's examine a few of them.

---

623 The above quotes are from Goldstein, *Incompleteness*, 156.

624 Daniel Rockmore, "The Style of Numbers behind a Number of Styles," *Chronicle of Higher Education*, June 9, 2006, B11.

The Arts in General

Paul Oskar Kristeller reminds us that a "creative" work of art must be more than original:

> Originality as such does not assure the excellence of a work of art, or for that matter, of any human product. In the field of the arts, there are many works that are quite original but not especially good, and there are works of limited originality that attain a high degree of artistic quality.[625]

He then enumerates "criteria other than originality that may be used to judge the excellence of a work of art":

> beauty, form, style, imitation of nature and of previous works of art, or of intelligible essences, good taste, human relevance, emotional power, truthfulness, moral and social consciousness, playfulness, usefulness, entertainment, craftsmanship, and many other features.[626]

Which work of art can you think of that has these qualities? Which does not?

In this chapter, as elsewhere in the book, I'll share a few of my favorites.

Painting

Painting works with the elements of composition. As listed in *Wickipedia*,[627] they are familiar to any undergraduate taking humanities or art appreciation:

- Line—the visual path that enables the eye to move within the piece

---

625 Paul Oskar Kristeller, "'Creativity'" and 'Tradition,'" *Journal of the History of Ideas,* 44, no. 1 (January March 1983), 110.

626 Ibid.

627 *Elements of Composition*, http://en.wikipedia.org/wiki/Composition_(visual_arts), retrieved April 11, 2007.

- Shape—areas defined by edges within the piece, whether geometric or organic
- Tone—the lights, midtones and darks throughout the piece
- Texture—surface qualities which translate into tactile illusions
- Color—hues with their various value and intensities
- Direction—visual routes which take vertical, horizontal, or diagonal paths
- Size—the relative dimensions and proportions of images or shapes to one another.

In addition to these visual elements, the artist uses other "primary elements":

- The area within the picture used for the illustration
- The perspective, relating to spatial arrangements of objects within a picture, creating depth of field or giving the illusion of dimension or depth on a two–dimensional surface
- The line or direction followed by the viewer's eye when they [sic] observe the image
- The value, or degree of lightness and darkness, used within the picture.

The creativity of the artist determines how these elements will combine in a form both original and apt. The *Wikipedia* entry reminds us that "The artist determines what the points of focus of the art will be, and composes the work accordingly. The eyes of the viewer will then tend to linger over these points of focus. The illustration can be arranged in a harmonious whole that works together to produce a statement."

As an illustration I'd like to present Botticelli's *La Primavera* (1482). This painting has always been one of my favorites, but when I saw the real work as opposed to a reproduction, I was astonished at the delicate textures of the brushstrokes and the vivid hues of the reds and greens. In my analysis I will quote partially from a journal entry I made on August 3, 2005, and partially from my memory of having once taught a humanities course. Much of the symbolism was explained by a Florentine guide whose name I did not catch.

The principal focus of the painting is *La Primavera* herself, archetype of

Google Art Project, courtesy of Wikimedia Commons

the spring. In true Renaissance fusion[628] she exhibits the iconography of both Venus and Madonna. She is pregnant, her hand raised in a gesture of blessing like the Virgin's, but over her hovers not a Christ Child but a Cupid. To the left the three Graces dance, and the Cupid is about to wound the only one that is not pregnant. She is gazing longingly at a youth garbed as Hermes: a depiction of Giuliano Medici, who died young. Note that our eyes travel from her to him, partially because of the red repeated in their draperies and partially because of the sight lines from Cupid's arrow.

To the right Flora is being grasped by a lustful goblin, and just to their left is the result: a pregnant Flora strewing flowers. In Botticelli's original, the green leaves and pink blossoms have an exquisite raised texture, their contrasting values of light and dark hues repeated in the gowns of the ladies and the dark of the background.

As well as being an allegory of spring, this painting represents the

628 During the Renaissance, Christian symbolism from the Middle Ages, such as the ubiquitous Madonna and Child, was reinforced or replaced by imagery from pagan Greece and Rome.

blessings of Florence under the rule of the Medici. Giuliano on the left plucks the fruit of Medici rule, symbolizing protection from the dark clouds that threaten in the background. Pregnant Flora strews flowers that represent not only the Renaissance but also the rebirth of Florence with Medici influence. Zephyr on the right may even be Lorenzo de Medici, about to render Florence (alias Flora) pregnant with the arts. Hence the painting is partially a tribute to Botticelli's patrons.

The creativity of this work lies in the way that color, value, texture, and sight lines reinforce the image of a world in rebirth: the spring of the season and the spring of the epoch, reinforced by the spring of Florence. *La Primavera* has exquisite beauty and composition, but it also has meaning as well. When I looked up a description of it in *The Secret Language of the Renaissance*, I saw yet another meaning!

The garden represents the Garden of the Hesperides, and the oranges are a symbol of the Medici family. The three Graces depict the idea of our deeds returning to us, and their dance signifies that as one gives, the next one receives, and vice versa. Venus's pregnancy "is an illusion created by her gown." Flora is indeed pregnant and strewing flowers, but the "nymph" to the far right should be called Chloris, the name Flora used before she had been raped and impregnated by Zephyr. In representing the rape and then the pregnancy, Botticelli uses "continuous narrative." The entire painting is an allegory of—"love and marriage!"[629]

A great work of art often contains multiple meanings, layered like the petals of a rose, slightly different for each viewer or reader. A sad footnote to Botticelli's art is that it came to have a heretical or even blasphemous meaning to him. He had created beauty from a fusion of Christian and classical imagery, and he fell prey to the depredations of the mad monk Savonarola, who lashed Florence with imprecations to repent, condemned the Medici as pagans, and launched a kind of inquisition, urging Florentines to cast their jewelry and art objects and other precious belongings into his "Bonfire of the Vanities." Botticelli was eventually made to repent, and he cast many of his paintings into Savonarola's bonfire.

Of course, much art from the twentieth century on concerns itself

---

629 Stemp, *The Secret Language of the Renaissance*, 156-57.

with elements such as color and shape and makes no pretense of meaning. But when we turn to our next domain, we will see that meaning becomes an important foundation of all the "elements of composition."

Literature

What makes a work of literature aesthetically pleasing?

First, we may know that we like a story without knowing why. Scholes and Kellogg remark, "All readers of literature carry around with them notions about character and incident, in the form of unconsciously consulted touchstones which shape their evaluations of literary works."[630] Wayne Booth says we would use "different general values," depending on the focus of our inquiry. Inadvertently, perhaps, he alludes to the "Big Three": a representational work could be evaluated by its "truth" to reality [Truth]; an authorial presence could be judged by "sincerity or expansiveness" [Goodness]; a "formal" evaluation would include "coherence, complexity, unity, or harmony [Beauty]."[631]

Whereas painting and sculpture are static, literature is dynamic. The meaning changes as the words, pictures, or narrative line move us from one space to another. Archibald Leach's *Ars Poetica* (ll. 10–16) explains this movement in poetry:

> A poem should be motionless in time
> As the moon climbs,
>
> Leaving, as the moon releases
> Twig by twig the night-entangled trees,
>
> Leaving, as the moon behind the winter leaves,
> Memory by memory the mind—
>
> A poem should be motionless in time
> As the moon climbs.

---

630 Robert Scholes and Robert Kellogg, *The Nature of Narrative* (London: Oxford University Press, 1966), 160.

631 Wayne Booth, *The Rhetoric of Fiction* (Chicago: University of Chicago Press, 1961), 124.

Just as we do not see the moon climb, we do not notice the movement of a poem until, image by image, it has carried us to a new place.

The different genres of literature, of course, have different elements of composition. Poetry and cinema and (to a lesser extent) fiction use imagery; the most creative artist is the one who devises an image that is both original and inevitable. Who among us has not seen the moon rise, yet who would observe it so closely and think to describe it in those words?

Language is, of course, the medium of literature; a successful artist should have a wide-ranging vocabulary as a painter should be sensitive to color. The combinations of language should be apt yet surprising. In the selection above, for instance, "night-entangled" is both original and pleasing, and our mind's eye sees the contrast between black night and ivory moon.

Rhythm, sound devices, figurative language, and appropriate structure are other elements in poetry. In the selection above, the rhythm mimics the slow rise of the moon, a movement reinforced by the short lines and long vowels. The poem is compared figuratively to the moon in a device known as a simile (the comparison of dissimilar items using *like* or *as*). The structure of the poem consists of various similes and other figures to evoke the feeling of the poem as image and conclude with the abstraction: "A poem should not mean/But be." (A poem should be not a didactic abstraction but a palpable image that evokes associations and feelings, a simulacrum of experience itself.)

Narrative elements such as plot, character, and setting are elements of composition in cinema, theater, and fiction. David Mamet says that manipulating these elements is easy: "Story telling is like sex. We all do it naturally. Some of us are better at it than others." He explains that dramas are based on the "bedtime stories" we heard as children, with all plots following the same format: "once upon a time, and then one day, and just when everything was going so well, and just at the last moment, and they all lived happily ever after." [632]

We are the heroes of our own stories, he claims, and we learn how

---

632 David Mamet, *Bambi vs. Godzilla: On the Nature, Purpose, and Practice of the Movie Business* (New York: Pantheon, 2007), 89.

to spin yarns to achieve our goals:

> On our way to the goal (the wedding party, the discount, the week-
> end in Vegas), we encounter resistance, we find unforeseen reserves
> of strength and cunning, we are almost undone by some evil force
> (nature, fate, the traffic cop), and we eventually triumph by recourse to
> those basic precepts or powers that we were apprised of at the story's
> opening.
> Our simplicity allows us to inform the king that he has no clothes;
> our inventiveness, to charm the cop; our work ethic, to deliver a superior
> product at an economical price and so become rich.
> And that's it. That's all drama comes down to.[633]

So why, if storytelling is so natural, "are some folks challenged in creating it?"

Mamet has "two answers: (1) everybody can throw a ball, but not everybody can throw like Sandy Koufax; and (2) self–consciousness doth make dullards of us all."[634] (See Chapter 3!)

Of course, not every plot has a happy ending. Mamet explains in a parenthesis that

> (In the case of certain drama and tragedy, the happily ever after is, of
> course, altered, per case, to, for example, "And then they all lived sadder
> but wiser [the drama] or "And then, finally realizing the essence of the
> human condition, they put their eyes out and wandered around for a
> while as a blind beggar" [tragedy].)[635]

Naturally, there are different types of poetry: ballads, epics, *epitha-lamia*, haiku, rap rhymes, sonnets, and many others. And there are different kinds of plots. Christopher Booker has categorized seven: Overcoming the Monster, Rags to Riches, The Quest, Voyage and Return, Comedy, Tragedy, and Rebirth.[636] Sometimes they combine. In *Lord of the*

---

633 Mamet, *Bambi vs. Godzilla*, 90.

634 Ibid.

635 Ibid., 91.

636 Christopher Booker, *The Seven Basic Plots* (New York, London: Continuum, 2004).

Rings Frodo the Hobbit undertakes a quest to overcome the monster on Mount Doom and in himself, then writes a memoir of voyage and return like Bilbo's "There and Back Again." Frodo also experiences a rebirth from an innocent to someone "sadder but wiser." Comedy and tragedy often feature rebirth: comedy, into a wiser and more just society; tragedy, into "realizing the essence of the human condition."

Shakespeare's *Merchant of Venice* is a problem play because it combines these two forms. As in classical comedy, the play ends with the union of lovers in marriage; a blocking figure who has been in control of the society and promoting injustice has been vanquished. As in tragedy, a flawed figure has been overcome and ruined. Shylock is the hinge on which this ironic juxtaposition of opposites turns; he is both blocking figure (the Monster saying that he will have his bond, a pound of flesh from Antonio's breast) and a figure of tragedy (a Jew mocked and spat upon for his religion, bereft of his daughter, bankrupt, and forced to turn Christian). The Rags to Riches plot in this drama involves the hero Bassanio, who asks his friend Antonio for money, which he borrows with the bond from Shylock. With these funds Bassanio is able to court and win Portia, a heroine who is fair, wise, and rich.

In Chapter 1 we saw that Harold Bloom's test of literary greatness is the effect of the work:

> **The question we need to put to any writer must be: does she or he augment our consciousness, and how is it done? I find this a rough but effectual test: however I have been entertained, has my awareness been intensified, my consciousness widened and clarified? If not, then I have encountered talent, not genius. What is best and oldest in myself has not been activated.**[637]

The three criteria he cites are "aesthetic splendor, cognitive power, wisdom."[638] In literature the acknowledged master is Shakespeare. He is a virtuoso of language and a master of depth, combining plots, images, and characters in layers of meaning. Of course, his plays are never his creation alone. In the performing arts such as theater, cinema, dance,

---

637 Bloom, *Genius*, 12.
638 Bloom, *Dramatists and dramas*, ix.

and music, many artists contribute to the final version.

Music

Pythagoras, who believed that mathematics underlay the secret design of the universe, was the first to codify the relationship between intervals of numbers and music. By dividing a vibrating string into ratios of 2:1, he discovered first the octave, then the secret of harmony: "the simpler the numerical ratio between vibrating bodies, the more blended and therefore, the more consonant the sounds."[639]

Melodies and chords are arranged by intervals: steps in a scale, with the count beginning at one. Hence, going from C to E "would be an interval of a third."[640] A major chord consists of a 1st and 3rd and 5th; in a minor chord, the 3rd is lowered ½ a tone.[641] "Harmony is 'a pleasing interval of 2 notes.'" In a Triad, 3 or more notes are "pleasing to the ear." [642]

Musical patterns may differ by culture, of course; an East Indian *raga* has a varied structure quite different from the mathematical precision of the baroque fugue. Like literature, music also takes many forms, from the fugue to the rap lyric. The sonata form, a staple in the nineteenth century, still endures in pop music such as The Beatles' "Yesterday," which uses the structure AABA.

Professor Robert Greenberg tells us that music is a language, with its own syntax.[643] It may best be defined as "sound in time," and its chief components are as follows:

- Timbre, "the actual physical sound, or tone color": the "'voice'" produced by one or more instruments, classified by sound quality into five groups: stringed, woodwind, brass, percussion, keyboard;[644]

---

639 Robert Greenberg, *Understanding the Fundamentals of Music*, two vols., transcription of a 16-DVD series (Chantilly, VA: The Teaching Company, 2007), part 1, 122.

640 Joseph Brye, *Basic Principles of Music Theory* (New York: Ronald Press, 1965), 18.

641 Harry Paine, personal communication, May 27, 2007.

642 Ibid.

643 Greenberg, *Understanding the Fundamentals of Music*, part 1, 8-12.

644 Ibid., 13-15.

- Beat, the smallest unit of time to which you can move your body in synchronization to the music;
- Tempo, the pace of the music, whether fast or slow or moderate;
- Meter, as defined by "emphasis" or "accent," such as triple time for the waltz and minuet;[645]
- Pitch, "a discrete sound" with "a fundamental frequency, with the attribute of timbre": defined in the West as major, minor, and chromatic "collections;" separated from other pitches by specific intervals, such as the octave, in a series commonly called a scale;
- Mode, either major or minor;[646]
- Melody, "any succession of pitches";
- Functional harmony, a "system" "codified "during the baroque period," dependent upon chords called "tonic, dominant, and subdominant" and "comparable to the three primary colors used by the artist: red, yellow, and blue."[647]

For instance, the Beatles combined the stringed instruments of guitar and bass with the percussion instrument of the drum and cymbals and, sometimes, the keyboard. They also created unusual *timbre* with idiosyncratic sounds such as a rooster crowing or a tape loop running backward. The strong *beat* of their music became associated with what, in the 1960s, was called "the Liverpool sound." Initially their song "I want to hold your hand" had a slow *tempo*, and it was their mentor and producer George Martin who demanded they speed it up, with the result being a break-through hit. The *meters* they used tended to have many strong accents; they often used unusual minor tones that are hard to sing, such as in "Girl." (In the movie *The Doors*, the breakthrough song "Light my Fire" becomes artistically complete when the *mode* is changed from major to minor.) Sir Paul was said to have the gift of creating strong *melodies*, and the Beatles were said to have crafted their distinct sound of tight *harmonies* during their exhausting apprenticeship in Hamburg.

---

645 Greenberg, *Understanding the Fundamentals of Music*, part 1, 63-78.

646 Ibid., 109-54.

647 Ibid., part 2, 152-53.

The above is an application by a musical novice. For a full discussion of all of these musical elements, watch the DVD series that professor Greenberg has filmed for the Teaching Company.

The definition of literary genius is Shakespeare; the definition of musical genius is Mozart. In *Amadeus*, we see that a Mozart masterpiece is like one by Shakespeare or Botticelli: a work that is both harmonious and complex, fresh and inevitable.

Notable is a scene during which the court composer Salieri presents a new tune to his patron, Emperor Joseph II of Austria. Mozart is being introduced to the court; Salieri says, "I've written a little march of welcome in his honor." Joseph himself plays the tune as Mozart enters. There are introductions and bows. At the end of the conversation, Joseph tries to hand the sheet music to Mozart: "It's yours."

Mozart says, "Keep, it, majesty; it's already here in my head."

"On one hearing only?"

Mozart replies, "I think so, sire. Yes."

Joseph commands, "Show us."

Mozart sits down to play the simple melody, then speeds it up and says, "The rest is just the same, isn't it?" There is a pause, and Salieri stops smiling. "Doesn't really work, does it?" There's another pause, and Mozart plays a surprising interlude. "Did you try? . . . Shouldn't it be a bit more?" He plays another astonishing variation. "Or this . . . yes." He plays a magnificently complex piece. "Better? What do you think?" He continues to play variations on the melody, adding counterpoint after counterpoint, complexity after complexity. Salieri is devastated.

Whether the scene is true or not, it makes a powerful point about genius. The second-rate artist never sees the variations, never devises the original combinations that lift his compositions from the realm of the ordinary.

In fact, as the movie opens, Salieri is attempting suicide. Confined afterward in an institution, he tries to explain that he was once a famous composer. He asks a priest indignantly, "Do you know who I am?" Getting no satisfactory response, he asks if the priest was trained in music. The priest acknowledges he knows "a little" and studied "here in Vienna."

Salieri says, "Then you must know this." He plays a tune on a harpsichord.

"I can't say that I do. What is it?"

"It was a very popular tune in its day. I wrote it."

The priest nods, with a sympathetic smile.

"Here. How about this?" Salieri plays another tune. "This one brought down the house."

"I regret it is not too familiar."

Exasperated, Salieri asks, "Can you recall no melody of mine? I was the most famous composer in Europe. I wrote forty operas alone." There is a pause. "Here!" he exclaims. "What about *this* one?" He begins to play an instantly recognizable tune, which the priest finishes by humming.

The priest, humming the rest of the tune, cries, "Yes, I know that! That's charming! I'm sorry; I didn't know you wrote that."

"I didn't." There is a pause. *"That,"* says Salieri softly, "was *Mozart."*

In the scene after the humiliation of the welcome march, Salieri rails at a crucifix and complains, "All I ever wanted was to sing to God."

But that is *not* what he wanted.

Peter Schafer's script makes the point that Salieri prayed for musical talent because he wanted to be known forever. He tried to make a bargain with God for the sake of his own ego. Instead God favored whom He chose—Mozart. In this script the choice is made to seem ironic and Mozart, an unworthy and coarse vessel: a "giggling, dirty-minded creature." The irony is effective, but perhaps at the expense of truth. Swami Kriyananda often says that someone with a divine gift like Mozart's would not have such a crude personality.

The Dance

Howard Gardner says the dance may be "the original art form, the one "practiced by the first human beings."[648] It depends on kinesthetic skill: one of his ten major intelligences. The truly gifted artists, such as ballet greats Nureyev or Baryshnikov, make of their bodies subtle instruments expressing grace and power, surpassing the usual in new interpretations that engage and surprise. Sometimes, like Isadora Duncan or Martha Graham, they can develop a style totally original. Duncan danced barefoot, with "flowing veils," invoking the spirit of

---

648 Gardner, *Creating Minds*, 266.

ancient Greek myths and the lush nature of Botticelli's *Primavera*.[649] Graham, in deliberate contrast to the "effortless" pirouettes of classical ballet, danced with "dynamic, irregular forms" that showed the dancer's "strain."[650] At its best, says the old proverb, "the dancer becomes the dance": the ballerina or Irish step dancer merges totally with her movements and forgets body and self in an ecstatic merging of subject and object, a meditative wholeness.

As a performing art, the dance depends on many contributors. The dancer uses his or her body as a musician uses an instrument; the choreographer develops patterns as a dramatist does plots or a poet does images. Whether the dance is modern, classical, or folk, the patterns symmetrical or contrasting or sequential, the movements create beauty and pleasure. In a like way, an inventive choreographer can devise new movements and patterns that express surprising new idea.

A renowned collaboration between choreographer and ballerina was that between George Balanchine and Suzanne Farrell.[651] Only through the blending of their selves could their highest level of creativity could have occurred. Farrell said, "I think how you dance is who you are," an echo of Parker Palmer's famous statement, "We teach who we are."[652] While instructing a class, Farrell used the metaphor of a rose opening up and blooming, becoming something different all day. The same is true of her collaboration with Balanchine.[653]

Though he was forty-two years older, he was her mentor and lover; she was his Muse.

Painting vs. Sculpture

During the Italian Renaissance it was common to debate the merits of painting vs. sculpture. We tend to lump them together as visual arts, and they do require somewhat similar skills, but there are significant differences. For one thing, a painting is executed on a flat surface, and a

---

649 Gardner, *Creating Minds*, 267.

650 Ibid., 297.

651 The information about Farrell and Balanchine comes from *Suzanne Farrell: Elusive Muse*.

652 The tile of Chapter 1 in Palmer, *The Courage to Teach*.

653 For this insight I am indebted to Dr. Jack Clemes.

sculpture is usually viewed from all angles. The *David* makes an impact from every point at which the viewer stands; and, in fact, observers are encouraged to walk slowly around him, viewing the perfection of his buttocks, the veins in his arms, the musculature of his legs. The impulse to touch, almost irresistible, is restrained because the lower part of the statue is surrounded by a small fence. (What amused me as I gawked at the *David* is that many spectators, eschewing the statue itself, were crowded around a digital showcase of it, viewing as if hypnotized the rotating images expressing its different views. So mediated have some of us become that we cannot, as was once said of Newton, "look on beauty and see it whole.")

At any rate, the talents required of sculpting and painting are different. The sculptor, especially in earlier eras, had to be strong and work with physically challenging materials, which were often quite expensive. A painter can cover a mistake, but a sculptor can ruin a block of marble with one wrong blow.

During the early fifteenth century, the rivalry between Leonardo and Michelangelo sometimes manifested as a debate about which was the better art: sculpting or painting. Ross King has an engaging account:

> **The surly Michelangelo had once taunted Leonardo in public for having failed in his attempt to cast a giant bronze equestrian statue in Milan. Leonardo, meanwhile, had made it clear that he had little regard for sculptors. "This is a most mechanical exercise," he once wrote, "accompanied many times with a great deal of sweat." He further claimed that sculptors, covered in marble dust, looked like bakers, and that their homes were both noisy and filthy, in contrast to the more elegant abodes of painters.[654]**

When Pope Julius II commanded Michelangelo to paint the ceiling of the Sistine Chapel, he agreed reluctantly; though once apprenticed to a painter, he had had little experience with a brush and considered himself a sculptor. In particular, he had had no experience at all with *fresco*, a demanding technique that required painting on fresh plaster.[655]

---

654 Ross King, *Michelangelo and the Pope's Ceiling* (New York: Walker, 2003), 23-24.
655 Ibid., 22-23.

Leonardo himself had failed with fresco while trying a new technique in *The Last Supper* (1495–1498), which had already disintegrated to what Vasari called "a glaring spot" seventy years later. Leonardo's desire for innovation had caused him to reject the technique of *"buon fresco"* and paint "in tempura and oil," which he could do in his own "erratic rhythm"[656] rather than being forced to work quickly while the plaster was wet.

Integrative Arts

A truly integrative art is opera, which combines imagery, storytelling, music, dance, acting, costume, and setting. The greatest operas are able to enchant with spectacle and suspense while still promoting a theme.

One of my favorites, Wagner's *Ring* series, boasts crashing chords of melody while it tells a powerful story of good and evil, greed and the downfall of the gods, in the context of spectacular sets including the River Rhine, a ring of fire, and a cast of giants and dwarves. Bryan Magee describes Wagner's "sound-worlds" in a way reminiscent of Coleridge's definition of the "Primary Imagination" (Chapter 5):

> **The creation not just of a world but of worlds, a unique world with each work, is something few artists achieve. Shakespeare did it, but not many others have. Most great artists inhabit a world of the imagination that is distinctively and recognizably theirs, and from which all their works come.[657]**

Magee says that the greatest opera has a strong narrative line and melodic tunes that stand alone as art by themselves. "The key to the nature of opera in general is that it is a form of drama in which the primary means of expression is music . . . And if it is true, as has been said so often, that music has the power to go deeper than words, this means that opera can go deeper than non-musical forms of drama, at least in some respects."[658]

---

656 Pedretti, *Leonardo da Vinci*, 188.

657 Bryan Magee, *The Tristan Chord: Wagner and Philosophy* (New York: Henry Holt, 2000), 17.

658 Ibid., 7.

As the author of his own libretti, Wagner composed music to support the emotions of the characters:

> He had a highly sophisticated dramatic sense that enabled him to filter emotional insight through compositional technique into music that was compellingly effective in the theater, articulating not just character, motive, emotion and situation, but complex character, ambiguous motive, conflicting emotion and unresolved situation. At one moment the music soars with open, full-hearted rapture—and then a shift in the harmony casts doubt on a relationship; or the cut of a phrase will open up the difference between confidence and swagger, or between indifference and insensitivity; or perhaps something unnameable in the orchestral sound suggests a bubble of hollowness in a declaration of love. As well as being able to depict, support, and assert, this music can also allude, undercut, and evade. Often it goes against the words: while a character is assuring us of something, his music may convey to us that he intends something different. Given that, in addition to the music, the whole gamut of words and verse forms is also lying there for the using, a medium of dramatic expression of almost unlimited complexity and potential is made available to those who know how to use it.[659]

So whereas the "beautiful" equation or experiment has simplicity, the great works of art often depend upon complexity: upon ironies, levels of interpretation, contrasts of color and form.

To watch a truly integrative work—one combining painting, sculpture, acting, music, and dance—check out *Prospero's Books*, Peter Greenaway's version of *The Tempest*. This visually rich and totally original rendition of Shakespeare is almost unwatchable in one sitting, in the same way that one would surfeit upon eating a gallon of ice cream all at once. Each frame is composed like a painting: bodies sculpted and posing like statues, narration appearing on manuscript leaves of a magic book, the demi–devil Caliban twisting his body in the contortions of modern dance, and processions of nude bodies promenading to music.

---

659 Bryan Magee, *The Tristan Chord: Wagner and Philosophy*, 8.

Universal vs. Spirit of the Age?

Is art great because it is universal—or because it expresses the spirit of an age? Does the greatest art do both? What about science? Do Newton's mechanistic laws express the spirit of one age and Einstein's relativity, another? Does quantum mechanics express the spirit of still another age? But are they all reflective of universal laws at the same time? We will ponder these questions shortly.

"The Big Three," Revisited

Though this chapter has considered the aesthetic Thing–in–Itself to be located in the Upper Right quadrant, Wilber himself would locate its impact differently. Separating Beauty and Truth, he locates the aesthetic in the Left-hand path. Interestingly, he says that "It is not the object expressed, but the depth of the subject expressing it, that most defines art." He reminds us that art is created and viewed by individuals (Upper Left) and embedded in the *"worldview"* of the era (Lower Left). He explains, "Within these worldviews, we still possess abundant freedom of choice, but worldviews generally constrain what we will even consider choosing." In essence, "Each worldview, operating for the most part collectively and unconsciously, simply presents the world as if it were the case. Few question the worldview in which they find themselves."[660]

For example, if you were an artist in thirteenth–century Italy, you would be painting biblical subjects—especially the Holy Family or Madonna and Child. It would not occur to you to produce the distorted faces of Pablo Picasso or the random paint splatterings of Jackson Pollock. It was even a major break with tradition when artists like Botticelli began painting scenes from Greek or Roman mythology! So notable was this fourteenth–century innovation that it is considered the beginning of a new era in art: the Renaissance.

What kind of art do we never consider because it is beyond our awareness?

---

660 Ken Wilber, "To See a World: Art and the I of the Beholder," *The Journal of Transpersonal Psychology,* *29.2* (1997), 143, 144.

Wilber asks, somewhat plaintively,

> Who will show us now the objects of the transpersonal landscape? Who will open themselves to such depths that they may scale these new heights, and return to tell those of us silently waiting what they have seen? Who can stand so far aside from self and same, ego and shame, hope and fear, that the transpersonal comes pouring through them with such force it rattles the world? Who will paint what reality looks like when the ego is anaesthetized, when settling into the corpse pose, it dies to its own wonderment and beholds the world anew? Who will paint that rising landscape? Who will show us that?[661]

He reminds us of the key point in Chapter 5: we create from our own stages of development—and sometimes, yes, even from our shadow. A work may have energy, but if its energy is negative, its impact destructive, can it really represent the Good, the Beautiful, and the True? Or is it like the heavy metal music that causes deformed crystals to grow?

Creativity in the Artistic Product: A Conclusion

So to recap, we have seen that the creative product has commonalities, no matter what the domain: that, in fact, some of these universals may be rooted in nature itself, even the nature of the universe. We have seen that math, science, and engineering can be "beautiful," but that they also reside in both the True and the Good. We have seen that the arts differ from one another as well as from the sciences. The beauty of the arts arises from novelty within familiar patterns, from its creation of a new and pleasing whole out of given formulas and genres.

I would like to repeat myself here and make a point I did earlier, during our discussion of levels of consciousness. It is my belief that the greatest art also supports "The Good." It elevates and broadens the awareness, evokes the sublime, and leaves us feeling cleansed. This is not to say that I recommend what Poe called "the heresy of the didactic": moral lessons concealed as literature. Few of us read *Pilgrim's Progress* any more, even if we are literature majors! No, I mean that the best

---

661 Ken Wilber, "To See a World: Art and the I of the Beholder," 149.

art both uplifts and strengthens us: makes us new by uncovering the Beauty, Truth, and Goodness at the heart of the universe.

"And that is all ye know," as Keats said to the Grecian Urn, "and all ye need to know."

Exercises

1. What would you say about the relation of "The Big Three" to one another? For instance, is Beauty objective—or subjective? What is its relationship to Truth?
2. To what extent is aesthetics dependent on the person (Upper Left), and to what extent is it dependent on objective universal principles (Upper Right)? Explain.
3. Have you ever felt awe in the presence of beauty? Explain.
4. Explain other applications of mathematics to the arts.
5. Explain other examples of energy in the arts.
6. Explain other examples of juxtaposition and contrast in the arts.
7. Explain other examples of pattern recognition in the arts.
8. Explain some additional principles and examples of music theory.
9. The examples in this chapter draw heavily on the Renaissance and baroque periods. What more up-to-date examples can you furnish?
10. Furnish some more examples and principles of the dance.
11. List some of the puzzling or unclear ideas in Chapter 11. Ask questions about them.
12. Explain what you think is most important in Chapter 11.
13. React to some of the ideas in Chapter 11. Debate, support, analyze, and/or reflect.
14. Give evidence from your own life or background experience about the ideas in Chapter 11. (Don't repeat what you have written in another exercise.)

The Domain or System (Its or They)

Synergistic Interlude

Alice in Wonderland Chapter VIII:
"The Queen's Croquet-Ground"

"A large rose-tree stood near the entrance of the garden: the roses growing on it were white, but there were three gardeners at it, busily painting them red. Alice thought this a very curious thing, and she went nearer to watch them, and just as she came up to them she heard one of them say, 'Look out now, Five! Don't go splashing paint over me like that!'

"'I couldn't help it,' said Five, in a sulky tone; 'Seven jogged my elbow.'

"On which Seven looked up and said, 'That's right, Five! Always lay the blame on others!'

"'YOU'D better not talk!' said Five. 'I heard the Queen say only yesterday you deserved to be beheaded!'

"'What for?' said the one who had spoken first.

"'That's none of YOUR business, Two!' said Seven.

"'Yes, it IS his business!' said Five, 'and I'll tell him——it was for bringing the cook tulip-roots instead of onions.'

"Seven flung down his brush, and had just begun 'Well, of all the unjust things——'when his eye chanced to fall upon Alice, as she stood watching them, and he checked himself suddenly: the others looked round also, and all of them bowed low.

"'Would you tell me,' said Alice, a little timidly, 'why you are painting those roses?'

"Five and Seven said nothing, but looked at Two. Two began in a low voice, 'Why the fact is, you see, Miss, this here ought to have been a RED rose-tree, and we put a white one in by mistake; and if the Queen was to find it out, we should all have our heads cut off, you know. So you see, Miss, we're doing our best, afore she comes, to——' At this moment Five, who had been anxiously looking across the garden, called out 'The Queen! The Queen!' and the three gardeners instantly threw themselves flat upon their faces. There was a sound of many footsteps, and Alice looked round, eager to see the Queen.

"First came ten soldiers carrying clubs; these were all shaped like the three gardeners, oblong and flat, with their hands and feet at the corners: next the ten courtiers; these were ornamented all over with diamonds, and walked two and two, as the soldiers did. After these came the royal children; there were ten of them, and the little dears came jumping merrily along hand in hand, in couples: they were all ornamented with hearts. Next came the guests, mostly Kings and Queens, and among them Alice recognised the White Rabbit: it was talking in a hurried nervous manner, smiling at everything that was said, and went by without noticing her. Then followed the Knave of Hearts, carrying the King's crown on a crimson velvet cushion; and, last of all this grand procession, came THE KING AND QUEEN OF HEARTS.

"Alice was rather doubtful whether she ought not to lie down on her face like the three gardeners, but she could not remember every having heard of such a rule at processions; 'and besides, what would be the use of a procession,' thought she, 'if people had all to lie down upon their faces, so that they couldn't see it?' So she stood still where she was, and waited.

"When the procession came opposite to Alice, they all stopped and looked at her, and the Queen said severely 'Who is this?' She said it to the Knave of Hearts, who only bowed and smiled in reply.

"'Idiot!' said the Queen, tossing her head impatiently; and, turning to Alice, she went on, 'What's your name, child?'

"'My name is Alice, so please your Majesty,' said Alice very politely; but she added, to herself, 'Why, they're only a pack of cards, after all. I needn't be afraid of them!'

"'And who are THESE?' said the Queen, pointing to the three gardeners who were lying round the rose-tree; for, you see, as they were lying on their faces, and the pattern on their backs was the same as the rest of the pack, she could not tell whether they were gardeners, or soldiers, or courtiers, or three of her own children.

"'How should I know?' said Alice, surprised at her own courage. 'It's no business of MINE.'

"The Queen turned crimson with fury, and, after glaring at her for a moment like a wild beast, screamed 'Off with her head! Off——'

"'Nonsense!' said Alice, very loudly and decidedly, and the Queen was silent.

"The King laid his hand upon her arm, and timidly said 'Consider, my dear: she is only a child!'

"The Queen turned angrily away from him, and said to the Knave 'Turn them over!'

"The Knave did so, very carefully, with one foot.

"'Get up!' said the Queen, in a shrill, loud voice, and the three gardeners instantly jumped up, and began bowing to the King, the Queen, the royal children, and everybody else.

"'Leave off that!' screamed the Queen. 'You make me giddy.' And then, turning to the rose-tree, she went on, 'What HAVE you been doing here?'

"'May it please your Majesty,' said Two, in a very humble tone, going down on one knee as he spoke, 'we were trying—'

"'I see!' said the Queen, who had meanwhile been examining the roses. 'Off with their heads!' and the procession moved on, three of the soldiers remaining behind to execute the unfortunate gardeners, who ran to Alice for protection."

Courtesy of Lenny's Alice in Wonderland Site, http://www.alice-in-wonderland.net/

Questions to ponder

1. What characteristics of the classic bully does the Queen depict?

2. Why do you suppose she backs down and looks for a different target when Alice confronts her?

3. Have you ever had a "bully boss" like the Queen—someone who shouts the equivalent "off with their heads!" at each mistake? How did that impact your creativity?

4. How are the underling cards attempting to deal with the Queen's threats and demands? Does their method work? Why or why not?

12

The Structure and Function of Institutional Teams: Creativity in the Lower Right, Part 1

"In all but the rarest cases, one is too small a number to produce greatness."

—Bennis and Biederman,
Organizing Genius, 3

Toxic or Nurturing?

Stanford University Professor Robert Sutton has written a handy guide called *The No Asshole Rule: Building a Civilized Workplace and Surviving One That Isn't*. Regrettably, the need for his book is so great that as of its release during the week of February 24, 2007, it had already been translated into a dozen languages, with the author's blog[662] having attracted the testimonials of 30,000 "Asshole" victims. The publication of the book warranted front-page coverage in the *San Francisco Chronicle*,[663] with an accompanying list of the "dirty dozen" techniques of the perpetrators. Anyone interested in knowing his or her "Asshole" quotient

---

662 Robert Sutton, author's blog, www.bobsutton.typepad.com./my_weblog/.

663 Jessica Guynn, "Crusade against the Jerk at Work: Some Companies Seek to Filter out Toxic Employees," *San Francisco Chronicle*, February 24, 2007, A-1, A6, accessed April 4, 2014, http://www.sfgate.com/default/article/Crusade-against-the-jerk-at-work-Some-companies-2646586.php.

can take an online quiz.[664]

According to Sutton, even one toxic personality can destroy the productivity and morale of an organization. The worst of them seem to take a perverse delight in interfering with workers' ability to do their jobs. Their egos are titillated as they see the magnitude of the impact they can cause. (Think of the pointy–haired boss in *Dilbert*.)[665]

While it can be therapeutic to point fingers at the pointy–haired boss who is "managing" his staff into mediocrity or worse, our focus in this chapter is different: the Lower Right (LR), the realm of systems, the plural *its*. Whereas the Lower–Left quadrant (LL, Chapters 5 and 6) deals with "the *cultural* dimension (or the inside awareness of the group—its worldview, its shared values, and so forth) . . . the Lower Right [encompasses] the social dimension (or the exterior forms and behaviors of the group, which are studied by 3rd–person sciences such as systems theory)."[666] Alan Combs reminds us that this dimension, systems analysis, didn't develop until the latter half of the twentieth century.[667]

As we explore a few models, we will see what characteristics enable workers to use all of their minds instead of shutting down in frustration. Hence our study applies not only to creativity but to productivity and efficiency as well. We will also see the truth of Keith Sawyer's claim: "Collaboration is the secret to breakthrough creativity . . . *collaborative webs are more important than creative people* . . . the whole is greater than the sum of the parts."[668]

Great Groups That Make a Significant Impact

Every so often a master team assembles: a collaboration of geniuses that shatter paradigms and change the world. Bennis and Biederman, who have tagged these teams as "Great Groups," says that they share twelve characteristics.

---

664 Online quiz, www.electricpulp.com/guykawasaki/arse/.

665 Lee G. Bolman and Terence E. Deal, *Reframing Organizations: Artistry, Choice, and Leadership*, 3rd ed. (San Francisco: Jossey-Bass, 2003), 115. They mention the popularity of *Dilbert* as evidence of pervasive poor management.

666 Wilber, *Integral Spirituality*, 23.

667 Combs, "Horizontal Evolution and Collective Intelligence," 41.

668 Sawyer, *Group Genius*, ix, 185.

1. Greatness starts with superb people. Bob Taylor, the leader of the Great Group at PARC, liked to say, "You can't pile together enough good people to make a great one." ... Recruiting the most talented people possible is the first task of anyone who hopes to create a Great Group ... They tend to be deep generalists, not narrow specialists ...

2. Great Groups and great leaders create each other. ... Edison worked hard at maintaining the illusion that his inventions had sprung fully developed from his fecund brain, but he had many collaborators, albeit unsung ones. In our constantly changing, global, highly technological society, collaboration is a necessity. The Lone Ranger, the incarnation of the individual problem solver, is dead ...

3. Every Great Group has a strong leader. ... This is one of the paradoxes of creative collaboration. Great Groups are made up of people with rare gifts working together as equals. Yet, in virtually every one there is one person who acts as maestro, organizing the genius of the others ... Ironically, the leader is able to realize his or her dream only if the others are free to do exceptional work. Typically, the leader recruits the others ... Oppenheimer couldn't do the individual tasks required to make the bomb, but he knew who could ... Such leaders are like great conductors.

4. The leaders of Great Groups love talent and know where to find it. ... The talented smell out places that are full of promise and energy, the places where the future is being made ... Certain schools and academic departments are lodestones for talent. Certain cities attract it as well ... Many Great Groups [also] start with great Rolodexes. Oppenheimer knew the physicists he wanted for the Manhattan Project because he was part of an international community of physicists ...

5. Great Groups are full of talented people who can work together. ... This may seem obvious, but talent can be so dazzling, so seductive, that the person who is recruiting may forget that not every genius works well with others ...

6. Great Groups think that they are on a mission from God. Whether they are trying to get their candidate elected to the White House or trying to save the free world, Great Groups always believe that they are doing something vital, even holy ...

7. Every Great Group is an island—but an island with a bridge to the mainland. Great Groups become their own world. They also tend to be physically removed from the world around them . . .

8. Great Groups see themselves as winning underdogs. They inevitably see themselves as the feisty David, hurling fresh ideas at a big, backward–looking Goliath.

9. Great Groups always have an enemy. Sometimes, of course, they really do have an enemy, as the scientists of the Manhattan Project had in the Axis powers. But when there is no enemy, you have to make one up . . .

10. People in Great Groups have blinders on. The project is all they see . . .

11. Great Groups are optimistic, not realistic. . . . Such groups are often youthful, filled with talented people who have not yet bumped up against their limits or other dispiriting life lessons . . .

12. In Great Groups the right person has the right job. . . . Too many companies believe that people are interchangeable. Truly gifted people never are . . . .[Harry Paine, in a personal communication, June 2007, said, "This is so true." He quoted a friend of his from a prominent oil company: "Why do they (management) always think that a guy with a doctorate in infrared rings is a great candidate to head the marketing department?"]

13. The leaders of Great Groups give them what they need and free them from the rest. . . . Successful leaders strip the workplace of nonessentials . . . Time that can go into thinking and making is never wasted on activities, such as writing reports, that serve only some bureaucratic or corporate function outside the group. . .

14. Great Groups ship. Successful collaborations are dreams with deadlines. They are places of action, not think tanks or retreat centers devoted solely to the generation of ideas . . .

15. Great work is its own reward. . . . Some primal urge to explore and discover, to see new relationships and turn them into wonderful new things drives these groups. They payoff is not money, or even glory . . . [669]

---

669 Bennis and Biederman, *Organizing* Genius, "Characteristics of Great Groups," 197-215. The above list is a direct quote, with ellipses for missing material.

We will see how these principles operate in a few case studies. The number of the applicable principle will appear italicized and in parentheses after the relevant detail.

Troupe Disney.[670] In the student life building at the University of Houston, there is a mural of Walt Disney emerging from a cloud to touch his finger to the upraised finger of Mickey Mouse. It has always been one of my favorite emblems of creativity. Coleridge would call it a celebration of the Primary Imagination, mimicking the primal act of creation: a whole world manifested from the vivification of a famous mouse.

Bennis and Biederman summarize the magnitude of Walt Disney's accomplishment:

> With its theme parks (a Disney invention), its television network, its Broadway musicals and road shows, its retail stores, its publishing house, its interactive media division, and its ice hockey team (by no means an exhaustive list of Disney's many parts), the company has given new meaning to the term *synergy,* the process of orchestrating entertainment production, distribution, and marketing into a lucrative whole (a department of corporate synergy is officially responsible for that orchestration).[671]

And all of it began with one mouse in a 1928 cartoon, *Steamboat Willie.*[672]

What created the extraordinary power of the Disney empire? A simple answer is the visionary consciousness of Walt, who could imagine what no one else could (*3: "A Strong Leader"*). He was the first to imagine a feature-length animated film. His biographer Leonard Mosley recounts his challenge to his animators:

> ". . . they would be called on to provide not just gags and comic tricks but the impression of fantasy combined with a real world of real people

---

670 This colorful name is the brainchild of writer Pat Hollister, who wrote an *Atlantic Monthly* profile of Walt Disney in 1940. See Bennis and Biederman, 47.

671 Bennis and Biederman, *Organizing Genius*, 34.

672 In this discussion of Disney, I follow Bennis and Biederman, *Organizing Genius,* 31-62.

doing believable things. Walt stressed that this would not be simply a cartoon film but drama, theater, with characters coming alive on the screen as never before in an animated film."[673]

Walt sold the idea to his troupe by acting out *Snow White*, scene by scene:

One evening in 1934 he gathered his artists together in an empty soundstage and, under a naked lightbulb, he acted out the entire story. Sitting on folding chairs, the men saw and heard it all: Snow White's first encounter with the Seven Dwarfs, the individual foibles of the seven little men, the transformation of the beautiful but wicked Queen into the cronelike Wicked Witch, the brandishing of the poison apple, even the final kiss that brings the comatose heroine back to life.

We are not talking here about a recitation. Walt apparently brought all the dramatic powers of an amateur Lon Chaney to the drama . . . When Walt, as Snow White, was awakened by the Prince's kiss, grown animators are said to have wept . . . The hours-long performance was the living script the animators turned to again and again as they struggled to complete the script.[674]

Midway through the project, Walt repeated "his one–man show" in order to get funding from the Bank of America. Joseph Rosenberg, who wrote the check, said, "'Pity we won't be seeing Walt up there on the screen. It's the best performance I've seen since Lillian Gish in *Way Down East.*'"[675]

Walt also knew how to make his dreams a reality. He experimented with animated shorts in his Silly Symphony series; and in one, "Flowers and Trees," he even used a new technology other studio moguls were afraid to touch: a process called Technicolor. The resultant film garnered the first animation Oscar in 1932 (8: *"Winning Underdogs"*).

In addition, Walt recruited three hundred gifted animators (4: *Recruiting "Talent"*), then saw to it that they were trained. He first sent them "to

---

673 Quoted in Bennis and Biederman, *Organizing Genius*, 38.

674 Ibid., 41-42.

675 Mosely, quoted in Bennis and Biederman, *Organizing Genius*, 42.

night classes at the prestigious Chouinard Art Institute of Los Angeles, sometimes driving them back and forth in his own car,"[676] and at last established an in-house academy (1: "Superb People"). In all, 750 artists worked on the film. No pains were spared, including the construction of a special camera and the modeling provided by dwarfs and a "graceful" dancer (2: Interaction of "Great Groups" and "Great Leader," 11: Optimism).

Louis B. Mayer forecast disaster for the project (8: "Winning Underdogs"): "'Who'd pay to see a drawing of a fairy princess when they can watch Joan Crawford's boobs for the same price at the box office?'"[677] Nevertheless, in 1939 Snow White and the Seven Dwarfs garnered "a special Academy Award . . . symbolized by one big Oscar and seven little ones"[678] (14: Place "of Action").

Throughout the process, Walt remained the idea-man, the general supervisor, as he did with all other projects (12: Right Job for Right Person). He never gave individual credit to the artists, the models, or the songwriter. His rationale was that he wanted Americans to associate only one name—Disney—with the products of his studio (3: "Strong Leader"). He explained his reasoning in a National Geographic article in August 1963:

> You know, I was stumped one day when a little boy asked, "Do you draw Mickey Mouse?" I had to admit I do not draw any more. "Then you think up all the jokes and ideas?" "No," I said, "I don't do that." Finally, he just looked at me and said, "Mr. Disney, just what do you do?"
>
> "Well," I said, "sometimes I think of myself as a little bee. I go from one area of the studio to another and gather pollen and sort of stimulate everybody." I guess that's the job I do. I certainly don't consider myself a businessman, and never did believe I was worth anything as an artist.[679]

While Walt was alive, he worked the same magic on all of the Disney projects. His "thumbs-up" or "thumbs-down" on a project was all his workers needed from him (2: Interaction of "Great Groups" and "Great Leader").

---

676 Bennis and Biederman, Organizing Genius, 39.
677 Quoted in Bennis and Biederman, Organizing Genius, 38.
678 Ibid., 43.
679 Ibid.

He was free to provide inspiration while his brother Roy watched the books and finances (12: *Right Job for Right Person*). After Walt's death, it took the studio awhile to regain its creative impact—and some will say it never quite did.

The Manhattan Project. Also pervasive and universal in its impact is the Los Alamos Manhattan Project.[680] Surprisingly, the team that created the atomic bomb (14: *Place "of Action"*) had much in common with the team that created *Snow White and the Seven Dwarfs*.

First, it had the right leader (3: *"Strong Leader"*). Howard Gardner says that Oppenheimer "possessed the optimal combination of personal and intellectual gifts" and that "no one else was nearly as likely to be able to preside over a disparate collection of scientists and technicians and get them to work together smoothly and effectively."[681] Physicist Hans Berthe stressed the magnitude of this achievement:

> The success of Los Alamos rested largely on its teamwork and the leadership of its Director . . . What was called for from the director of Los Alamos at that time was to get a lot of prima donnas to work together, to understand all the technical work that was going on, to make it fit together, and to make decisions between [sic] various lines of development. I have never seen anyone who performed these functions as brilliantly as Oppenheimer.[682]

Rabi called Oppenheimer "'a born leader . . . [who, with the Manhattan Project,] created an atmosphere of excitement, enthusiasm, and high intellectual and moral purpose that still remains with those who participated, as one of the great experiments of their lives'"[683] (6: *Divine "Mission*," 15: *Intrinsic Motivation*).

Next, the Manhattan Project had the right combination of talent and attitude.

General Groves held the world at bay, negotiated its practical de-

---

680 In this discussion of the Manhattan Project, I follow Bennis and Biederman, *Organizing Genius*, 171-95, except for clearly indicated citations from Howard Gardner, *Leading Minds: An Anatomy of Leadership* (New York: Basic Books, 1995).

681 Gardner, *Leading Minds*, 95.

682 Quoted in Gardner, *Leading Minds*, 96.

683 Another physicist, co-author of *Oppenheimer*, quoted in Gardner, *Leading Minds*, 96.

mands, and left the collaborators free to think in an isolated environment. Like the combination of Roy and Walt Disney, "Groves and Oppenheimer had complementary virtues that allowed them to work independently and efficiently toward the same goal"[684] (*2: Interaction of "Great Groups" and "Great Leader," 3: "Strong Leader," 7: Isolated "Island," 12: Right Person for the Right Job, 13: Focus on Essentials*). Like Troupe Disney, the collaborators on the Manhattan Project were the best (*4: Talent*). The roll call at Los Alamos includes some of the greatest names in twentieth-century science: Nils Bohr, Werner Heisenberg, and Richard Feynman (*1: Superb People*). It was said of Los Alamos that "'more scientific talent was accumulated there than at any time since Isaac Newton dined alone.'"[685] Both the Disney and Los Alamos teams were infected with a revolutionary and messianic zeal (*9: Identification of an Enemy, 10: Single-Minded Focus*). At Los Alamos "Almost everyone knew that this job, if it were achieved, would be part of history."[686] (*6: Divine Mission*).

"Great Groups" in Sports Teams. Some famous, high-achieving sports teams have the characteristics of "Great Groups." One example is the UCLA basketball team led by Coach John Wooden, named "Coach of the Century" by ESPN. Under his guidance the team "won ten NCAA national championships (including seven in a row), eighty-eight straight games, and had four perfect seasons. He is the only basketball Hall-of-Famer to be inducted as both a player and a coach."[687]

Wooden compiled a "Great Group" by recruiting the best people (*1: Superb People*), co-creating success with them (*2: Co-Creation*), being a strong leader (*3: Strong Leader*), teaching them teamwork (*5: Talented People Working Together*), and insisting that they focus on the effort rather than on winning (*15: Great Work its Own Reward*). One of his players summarizes these principles (and others) as pithy "secrets": "The team with the best players almost always wins;" "A good leader is, first and foremost, a teacher;" "Teamwork is not a preference, it's a necessity;" "Focus on

684 Bennis and Biederman, *Organizing Genius*, 175.

685 Editors Lawrence Badash, Joseph O. Hirschfelder, and Herbert P. Broida, quoted in Bennis and Biederman, *Organizing Genius*, 177.

686 Ibid.

687 John Wooden, *They Call Me Coach,* with Jack Tobin, Contemporary Books (New York: McGraw Hill, 2004), back cover.

effort—not winning." [688] Perhaps Wooden's most famous legacy is his "Pyramid of Success," a triangular graphic of success skills, which he insisted be made available free to anyone who wanted it. (The pyramid is readily available on the Internet.)

The film *Hoosiers* narrates a similar tale of basketball success. The coach, played by Gene Hackman, insists on teamwork (*5: Talented People Working Together*) and tells his team to focus on the effort rather than on winning (*15: Great Work its Own Reward*): "I'm sure going to the state finals is beyond your wildest dreams. So forget about the crowds, the size of the school, their fancy uniforms . . . Focus on the fundamentals . . . Don't get caught up in thinking about winning or losing this game." He stresses that the most important thing is playing to their "potential."

Though it may seem as if the Disney Corporation, the Manhattan Project, and the Wide World of Sports are fields far-flung from creativity, they illustrate principles that are significant. All of these systems involve creation on a high level. In each case the group created something new that changed the field. The individuals banded together (*Lower Left*) to create a systemic synergy (*Lower Right*) that exhibited creative adaptations to achieve goals. In so doing, they defined the field and provided inspirational exemplars for those who were to follow.

Structures of Teams in Institutions

Though not "Great Groups" in the legendary sense described by Bennis and Biederman, other high-functioning teams help to form a creative synergy that makes the enterprise of their institution work. Kelly Gachet[689] describes her workplace at Microsoft as a system of teams, each specializing in a certain area, such as "Cut and Paste" or "Testing." After Microsoft determines consumers' needs by watching them use software or other products, then decides what innovations to introduce to make work easier, the various teams decide what they must contribute to make the whole system work. Ryan Gachet,[690] her husband, works for a computer consulting firm dedicated to helping

---

688 Hall, pp. 63, 96, 136, 177.

689 Personal Communication, November 22, 2007.

690 Personal Communication, November 22, 2007.

customers make the best use of technology. The teams in his company are fluid, with experts in various specialties banding together on an *ad hoc* basis for individual projects.

If such a group is functioning well, it probably uses the appropriate organizational structure to meet its needs. Bolman and Deal describe five organizational structures, each best for a particular purpose. [691] We'll examine the use of two of them.

Bridge Resource Management in Maritime Higher Education and Practice: The All-Channel Network or Star. You are on the bridge of a ship, maneuvering her into the San Diego harbor, and all at once a crucial member of your team falls down, writhing, suffering a heart attack. What would you do?

Professor Tuuli Messer–Bookman, who trains college students to be officers in the Coast Guard and merchant marine, regularly confronts her charges with such challenges. The professor teaches at Cal Maritime, a campus of the California State University, thirty–five miles northeast of San Francisco. And she doesn't just facilitate discussions. She puts teams of four into a bridge simulator, a virtual reality machine, and they are *there* in the harbor, chugging away fast, with a wraparound view of the harbor, the traffic coming at them and directional buoys indicating that it is time to make a decision, *now*.

This is not some computer game. Says Professor Messer–Bookman, "The simulator is treated as a real ship. It counts for sea time." When students make an egregious mistake, such as running the ship aground, professors assemble for a mock trial. The quaking and formally garbed students confront the licensed faculty, in full uniform and beribboned regalia, for the simulacrum of a full–blown Coast Guard investigation. The *F* in the class seems tame by comparison.

Professor Messer–Bookman says that stress is the greatest catalyst for creative and critical thinking in simulator teams. "If there's no urgency to the situation, the groups don't seem to gel as fast." She said that she is willing to be "the enemy" to provide that stress. She'll tell one team member to simulate a heart attack. She'll send a note to the brightest, most outgoing member of the team to say, "The captain wants you in

---

691 See Appendix 2.

her quarters now." She may tell the smart student, "I want you to give *very* wrong information."

She stresses the importance of team synergy in helping the students deal with sudden crises. We may think that the maritime world is all about following orders in a rigid chain of command, but Professor Messer–Bookman says that nothing could be further from the truth.

Teaching teamwork in simulator entails "Bridge Resource Management, an internationally accepted practice required at the senior level of management." The concept comes from the US Navy, which originally used "hierarchical management": says Professor Messer–Bookman, "You wouldn't address the captain even if you had a hunch something was wrong." The rigid hierarchy[692] had had the effect of "chilling information": "maybe the cook has an acute sense of smell and smells land!" She cites a possibly apocryphal anecdote: "Everyone on the bridge had a gut feeling something was wrong" but had "no direct evidence." As a result the ship went aground. Hence a new concept became operative: "Sir, I recommend . . . ." Anyone can say it.

As a result, since the 1980s, the organizational chart of the modern merchant ship is "not a pyramid but a circle." Everybody is on the bridge "so everybody is in the loop, on the same page." "Also you have a synergy developing; when a problem does evolve everybody's on the same page. It only works if everybody is at same level of situational awareness."

With "Bridge Team Management," she says, "Just because you're senior you're not the best necessarily to handle the problem." When a problem develops and the crew members on bridge call the captain, they don't just step back and relinquish responsibility. "The Captain inserts himself into the circle, which accommodates an additional brain. Everybody is contributing information into the pot." The crew will know more about how the problem developed and may be able to provide crucial information. (*See Figure 11.1.*)

---

692 In a personal communication, June 2007, Harry Paine, who served in the Navy during World War II, cited the Caine Mutiny as a good example of a hierarchical Navy structure.

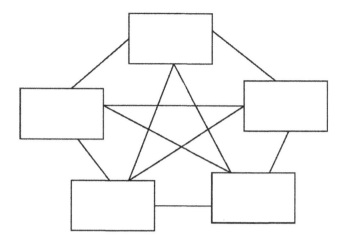

Figure 11.1
All-Channel Network or Star

Bolman and Deal would call this structure not a Circle but an All–Channel Network or star. Everyone in the group has access to everyone else, and information can flow freely from any one person to any other. In a Circle, as they define it, information passes only from one person to the next and never jumps to another part of the curve. [693]

(These diagrams are reproduced, with those of three other models, in Appendix 1.)

Professor Messer–Bookman trains her students that "Everybody must be cross checking everybody else." The motto is, "Trust but verify." What is optimum is "a circular flow of energy, almost like a magnetic field, [while] everybody's cross checking." Bolman and Deal say that in the Circle, as they conceive it, "the weakest link" can kill the information flow. In Professor Messer–Bookman's version of the All–Channel model, "The saying 'You are only as strong as your weakest link' is not true." Others will "take up the slack." "The four [members of the simulator team] working together are more effective than each working independently; [that] means we have a little room if one isn't as strong in an area."

---

693 Bolman and Deal, *Reframing Organizations*, 101.

One problem noted by Professor Peter Hayes, who also teaches the course, is that teams can exhibit "a lot of groupthink, where the team is swayed by one assertive personality."[694] Professor Messer–Bookman says, "If we have a personality type that shuts someone down, we'll talk about that during the brief" (a post–mortem that follows the experiential session).

Personality types matter. Professor Jim Buckley,[695] who also teaches the course, notes that an intelligent Asian female may defer to the males even if they have the wrong solution. Women tend to use creative problem–solving techniques that are based on talk, whereas the men plunge into action then act again to correct their mistakes. For example, in one scenario, "the ship was on a collision course with another vessel. The men automatically turned, which correctly avoided the situation. After they made the turn they realized that they were going toward a shoal, and that was a separate problem. They turned to miss the shoal, but then that put them in the shallows. They looked at what they were going to do with the shoal and they were headed toward the ship again. They then made a third decision, which was to slow down." This action-reaction pattern took seventeen minutes.

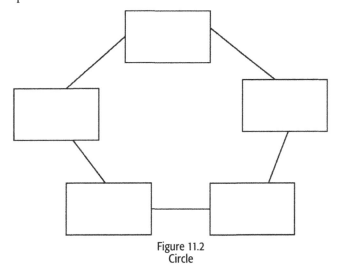

Figure 11.2
Circle

---

694 Professor Hayes' remarks come from an interview, March 20, 2007.
695 Professor Buckley's remarks from an interview, March 20, 2007.

In contrast, the women spent time discussing their options and then took a single action: to slow down. "They looked at the big picture and they looked at all the options and they considered everything before they ultimately made a decision." At the seventeen-minute point they slowed down. "The men made two or three different decisions to get to the exact same place the women made in one." In this instance Professor Buckley was monitoring stress levels by "finger pulse and blood pressure." Understandably, the men's stress level went up when the women were in charge, and vice versa.

The "ship-to-shoal" scenario demonstrates that with creative thinking, more than one solution may be possible. Hence the optimum group is one in which all channels in the "All-Star-Network" are operative. For simulator training Professor Bookman-Messer prefers a "random group," in which students are assigned to course sections, rather than a system of choice, which often puts high-performing friends in the same team together and leaves the weaker students to flounder by themselves. Diversity can also help to stop the "groupthink."

And does Bridge Resource Management work in the real maritime industry? You bet it does. The professor said she witnessed this system during a recent cargo transfer and was amazed at the collaborative synergy: "Licensed and unlicensed together, all discussed what was going to happen and who was responsible for what, everyone from deckhand to captain involved, [a system] unheard of 20 years ago."

Film Cutting: The Dyad or Circle. As the stars and directors never fail to say while clutching their Oscars, it takes a whole team to create a movie. One example is the art of film cutting.[696]

According to the narrator in *The Cutting Edge*, "The first cutters were considered hands for hire rather than creative partners." They would look at the images "by holding them up to the light and then check their work by running it through a projector." At the turn of the twentieth century, D.W. Griffith and his cutter Jimmy Edward Smith "worked far into the night" together and then the next day. Jimmy met his bride-to-be Rose when she went to work with him. "The Smiths married during the cutting of *Intolerance*. For their wedding, Griffith allowed them the weekend off."

---

696 The information in this section comes from *The Cutting Edge*.

In the 30s and 40s directors usually didn't come into the technical studios. Irving Thalberg "was the first to call cutters film editors." Today the editor is the director's "key collaborator. No other crew member spends as much time working alone with the director." Ridley Scott, director of *Alien* and *Gladiator*, says that choosing an editor is like getting married: if it doesn't work, "there's going to be a sticky divorce."

Steven Spielberg, while directing *Jaws*, said the cast referred to Verna Fields as "mother cutter." "She was very earthy, very maternal." He would suggest a cut in one place and she in another; whenever they noted the same place, they marked it with an x as "certain." She was in favor of "less is more," but he wanted to include more of the shark "because it took me days to get the one shot." The shark "looked real at thirty-six frames," not thirty-eight. The two-frame difference, says Spielberg in colorful language, is "the difference between something that looked really scary and something that looked like a great white floating turd."

Director James Cameron discovered the benefit of collaboration when, desperate to shorten *Terminator 2* to a manageable length, he decided to take out one frame a second, one in every twenty-four. "And the editors looked at me like I was nuts . . . It was a mess. There were jerks; there were cuts in the wrong places."

Quinton Tarantino, director of *Reservoir Dogs*, says he wanted a "female editor" who "would be nurturing me through this process rather than pushing a point of view" or "trying to win their [sic] battles." His editor Sally Menke says she "work[ed] with him" to implement what he wanted. But according to both of them, she still kept advising him to "bring it down" more. She says, "I see him more than my husband." He says, "Sometimes I get mad at her for not reading my mind 100% of the time."

Alexander Payne, director of *Election* and *About Schmidt*, says that by the time he's dealt with casting and filming, "It feels like I've washed up on shore. I'm so happy to be here, because I now think we can start making the film." In *Election*, in the principal's office, he wanted a series of shots as in *The Good, the Bad, and the Ugly*, "holding onto faces for a long time." His editor Kevin Trent wanted to cut fast. Trent said, "I'll pay you $25."

"No."

"$50?"

"No."

"$75?"

"Okay."

The short cuts prevailed, but Payne didn't collect. He remarks, "I think successful editors are really sly politicians."

As well as collaborating with the director, the editor may work with other technicians. In *Dante's Peak* the music editor tried to insert a tune as a tunnel was collapsing. Film cutter Hirsch said that didn't work because the audience needs to hear the "tiny sound" of sand falling to increase the suspense. Carol Littleton, of *Places in the Heart*, says that sometimes what is needed is silence to let the mood build. She held camera and point of view on the new widow as she washed her husband's body on the kitchen table.

Editing also controls the image of the actor on screen. The editor has to find the best performance in each take and splice them together. Sharon Stone's performance in *Basic Instinct* was the result of this method. In the famous scene when she crossed her legs, the editing cut back and forth between her comments and Michael Douglas' and the other man's reactions. Simply focusing on one person talking would have been boring. Sharon Stone wanted to cut "that scene," "the interrogation scene," but was told, "That scene will make you a star."

Martin Scorsese used an improvisational method in *Raging Bull*; his editor had to carve a story out of all the documentary scenes. "The emotional impact of the picture" is what Scorsese wanted her to look for. A director will also deal with questions of continuity, such as, "Why aren't we caring about this character as much as we did earlier?" This checks-and-balances system is like the immune system saying, "Yes, this is good for the body" or no.

Director Steven Spielberg thinks that "the editor has the most objective eye in that creative environment" because he/she hasn't been involved in all the work beforehand. In *Schindler's List* the pacing in the scene with the first drink together was all done in the editing: "how long to let the characters look at one another." He says he himself has trouble cutting and pacing, always shoots a lot, and dislikes decisions about whether the scene is comic or dramatic, slow or fast.

An editor can reconfigure a sequence and make it something totally different. The opening scene of *Apocalypse Now* changed in the editing room, as did Martin Sheen's character. The scene with the mirror was an improvisation. During the dissolve from Willard in his room to the napalm in the jungle, the fan dissolved into the helicopter, and the editor "almost jumped" when he saw the effect. That sound—is it from the helicopter—or the fan?

Some directors are hesitant about taking actors' suggestions for cutting. Jodie Foster says, "I have never let an actor into the editing room." She feels it's "inappropriate." *Home for the Holidays* was interesting because it had "six great actors," all with different style and pacing, all with gestures that add up to a complete interpretation. When the turkey falls to a floor, which shots do you show? Sean Penn would allow Jack Nicholson (*The Pledge*) into the editing room because he had good ideas and could recall things he'd done.

So, in essence, the film editing team may differ from one movie to the next—sometimes representing the dyad of cutter and director and sometimes representing the Star or Circle, as actors, music editors, sound technicians, and perhaps even writers and producers are introduced into the mix.

Sally Menke, who worked on *Reservoir Dogs* and *Pulp Fiction*, says that editing is called "the invisible craft." Craig McKay, editor of *Silence of the Lambs* agrees: "We call it the invisible art." "Unfortunately," says the narrator of *The Cutting Edge*, this style "kept editors invisible—and unappreciated as well." Whether invisible or not, film editors do a crucial job of creating the films we actually see, like Michelangelo carving from his block of marble or a novelist crafting a work of fiction from a heap of journals.

In Chapter 13 we will move from creative teams to larger institutional systems. Our focus will still be the Lower Right—exploring structures that work creatively—but will take a broader view.

Exercises

1. Go to the website on Dr. Sutton's book about "Assholes:" www.bobsutton.typepad.com./my_weblog/.
   What did you find out? What can you add, based on your experience?
2. Explain a good and/or bad system of which you are aware. What characteristics in your example/s help creativity and productivity? What characteristics stifle them? Do you see any characteristics of "Great Groups"?
3. Watch the film *Hoosiers* or another film about a successful coach and team. What principles caused synergy to happen? What did the team create that was new and important in the field?
4. Explain your own experience with "creative synergy" in a team. What caused the team to gel and be creative? What systemic principles were involved (Lower Right) as opposed to just the feeling of camaraderie (Lower Left)?
5. List some of the puzzling or unclear ideas in Chapter 12. Ask questions about them.
6. Explain what you think is most important in Chapter 12.
7. React to some of the ideas in Chapter 12. Debate, support, analyze, and/or reflect.
8. Give evidence from your own life or background experience about the ideas in Chapter 12. (Don't repeat what you have written in another exercise.)
9. Form a team, and do a brainstorming exercise to solve a problem. In brainstorming, everyone feels free to call out ideas, and someone writes them down. At this stage there is no judgment; often the best ideas emerge after people have felt free to be silly awhile. In fact, you may want to establish the rule that outrageous ideas are welcome. After the brainstorming session is over, then all of you can evaluate what you have and decide which idea/s to use. (It might be helpful to "sleep on" the ideas first.)

Synergistic Interlude

Through the Looking Glass
Chapter II: "The Garden of Live Flowers"

"For some minutes Alice stood without speaking, looking out in all directions over the country —and a most curious country it was. There were a number of tiny little brooks running straight across it from side to side, and the ground between was divided up into squares by a number of little green hedges, that reached from brook to brook.

"'I declare it's marked out just like a large chessboard!' Alice said at last. 'There ought to be some men moving about somewhere—and so there are!' She added in a tone of delight, and her heart began to beat quick with excitement as she went on. 'It's a great huge game of chess that's being played—all over the world—if this is the world at all, you know. Oh, what fun it is! How I wish I was one of them! I wouldn't mind being a Pawn, if only I might join— though of course I should like to be a Queen, best.'

"She glanced rather shyly at the real Queen as she said this, but her companion only smiled pleasantly, and said, 'That's easily managed. You can be the White Queen's Pawn, if you like . . . " —Just at this moment, somehow or other, they began to run.

"Alice never could quite make out, in thinking it over afterwards, how it was that they began: all she remembers is, that they were running hand in hand, and the Queen went so fast that it was all she could do to keep up with her: and still the Queen kept crying 'Faster! Faster!' but Alice felt she could not go faster, thought she had not breath left to say so.

"The most curious part of the thing was, that the trees and the other things round them never changed their places at all: however fast they went, they never seemed to pass anything. 'I wonder if all the things move along with us?' thought poor puzzled Alice. And the Queen seemed to guess her thoughts, for she cried, 'Faster! Don't try to talk!'

"Not that Alice had any idea of doing that. She felt as if she would never be able to talk again, she was getting so much out of breath: and still the Queen

cried 'Faster! Faster!' and dragged her along. 'Are we nearly there?' Alice managed to pant out at last.

"'Nearly there!' the Queen repeated. 'Why, we passed it ten minutes ago! Faster!' And they ran on for a time in silence, with the wind whistling in Alice's ears, and almost blowing her hair off her head, she fancied.

"'Now! Now!' cried the Queen. 'Faster! Faster!' And they went so fast that at last they seemed to skim through the air, hardly touching the ground with their feet, till suddenly, just as Alice was getting quite exhausted, they stopped, and she found herself sitting on the ground, breathless and giddy.

"The Queen propped her up against a tree, and said kindly, 'You may rest a little now.'

"Alice looked round her in great surprise. 'Why, I do believe we've been under this tree the whole time! Everything's just as it was!'

"'Of course it is,' said the Queen, 'what would you have it?'

"'Well, in our country,' said Alice, still panting a little, 'you'd generally get to somewhere else—if you ran very fast for a long time, as we've been doing.'

"'A slow sort of country!' said the Queen. 'Now, here, you see, it takes all the running you can do, to keep in the same place. If you want to get somewhere else, you must run at least twice as fast as that!'"

Courtesy of Lenny's Alice in Wonderland Site, http://www.alice-in-wonderland.net/

Questions to ponder

The Red Queen's last speech is a great summary of what we call "the rat race." In some jobs or creative efforts, "it takes all the running you can do, to keep in the same place."

1. When have you felt that it took all the running you could do to stay in the same place?

2. How were your efforts helped or harmed by the organizational structure or rules within which you were operating?

3. How did your boss, supervisor, leader, or coach help or harm you?

4. How did teammates help or harm you?

5. How is life like a chess board?

13

Systemic Support: Creativity in the Lower Right, Part 2
Patrons and Institutions
Nurturing vs. Toxic Systems

Creativity is a delicate hothouse flower. *Depression, blocking, perceived failure, inability to focus*: all of these and more can impair the self-confidence and will needed to create. Another distracter can be *"the day job,"* the business to which the artist has sold his or her body in order to pay the bills. Waiting on tables may not interfere with appearing for auditions, but teaching can drain the creative energy needed for writing—hence the sabbatical, without which I would not have been able to write this book!

Vera John-Steiner reminds us,

> In addition to their personal powers of drive and regeneration, creative individuals need external supports. "Literature is not created in mid-air," is an often-quoted line from Virginia Woolf; she reminded us that creative work is rooted in the material conditions of existence, such as space, money, and experience.[697]

697 John-Steiner, *Notebooks of the Mind*, 79.

In Chapter 12 we saw that corporations like Disney nurtured creativity in teams. In this chapter we will look at other forms of creative
support: patronage and institutional structure.

Patronage

James M. Saslow, City University of New York, explains that in the
Renaissance, "You didn't put art into the shop window and then wait
for someone to buy it. You only made art when somebody commis-
sioned it from you and paid you for it, more or less in advance."[698] One
family did more than that. The Medici of Florence not only awarded
commissions but even provided financial support and nightly informal
symposia. Their beneficiaries included Leonardo, Botticelli, Michelangelo, Brunelleschi, Machiavelli, Galileo—"cultural revolutionaries" with
"breathtaking ideas."[699]

The Medici. The Medici wealth came from their status as the
pope's bankers;[700] the Medici largesse came from their values. In 1433
Cosimo di Gionanni (1389–1464), styled *pater patriae*, was rumored to be
one of the world's richest men.[701] His lucrative relationship with the
Vatican began during the time of Pope John XXIII (1410–1415); and, with
some setbacks, managed to weather two shifts in the papacy thereafter, as well as threats from the rival Albizzi clan.[702] By 1435 the church
dignitary who was to become Pope Pius II in 1458 said of Cosimo, "'He
is King in everything but name.'"[703]

In addition, Cosimo was a humanist, with a "deep respect for classical
learning and classical ideals."[704] Great Florentine merchants were expected
to be generous,[705] and Cosimo became a patron of what was already be-

698 Quoted in *Empires: The Medici: Godfathers of the Renaissance*, Part 1 (PBS, 2004).

699 Ibid. This source claims that the motive of the Medici patrons was to demonstrate their power and enhance their prestige.

700 Chistopher Hibbert, *The House of Medici: Its Rise and Fall* (New York: Harper Perennial, 2003), 35.

701 Ibid., 19.

702 Ibid., 35-63.

703 Ibid., 63.

704 Ibid., 37.

705 Ibid., 29.

ing discussed as the *Rinascaimento*: a great rebirth of art and philosophy.

> **The presence of so many Greek scholars in Florence provided an incalculable stimulus to the quickening interest in classical texts and classical history, in classical art and philosophy, and particularly in the study of Plato, that great hero of the humanists, so long overshadowed by his pupil, Aristotle.**[706]

One of Cosimo's protégés had inestimable value in this enterprise. Discovering a youth who loved Plato, Cosimo subsidized the rest of his education and installed him in "the villa known as Montevecchio where, in the peace of the country, the young man was to study Greek and to translate all Plato into Latin."[707] Periodically the young man was invited "to the nearby villa of Careggi," to discuss philosophy "far into the night" with Cosimo and his friends. These discussions formed the basis of the Platonic Academy. This young scholar was to become the great Ficino, whose work was to make Plato accessible for the rest of Renaissance Europe.[708] In addition, Cosimo collected books: hundreds of rare volumes gathered from all over Europe and the Near East and made available to his friends for study.[709]

The Medici also supported great works of art and architecture. The list is long.

Notable was *Il Duomo*, the red–ribbed cathedral dome that has come to be synonymous with pictures of Florence. This marvel of engineering and architecture, 138 feet in diameter, took sixteen years (1420–1426) to complete,[710] and it was created by Filippo Brunelleschi, who used the Pantheon as a model. Biographer Ross King comments, "We're reluctant to use "the G–word, genius," but it fits him.[711]

"Like other geniuses"[712] he wasn't easy to get along with, but the

---

706 Hibbert, *The House of Medici,* 68.

707 Ibid.

708 Ibid., 69.

709 Ibid.

710 Ibid., 72.

711 Quoted in *Empires: The Medici: Godfathers of the Renaissance,* Part 1.

712 The following information comes from *Empires: The Medici: Godfathers of the Renaissance,* Part 1.

Courtesy of Wikimedia Commons

Medici "were not daunted by the temper of a maverick architect." They became his patrons, "willing to gamble on his judgment."

In order to get the commission, Brunelleschi had to convince a committee that he knew how to solve an "unprecedented" engineering problem that "had no certainty of success."[713] Irritated by the skepticism of these ignorant judges,

> **Brunelleschi produced an egg, announcing that only he knew how to make it stand on its end: when all the others had confessed their failure to do so, he cracked its top on the table and left it standing there. "But we could have all done that," they protested. "Yes," replied Brunelleschi crossly, "and you would say just that if I told you how I propose to build the dome."[714]**

He got the commission.

As the dome and its supports rose, people gathered by the building site to watch, in amazement, because they had never seen anything built like this before. "Even the recipe for concrete had been lost since the fall of Rome." Brunelleschi solved a major engineering problem when he conceived two domes and rings to hold them together "like a barrel." [715]

James M. Saslow sums up the Medici contribution to this project: "Brunelleschi and Cosimo were very close. . . .It was very much about recreating a great classical city . . . Cosimo would publicly support him."[716]

Another example is Cosimo's love for Donatello, who produced the delicate and effeminate *David*, which was not only an astonishingly beautiful and emotive work of art; it was also a remarkable innovation, the first free-standing figure cast in bronze since classical times.

Some of his contemporaries found it shocking. That Donatello was a homosexual was bad enough; that he should have portrayed the

---

713 *Empires: The Medici: Godfathers of the Renaissance*, Part 1.

714 Hibbert, *The House of Medici*, 72. This anecdote is also narrated in *Empires: The Medici: Godfathers of the Renaissance*, Part 1.

715 *Empires: The Medici: Godfathers of the Renaissance*, Part 1.

716 Ibid.

young male form so lovingly, realistically and sensually, with so obvious a delight in the flesh, was outrageous. To Cosimo such objections seemed wholly unreasonable, obtusely at variance with those classical Greek ideals which were Donatello's inspiration.[717]

Donatello's *David*
Courtesy of Wikimedia Commons

Lorenzo the Magnificent (1449–1492), Cosimo's son,[718] instituted "the Council of Florence . . . the greatest mix of thinkers, artists, merchants, and churchmen that the world had ever seen." "And bankrolling it all, was Cosimo De Medici," including paying "travel expenses" as guests

717 Hibbert, *The House of Medici*, 91.

718 The information in this paragraph comes from *Empires: The Medici: Godfathers of the Renaissance*, Part 1.

came from all over the globe to wonder at the beauty that was Florence. In the words of Saslow, Lorenzo presided over "an open house where writers and artists, and other interesting people were free to come and partake of his bounty."

Invited to this table was a talented young artist whom Lorenzo had discovered and spirited away, to train in his Garden of San Marco, a school of "sculpture and the liberal arts."[719] The Medici patron even brought this precocious thirteen–year–old into his family, with "the young artist . . . given his own rooms at the Medici palace to grow up alongside Lorenzo's seven children."

Lorenzo and this prodigy, Michelangelo, had "a close relationship . . . They seemed to seek each other almost every day," and Michelangelo "became invested in Lorenzo's approval."[720] Jeffrey Brotton, Queen Mary University of London, says this situation represents "something new: a very intimate relationship between patron and artist. Lorenzo would invite Michelangelo to his dinner table." He would sit there and listen, to Botticelli and Ficino, "about humanist theory, about neoclassical antiquities, and he absorbed all that, and you can see it coming out, in the sculptures and in the drawings and in the paintings."[721]

And so he joined a refined court in which the leading artists and thinkers of the day dwelt, enriching one another's perspectives with a cross–fertilization of ideas. At this sanctuary one need do nothing except practice his art and engage in intellectual discussion!

In 1402 Cosimo's father, Giovanni di Bicci, served as a judge in one of the most stupendous contests in art history. He helped to decide who would design the figures on the Baptistery Doors. These doors, planned for the northern front of the Church of San Giovanni Battista, "were to be cast in bronze of the most exquisite workmanship, and seven of the leading artists of the day had each been asked to submit a design."[722] The topic was to be the sacrifice of Isaac by Abraham.

So "exquisite" were the designs of the two runners–up, Lorenzo Ghiberti and Filippo Brunelleschi, that they have been preserved for

---

719 King, *Michelangelo and the Pope's Ceiling*, 22.

720 *Empires: The Medici: Godfathers of the Renaissance*, Part 1.

721 Ibid.

722 Hibbert, *The House of Medici*, 70.

viewing behind a museum glass. The execution of the eventual project by Ghiberti is one of the treasures of world art. So precious is it that a copy now graces the Baptistery Doors and the original is, ironically, preserved in the museum of *Il Duomo*—under the dome created by the angry runner-up, Brunelleschi! The incomparable Baptistery Doors are a testament not just to Medici values—but the values of an entire city that cared about beauty, creativity, and culture.

Alas, those days are gone! They were already dwindling by 1491, when the apocalyptic preaching of the crazed monk Savonarola electrified Florence with his proclamations of doom. By the time of Lorenzo's death in 1492, the mad monk held Florence captive. "Michelangelo as an old man was to say that he could still hear the friar's voice ringing in his ears." [723] And so died a great humanist Republic that respected philosophy and the arts.

Other patrons. Michelangelo had another patron of sorts in the choleric "emperor Pope" Julius II. Engaged to sculpt statues for the pope's tomb—a prestigious commission—Michelangelo was irritated and frustrated to be pulled out of his Florentine workshop, with its marble and partially finished statues, to be summoned to Rome in 1508 for another of Julius' projects: the ceiling of the Sistine Chapel. In those days the painting of vaults was the purview of lesser artists; a greater honor was to paint walls.[724] In the end Michelangelo submitted; indeed he had no other choice. He might grumble at Julius and quarrel with him but could not strictly disobey the most powerful figure in Christendom, even when that figure demanded Michelangelo leave a town and project he loved for the inferior art of painting, in which he'd had small practice, in a town with "bad air" and brutally hot summers.[725] In departing, he even left behind other unfinished commissions, "an incredible thirty-seven statues and reliefs of various sizes."[726]

It is difficult to imagine that sort of patronage in the United States today. Though cities do grant commissions for "public art," how many

---

723 Hibbert, *The House of Medici*, 181.

724 King, *Michelangelo and the Pope's Ceiling*, 27.

725 Ibid., 74-78. King notes that Michelangelo's allusions to "bad air" may have been a ruse to discourage family members from staying with him.

726 Ibid., 31.

sculptors can make their living that way? How many get the increasingly rare NEH grants? Other countries are more generous as patrons. Community of Service (cos.com), a grants database, lists a plethora of opportunities for artists native to Great Britain, Canada, and Australia.

Fortunately, some wealthy patrons still remain. In San Francisco an example is the socialite Dede Wilsey, who has been called "one of the nation's pre–eminent fundraisers."[727] In 1998 when voters turned down Measure A, designed to restore "the earthquake–damaged de Young Museum in San Francisco's Golden Gate Park," Wilsey decided that the renovation would have to be funded by private donors. When it opened on October 15, 2005, she had raised $190 million.[728] As of April 2, 2007, she had raised over $10 million more and was focusing on a new project: a $1.2 billion dollar hospital complex at the University of San Francisco Medical Center.[729]

Many anecdotes are related of her. Once as she was arriving at a gathering of the rich and famous "to welcome [symphony conductor] Michael Tilson Thomas back from London," she realized she had brought no money and asked if anyone nearby had two dollars to tip the valet parker. Denise Bradley, executive director of the Museum of the African Diaspora, humorously remarked, "I'll give you two dollars if you give me a thousand!"[730]

Patrons, like Wilsey, foundations set up by early tycoons like Carnegie, and philanthropists like the MacArthurs, take the place of the Medici today—but there are not enough of them. In *quattrocento* Florence, art was blooming, and patrons were generous. Alas, artists in the

---

727 Julian Guthrie, "San Francisco: New UCSF Hospital Planned: Mission Bay Facility to Focus on Women, Children, Cancer." *San Francisco Chronicle* (April 2, 2007), B-1, accessed April 4, 2014, http://www.sfgate.com/default/article/SAN-FRANCISCO-New-UCSF-hospital-planned-2605079.php.

728 Julian Guthrie, "De Young's Rebirth: It Had to Overcome Design Challenges, Lawsuits, and a Lack of Funds. S.F.'s New Museum Opens Today, a Triumph of Creativity and Commitment," *San Francisco Chronicle*, October 15, 2005, A-1, accessed April 4, 2014, http://www.sfgate.com/default/article/De-Young-s-rebirth-It-had-to-overcome-design-2564985.php.

729 Guthrie, "San Francisco: New UCSF Hospital Planned."

730 According to Garchick, who covers gossip about the elite of San Francisco for the local newspaper. The super-rich don't seem to carry cash. The Queen of England is said to carry a hanky in her pocketbook. John Lennon said the Beatles never carried cash and he himself didn't know how to write a check. My husband Jack and I once saw a television program that featured Michael Jackson walking around a showroom of fabulously expensive antiques and pointing at what he wanted.

US today must learn to market themselves and do spin–off projects like postcards, signed lithographs, calendars, and refrigerator magnets.[731] (I have seen such marketing in Montreal and British Columbia as well.) And then, there is always the "day job." In fact, creativity of whatever sort in the US today tends to occur, like Troupe Disney, in businesses and educational institutions. But they, of course, can either encourage or discourage it, based on their mores, personnel, and structure.

Contemporary Support for Creativity: Toxic and Nurturing Institutional Structures

Toxic Structures. Unfortunately, these are rife in business, education, and government.

TQM. In fact, the assumption of the Total Quality Movement (TQM) is that workers want to do their jobs well but are prevented from doing so by a dysfunctional system. I quote from an earlier article of mine[732] with an amusing example, "the bead game":

> A large bowl contains 1,600 white beads and 400 colored beads. Colored beads are defects. Employees are equipped with a paddle containing 50 bead-sized indentations. They scoop the paddle into the bowl, and it comes out containing 50 beads. The beads are hot, so workers cannot touch the beads or container.

The goal is to have no more than five defects for each immersion of the paddle. The flaw in the process soon becomes evident: the beads are scooped out randomly, and nothing the players do can make a difference. By sheer chance, some workers scoop out more than five flawed beads.

---

731 I discussed this situation with contemporary artist Anton Nemeth.

732 Bunny Paine-Clemes, "What is Quality in a Maritime Education?" paper presented October 25, 2005, in Malmö, Sweden, and published in *Maritime Security and MET: Proceedings of the International Association of Maritime Universities: IAMU 6 General Assembly and Conference, World Maritime University, Malmö, Sweden, 24-26 October, 2005*, edited by Detlef Nielsen (Southampton, U.K.: WIT Press, 2005), 267-76. Rpt. in *The IAMU Journal* 2, No. 4 (March 2006): 23-30.

> People who play the Bead Game soon recognize both its parallels with actual work situations—setting goals, trying hard, motivating, warning—and its hopelessness. Ultimately, the best and perhaps the only way to obtain lower defect rates is lowering the proportion of colored beads in the bowl. But the workers cannot lower the proportion, for they are dippers, not process designers, purchasers, or managers.

Hence, for TQM, "The primary job of administration is to remove the barriers that prevent people from achieving quality work processes."[733]

"Assholes" Poisoning the System. One of these barriers is the power-mad, ego-driven, truculent bully boss. He can poison a whole system by leaving in his wake dispirited, disempowered victims. Robert I. Sutton calls the worst cases "certified assholes," and he claims that you can identify one by his "persistent pattern" of leaving "one 'target' after another feeling belittled, put down, humiliated, disrespected, oppressed, deenergized, and generally worse about themselves." [734]

Unfortunately, I have known my share of these. One Dean said that his purpose was to make the faculty afraid of him so they would do their jobs. He would dock their pay if they missed the Christmas party. He left, accompanied by a cluster of lawsuits, for another job. His co-workers had given him a glowing evaluation in order to get rid of him.

If you can't leave or get him to do so, there are resources to help you cope and vent: not only Sutton's popular book but also Gary and Ruth Namie's *The Bully at Work*.

Theory X. What is it? Something out of science fiction? An algebra equation? A dose of toxic rays?

In essence, the last alternative is correct. Theory X concerns managerial assumptions that disempower employees and thwart their creativity.

Citing Professor Douglas McGregor, Bolman and Deal categorize these assumptions as follows: "subordinates are passive and lazy, have little ambition, prefer to be led, and resist change." McGregor believes

---

733 Quoted in Paine-Clemes, "What is Quality in a Maritime Education?" 23-30. Harry Paine, my father, reading this anecdote about the Bead Game, added, "And then someone comes up to the bowl and throws in a handful of jackpeas. That's called a consultant!"

734 Sutton, *The No Asshole Rule*, 11.

that "Most conventional management practices" have "either hard or soft versions of Theory X. The hard version emphasizes coercion, tight controls, threats, and punishments." The "soft version" results in "superficial harmony with undercurrents of apathy and indifference."[735] Either way, the creativity of employees shuts down in the face of a managerial stance devaluing their motives and contributions.

Theory X managers—whom Bolman and Deal also call Model 1 bosses—are uncomfortable with democratic processes, worker autonomy, and employee input. They may say that they hold these values, but their behavior tells a different story.

Bolman and Deal narrate a sad example. Morale and productivity were down in a factory where women painted dolls.

> In a reengineered process, each woman took a doll from a tray, painted it, and put it on a passing hook. The women received an hourly rate, a group bonus, and a learning bonus. Although management expected little difficulty with the new system, production was disappointing and morale worse. Workers complained that the room was too hot and the hooks moved too fast.
>
> Reluctantly, the foreman followed a consultant's advice and met face to face with the employees. After hearing the women's complaints, the foreman agreed to bring in fans.

Despite the expectations of the foreman and "industrial engineer who designed the new manufacturing process," morale improved significantly. Then "after several [more] meetings, the employees came up with a radical suggestion: let them control the belt's speed."[736]

Now, this example of creativity is modest: scarcely the "Creativity with a capital C" of the Florentine Renaissance. Nevertheless, it is creativity. Workers were encouraged to "think outside the box," to devise suggestions undreamt of by management. And the one they devised worked splendidly. "The employees developed a complicated production schedule: start slow at the beginning of the day, increase the speed once they had warmed up, slow it down before lunch, and so on." The

---

735 Bolman and Deal, *Reframing Organizations*, 118.
736 Ibid., 145.

foreman had been dubious about this plan; the engineer had argued adamantly against it. Nevertheless,

> **Results of this inadvertent experiment in participation were stunning. Morale skyrocketed. Production increased far beyond the engineer's most optimistic calculations. The women's bonuses escalated so much that they were earning more than many workers with significantly higher levels of skill and experience.**
>
> **So guess what happened?**
>
> **The women's production and high pay became a problem because higher-skilled workers in the rest of the plant protested. To restore harmony, management reverted to the engineer's earlier recommendation: a fixed speed for the belt. Production plunged, morale plummeted, and most of the women quit.[737]**

I wish I could say that this example is an anomaly. Instead, many organizations work to destroy the initiative and creativity of their workers and then complain about the unproductive, listless workforce they themselves have created—employees who are simply putting in a day's work to collect their paychecks because they are discouraged from reaching their potential.

In contrast is Theory Y, Professor McGregor's notion that workers seek to satisfy inherent needs. McGregor draws on Abraham Maslow's famous hierarchy[738] to stress that after biological and safety needs are met, human beings want to satisfy needs for belonging, esteem, and self-actualization. In other words, as human beings we are hard wired to make the most of our potential, to be all that we can be. A system that frustrates this need is not only sabotaging itself; it is in the business of soul murder.

Bolman and Deal, following the work of Argyris, list the ways in which employees try to cope with such a demoralizing system. I have used the wording of the categories but omitted the examples (which you may be able to furnish from your experience yourself, as I, too, often can):

---

737 Bolman and Deal, *Reframing Organizations,* 145.
738 Ibid., 118-19.

1. *They withdraw—through chronic absenteeism or simply by quitting.*
2. *They stay on the job but withdraw psychologically, becoming indifferent, passive, and apathetic.*
3. *They resist by restricting output, deception, and featherbedding.*
4. *They try to climb the hierarchy to better jobs.*
5. *They form alliances (such as labor unions) to redress the power imbalance.*
6. *They teach their children to believe that work is unrewarding and hopes for advancement are slim.*[739]

With which of these sad consequences are you familiar?

In academic workplaces that turn toxic, I personally have never seen employees resort to Options 3 and 6. My husband, though, once knew a K–12 principal who hid in a closet and slept (Option 3), and in *Catch-22*, Major Major jumped out of the window if anyone entered his office. (His secretary was trained to tell would-be visitors that he was in only when he was out, and when he was in, he wasn't in for appointments.) In neighborhoods of "at-risk" children, parents may also opt for the defense mechanism of Option 6. It is easier not to care if you are repeatedly disappointed.

In higher education, the other options are common. In one toxic environment of which I know, Item 1 became so chronic that I would tell friends, "The rats are leaving the sinking ship again." The campus became a sieve through which employees leaked as all those with the chance to leave fled for other colleges. Those who couldn't leave racked up more absences (secretaries) or worked from home as much as possible (faculty). Option 2, staying on the job but withdrawing emotionally, became common for staff; faculty still projected energy, perhaps because they got it from the students or needed to simulate it for classroom performance. Some faculty members tried to jump to administrative jobs, either at this toxic workplace or at another school: administrators are paid better and have more freedom. At last the bully left, in a promising career move. But he created such a toxic environment at his new job that his position was eliminated!

Nurturing Systems. Fortunately, not all systems are toxic. Some support creativity.

---

739 Bolman and Deal, *Reframing Organizations*, 121-23.

The Scientific Institute. If true contemporary patronage exists, it probably occurs most often in the scientific institute or "think tank." Examples in the twentieth century are the Princeton Institute for Advanced Study that nurtured Einstein and Gödel, the Cambridge Cavendish Laboratory that sponsored Watson and Crick, and the Carnegie Cold Spring Harbor laboratory that employed Barbara McClintock. In these places the most brilliant of scientists were expected simply to experiment and think—unlike academia, where they would be expected to carry the dreaded "teaching load."[740]

These havens not only furnished financial support; they also provided intellectual stimulation—a twentieth-century version of Lorenzo's dinner table. Einstein and Gödel became friends; they took walks together in suburban Princeton and discussed ideas.[741] To work with Crick at Cambridge, Watson broke the funding rules of his fellowship, which required he study in Copenhagen.[742] McClintock, by disposition a loner, was still able to have as much company as she wished (and sometimes more!) during the annual summer symposium.[743]

In fact, her situation at Cold Harbor seems ideal for a reclusive scientist. Her biographer Nathaniel C. Comfort calls it "possibly the only institution at which McClintock could have been happy and productive." A fellowship from the Carnegie Institute of Washington, then later a National Research Council Fellowship, freed her to work uninterrupted wherever she chose; she need not bother with teaching, which she disliked; the "bucolic" and remote setting of Cold Harbor meant that she was enough out of the mainstream to be mostly uninterrupted; she had a field in which to grow her experimental maize plants.[744] It was the twentieth-century equivalent of Medici patronage! Speaking about the National Research Council Fellowship, she said, you could "'do something where you wanted to, when you wanted to, no restric-

---

740 A word of explanation here: I, myself, unlike many renowned scientists, actually enjoy teaching. But I also enjoy writing, and it is difficult for most people to do them both at the same time.

741 Goldstein, *Incompleteness*, 13-14, 219.

742 James D. Watson, *The Double Helix: A Personal Account of the Discovery of the Structure of DNA*, A Mentor Book (New York: New American Library, 1969), 34.

743 Comfort, *The Tangled Field*, 78-80.

744 Ibid., 9, 66, 76-80, 120-21.

tions, no obligations, you could work all night if you wanted. You did not have to get up and teach the next morning. To do what you wanted and really have a wonderful time doing it.'" She recommended such fellowships for any creator in art or science.[745]

"Idea–Spaces" and Open Systems. Why did the VHS format conquer the superior Betamax? Why do we have Monopoly, Frisbees, televisions, airplanes, and personal computers? According to Keith Sawyer, the reason is the same. All of these successful innovations arose from shared ideas.

Sawyer remarks, "The key to understanding innovation is to realize that *collaborative webs are more important than creative people*."[746] Sony introduced the first video recorder, the Betamax, in 1975; but rival JVC "made a key strategic decision in 1976: They would openly share their technology with companies and allow a collaborative web to emerge."[747] Monopoly arose from Quaker communities who shared the game, changing it as it moved from one group to another. Frisbees began as pie plates that college students decided to toss around. Television arose from a "collaborative web" "extending back for decades." Though unveiled by RCA at the 1939 World's Fair, it had begun as an idea in 1872.[748] The Wright Brothers may have gotten their plane off the ground, but it didn't fly far. The idea of ailerons came from a collaborative web established by Glen Curtiss while the Wrights themselves were busy filing patent infringement suits.[749] The personal computing revolution is based on a long series of innovations, beginning with enormous computers used by the Department of Defense. The computers were linked by an ARPANET, and then Ray Tomlinson decided to use the @ sign to route work to a particular computer.[750]

Sawyer's thesis is that companies thrive when they encourage collaborative webs. He especially recommends sharing "idea–spaces" with customers, as Kimberly–Clark did with its Kleenex Kerchiefs. Originally

---

745 Comfort, *The Tangled Field*, 101-2.

746 Sawyer, *Group Genius*, 185.

747 Ibid., 188-89.

748 Ibid., 184.

749 Ibid., 190-91.

750 Ibid., 194-95.

designated as tissues for make–up removal, they were remarketed as handkerchiefs for colds because customers wrote in to admit they were using "this 'feminine' product in secret" "to blow their noses." The invention of the pop–up tissue box in 1921 cinched the idea, though it was 1930 before the company put the new marketing program into action.[751]

Sawyer recommends that companies "do ten things that foster collaboration":[752]

> "1. *Keep Many Irons in the Fire.*" "Cisco encourages employees to try put together pilot projects and try them out . . . Most new ideas will never pan out . . . But it's a law of innovation that successes can't go up unless failures go up, too."
>
> "2. *Create a Department of Surprise.*" Royal Dutch/Shell has teams to which other units "email their new ideas . . . These teams have created more than half of the company's innovations."
>
> "3. *Build Spaces for Creative Conversation.*" General Computer Corporation, known for Pacman, had its offices arranged around an open "stairway atrium" so employees could stop by and chat about their projects.
>
> "4. *Allow Time for Ideas to Emerge.*" "Many people say that they work best under pressure," but Teresa Amabile's research shows otherwise. She studied 177 companies and found that though people *claimed* to work best under pressure, their "daily work diaries . . . showed that creativity on high–pressure days happened less than half as often as it did on low–pressure days. And creativity remained depressed for at least two days after a high–pressure event."
>
> "5. *Manage the Risks of Improvisation.*" There are three dangers: time away from planned chores, loss of a core mission, and addition of too many product features. Businesses should be aware of these problems and plan to circumvent them.
>
> "6. *Improvise at the Edge of Chaos.*" Maintain a balance: "not too rigid to prevent emergent innovation, but not too loose to result in total chaos."
>
> "7. *Manage Knowledge for Innovation.*" "Good jazz improvisers have

---

751 Sawyer, *Group Genius*, 206.

752 The following list comes from Sawyer, *Group Genius*, 160-78.

years of experience. Through years of practicing alone and playing with others, they build a repertoire of phrases, overall forms,
and memories of other musicians' famous solos and recordings
. . . The collaborative organization excels at transferring to other
groups the ideas that emerge from good improvisations."

"8. *Build Dense Networks.*" "Cisco has turned the common practice of
electronic connection into an art form. For example, Cisco's online directory is used about four million times each month, and
even CEO John Chambers' record in the directory gives his email
address and a link that, with one click, will beep his electronic
pager."

"9. *Ditch the Organizational Chart.*" Research in the 1980s "showed that
more interconnection led to greater innovation."

"10. *Measure the Right Things.*" A 2005 study of "the world's one thousand biggest corporate spenders" showed "no relationship between the amount of R&D spending and the usual measures of
performance: sales growth, gross profit, operating profit, total
shareholder return."

All of these structural suggestions encourage what Richard Ogle
calls "idea–spaces": spaces where ideas can be shared between people.
In language reminiscent of that in Chapter 2, he says,

> **The mind—seat and organ of human intelligence—is broader and deeper
> than we thought. It extends far out into the world, more outside than
> inside. Even without our being aware of it, this extended mind engages
> closely with our individual mind, shaping and organizing our think-
> ing.**[753]

The Best Damn Ship in the Navy. That's what US Captain
D. Michael Abrashoff called the *Benfold* under his command. Abrashoff
knew that it was his job to get out of his crew's way and encourage their
creativity and autonomy. He says, "It's funny how often the problem
is you."[754]

---

753 Ogle, *Smart World*, 13.

754 Abrashoff, *It's Your Ship*, 33.

Often, he claims, leaders operate out of their own "fears, ego needs, and unproductive habits." However, "My experience has shown that helping people reach their full potential can lead to attaining goals that would be impossible to reach under command–and–control."[755] The title of his book, a "watchword" he often repeated to the crew, gave them ownership of their workplace: *It's Your Ship.*

His method encouraged creativity. He endorsed fun and play. At one time, in defiance of the regulations, he brought beer[756] on board. At another time the crew figured out how to rig a giant outdoor theater. He espoused the philosophy attributed to Cosimo de Medici by James M. Saslow: "One of the things that Cosimo understood is that you get better work out of people when people are happy." [757]

Abrashoff also invited ideas:

> **I began with the idea that there is always a better way to do things, and that, contrary to tradition, the crew's insights might be more profound than even the captain's . . . I asked everyone, "Is there a better way to do what you do?" Time after time, the answer was yes, and many of the answers were revelations to me.[758]**

The *Benfold* system paid off. Here are a few of the results.

First, the crew and ship kept winning all manner of awards. In all naval contests, "Time after time, *Benfold* outperformed *Lake Champlain*," a ship with which it had "a strong case of sibling rivalry." Abrashoff gloats, "Actually, I didn't consider it rivalry; I didn't have any rivals. I was in competition only with myself, to have the best ship we possibly could."[759]

A Theory Y manager, he encouraged self–actualization.

---

755 Abrashoff, *It's Your Ship*, 4, 5.

756 A clarification: the beer was locked up and only brought out when the ship was stalled on New Year's Eve near an island. The crew went ashore and had a cookout, enjoying the beer and a nice meal on the beach. The captain's intuition had told him there might be a time when the beer would come in handy.

757 Quoted in *Empires: The Medici: Godfathers of the Renaissance,* Part 1.

758 Abrashoff, *It's Your Ship*, 15.

759 Ibid., 123.

He arranged for his crew to take SAT tests and "college courses via CD-ROM." He says,

> To my surprise, it spurred my sailors to keep taking other tests—Navy advancement tests—and Benfold soon had a promotion rate two and a half times the Navy average. By upgrading their skills, the crew accomplished all sorts of things. We challenged their minds, which made shipboard life more fun. They boosted their chances of getting good jobs in the civilian economy, removing the specter of flipping burgers from their futures. And they clearly enriched the ship's skills pool, which in turn improved readiness.[760]

He adds,

> For my mid-level managers, my officers and chief petty officers, I set up clear and concise guidelines as to what I expected from them. I told them that I expected them to be experts in their own fields and that I would check on whether or not they were. Furthermore, they were expected to take on a project or two that would improve the ship's quality of life, or a military process that affected the entire organization . . . If you want to climb the ladder, you have to do more than your own specific job; you have to do things that affect the lives of others in the organization.[761]

He then says, in language reminiscent of Bridge Resource Management (Chapter 12),

> History records countless incidents in which ship captains or organization managers permitted a climate of intimidation to pervade the workplace, silencing the subordinates whose warnings could have prevented disaster. Even when the reluctance to speak up stems from admiration for the commanding officer's skill and experience, a climate to question decisions must be created in order to foster cross-checking.

---

760 Abrashoff, *It's Your Ship*, 160.

761 Ibid., 163.

He urges, "Make your people feel they can speak freely, no matter what they want to say." Sample phrases are as follows: "'Captain, have you thought of this?'" or 'Captain, I'm worried about something, 'or even 'Captain, I think you're dead wrong, and here's why.' Yes-people are a cancer in any organization, and dangerous to boot."[762]

He sums up his management style:

> I worked hard to create a climate that encouraged quixotic pursuits and celebrated the freedom to fail. I never once reprimanded a sailor for attempting to solve a problem or reach a goal. I wanted my people to feel empowered, so they could think autonomously.[763]

He also pushed the envelope on navy procedure more than once.

A higher-up in the navy (who wishes to remain anonymous) says that Abrashoff often defied the rules of the system and adds, "I'm glad I didn't have to relieve him."

Which brings us to . . .

The System. The System matters. Just ask Philip Zimbardo. In 1971 Dr. Zimbardo created the famous Stanford Prison Experiment. He placed an ad offering $15 a day to students willing to participate in an experiment in prison simulation. After interviewing and testing his subjects to confirm that they were mentally healthy, he had them randomly assigned to roles as guards or prisoners.

What he discovered was startling even to him. These sensitive, intelligent young men became completely identified with their roles. The experiment, scheduled to run for two weeks, had to be stopped after four days because the guards were becoming brutal and the prisoners were suffering breakdowns. Zimbardo, who calls this phenomenon the Power of the Situation, has this to say about Systems:

> Systems provide the institutional support, authority, and resources that allow Situations to operate as they do . . . a key question is rarely asked: Who had the power to design the behavioral setting and to maintain its operation in particular ways? Therefore, who should be held responsible

---

762 Abrashoff, *It's Your Ship*, 92, 89.
763 Ibid., 94.

for its consequences and outcomes? . . . finding that answer is not such a simple matter when we deal with complex organizations, such as failing educational or correctional systems, corrupt megacorporations, or the system that was created at Abu Ghraib prison.[764]

The Medici created a system nurturing creativity. So did the benefactors who established scientific institutes and foundations. The foreman at the doll factory did the opposite. Captain Abrashoff had the unusual perspicacity to understand what sort of system he was creating: to know exactly what he was doing and what effects it would have. Most of us can't direct the process so well. We educators think we know what we are doing when we set up the rules and procedures for a class, but all too often we are surprised at the system that develops.

So we have seen that individuals can enhance their creativity by following certain processes and monitoring their states, stages, shadows, and egos (Chapters 1–6). We have seen that *Creative Synergy* can operate between the Field and the individual (Chapters 1–4), between parts of the individual (Chapters 5–6), between members of a group (Chapters 7–8), between parts of the Thing–in–Itself (Chapter 9–11), and between parts and a system (Chapters 12–13).

What Next?

And now for something completely different: the wrap–up. What have we learned, and what is the possible future of creativity in this new century?

---

764 Philip Zimbardo, *The Lucifer Effect: Understanding how Good People Turn Evil* (New York: Random House, 2007), 226.

Exercises

1. Write about systems of patronage that are not mentioned in this book.
2. Do some research about the Medici and the artists they supported. Report on the results.
3. What toxic systems have you encountered, either in your own life or in the lives of others? (It might be a good idea not to name names specifically.) Evaluate the system/s in terms of TQM, "Assholes," Theory X, and/or the six coping mechanisms. How did the system/s squelch creativity?
4. What nurturing systems have you encountered, either in your own life or in the lives of others? What made them nurturing? How did they encourage creativity?
5. As a leader, how would you (or do you) establish a system that is nurturing and supports creativity?
6. Sawyer mentions innovations such as the mountain bike that resulted from modification to existing products. Modify something to make something new and useful.
7. List some of the puzzling or unclear ideas in Chapter 13. Ask questions about them.
8. Explain what you think is most important in Chapter 13.
9. React to some of the ideas in Chapter 13. Debate, support, analyze, and/or reflect.
10. Give evidence from your own life or background experience about the ideas in Chapter 13. (Don't repeat what you have written in another exercise.)

Synergistic Interlude from Jonathan Young:

"Once Upon a Time:
How Fairy Tales Shape Our Lives"

"Poet William Stafford had a favorite image. He said that the work of creativity is to 'follow the golden thread.' Something catches your attention, a feeling, an image, an idea, the events of a moment. The challenge is to pay attention to that subtle urge and follow it gently. We must roll out the golden thread with care or it will break. Opening ourselves to greater significance in familiar stories requires a certain tenderness of spirit. The notions will be fragile at first. We must hold them gently for a time until they deliver their message to us. The effects of what we learn might well last for a lifetime."

—Inside Journal *magazine*, Fall 1997[765]

Questions to Ponder

1. How is creativity like a golden thread?

2. In the practice of your own creativity, have you ever felt that you were following a delicate thread without knowing where it would lead? Explain.

3. How is this metaphor similar to the tale of the golden key at the beginning of Chapter 1?

4. Of what fairy tales or folktales does the metaphor of the golden thread remind you?

---

765 Jonathan Young, from the web site for story and symbol: http://www.folkstory.com.

14

Conclusion: Synthesis, Summary, and Resources

So what have we learned about how to be more creative? And what's in store for the field of creativity in the future? Can we look into our crystal ball and draw some conclusions?

Creative Synergy: The Philosophy

In one interview Ken Wilber explains the cooperation of the forces of synergy and evolution: "Self and culture and nature go together. We have to liberate all three of them, or none at all . . . Indeed, there *is* this drive toward perfection, or this drive toward something better, this intuition that there's something fully whole that I can reach for that is better than anything that has gone before."[766] It is the drive to self–actualize, to evolve, to be more fully creative. It is the desire to stand in the presence of Beauty, Truth, and Goodness—to experience the creativity that Ken Wilber says "is part of the basic ground of the universe."[767]

And part of this "basic ground" is *Creative Synergy*—the principle that the whole is greater than the sum of the parts. When we act in cooperation with "the Force"—when we integrate the parts of our own being—when we act in cooperation with culture and systems and create

---

766 Cohen and Wilber, "The Guru and the Pandit: Dialogue XV: Creative Friction," 56.
767 Wilber, *CW*, vol. 7, *A Brief History of Everything*, 25.

"what is trying to happen"—then we can aid our own self-actualization as well as the continuing evolution of life and culture on this planet. We become whole as we make others and the culture more whole. We understand our life's mission and our part in something larger. Andrew Cohen calls the process "Creative Friction": "the definition of deep spiritual, psychological, and emotional health and vibrancy in a community or intersubjective context."[768]

So this is the underlying philosophy. On a more practical side, here are some techniques to aid in the journey.

How to Be More Creative: Twenty Tips

1. *Make the decision (Ch. 1).* Commit to being creative.[769] Remember Amabile's Intrinsic Motivation Principle: "Intrinsic motivation is conducive to creativity; controlling extrinsic motivation is detrimental to creativity, but informational or enabling extrinsic motivation can be conducive, particularly if initial levels of intrinsic motivation are high."[770] Even if you have an extrinsic deadline, cultivate "Task Motivation."[771]

2. *Court the wind, but put in the sweat (Ch. 1).* Begin working on a project, put in the time, and trust that inspiration will come. Jim Buckley, a professor of Maritime Transportation at the California Maritime Academy, advises his students to begin writing as soon as they receive an assignment for a paper and to write every day thereafter. Any sort of writing—whether making notes, jotting down ideas, or creating mind maps—will keep the ideas coming. (For mind maps, see the Alternative Exercises in the Appendix.)

3. *Practice the formulas of your domain (Chs. 1, 3).* Practice your craft. When you are proficient, you will be able to use your tools without thinking. If you are intrinsically motivated to enjoy a domain, you will practice it for fun and get better. As a musician and artist of my acquaintance said, "You either have that desire

---

768 Cohen and Wilber, "The Guru and the Pandit: Dialogue XV: Creative Friction," 60.
769 Sternberg, *Creativity as a Decision.*
770 Amabile, *Creativity in Context*, 119.
771 Ibid., 82-83, 77.

for it or you don't have it . . . Some of it is innate, but you still have to have a theoretical background." [772]

4. *Focus on your project (Ch. 1).* Become obsessed. Think about your project every day. Edison neglected his family and lived in his laboratory. Einstein was so involved in his theories he neglected his appearance and forgot his suitcases. Pavlov, who discovered the basic principles of behaviorism by studying the digestion of dogs, often forgot to bring home his paycheck, even though his family was destitute. These are extreme examples, but some degree of obsessed focus is necessary.

5. *Keep a notebook (Exercises).* Many great creators, such as Leonardo and Edison, kept one. In some cases the notebooks are still creating, decades or centuries after the thinker's death. Would-be engineers are still constructing machines from Leonardo's notebooks,[773] and Howard Gruber has made a career from Darwin's, which inspired his "evolving systems approach" to creativity.[774] Notebooks—such as the one I kept while writing this book—contain seeds of ideas that may germinate later. As I revisited portions of my notebook written months before, I often saw ideas I had forgotten.

6. *Center your awareness. (Chs. 1, 3).* Ask, "What is trying to happen here?" Meditate or concentrate. Focus on the Form that is trying to come through. Redefine the problem.

7. *Allow time for incubation (Chs. 1, 3).* Start early, and understand that you will hit blocks from time to time. Blocks often dissolve suddenly in the bathroom, during a physical activity, or after a good night's sleep. Leave time for the process to work naturally rather than trying to force yourself through a block.

8. *Use your dreams (Ch. 2).* Before you go to sleep at night, hold a creative problem or project in your mind, and ask for a dream to help you. Keep writing materials beside your bed so you can jot down ideas and dream fragments as soon as you awaken.

9. *Cultivate the "Flow" state (Ch. 3).* Choose a creative task that is de-

---

772 Harry Paine, personal communication, May 27, 2007.

773 *Leonardo's Dream Machines.*

774 See references and Appendix 1.

manding but not too hard. Concentrate fully and mindfully on it until time disappears and you feel joy. Be aware of what conditions create "Flow" for you.

10. *Be aware of your individual self and its influence (Chs. 1, 2, 4).* Is your personality helping you—or hindering you? What characteristics of the creative personality can you cultivate? What stage or state of awareness does your art reflect? Is your shadow getting in the way? Which of the multiple intelligences do you have? Are you cultivating them consciously? Are you working on those that are not natural to you?

11. *Be aware of your ego and its influence (Ch. 5).* Can you take multiple perspectives on your work, or are you locked into one of view? Is your ego blocking the "Flow" state? Can you take feedback without reacting personally? While practicing your creative work, are you fulfilling what you believe to be your life's mission or function?

12. *Cultivate a balance of energetic action and surrender (Ch. 3).* Act, but be receptive to nudges from "the Force" and "what is trying to happen." Practice "Mindfulness" or "bare awareness." Try meditation. Keep a notebook of your insights.

13. *Take advantage of serendipity and synchronicity (Ch. 3).* Watch for lucky breaks, and take advantage of them. They may be a sign that "the Force" is cooperating with you. Keep a notebook of your insights.

14. *Find a model (Examples in all Chs. and the Exercises).* Study the life and work of a creator. Imitate his or her process and/or product. Find someone whose thinking is like yours. For instance, Einstein thought in pictures and flashes of insight. Isabel Allende feels her books somatically, in her "belly." I receive inspiration in language and thoughts. Feynman enjoyed working out the math, whereas Einstein did not.

15. *Synthesize (Ch. 1).* Practice combining unlike ideas and images. The idea for the Nike shoe came from a synergistic combination of an athletic shoe and a waffle iron![775] (See the Alternative Exercises for practice in "Janus–thinking.")

---

775 Kurt Hanks and Jay A. Parry, *Wake up Your Creative Genius* (Los Altos, CA: William Kaufman, 1983), 7-8.

16. *Collaborate (Chs. 6-7, 11, 1).* Work in a team, or establish a support network. Discuss your project with others. Ask them for feedback. Be aware of how others may be hindering as well as helping your creativity. Be aware of group dynamics and acknowledge when the team is disintegrating. Help others with their creativity.

17. *Evaluate the product. (Chs. 1, 8-10).* Does it have universal qualities? Is it new and useful? Is it beautiful? Does it cultivate what is good? Does it follow the formal and/or functional rules of its domain?

18. *Try it out (Chs. 1, 3).* Try your project out in the real world. Does the model of the plane fly? Does the art gallery accept the paintings? Do people visit the blog?

19. *Get a patron (Ch. 12).* Get a grant. Find a job that supports your creativity. Analyze the system in which you are working to see whether it is nurturing or toxic. If it is to some degree toxic, decide how you will cope.

20. *Go to other resources to become more aware of "Creativity-Relevant Processes." Read other books on creativity, and watch movies or documentaries about creators. (Ch.1, Alternative Exercises, Bibliography).* Every book takes a different slant. Some are "puzzle books" of exercises; some are lists of practical tips; some are scholarly or biographical studies. Many, if not most, will contain something useful for you. So will films. They may inspire you as well as providing insight into how someone successful creates.

Creativity in the Future

New Combinations

The Introduction and Chapter 1 explain the new synthesis of disciplines occurring in higher education. I predict that these creative combinations will continue. We have had a few centuries in which to refine the boundaries between disciplines and to practice discipline-specific methodologies—even to create disciplines within disciplines, such as neuroscience. Now new mergers are taking place.

For instance, the domain of English is in a crisis because it has disintegrated into subfields that are merging in new ways with the social sciences, language arts, and communications. We now have Black Studies, Gay Studies, East Asian Studies, Hispanic Studies; we have English as a Second Language, Critical Thinking, Media, Writing in the Disciplines and Across the Curriculum. We don't have–at least in any sphere I frequent–the field for which I was trained in the 1970s: specialist in the literature of the Renaissance, Eighteenth Century, or Middle Ages. Is this a good thing? Is it a bad thing? Experts disagree. The point is, something is happening, and new syntheses are occurring.

Here's another example of this new wave of interdisciplinary thinking.

Stanford Professor Jonathan Berger, a composer, began to study how listening to complex sounds can influence behavior. While teaching his students how to draw a bow across a stringed instrument, he realized that no amount of verbal instruction would help. The only procedure that worked was for the would–be violinist or cellist to make the correct movement and hear the desired sound. This dual combination of movement and sound acted on the brain to embed the experience, which could then be repeated. Berger realized that this method could be used in medical or behavioral science. By hooking actions to accompanying sounds, he could help golfers improve their swings and disabled children walk. He has created a machine to implement this idea and is working with professors from the sciences to perfect the mechanism. He is now also founder of the Stanford Institute for Creativity in the Arts, created in 2006.[776]

We are also achieving new insights by what is called the Scholarship of Integration. An example is this book, which integrates the concepts of many domains formerly separate: math, science, the arts, spirituality, sports, and business. Ed Nuhfer (California State University of the Channel Islands) explains the value of "unifying concepts":

> **The value of unifying concepts is less about unique discoveries than about their effects in making dispersed information more relevant and accessible. For example, the unifying concept of plate tectonics in geology did not accompany a specific discovery involving rocks, ore deposits, field geology, geochemistry, geophysics, oceanography, seismology, vulcanology, stratigraphy, and so on. Each of these specialties contributed knowledge and made impressive discoveries without any**

---

776 Carrie Sturrock, "Stanford: Professor Decodes Life Note by Note," *San Francisco Chronicle*, February 5, 2007, accessed April 5, 2014, http://www.sfgate.com/default/article/STANFORD-Professor-decodes-life-note-by-note-2651438.phpvvv.

unifying theory. However, once plate tectonics made obvious the connections among these specialties, it greatly expedited understanding . . . The concept had a profound effect from the level of individual scholar to the entire disciplinary profession.[777]

Web 3.0

Csikszentmihalyi's "systems view of creativity" emphasizes the importance of gatekeepers, those who guard the field by evaluating creative products before they get to an audience. The art gallery decides whether or not to accept the pictures; the publisher decides whether or not to accept the writing.

Those days are over.

Web 3.0 is here, and it is helping to create the "flat earth" mentioned in the Introduction: a level playing field on which anyone can compete.

Web 1.0 focused on providing one–way information from limited sites. Web 2.0 extended that network and became interactive, offering the opportunity for anyone to be an instant star. With Web 2.0 we could create information and share it, network with groups and people all over the planet, post our writing or videos, blog on any subject.

Alternative websites like *Daily Kos* began competing with traditional print newspapers. Bill Clinton courted the youth vote by playing the saxophone on MTV; the major candidates for the 2008 election had sites on My Space. Now anyone can become famous (or exposed) by a video posted on YouTube. Anyone can meet someone through postings on My Space or Facebook. Anyone can sign up to receive email messages from President Obama and respond with feedback. A disaster can be recorded by phone cameras and posted online within minutes. One spin–off was Lunch 2.0. After Silicon Valley geeks began sneaking into lunchrooms of rival tech companies and blogging about their experiences, many firms formalized and endorsed the movement by inviting the crashers to lunch, thereby instituting communal brainstorming and sharing.[778]

---

777 Ed Nuhfer, "The ABCs of Fractal Thinking in Higher Education," in *To Improve the Academy,* ed. Douglas R. Robertson and Linda B. Nilson, POD Network (Boston: Anker, 2007), 75-76.

778 Jessica Guynn, "Lunch 2.0: Free Food, A Side of Tech Talk," *San Francisco Chronicle,* May 25, 2007, A-1, A-14, accessed April 4, 2014, http://www.sfgate.com/default/article/Lunch-2-0-free-food-a-side-of-tech-talk-2591946.php,. See the bloggers' web site at www.lunch20.

With Web 3.0, the interactivity has intensified, Csikszentmihalyi's gatekeepers are disappearing. A blogger can become a famous writer. A self–published author can order a book at a time from a digital copy rather than spending $10,000–$20,000 on a garage full of books. Third graders know how to construct Web sites with software that make it increasingly easier for anyone to sell to anyone. Todd Lubart (Université René Descartes, Paris) says that with the advent of the twenty–first century, *homo sapiens* has become *homo creativus.*[779]

A young man in San Francisco became famous by recording all the events of his life as they happened and posting them on his website: *Justin TV.*[780] Another young man became famous by editing an old ad, spinning it into an endorsement for Barack Obama, and posting it on YouTube. Political candidates, public officials, and other celebrities find themselves in a constant circuit of apologies because something they said or did is suddenly recorded online. A troubled young man massacres classmates at Virginia Tech, sends a video of himself to NBC news, and achieves his desired fame. A Syracuse communications professor writing in *The Chronicle of Higher Education* observes, "In the age of the Internet and the 24/7 news cycle, it is reasonable to anticipate that the next wave of attackers will not merely copy Cho's efforts but will try even harder to shock the audiences following news of their violent misdeeds." The question then is, "How will the news media decide whether and when to provide platforms for such communications?"[781]

And what is happening to copyright during this digital revolution? The music and movie industries are trying to control illicit copying and pirating—without success. Cory Doctorow, lecturer at USC, asks on his communications syllabus, "'Is everyone on campus a criminal?'"[782] Stu-

779 Ted Lubart, "Creativity, Culture, and Assessment of Potential Creativity with EPoC," Keynote Address, International Centre for Innovation in Education, 3rd Annual Conference, Athens, Greece, June 9, 2010.

780 After two months he grew bored and passed the torch to a new video autobiographer: Justine. See Jessica Guynn, "Can't Get Enough Justin? You Can Watch Justine," *San Francisco Chronicle*, May 29, 2007, C-1, C-4, accessed April 4, 2014, http://www.sfgate.com/default/article/Can-t-get-enough-Justin-You-can-watch-Justine-2573698.php.

781 Joan Deppa, "Coping with a Killer's 'Manifesto,'" *Chronicle of Higher Education*, May 11, 2007, B14.

782 Brock Read, "A Blogger Infiltrates Academe," *Chronicle of Higher Education*, April 6, 2007, A30.

dents share music and videos; instructors copy online texts and pictures onto handouts. Hired to teach a class because of his popular blog Boing Boing, Doctorow advocates a "minimalist" view of copyright as realistic, given the new technology.[783] Keith Sawyer agrees.

Creativity—both positive and negative—is expanding exponentially. Now almost anyone has a chance to be heard. Carter Phipps says that "the advent of the internet" represents an evolution of "something much more profound . . . than simply greater and personal and social productivity." Quoting Fred Turner's book *From Counterculture to Cyberculture*, Phipps cites "a 'countercultural dream of empowered individualism, collaborative community, and spiritual communication' that hovers around the idea of the internet and computing like a mythological halo.'"[784] *Time Magazine* named its 2006 cover person as "You" and called Web 2.0 "'a massive social experiment'": "'There's no road map for how an organism that's not a bacterium lives and works together on this planet in numbers in excess of 6 billion.'"[785]

What 2.0 is next? We already have one in education: the Classroom Management System, which offers chat rooms and electronic office hours—not to mention the new explosion in Distance Learning, which takes full advantage of the technology. These tools become 3.0 as students are asked to use Google apps and create wikis.

Michael Auer (Carinthia University of Applied Sciences, Villach, Austria), has described the development of the Internet:

Web 1.0: many Web sites containing much unstructured textual content
Web 2.0: a few large Web sites allowing users to share
Web 3.0: many Web sites containing semantically controlled content.

Web 3.0, says Auer, is a "social–semantic web," with "interactive technology, game–based learning, collaborative virtual environments and learning, 3D synchronous network, 3D visualization and learning," as well as "i–labs, real labs that are accessed through the Internet from

---

783 Brock Read, "A Blogger Infiltrates Academe," April 6, 2007, A30.

784 Carter Phipps, "Dreams of a Digital Utopia," *What is Enlightenment?* 36 (April-June 2007), 114.

785 Quoted in Phipps, 116.

anywhere at any time." "The core of web 3.0 is not technology but a new way of using technology."[786]

Keith Sawyer says,

> Group genius is, ultimately, the genius of all humanity. Our success in solving the most critical problems and needs that we face, today and in the future, depends on our ability to tap into the creative power of collaboration.[787]

"May the Force Be With You"

Mira Nair is an East Indian director who has achieved worldwide fame with films such as *Salaam Bombay, Mississippi Masala, Monsoon Wedding,* and *The Namesake.* In 2007 she began work on a new project: the story of the Beatles' 1968 sojourn in the Rishikesh ashram of Maharishi Mahesh Yogi, a period during which they wrote the songs that would become the two–disc *White Album.* Her subject is, she says, "about the nature of inspiration. 'Why do these moments of inspiration happen?'" She adds a theory: "It's a synergy of things, and sometimes the Force is with you."[788]

What she has said in a few sentences, I have drawn out to over 300 pages. Cultivate synergy. Be mindful. And "may the force be with you."

This text was used in creativity classes at Cal State Maritime. In the spring semester of 2014, the students agreed to share some representative examples of their art work during a 50–minute lab session. I provided the names of the art works.

---

786 Michael Auer, "Online Laboratories in Education and the Transition from Web 2.0 to Web 3.0," Keynote Address, International Centre for Innovation in Education, 3rd Annual Conference, Athens, Greece, June 10, 2010.

787 Sawyer, *Group Genius*, 219.

788 "Here, There, and Mira Nair," *What is Enlightenment?* 36 (April-June 2007), 24.

Spaghetti uses the curves mentioned in Chapter 9

Artist: Vanessa Parke
Photographer: Michael Midgley

Alien shows engineering, ability, spatial reasoning and unique combinations of materials

Artist and Photographer: Grant Innis

Addict shows an original vision and unique combinations of materials

Artist: Sean Boston
Photographer: Madeleine Wolczko

Totem shows an original vision and unique combinations of materials

Artist and Photographer Austin Koucek

Exercises

1. In *How to Think Like Leonardo da Vinci,* Michael J. Gelb lists "Seven da Vincian Principles":

   Curiositá—An insatiably curious approach to life and an unrelenting quest for continuous learning.

   Dimostrazione—A commitment to test knowledge through experience, persistence, and a willingness to learn from mistakes.

   Sensazione—The continual refinement of the senses, especially sight, as the means to enliven experience.

   Sfumato (literally "Going up in Smoke")—A willingness to embrace ambiguity, paradox, and uncertainty.

   Arte/Scienza—The development of the balance between science and art, logic and imagination. "Whole-brain thinking."

   Corporalia—The cultivation of grace, ambidexterity, fitness, and poise.

   Connessione—A recognition of and appreciation for the interconnectedness of all things and phenomena. Systems thinking.[789]

   Where have you seen these principles demonstrated or explained in this book? And/or how can you practice them in your life, education, or career?

2. See the tips on "How to be more creative." Which have you practiced or do you plan to practice? How? Be specific.

3. What experience have you had with Web 3.0? Has it enabled you to be more creative? Explain.

4. Listen to Dr. Jonathan Berger's podcast at www.sfgate.com/blogs/podcasts. Report on the results.

5. In *Notebooks of the Mind,* Vera John-Steiner explains various modes of creative thinking: visual thinking, verbal thinking, and thinking with movement and sound. She notes that there is also *condensed thought across several modalities,*[790] as in Darwin's notebooks of sketches and observations. Which modalities do you typically use, and how?

6. Read the one or both of these articles on Art and the Unconscious: S.

---

789 Gelb, *How to Think Like Leonardo da Vinci*, 9.

790 John-Steiner, *Notebooks of the Mind*, 215.

Winn, "Painting a Picture of the Creative Mind" (2007, May 28.) *San Francisco Chronicle,* B-1, B-2. Available at www.sfgate.com.

_____. "What Happens to Us When Art Connects to the Unconscious" (2007, May 29.) *San Francisco Chronicle,* D-1, D-2. Available at www. sfgate.com.

Write a reaction to what you have read, and apply some of the insights from this book.

Appendices

Appendix 1

Structures of Organizations

Bolman and Deal describe five organizational structures, each best for a particular purpose.

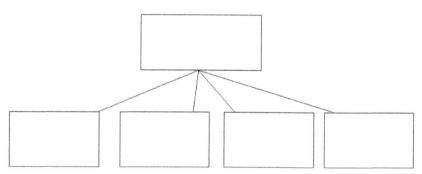

Figure 14 represents the "One Boss" structure, useful in small start-ups. The tasks are simple and uncomplicated; the organization is so small that a few employees can report directly to the boss. A danger is that the boss could become overloaded and stretched too thin.

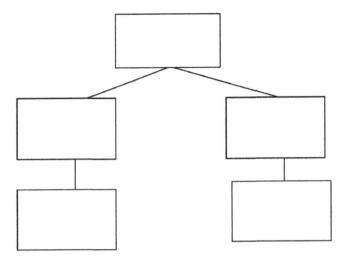

Figure 15 represents the Dual Authority model, with two chains of command. The boss is free to concentrate on the mission and strategic planning, leaving day-to-day management under control of two subordinates. The danger is that, with one more level of management added, the workers on the front line might not have ready access to the boss with their ideas and complaints.

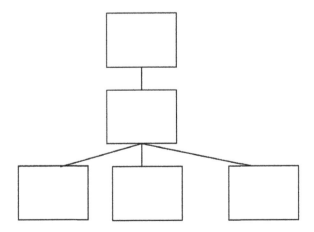

Figure 16 represents a Simple Hierarchy. One manager reports to the boss and supervises various areas. Problems can arise, however, if the middle managers attempt to usurp the power of the "top-level manager" above them.

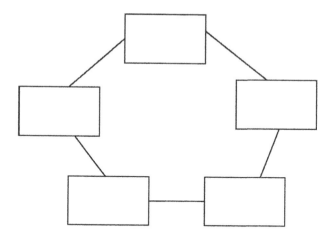

Figure 17 represents a Circle. Information, help, and ideas can flow readily from one person to the next, but "one weakest link can undermine the entire enterprise."

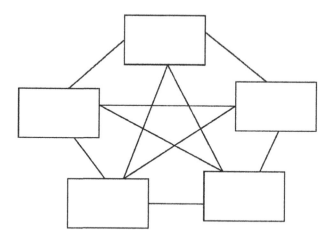

With **Figure 18**, the Circle has become a Star or All-Channel Network. In this "web of inclusion," all of the members of the group can help one another with ideas, suggestions, and information.

Appendix 2

Alternative Exercises

1. Visit MIT's website of open courseware at www.ocw.mit.edu. Search a term like "creativity," and download or print out some course material. Write a response—or, if you're taking a class, bring the material to class for a demonstration.

2. Do an exercise from a creativity book. Recommended are those by von Oech, Koberg and Bagnall, Buzan, Hanks and Parry, DeBono, Pink, and the Root-Bernsteins. (See the Bibliography.) Note: the MIT site has some great PowerPoint slides from Buzan.

3. Convert a writing exercise to another modality, based on your preferred type of intelligence or learning style. Do a dance, write a song, draw a picture, or make a sculpture or invention. Do research, or try something out.

4. Do an interview with someone who is creative. Report on the results.

5. Explain how a cartoon comments on creativity.

6. Research a "Creation Myth." Summarize it, and explain its meaning.

7. Investigate a company you think is creative. Report on why. (Some examples are Microsoft, Dell, and Apple.)

8. Make a Mind Map or Cluster of a Project on which you are working. In the center of a page, write your main topic, and draw a circle around it. Then brainstorm subtopics and draw circles around them, as well as lines to the main topic. Do the same for subtopics and even smaller subtopics. Here's a simple example. (I made a cluster for each chapter of this book.)

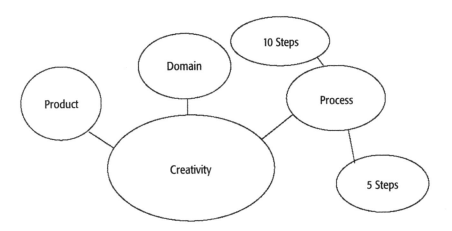

Bibliography

Abrashoff, D. Michael. *It's Your Ship: Management Techniques from the Best Damn Ship in the Navy*. New York: Time Warner, 2002.

Advancing Faculty Learning through Interdisciplinary Collaboration, Edited by Elizabeth G.Creamer and Lisa R. Lattuca. New Directions for Teaching and Learning, Number 102. San Francisco: Jossey–Bass, Summer 2005.

Albert, Robert S., and Mark A. Runco. "A History of Research on Creativity." In *Handbook of Creativity*, edited by Robert J. Sternberg, 16–31. Cambridge, Massachusetts: University Press, 1999.

Alexander, Christopher. *The Nature of Order: An Essay on the Art of Building and the Nature of the Universe*. Vol 3. *The Phenomenon of Life*. Berkeley: The Center for Environmental Structure, 2002.

Amadeus, directed by Peter Shaffer. Amadeus Productions, 1984.

Allende, Isabelle. In *Writers Dreaming*, edited by Naomi Epel, 7–24. New York: Carol Southern, 1993.

Amabile, Teresa M. "Beyond Talent: John Irving and the Passionate Craft of Creativity." *American Psychologist* 56 (April 2001): 333–36.

———. *Creativity in Context*. Boulder, Colorado: Westview Press, 1996.

American Heritage Dictionary of the English Language. 4th ed. Boston: Houghton Mifflin, 2000.

Andreason, Nancy C. *The Creative Brain*. New York: Penguin, 2006.

Arieti, Silvano. *Creativity: The Magic Synthesis*. New York: Basic Books, Harper Colophon, 1976.

Ashliman, D.L., ed. *Folklore and Mythology: Electronic Texts*. Accessed April 3, 2014.http://www.pitt.edu/~dash/folktexts.html.

Astin, Alexander, and Helen Astin. *The Spiritual Life of College Students: A National Study of College Students' Search for Meaning and Purpose*. Higher Education Research Institute, U.C.L.A. PDF file of Report, 2003–2005. Accessed April 3, 2014. http://spirituality.ucla.edu/.

Atwater, P.M.H. *Future Memory*. Charlottesville, VA: Hampton Roads Publishing Company, 1999.

Auer, Michael. "Online Laboratories in Education and the Transition from Web 2.0 to Web 3.0." Keynote Address. International Centre for Innovation in Education. 3rd annual conference, Athens, Greece, June 10, 2010.

Aurobindo, Sri. *A Greater Psychology.* Edited by A.S. Dalal. New York: Tarcher–Putnam, 2001.

Ayral–Clause, Odile. *Camille Claudel: A Life.* New York: Henry N. Abrams, 2002.

Barzun, Jacques. "The Paradoxes of Creativity." *American Scholar* 58, no. 3 (Summer 1989): 337–51.

Baxter Magolda, Marcia B. *Knowing and Reasoning in College: Gender-Related Pat-terns in Students' Intellectual Development.* San Francisco: Jossey–Bass, 1992.

Beauvoir, Simone de. *Hard Times: Force of Circumstances, 1952-1962 (Autobiography of Simone de Beauvoir).* Harmondsworth: Penguin Books, 1963.

Beck, Don. *Spiral Dynamics Integral.* 6–CD set. Boulder, Colorado: Sounds True, 2006.

Belenky, Mary Field, Blythe Mcvicker Clinchy, Nancy Rule Goldberger, and Jill Mattuck Tarule. *Women's Ways of Knowing: The Development of Self, Voice, and Mind.* New York: Basic Books, 1986.

Bell, Derek. "The Divine Gift of Melody." Interview. *Clarity Magazine,* Number 2 (1999): 8–10.

Bennis, Warren, and Patricia Ward Biederman. *Organizing Genius: The Secrets of Creative Collaboration.* Reading, MA: Addison–Wesley, 1997.

Bensaude–Vincent, Bernadette. "Star Scientists in a Nobelist Family: Iréne and Frédéric Joliot–Cure." In *Creative Couples in the Sciences,* edited by Helena M. Pycior, Nancy G. Slack, and Pnina G. Abir–Am, 57–72. New Brunswick, NJ: Rutgers University Press, 1996.

Berman, Richard. "Surviving a Bad Boss: Certain Management Styles Can Create Real Trauma. *San Francisco Chronicle,* April 15, 2007, H–1. Accessed April 4, 2014. http://www.sfgate.com/default/article/Surviving-a-Bad-Boss-Certain-management-styles-2602737.php.

Bhatt, Nilkanth. Class on Sankaracharya's *Tattva Bodha.* Sponsored by Chinmaya Trust. Houston, Texas, December 18, 1983.

Block, Larry. *Affirmations for Writers.* Privately produced audiotape, 1986.

_____. *Write for Your Life: The Book about the Seminar*. Privately printed, 1986.

Bloom, Harold. *20th Anniversary Edition: Dramatists and Dramas*. New York: Readers Subscription Book Club, 2006.

_____. *20thAnniversary Edition: Essayists and Prophets*. New York: Readers Subscription Book Club, 2005.

_____. *Genius: A Mosaic of One Hundred Exemplary Minds*. New York: Warner, 2002.

Bly, Robert. "The Long Bag We Drag Behind Us." In *Meeting the Shadow: The Hidden Power of the Dark Side of Human Nature*, edited by Connie Zweig and Jeremiah Abrams, 6–12. Los Angeles: Tarcher, 1991.

Bohm, David. *Wholeness and the Implicate Order*. London: Ark Paperbacks, 1983.

Bolman, Lee G., and Terence E. Deal. *Reframing Organizations: Artistry, Choice, and Leadership*. 3rd ed. San Francisco: Jossey–Bass, 2003.

Booker, Christopher. *The Seven Basic Plots*. New York, London: Continuum, 2004.

Booth, Wayne. *The Rhetoric of Fiction*. Chicago: University of Chicago Press, 1961.

Boyer, Ernest. *Scholarship Reconsidered: The Priorities of the Professoriate*. Carnegie Foundation, 1990.

Braden, Gregg. *Awakening to Zero Point: The Collective Initiation*. rev. ed. A Sacred Spaces/Ancient Wisdom Book. Bellevue, Washington: Radio Bookstore Press, 1997.

_____. *The Divine Matrix: Bridging Time, Space, Miracles, and Belief*. Carlsbad, California: Hay House, 2007.

Bride of the Wind. Directed by Bruce Beresford. Paramount Classics. Total Film Group, 2001.

Brye, Joseph. *Basic Principles of Music Theory*. New York: Ronald Press, 1965.

Cabanatuan, Michael. "Net Seems Likelier for Bridge Suicide Barrier." *San Francisco Chronicle*, October 4, 2008, B-1.

Camille Claudel. Directed by Bruno Nuytten. Distributed by Orion Home Video, 1989.

Campbell, David. *Take the Road to Creativity*. Allen, TX: Argus, 1977.

Capra, Fritjof. *The Turning Point*. New York: Simon and Schuster, 1982.

Carrington. Directed by Christopher Hampton. Freeway Films, 1995.

Castaneda, Carlos. *Tales of Power*. A Touchstone Book. New York: Simon and Schuster, 1974.

Chaitanya, Svarupa. Commentary based on discourses by H.H. Swami Dayanandaji. *Tattva Bodha of Sankaracharya*. Bombay, India: Central Chinmaya Mission Trust, n.d.

Cheever, Susan. *American Bloomsbury: Louisa May Alcott, Ralph Waldo Emerson, Margaret Fuller, Nathaniel Hawthorne, and Henry David Thoreau: Their Lives, Their Loves, Their Work*. New York: Simon and Schuster, 2006.

Chidbhavananda, Swami. Commentary accompanying verses and translation of *The Bhagavad Gita*. Tamil Nadu, India: Sri Ramakishna Tapovanam, 1982.

Christy, Lynn Sparrow. *Beyond Soul Growth*. Virginia Beach, VA: A.R.E. Press, 2013.

Combs, Allan. "Horizontal Evolution and Collective Intelligence. Integral Ideas." *What is Enlightenment?* 36 (April–June 2007), 40–42.

_____, and Mark Holland. *Synchronicity: Science, Myth and the Trickster*. New York: Paragon House, 1990.

Cohen, Andrew, and Ken Wilber. "The Guru and the Pandit: Dialogue XIV: A Living Experiment in Conscious Evolution." *What is Enlightenment?* 35 (January–March 2007), 47–58.

_____. "The Guru and the Pandit: Dialogue XV: Creative Friction: Community and the Utopian Impulse in a Post–Modern World." *What is Enlightenment?* 36 (April–June 2007), 52–66.

_____. "The Guru and the Pandit: Dialogue XXI: The Interdynamics of Culture Consciousness." *What is Enlightenment?* 42 (December–February, 2008–2009), 40–52.

Coleridge, Samuel Taylor. *Biographia Literaria*. Project Gutenberg. Original work 1817. Retrieved from http://www.gutenberg.org/files/6081/6081-h/6081-h.htm.

Comfort, Nathaniel C. *The Tangled Field: Barbara McClintock's Search for the*

Patterns of Genetic Control. Cambridge, MA: Harvard University Press, 2003.

"Construction Data." Accessed April 8, 2007. http://goldengatebridge. org/research/factsGGBDesign.php.

Coppola, Eleanor, and Francis Ford Coppola, Producers, Writers, and Directors. *Hearts of Darkness.* Motion Picture. United States: American Zoetrope, 1991.

Coppola, Francis Ford. Producer, Writer, and Director. *Apocalypse Now.* Motion Picture. United States: American Zoetrope, 1979.

Covey, Stephen R. *The 7 Habits of Highly Effective People.* New York: Simon and Schuster, 1989.

_____. *First Things First.* New York: Simon and Schuster, 1994.

Crease, Robert P. *The Prism and the Pendulum: The Ten Most Beautiful Experiments in Science.* New York: Random House, 2003.

Creativity: Touching the Divine. Instructional Video. The Catholic Communication Campaign. Interfaith Broadcasting Communion. Alexandria, VA: Journey Communications, 1994.

Crick, Francis. *What Mad Pursuit: A Personal View of Scientific Discovery.* Alfred P. Sloane Foundation Series. New York: Basic Books, 1988.

Cropley, Arthur. *Creativity in Education and Learning: A Guide for Teachers and Educators.* London: Kogan Page, 2001.

Csikszentmihalyi, Mihaly. *Creativity: Flow and the Psychology of Discovery and Invention.* New York: HarperCollins, 1996.

_____. *Flow: The Psychology of Optimal Experience.* New York: Harper and Row, 1990.

_____. "Society, Culture, and Person: A Systems View of Creativity." In *The Nature of Creativity*, edited by Robert J. Sternberg, 325–39. Cambridge, Massachusetts: University Press, 1988.

The Cutting Edge: The Magic of Movie Editing. Directed by Wendy Apple. Starz Encore Entertainment. ATCEP, Inc., Production. In association with ACE. Produced by NHK and the BBC, 2004.

Dalai Lama, His Holiness. "Contemplative Mind, Hard Science." *Shift: At the Frontiers of Consciousness, Journal of the Institute of Noetic Sciences*

(December–February 2005–2006), 24–28.

———. *The Universe in a Single Atom: The Convergence of Science and Spirituality.* New York: Morgan Road Books, Random House, 2005.

The Dark Secrets of Newton. PBS. Nova. WGBH, 2005.

De Bono, Edward. *Lateral Thinking.* Boston: Little, Brown, 1973.

———. *Six Thinking Hats.* New York: Harper Colophon, 1985.

Delaney, Gayle. *Breakthrough Dreaming: How to Tap the Power of Your 24-Hour Mind.* NewYork: Bantam, 1991.

Deppa, Joan. "Coping with a Killer's 'Manifesto.'" *Chronicle of Higher Education*, May 11, 2007, B14.

De Rooy, Lenny. *Alice in Wonderland.* Lenny's Alice in Wonderland site. Accessed April 4, 2014. http://www.alice-in-wonderland.net/.

De Salvo, Louise. "'Tinder-and-Flint': Virginia Woolf & Vita Sackville-West. In *Significant Others: Creativity & Intimate Partnership*, edited by Whitney Chadwick and Isabelle De Courtivron, 83–95. New York: Thames and Hudson, 1993.

Dewey, David. "Introduction to the Mandelbrot Set: A Guide for People with Little Math Experience. Accessed April 4, 2014. http://www.ddewey.net/mandelbrot/.

Discovering Psychology. Annenburg/CPB Collection featuring Philip Zimbardo. Video 4, Program 20: "Constructing Social Reality." VHS tape. WGBH, Boston: PBS Educational video in association with the APA, 1989.

Dobnik, Verena. "Hilton Dead in Provocative NYC Statue." *San Francisco Chronicle*, May 9, 2007.

Dunker, Karl. "On Problem Solving." *Psychological Monographs, 68(5)*, whole issue 270, 1945.

Editors of *Rolling Stone. The Ballad of John and Yoko.* Dolphin Books. Garden City, New York: Doubleday, 1982.

Edwards, David. *Artscience: Creativity in the Post-Google Generation.* Cambridge, Massachusetts: Harvard University Press, 2008.

Elements of Composition, http://en.wikipedia.org/wiki/Composition_(visual_arts), retrieved April 11, 2007.

Emoto, Masaru. *The Hidden Messages in Water*. Translated by David A. Thayne. Hillsboro, Oregon: Beyond Words, 2001.

Empires: The Medici: Godfathers of the Renaissance. Actors Ross King and Mario Biagioli. Two Parts. PBS, 2004.

Epstein, Mark. *Thoughts without a Thinker: Psychotherapy from a Buddhist Perspective*. New York: HarperCollins, Basic Books, 1995.

Estés, Clarissa Pinkola. *The Creative Fire: Myths and Stories about the Cycles of Creativity*. The Jungian Storyteller Series. Audiotape. Boulder, CO: Sounds True, 1991.

_____. *Warming the Stone Child: Myths and Stories about Abandonment and the Unmothered Child*. The Jungian Storyteller Series. Audiotape. Boulder, CO: Sounds True, 1990.

The Expanded Quotable Einstein, collected and edited by Alice Calaprice and Freeman Dyson. Princeton and Oxford: Princeton University Press, 2000.

Feist, Gregory J., and Mark A. Runco. "Trends in Creativity Literature: An Analysis of Research in the *Journal of Creative Behavior* (1967–1989)." *Creativity Research Journal* 6 (1993): 271–83.

Fellini, Federico. *Fellini: I'm a Born Liar*. Documentary movie of an interview translated with subtitles. First Look Media, 2003.

Feynman, Richard P. *Classic Feynman: All the Adventures of a Curious Character*. Edited by Ralph Leighton. New York, London: Norton, 2006.

French, R.M. *The Way of the Pilgrim and the Pilgrim Continues His Way*. New York: HarperCollins, 1954.

Frida. Directed by Julie Taymor. Distributed by Miramax Films. 2002.

Friedman, Thomas L. *The World Is Flat: A Brief History of the Twenty-First Century*, rev. ed. New York: Farrar, Straus, and Giroux, 2006.

Frishberg, Janet. "Suicide Net Needed on Gold Gate Bridge." *San Francisco Chronicle*, May 25, 2013. Updated June 7, 2013. http://www.sfgate.com/default/article/Suicide–net–needed–on–Golden–Gate–Bridge–3584667.php.

Gaffney, Mark H. *Gnostic Secrets of the Naassenes: The Initiatory Teachings of the LastSupper*. Rochester, VT: Inner Traditions, 2004.

Garchick, Leah. Untitled Column. *San Francisco Chronicle*, March 30, 2007, E-18.

Gardner, James N. "Should Science Study Religion? Voices from the Edge: The Spirit of Science." *What is Enlightenment?* 36 (April–June 2007), 36–38.

Gardner, Howard. *Creating Minds*. New York: Basic Books, 1993.

_____. *Leading Minds: An Anatomy of Leadership*. New York: Basic Books, 1995.

_____. *Intelligence Reframed: Multiple Intelligences for the 21st Century*. New York: Basic Books, 1999.

Gates, S. James, Jr., "Lecture 1, The Macro/Micro/Mathematical Connection." *Superstring Theory: The DNA of Reality*. 24 DVDs. Chantilly, Virginia: The Teaching Company, 2006.

Gayford, Martin. *The Yellow House: Van Gogh, Gauguin, and Nine Turbulent Weeks in Arles*. New York: Little, Brown, 2006.

Gelb, Michael J. *How to Think Like Leonardo da Vinci: Seven Steps to Genius Every Day*. New York: Delacorte, 1998.

Ghiselin, Brewster. "Introduction." In *The Creative Process*, edited by Brewster Ghiselin. Mentor Books. New York: New American Library, 1952.

Gilligan, Carol. *In a Different Voice: Psychological Theory and Women's Development*. Cambridge, MA: Harvard University Press, 1993.

Giuliano, Geoffrey. *Two of Us: John Lennon and Paul McCartney, Behind the Myth*. New York: Penguin, 1999.

"Golden Gate Bridge, Facts," http://goldengatebridge.org/research/facts. php#PaintedIntnlOrange.

"Golden Gate Bridge, Facts, History." Accessed April 7, 2014. http://gocalifornia.about.com/cs/sanfrancisco/a/ggbridge_4.htm.

"Golden Gate Bridge, Facts, Paint." Accessed April 7, 2014. http://gocalifornia.about.com/cs/sanfrancisco/a/ggbridge_3.htm.

http://gocalifornia.about.com/cs/sanfrancisco/a/ggbridge_4.htm.

"Golden Gate Bridge, Facts, Traffic." Accessed April 7, 2014. http://gocalifornia.about.com/cs/sanfrancisco/a/ggbridge_3.htm.

"The Golden Rectangle and Number 5, 1948, Jackson Pollock." Accessed April 4, 2014.http://www.gogeometry.com/wonder_world/golden_

rectangle_jackson_pollock_5_1948.html.

"Golden Ratio." Accessed May 12, 2014. http://en.wikipedia.org/wiki/Golden_ratio.

Goldstein, Rebecca. *Incompleteness: The Proof and Paradox of Kurt Gödel*. Great Discoveries Series. New York: Norton, 2005.

Görnitz, Thomas. "The Contribution of Quantum Theory to the Phenomena of Creativity in Science." Keynote Address. International Centre for Innovation in Education. 3rd annual conference. Athens, Greece, June 10, 2010.

Goswami, Amit. "Creativity and the Quantum: A Unified Theory of Creativity." *Creativity Research Journal* 9 (1996): 47–61.

_____. *Quantum Creativity*. Carlsbad, California: Hay House, 2014.

Gothic. Motion Picture. Directed by Ken Russell. Virgin Vision, 1986.

Greenberg, Robert. *Understanding the Fundamentals of Music*. Two vols. Transcription of a 16–DVD series. Chantilly, VA: The Teaching Company, 2007.

Gruber, Howard E. *Darwin on Man: A Psychological Study of Scientific Creativity*. 2nd ed. Chicago: University Press, 1981.

_____. and Doris B. Wallace. "Creative Work: The Case of Charles Darwin." *American Psychologist* 5 (April 2001): 346–49.

Guildford, John P. "Creativity." *American Psychologist*, 5 (1950): 444–54.

_____. "The Structure of Intellect." *Psychological Bulletin*, 53 (1956): 267–93.

Guthman, Edward. "The Allure: Beauty and an Easy Route to Death Have Long Made the Golden Gate Bridge a Magnet for Suicides." Part 1 of a 7–part series, *Lethal Beauty*. San Francisco Chronicle, October 30, 2005. Accessed April 4, 2014. http://www.sfgate.com/default/article/Lethal-Beauty-The-Allure-Beauty-and-an-easy-3302966.php#page-1.

Guthrie, Julian "De Young's Rebirth: It Had to Overcome Design Challenges, Lawsuits, and a Lack of Funds. S.F.'s New Museum Opens Today, a Triumph of Creativity and Commitment. *San Francisco Chronicle*, October 15, 2005, A-1. Accessed April 4, 2014. http://www.sfgate.com/default/article/De-Young-s-rebirth-It-had-to-overcome-design-2564985.php.

_____. "San Francisco: New UCSF Hospital Planned: Mission Bay Facility to Focus on Women, Children, Cancer." *San Francisco Chronicle* (April 2, 2007), B-1. Accessed April 4, 2014. http://www.sfgate.com/default/article/SAN-FRANCISCO-New-UCSF-hospital-planned-2605079.php.

Guynn, Jessica. "Can't Get Enough Justin? You Can Watch Justine." *San Francisco Chronicle*, May 29, 2007, C-1, C-4. Accessed April 4, 2014. http://www.sfgate.com/default/article/Can-t-get-enough-Justin-You-can-watch-Justine-2573698.php.

_____. "Crusade against the Jerk at Work: Some Companies Seek to Filter out Toxic Employees." *San Francisco Chronicle*, February 24. 2007, A-1, A6. Accessed April 4, 2014. http://www.sfgate.com/default/article/Crusade-against-the-jerk-at-work-Some-companies-2646586.php.

_____. "Lunch 2.0: Free Food, A Side of Tech Talk." *San Francisco Chronicle*, May 25, 2007, A-1, A-14. Accessed April 4, 2014. http://www.sfgate.com/default/article/Lunch-2-0-free-food-a-side-of-tech-talk-2591946.php.

Hanks, Kurt, and Jay A. Parry. *Wake up Your Creative Genius*. Los Altos, CA: William Kaufman, 1983.

Hart, P.D., Research Associates. *It Takes More Than a Major: An Online Survey among Employers Conducted by the Association of American College and Universities*. (April 10, 2013). Retrieved from www.aacu..org/leap/index.cfm.

Haunted Summer. Directed by Irving Passer. Distributed by Cannon Film, 1988.

Hayes, John R. "Cognitive Processes in Creativity." In *Handbook of Creativity*, edited by John A. Glover, Royce R. Ronning, and Cecil Reynolds, 135–45. New York: Plenum, 1989.

Hearts of Darkness: A Filmmaker's Apocalypse. Directed by Francis Ford Coppola. Narrated by Eleanor Coppola. American Zoetrope, 1991.

"Here, There, and Mira Nair." *What is Enlightenment?* 36 (April–June 2007), 24.

Herrera, Hayden. "Beauty to His Beast: Frida Kahlo and Diego Rivera." In *Significant Others: Creativity & Intimate Partnership*, edited by Whitney Chadwick and Isabelle De Courtivron, 119–35. New York: Thames and Hudson, 1993.

Hibbert, Chistopher. *The House of Medici: Its Rise and Fall*. New York: Harper Perennial, 2003.

Higonnet, Anne. "Myths of Creation: Camille Claudel and Auguste Rodin." In *Significant Others: Creativity & Intimate Partnership*, edited by Whitney Chadwick and Isabelle De Courtivron, 15–29. New York: Thames and Hudson, 1993.

Hill, Andrew, with John Wooden. *Be Quick—but Don't Hurry! Finding Success in the Teachings of a Lifetime*. New York: Simon and Schuster, 2004.

Hill, Napoleon. *Law of Success*. 4th ed. Chicago, IL: Success Unlimited, 1979.

Ho, Vivian. "Golden Gate Suicides Hit Record High—46." *San Francisco Chronicle*, February 25, 2014. Accessed April 5, 2014. http://www.sfgate.com/default/article/Golden–Gate–Bridge–suicides–hit–record–high–46–5263870.php.

Hoobler, Dorothy, and Thomas Hoobler. *The Monsters: Mary Shelley and the Curse of Frankenstein*. New York: Little, Brown, 2006.

Hoosiers. Directed by David Anspaugh. Orion. Hemdale Film Corp. Avid Home Entertainment, 1992.

The Hours. Directed by Stephen Daldry. Paramount Pictures, 2002.

Huber, Mary Taylor, Pat Hutchings, and Richard Gale. "Integrative Learning for Liberal Education." *Peer Review*, 7, no. 4 (Summer/Fall 2005): 4–7.

HumanMetrics. Jung Typology Test. Accessed April 5, 2014. http://www.humanmetrics.com/cgi–win/JTypes1.htm.

"In Other Words: Great Quotes on the Gate." *San Francisco Chronicle*, May 20, 2012. Accessed April 5, 2014. http://www.sfgate.com/default/article/In–other–words–Great– quotes–on–the–Gate–3571134.php.

Isaacson, Walter. *Einstein: His Life and Universe*. New York: Simon and Schuster, 2007.

Jackson, Peter, director. "Commentary. " *The Lord of the Rings: The Fellowship of the Ring*. Special Extended DVD Edition. New Line Platinum Series, 2001.

John Lennon and Yoko Ono: The Final Testament . . . Interviews by David Sheff. Edited by G. Barry Golson. New York: Berkeley Books, 1982.

Johnson, John, Jr. "A Glimpse at Personal Side of Einstein: Notes and Letters from a Troubled Man." *San Francisco Chronicle*, February 4, 2007, B-1. Accessed Aporil 5, 2014. http://www.sfgate.com/default/article/A-glimpse-at-personal-side-of-Einstein-Note-and-2619536.php.

John-Steiner, Vera. *Creative Collaboration*. New York: Oxford University Press, 2000.

_____. *Notebooks of the Mind: Explorations of Thinking*. rev. ed. New York: Oxford University Press, 1997.

Joyce, Susan. "On or about 1901 [sic]: The Bloomsbury Group Looks Back at the Victorians. " *Victorian Studies* 4, no. 6 (2004): 631–54.

Kaku, Michio. *Hyperspace: A Scientific Odyssey through Parallel Universes, Time Warps, and the 10th Dimension*. New York: Oxford University Press, 1994.

Keen, Sam. *Faces of the Enemy: Reflections of the Hostile Imagination*. San Francisco, California: HarperSanFrancisco, 1986.

Keller, Evelyn Fox. *A Feeling for the Organism*. Owl Books. NY: Henry Holt, 2003.

King, John. "Lethal Beauty: The Engineering Challenge: A Suicide Barrier Must Be Effective and Safe." Part 6 of a 7-part series, "Lethal Beauty." *San Francisco Chronicle*, November 4, 2005, A-1. Accessed April 5, 2014. http://www.sfgate.com/default/article/LETHAL-BEAUTY-THE-EN-GINEERING-CHALLENGE-A-2562115.php.

King, Ross. *Brunelleschi's Dome: How a Renaissance Genius Reinvented Architecture*. New York: Walker, 2000.

_____. *Michelangelo and the Pope's Ceiling*. New York: Walker, 2003.

Kirkpatrick, Sidney. Lectures. A.R.E. Northern California Conference at Asilomar, Pacific Grove, California, July 20, 2013.

Koberg, Don, and Jim Bagnall. *The All New Universal Traveler: A Soft-Systems Guide to Creativity, Problem-Solving, and the Process of Reaching Goals*. Los Altos, California: William Kaufman, 1972.

Koestler, Arthur. *The Roots of Coincidence: An Excursion into Parapsychology*. New York: Vintage, 1973

Kolb, David A. *Experiential Learning: Experience as the Source of Learning and Development*. Englewood Cliffs, NJ: Prentice Hall, 1984.

Kopytoff, Verne. "User Revolt at Digg.com shows Risks of Web 2.0. *San Francisco Chronicle*, May 3, 2007, A–1, A–7. Accessed April 5, 2014.http://www.sfgate.com/default/article/User–revolt–at–Digg–com–shows–risks–of–Web–2–0–2597628.php.

Kramer, Jerry with Dick Schaap. *Distant Replay*. New York: Putnam, 1985.

Kristeller, Paul Oskar. "'Creativity'" and 'Tradition.'" *Journal of the History of Ideas*, 44, no. 1 (January March 1983): 105–13.

Kriyananda, Swami. (Donald Walters). *Art as a Hidden Message: A Guide to Self-Realization*. Nevada City, CA: Crystal Clarity, 1997.

_____. *Cities of Light: A Plan for This Age*. Nevada City, California: Crystal Clarity, 1987.

_____. *Conversations with Yogananda*. Nevada City, California: Crystal Clarity, 2004.

_____. "Creativity, Music, and the Mystical Experience. " Excerpted from a talk given March, 1996. Interview. *Clarity Magazine*, Number 2 (1999), 5, 11–12.

_____. *Crystal Clarity: The Artist as Channel*. Nevada City, California: Crystal Clarity, 1987.

_____. *The Essence of the Bhagavad Gita, Explained by Paramhansa Yogananda, as Remembered by His Disciple, Swami Kriyananda*. Nevada City, California: Crystal Clarity, 2006.

_____. "*The Essence of the Bhagavad Gita*." Lecture, San Francisco California. Book launch, June 3, 2006.

_____. *The Essence of Self-Realization: The Wisdom of Paramhansa Yogananda*. Nevada City, California: Crystal Clarity, 1990.

_____. *The Hindu Way of Awakening: Its Revelation, Its Symbols*. Nevada City, California: Crystal Clarity, 1998.

_____. *Meditation for Starters*. Nevada City, California: Crystal Clarity, 1996.

_____. "Music, Creativity, and the Superconscious Experience." Lecture given in June 1996 in Toronto. Abstracted in *Ananda Clarity: Newsletter of Ananda Church of Self-Realization*, 5 (1996): 1 and 4.

_____. *Revelations of Christ Proclaimed by Paramhansa Yogananda*. Presented by his Disciple, Swami Kriyananda. Nevada City, California: Crystal Clarity, 2007.

_____. *Space, Light, and Harmony: The Story of Crystal Hermitage*. Nevada City, California: Crystal Clarity, 2005.

_____. *Superconsciousness: A Guide to Meditation*. Nevada City, California: Crystal Clarity, 1996.

Kuhn, Thomas. *The Structure of Scientific Revolutions*. 2nd ed. Chicago: University of Chicago Press, 1970.

Laszlo, Ervin. *Science and the Akashic Field: An Integral Theory of Everything*. Rochester, Vermont: Inner Traditions, 2004.

Lawrence, Brother. *The Practice of the Presence of God*. White Plains, New York: Peter Pauper Press, 1963.

Lethal Beauty. Seven-Part Series. *San Francisco Chronicle*, October–November 2005, www.sfgate.com.

Lehrer, Jonah. *How We Decide*. Mariner Books. Boston, New York: Houghton Mifflin, 2009.

Lenny's Alice in Wonderland site. Accessed April 4, 2014. http://www.alice-in-wonderland.net/.

Leonardo's Dream Machines. Instructional DVD. Directed by Paul Sapin. Channel 4 Television and PBS, 2003.

Levine, Arthur, and Jeanette Cureton. *When Hope and Fear Collide: A Portrait of Today's College Student*. San Francisco: Jossey-Bass, 1998.

The Life and Times of Frida Kahlo. Amy Stechlo, Producer and Editor. PBS/WETA, 2004.

Loevinger, Jane. *Ego Development: Conceptions and Theories*. The Jossey-Bass Behaviorial Science Series. San Francisco: Jossey-Bass, 1976.

Lubart, Ted. "Creativity, Culture, and Assessment of Potential Creativity with EPoC." Keynote Address. International Centre for Innovation in Education. 3rd annual conference. Athens, Greece, June 9, 2010.

Ludwig, Arnold M. "Creativity and Madness in the Arts and Sciences." *Creativity Research Journal*, 11 (1998): 93–102.

Magee, Bryan. *The Tristan Chord: Wagner and Philosophy*. New York: Henry Holt, 2000.

Maisel, Eric. *Creativity for Life*. California: New World Library, 2007.

Mamet, David. *Bambi vs. Godzilla: On the Nature, Purpose, and Practice of the Movie Business*. New York: Pantheon, 2007.

Man Ray: Prophet of the Avant Garde. Directed by Mel Stuart. American Masters Series. PBS, 1999.

Maslow, Abraham. *The Farther Reaches of Human Nature*. New York: Viking, 1971.

Matheson, Richard. "The Enemy Within." *Star Trek*. Season 1, episode 5. Directed by Leo Penn. Hollywood, CA: Paramount, 1991. Aired October 6, 1966. The Original and Uncut Television Series.

May, Rollo. *The Courage to Create*. New York: Bantam, 1976.

McTaggart, Lynne. *The Field: The Quest for the Secret Force of the Universe*. New York: HarperCollins, 2002.

McTaggart, Lynne. *Living the Field*. Boulder, Colorado: Sounds True, 2006. 4 CDs.

Mellor, Anne K. "Romanticism, Difference, and the Aesthetic." *Pacific Coast Philology*, 34, no. 2 (1999), Convention Program Issue, 127–141. Original Plenary Address 1998.

Miles, Barry. *Paul McCartney: Many Years from Now*. New York: Henry Holt, 1997.

Nardini, Bruno. *Michelangelo: Biography of a Genius*. Florence–Milan: Giunti, 1999.

Nolte, Carl. "Golden Gate Bridge: Monument, Work of Art, Star." *San Francisco Chronicle*, May 20, 2012. Accessed April 5, 2014. http://www.sfgate.com/default/article/Golden-Gate-Bridge-monument-work-of-art-star-3571131.php.

Novak, John. *How to Meditate: A Practical Guide Based on the Teachings of Paramhansa Yogananda and Sri Kriyananda*. Nevada City, California: Crystal Clarity, 1989.

Nuhfer, Ed. "The ABCs of Fractal Thinking in Higher Education." In *To Improve the Academy*, edited by Douglas R. Robertson and Linda B. Nilson, 70–89. POD Network. Boston: Anker, 2007.

Oblinger, Diana. "Boomers, Gen-Xers, and Milennials: Understanding the New Students." *Educause* (July–August 2003): 37–47. Accessed April

5, 2014. http://www.educause.edu/ero/article/boomers-gen-xers-and-millennials-understanding-new-students.

Ogle, Richard. *Smart World: Breakthrough Creativity and the New Science of Ideas.* Boston: Harvard Business School Press, 2007.

Osborn, Alex F. *Applied Imagination.* rev. ed. New York: Scribner's, 1953.

Paine-Clemes, Bunny. *Power Writing: Visualization Tapes for Writers.* Privately produced in Houston, Texas, with music by John Arthur, 1989.

_____. "*The Yugas*: Divine Agents of Change." *Joy: The Journal of Yoga*, 4, No. 3 (Summer 2005). Posted July, 2005, at www.journalofyoga.org/yugas.pdf.

_____. "What is Quality in a Maritime Education?" Paper presented October 25, 2005, in Malmö, Sweden, and published in *Maritime Security and MET: Proceedings of the International Association of Maritime Universities: IAMU 6 General Assembly and Conference, World Maritime University, Malmo, Sweden, 24-26 October, 2005*, edited by Detlef Nielsen. Southampton, U.K.: WIT Press, 2005. 267-76. Rpt. in *The IAMU Journal* 2, No. 4 (March 2006): 23-30.

Parallel Universes. Documentary series, *The Universe*, 7 seasons. Season 3, Episode 3. TLC/BBC, 2008.

Palmer, Parker J. *The Courage to Teach: Exploring the Inner Landscape of a Teacher's Life.* San Francisco: Jossey-Bass, 1998.

Pariser, David. "The Juvenile Drawings of Klee, Toulouse-Latrec, and Picasso." *Visual* Arts Research, 13 (1987): 53-67.

_____. "Review of *The Nature of Creativity: Contemporary Psychological Perspectives*," edited by Robert J. Sternberg, *Leonardo*, 26, no. 2 (1993): 141-44.
Parrish, Stephen Maxfield. "The Wordsworth-Coleridge Controversy." *PMLA*, 73, no. 4 (September 1958): 367-74.

Pedretti, Carlo. *Leonardo da Vinci: Artist, Scientist, Inventor.* Florence-Milan: Giunti, 2005.

Penrose, Roger. *The Road to Reality: A Complete Guide to the Laws of the Universe.* New York: Knopf, 2005.

Petroski, Henry. *Invention by Design: How Engineers Get from Thought to Thing.* Cambridge, MA: Harvard University Press, 1996.

Pfirman, Stephanie L., James P. Collins, Susan Lowes, and Anthony F.

Michaels. "Collaborative Efforts: Promoting Interdisciplinary Schol-ars." *The Chronicle of Higher Education.* February 2, 2005.

Phipps, Carter. "Dreams of a Digital Utopia." *What is Enlightenment?* 36 (April–June 2007), 112–16.

Pink, Daniel H. *A Whole New Mind: Moving from the Information Age to the Conceptual Age.* New York: Riverhead Books/Penguin, 2005.

Plotnik, Rod. *Introduction to Psychology.* 6th ed. Pacific Grove, California: Wadsworth–Thomson, 2002.

Poincaré, Henri. "Mathematic Creation." In *The Creative Process: Reflections on the Invention in the Arts and Sciences,* edited by Brewster Ghiselin, 33–42. New York: Mentor Books, New American Library, 1952.

Prospero's Books. Directed by Peter Greenaway. Miramax, 1991.

Pycior, Helena M. "Pierre Curie and 'His Eminent Collaborator Mme Curie': Complementary Partners." In *Creative Couples in the Sciences,* edited by Helena M. Pycior, Nancy G. Slack, and Pnina G. Abir–Am, 39–56. New Brunswick, NJ: Rutgers University Press,. 1996.

_____., Nancy G. Slack, and Pnina G. Abird–Am. "Introduction." In *Creative Couples in the Sciences,* edited by Helena M. Pycior, Nancy G. Slack, and Pnina G. Abir–Am, 3–35. New Brunswick, NJ: Rutgers University Press,. 1996.

Quality:Transforming Secondary Education, Report Three, 1992 ASHE–ERIC Higher Education Series, ERIC Clearinghouse on Higher Education, edited by Ellen Earle Chaffee and Lawrence A. Sherr, Washington, D.C., 1992.

Ray, Michael, and Michelle Myers, *Creativity in Business: Based on the Famed Stanford University Course That Has Revolutionized the Art of Success.* New York: Doubleday, 1986.

Read, Brock. "A Blogger Infiltrates Academe." *Chronicle of Higher Education,* April 6, 2007.

Rieger, James. "Dr. Polidori and the Genesis of Frankenstein." *Studies in English Literature, 1500-1900,* 3, no. 4 (Autumn 1963), *Nineteenth Century*: 461–72.

Rivers and Tides. Documentary by Thomas Reidelsheimer. Mediopolis, Skyline, 2003.

Robinson, Ken. *Out of Our Minds: Learning to be Creative.* Chichester, West Sussex: Capstone, 2011.

Rockmore, Daniel. "The Style of Numbers behind a Number of Styles." *Chronicle of Higher Education,* June 9, 2006.

Roemischer, Jessica. "The Never-Ending Upward Quest: A *WIE* Editor Encounters the Practical and Spiritual Wisdom of Spiral Dynamics: An Interview with Dr. Don Beck." *What is Enlightenment?* 22 (Fall/Winter 2002), 105–126.

Root-Bernstein, Robert, and Michele Root-Bernstein. *Sparks of Genius: The 13 Thinking Tools of the World's Most Creative People.* Boston: Houghton Mifflin, 1999.

Rosanoff, Nancy. "Intuition Workout: The Key to Creativity." *Intuition: A Magazine for the Higher Potential of the Mind,* Issue 8, 8–11, 54. No date specified on issue.

Rothenberg, Albert. "The Process of Janusian Thinking in Creativity." *Archives of General Psychiatry* 24 (1971): 195–205.

Rubin, Sylvia. "The Bikini at 60: Barely There." *San Francisco Chronicle,* July 2, 2006. Accessed April 5, 2014. http://www.sfgate.com/default/article/THE-BIKINI-AT-60-BARELY-THERE-2516337.php.

Salvesen, Christopher. Review. "*Coleridge and Wordsworth: A Lyrical Dialogue* by Paul Magnuson." *The Review of English Studies,* New Series, 41, no. 162 (May 1990): 266–267.

Sawyer, Keith. *Group Genius: The Creative Power of Collaboration.* New York: Basic Books, 2007.

Schindler, John. "Learning Styles Resource Site." Accessed April 5, 2014. http://www.calstatela.edu/faculty/jshindl/ls/.

Scholes, Robert, and Robert Kellogg, *The Nature of Narrative.* London: Oxford University Press, 1966.

Schwartz, Gary E. with William L. Simon, *The G.O.D. Experiments: How Science is Discovering God in Everything, including Us.* New York: Atria Books, 2006.

Seligman, Martin, and Christopher Peterson. *Character Strengths and Virtues: A Handbook and Classification.* Oxford, New York: Oxford University Press, in conjunction with the American Psychological Association, 2004.

Selvin, Joel. "Summer of Love 40 Years Later: Just a Season, but It Lives on—From Politics to Music to Sexuality—Even to the Way the PC was Designed—The Values are Ingrained in Our Culture." *San Francisco Chronicle*, May 23, 2007. Accessed April 5, 2014. http://www.sfchronicle.com/entertainment/article/SUMMER-OF-LOVE-40-YEARS-LATER-Just-a-season-2559193.php.

Servedio, Phil. "The Indra's Net: What is it?" Heart Space: The Web Site of Phil Servedio. Accessed April 5, 2014. http://www.heartspace.org/misc/IndraNet.html.

Shaw, Melvin P. "Affective Components of Scientific Creativity." In *Creativity and Affect*, edited by Melvin P. Shaw and Mark A. Runco, 3–43. Creativity Research Series. Norwood, New Jersey: Ablex, 1994.

Sheldrake, Rupert. *The Presence of the Past: Morphic Resonance and the Habits of Nature*. NY: Random House, Vintage Books, 1989. Original edition 1988.

Sheldrake, Rupert, Terence McKenna, and Ralph Abraham. *Chaos, Creativity, and Cosmic Consciousness*. Rochester, VT: Park Street, 1992.

Shelley, Mary. "Introduction to *Frankenstein*," 1831. Accessed April 5, 2014. http://www.rc.umd.edu/editions/frankenstein/1831v1/intro.

Simonton, Dean Keith. "Creativity as a Constrained Stochastic Process." In *Creativity: From Potential to Realization*, edited by Robert J. Sternberg, Elena L. Grigorenko, and Jerome L. Singer, 83–101. Washington, D.C.: APA, 2004.

_____. "Creativity from a Historiometric Perspective. In *Handbook of Creativity*, edited by R.J. Sternberg, 116–33. Cambridge, Massachusetts: University Press, 1999.

_____. *Genius, Creativity and Leadership: Historiometric Inquiries*. Cambridge, Massachusetts: Oxford University Press, 1984.

_____. *Origins of Genius*. New York: Oxford University Press, 1999.

Snyder, Neil, James J. Dowd, Jr., and Diane Morse Houghton. *Vision, Values and Courage: Leadership for Quality Management*. New York: The Free Press/Macmillan, 1985.

Stachel, John. "Albert Einstein and Mileva Mariæ: A Collaboration that Failed to Develop." In *Creative Couples in the Sciences*, edited by Helena M.

Pycior, Nancy G. Slack, and Pnina G. Abir–Am, 207–20. New Brunswick, NJ: Rutgers University Press, 1996.

Stemp, Richard. *The Secret Language of the Renaissance: Decoding the Hidden Symbolism of Italian Art.* London: Duncan Baird, 2006.

Sternberg, Robert J. "The Concept of Creativity: Prospects and Paradigms." In *Handbook of Creativity,* edited by R.J. Sternberg, 3–15. Cambridge, Massachusetts: University Press, 1999.

_____. "Creativity as a Decision." *American Psychologist* 57, no. 5 (May 2002): 376.

_____. "Creativity for the New Millennium." *American Psychologist* 56, no. 4 (April 2001): 332.

_____. "A Three–Facet Model of Creativity." In *The Nature of Creativity,* edited by Robert J. Sternberg, 125–147. Cambridge: Cambridge University Press, 1988.

_____. "What is the Common Thread of Creativity?" *American Psychologist* 56, No. 4 (April 2001): 360–62.

Sternberg, Robert J., and Elena A. Grigorenko. "Unified Psychology." *American Psychologist* 56, no.12 (December 2001): 1069–79.

Sternberg, Robert J., and Ted I. Lubart. "An Investment Theory of Creativity and Its Development." *Human Development,* 34 (1991): 1–31.

Stewart, Michael. "Prometheus." *Greek Mythology: From the Iliad to the Fall of the Last Tyrant.* November 14, 2005. Accessed April 5, 2014. http://messagenet.com/myths/bios/promethe.html.

Stokes, Patricia D. "Variability, Constraints, and Creativity: Shedding Light on Claude Monet." *American Psychologist* 56 (April 2001): 355–359.

Strathern, Paul. *The Big Idea Collected: 6 Revolutionary Ideas That Changed the World.* New York: Quality Paperback Book Club, 1999.

Stross, Randall. *The Wizard of Menlo Park: How Thomas Alva Edison Invented the Modern World.* New York: Crown, 2007.

Sturrock, Carrie. " Stanford: Professor Decodes Life Note by Note. *San Francisco Chronicle,* February 5, 2007. Accessed April 5, 2014. http://www.sfgate.com/default/article/STANFORD–Professor–decodes–life–note–by–note–2651438.phpvvv.

"Summer of Love: 40 Years Later." Series in the *San Francisco Chronicle*, May 19–23, 2007. (See also Selvin.)

Sutton, Robert I. *The No Asshole Rule: Building a Civilized Workplace and Surviving One that Isn't*. New York: Warner Business Books, 2007.

Suzanne Farrell: Elusive Muse. Seahorse Films, 2006.

Talbot, Michael. *The Holographic Universe*. New York: HarperCollins, 1991.

———. *Mysticism and the New Physics*. New York: Bantam, 1980.

Tart, Charles. *Waking up: Overcoming the Obstacles to Human Potential*. New Science Library. Boston: Shambhala, 1987.

Terry Gilliam. Director's series. Written, produced, and directed by Robert J. Emery. For the American Film Institute, 2000.

Thurston, Mark. *The Essential Edgar Cayce*. New York: Tarcher/Putnam, 2004.

Tickner, Lisa. "The 'Left-handed Marriage': Vanessa Bell and Duncan Grant." In *Significant Others: Creativity & Intimate Partnership*, edited by Whitney Chadwick and Isabelle De Courtivron, 65–81. New York: Thames and Hudson, 1993.

Toffler, Alvin. *The Third Wave*. New York: Bantam, 1981.

Tolle, Eckhart. *A New Earth: Awakening to Your Life's Purpose*. A Namaste book. New York: Dutton, 2005.

———. *The Power of Now: A Guide to Spiritual Enlightenment*. Novato: New World Library, 1999.

———. *Through the Open Door*. 2 CDs. Sounds True and Namaste Publishing, 2006.

Van Derberken, Jaxon. "Bay Bridge's New Problem: Leaks." *San Francisco Chronicle*, February 8, 2014. http://www.sfgate.com/default/article/Bay–Bridge–s–new–problem–leaks–5217783.php.

———. "Bolts along Bay Bridge Bike Path Fail." *San Francisco Chronicle*, May 29, 2013. http://www.sfgate.com/default/article/Bolts–along–Bay–Bridge–bike–path–fail–4555354.php.

———. "Caltrans Documents Tell of Bay Bridge Woes." *San Francisco Chronicle*, June 22, 2013. http://www.sfgate.com/default/article/Caltrans–documents–tell–of–Bay–Bridge–_woes–4615826.php.

von Oech, Roger. *A Kick in the Seat of the Pants: Using Your Explorer, Artist,*

Judge, and Warrior to Be More Creative. NY: Perennial, Harper & Row, 1986.

_____. *A Whack on the Side of the Head: How to Unlock Your Mind for Innovation.* New York: Warner, 1983.

Waserstrom, Jeffrey N. "Expanding on the I–word." *Chronicle of Higher Education,* January 20, 2005.

Watson, James D. *The Double Helix: A Personal Account of the Discovery of the Structure of DNA.* A Mentor Book. New York: New American Library, 1969.

Watson, J.R. Review. *"Coleridge, Wordsworth, and the Language of Allusion by Lucy Newlyn." The Review of English Studies,* New Series, 38, no. 152 (November 1987): 570–71.

The Way of the Pilgrim and The Pilgrim Continues His Way. Translated by R.M. French. San Francisco, CA: HarperSanFrancisco, 1965.

Weisberg, Robert W. *Creativity.* New York: Wiley, 2006.

_____. (1999). "Creativity and Knowledge: A Challenge to Theories." In *Handbook of Creativity,* edited by Robert J. Sternberg, 226–50. Cambridge, Massachusetts: University Press, 1999.

Wheel of Time. Directed by Werner Herzog (2003), Motion picture.

"Why Study Creativity?" The International Center for Studies in Creativity. Buffalo State, State University of New York, 2005. http://www. buffalostate.edu/orgs/cbir/readingroom/html/Why_study.html.

Wilber, Ken. *The 1 2 3 of God.* Sounds True. 4 CDs, 2006.

_____. *Boomeritis: A Novel That Will Set You Free.* Boston: Shambhala, 2002.

_____. *The Collected Works of Ken Wilber.* 8 vols. Boston: Shambhala, 1999–2000. Selections from these works will be cited as "CW," followed by the volume, work, and page.

_____. *Integral Operating System.* Boulder, CO: Sounds True, 2005. DVD, 2 CD–ROMS, booklet, and diagram

_____. "The Integral Operating System: An Integral or Comprehensive Map." (February 19, 2012). Retrieved from http://integrallife.com/integral–post/integral–operating–system.

_____. "The Integral Operating System: How It All Fits Together: The Four

Quadrants." (February 19, 2012). Retrieved from http://integrallife. com/integral–post/integral–operating–system.

_____. "The Integral Operating System, What Type?"(February 19, 2012). Retrieved from http://integrallife.com/integral–post/integral–operating–system.

_____. *Integral Spirituality*. Integral Books. Boston: Shambhala, 2006.

_____. *A Theory of Everything*. Boston: Shambhala, 2000.

_____. "To See a World: Art and the I of the Beholder." *The Journal of Transpersonal Psychology, 29.2* (1997): 143–49.

Willey, Basil. *The Seventeenth Century Background*. Garden City, New York: Doubleday Anchor, 1953.

Winn, Steven. "Painting a Picture of the Creative Mind." *San Francisco Chronicle*, May 28, 2007. Accessed April 7, 2014. http://www.sfgate. com/default/article/PAINTING–A–PICTURE–OF–THE–CREATIVE– MIND–It–s–2558336.php.

_____. "What Happens to Us When Art Connects to the Unconscious." *San Francisco Chronicle*, May 29, 2007. Accessed April 7, 2014. http:// www.sfgate.com/default/article/What–happens–to–us–when–art– connects–to–the–2591269.php.

Wolf, Fred A. *The Dreaming Universe*. New York: Simon and Schuster, 1994.

_____. *Dr. Quantum: A User's Guide to Your Universe*. 8–DVD set. Boulder, CO: Sounds True, 2005.

Wooden, John with Jack Tobin. *They Call Me Coach*. Contemporary Books. New York: McGraw Hill, 2004.

Woolf, Leonard. *Sowing*. London: Hogarth Press, 1961.

"The Worst Bridge Collapses in the Past 100 Years." (n.d.) *Time* Photos. Retrieved from http://content.time.com/time/photogallery/0,29307,1649646,00.html.

Yogananda, Paramhansa. *Autobiography of a Yogi*. Reprint of the 1946 Philosophical Library First Edition. Nevada City, CA: Crystal Clarity, 1994.

_____. "The Missing Link between Consciousness and Matter." In *Man's Eternal Quest*, 364–369. Los Angeles: Self–Realization Fellowship, 1975. (Self–Realization Fellowship includes an "a" in the name that Ananda spells "Paramhansa.")

_____. "Understanding the Unreality of Matter." In *Man's Eternal Quest*, 55–59. Los Angeles: Self-Realization Fellowship, 1975. (Self-Realization Fellowship includes an "a" in the name that Ananda spells "Paramhansa.")

_____. "A New Look at the Origin and Nature of Cosmic Creation." In *The Divine Romance*, 18–32. Los Angeles: Self-Realization Fellowship, 1986. (Self-Realization Fellowship includes an "a" in the name that Ananda spells "Paramhansa.")

Young, Jonathan. "The Lost Coin." Center for Story and Symbol. January 1996. Retrieved November 3, 2007, from http://www.folkstory.com.

_____. "Once upon a Time: How Fairy Tales Shape Our Lives." Center for Story and Symbol. Fall 1997. Retrieved November 3, 2007, from www.folkstory.com.

_____. "The Psychology of Creativity." Workshop. Sponsored by The Center for Story and Symbol, www.folkstory.com. Sacramento, California, May 16, 2006.

Zimbardo, Philip. *The Lucifer Effect: Understanding How Good People Turn Evil*. New York: Random House, 2007.

Zinko, Carolyne. "Three Options Offered for Suicide Barrier." *San Francisco Chronicle*, May 24, 2007. Retrieved from http://www.sfgate.com/default/article/Three-options-offered-for-bridge-suicide-barrier-2592326.php.

Zweig, Connie, and Jeremiah Abrams. "Introduction." In *Meeting the Shadow: The Hidden Power of the Dark Side of Human Nature*, edited by Connie Zweig and Jeremiah Abrams, xvi–xxv. Los Angeles: Tarcher, 1991.

Index

A

A-Field 39, 55
Abrashoff, Captain Michael D. xxv, 332, 333, 335, 336
Acting 281, 282
All-Channel Network or Star 301, 303, 358
Allende, Isabel 55, 60, 344
Amabile, Teresa 5, 10, 13, 16, 57, 143, 331, 342
Amadeus 277
Apocalypse Now 9, 19, 133, 307
Archimedes 14
Arieti, Silvano 13
Ars Poetica 271

B

Bach, Johann Sebastian 77, 223
Balanchine, George 132, 279
Baryshnikov, Mikhail 278
Basic Instinct 307
Bay Bridge, the 244
Bead Game, the 324, 325
Beatles, the 9, 16, 17, 53, 54, 167, 168, 190, 201, 262, 275, 276, 323, 350
Beauty 40, 75, 79, 80, 165, 207, 208, 231, 233, 236, 248, 250, 257, 258, 259, 260, 271, 283, 285, 286, 341
Beauvoir, Simone de 157, 158, 177, 184
Beck, Don 83, 85, 86, 87, 88, 89, 90, 91, 93, 115, 116, 117, 139
Beethoven, Ludwig von 77, 252, 253, 262
Bell, Derek 61, 65
Bhagavad Gita, the 28, 36, 143, 193
"Big Three" (the Good, the Beautiful, the True): *See* Integral Operating System xvi, 79, 80, 101, 207, 257, 258, 259, 271, 283, 286
Blake, William v, 221
Bloom, Harold 4, 15, 193, 274
Bloomsbury Group, the 191
Blue bindu, the 241
Bohm, David 35, 39
Botticelli, Sandro 268, 269, 270, 277, 279, 283, 316, 321
Braden, Gregg 41, 217, 218

Bridge Resource (or Team) Management xxv, 301, 302, 305, 334
Brontës, the 188
Brunelleschi, Filippo xxii, 15, 316, 317, 319, 321, 322
Buckley, James xxv, 304, 305, 342
Buddha, the xiii, 34, 65
Burning Man 195, 196, 197, 201

C

Cameron, James 306
Catch-22 328
Cayce, Edgar 41, 58, 59, 68, 93, 96, 109, 115, 123, 135, 145, 156, 174, 188, 189, 190, 208, 240, 259
Christy, Lynn Sparrow 93, 94
Circle (Management Structure) 302, 303, 304, 305, 359, 360
Claudel, Camille 160, 161, 162, 163
Cohen, Andrew 43, 198, 200, 342
Coleridge, Samuel Taylor 14, 17, 77, 109, 110, 140, 142, 159, 160, 177, 211, 241, 281, 295
Combs, Alan 199, 292
Coppola, Francis Ford 9, 19, 133, 155, 264
Covey, Stephen 52, 59
Crease, Robert 233, 234, 235, 236
Creativity
  Aspects (Ch. 1) 3
  Characteristics of a Creative Person (Ch. 1) 10
  Definition (Ch. 1) 16
  "Fundamental" vs. "Situational" (Ch. 2) 28
  Integral (Ch. 2) 34
  Janusian Thinking (Ch. 1) 13
  Motivation, Extrinsic and Intrinsic (Ch. 1) 5, 8, 19, 298, 342
  Mystical (Ch. 2) 35
  Paradigms (Ch. 2): Materialistic, Idealistic, Organismic 26
  Paradox (Ch. 1) 17
  Processes
    "Flow state" (Ch. 3) 55, 56
    10–step process (Ch. 3) 53

387

389

Who Was Edgar Cayce?
Twentieth Century Psychic and Medical Clairvoyant

Edgar Cayce (pronounced Kay-Cee, 1877-1945) has been called the "sleeping prophet," the "father of holistic medicine," and the most-documented psychic of the 20th century. For more than 40 years of his adult life, Cayce gave psychic "readings" to thousands of seekers while in an unconscious state, diagnosing illnesses and revealing lives lived in the past and prophecies yet to come. But who, exactly, was Edgar Cayce?

Cayce was born on a farm in Hopkinsville, Kentucky, in 1877, and his psychic abilities began to appear as early as his childhood. He was able to see and talk to his late grandfather's spirit, and often played with "imaginary friends" whom he said were spirits on the other side. He also displayed an uncanny ability to memorize the pages of a book simply by sleeping on it. These gifts labeled the young Cayce as strange, but all Cayce really wanted was to help others, especially children.

Later in life, Cayce would find that he had the ability to put himself into a sleep-like state by lying down on a couch, closing his eyes, and folding his hands over his stomach. In this state of relaxation and meditation, he was able to place his mind in contact with all time and space—the universal consciousness, also known as the super-conscious mind. From there, he could respond to questions as broad as, "What are the secrets of the universe?" and "What is my purpose in life?" to as specific as, "What can I do to help my arthritis?" and "How were the pyramids of Egypt built?" His responses to these questions came to be called "readings," and their insights offer practical help and advice to individuals even today.

The majority of Edgar Cayce's readings deal with holistic health and the treatment of illness. Yet, although best known for this material, the sleeping Cayce did not seem to be limited to concerns about the physical body. In fact, in their entirety, the readings discuss an astonishing 10,000 different topics. This vast array of subject matter can be narrowed down into a smaller group of topics that, when compiled together, deal with the following five categories: (1) Health-Related Information; (2) Philosophy and Reincarnation; (3) Dreams and Dream Interpretation; (4) ESP and Psychic Phenomena; and (5) Spiritual Growth, Meditation, and Prayer.

Learn more at EdgarCayce.org.

What Is A.R.E.?

Edgar Cayce founded the non-profit Association for Research and Enlightenment (A.R.E.) in 1931, to explore spirituality, holistic health, intuition, dream interpretation, psychic development, reincarnation, and ancient mysteries—all subjects that frequently came up in the more than 14,000 documented psychic readings given by Cayce.

The Mission of the A.R.E. is to help people transform their lives for the better, through research, education, and application of core concepts found in the Edgar Cayce readings and kindred materials that seek to manifest the love of God and all people and promote the purposefulness of life, the oneness of God, the spiritual nature of humankind, and the connection of body, mind, and spirit.

With an international headquarters in Virginia Beach, Va., a regional headquarters in Houston, regional representatives throughout the U.S., Edgar Cayce Centers in more than thirty countries, and individual members in more than seventy countries, the A.R.E. community is a global network of individuals.

A.R.E. conferences, international tours, camps for children and adults, regional activities, and study groups allow like-minded people to gather for educational and fellowship opportunities worldwide.

A.R.E. offers membership benefits and services that include a quarterly body-mind-spirit member magazine, Venture Inward, a member newsletter covering the major topics of the readings, and access to the entire set of readings in an exclusive online database.

Learn more at EdgarCayce.org.

EDGARCAYCE.ORG